D0966805

ISRAEL SINCE THE SIX-DAY WAR

Also by Leslie Stein

The Hope Fulfilled: The Rise of Modern Israel
The Making of Modern Israel: 1948–1967

ISRAEL SINCE THE SIX-DAY WAR

TEARS OF JOY, TEARS OF SORROW

LESLIE STEIN

polity

First published in 2014 by Polity Press

Polity Press
65 Bridge Street
Cambridge CB2 1UR, UK

Polity Press
350 Main Street
Malden, MA 02148, USA

ISBN-13: 978-0-7456-4726-5

A catalogue record for this book is available from the British Library.

Typeset in 10.75 on 14 pt Janson Text by
Servis Filmsetting Ltd, Stockport, Cheshire
Printed and bound in Great Britain by Clays Ltd, St Ives plc

The publisher has used its best endeavours to ensure that the URLs for external websites referred to in this book are correct and active at the time of going to press. However, the publisher has no responsibility for the websites and can make no guarantee that a site will remain live or that the content is or will remain appropriate.

Every effort has been made to trace all copyright holders, but if any have been inadvertently overlooked the publisher will be pleased to include any necessary credits in any subsequent reprint or edition.

For further information on Polity, visit our website: www.politybooks.com

To Clara with love

CONTENTS

Illustrations

PREFACE

This book provides a broad survey of the history of Israel from the Six-Day War in June 1967 to the end of the first decade of the twenty-first century. While paying particular attention to Israel's wars and military engagements, other topics have by no means been neglected. Israel's economic development and internal political matters, the nature of the PLO and the Palestinian Authority, Israeli settlements in the West Bank and Gaza, extremist Jewish movements, social protest in Israel, Russian and Ethiopian migrants, Israeli Arabs, the ultra-orthodox Haredi Jewish community, foreign workers, the kibbutz movement and social and economic disparities are all considered. Covering such an extensive range of issues over a 43-year period necessitated drawing upon largely secondary sources, both in English and in Hebrew. In the process an attempt was made to synthesize the material at hand to provide a cogent and reliable account of Israel's recent past that could well serve both students and general readers.

Given that the book covers only a part of Israel's post-independence history, background information relating to the period 1948 to 1967 is provided in the introductory chapter to facilitate an understanding of the later events in relation to previous ones. For the reader interested in pursuing the earlier period in more detail, recourse to my book *The Making of Modern Israel: 1948–1967* is suggested.

It was to my good fortune that I was able to receive advice and comments from renowned scholars in the field of Israel Studies who had either read the entire manuscript or a chapter or two, as well as from others who proffered clarifications on specific points. The scholars in question were Oz Almog, Ahron Bregman, Raphael Cohen-Almagor, Alan Dowty, Robert Freedman, Daniel Gordis, Raphael Israeli, Moshe Lissak, Derek Penslar, Daniel Pipes, Abraham Rabinovich, Anita Shapira and Colin Shindler. To all of them I am indebted for their valuable inputs, with, of course, the usual proviso that any faults and defects found in the book remain mine alone. In addition, I would like to thank Joe Devanny, editor at Polity Press, for his friendly guidance and cooperation, particularly at a time when I had been labouring under difficult personal circumstances. Furthermore, it has been to my good fortune to have had the manuscript copyedited by Caroline Richmond, who has combed through the text with exceptional care and exemplary professionalism.

Finally, words of gratitude fail me in expressing my appreciation to both my wife Clara (to whom this work is dedicated) and to my son Mark, who have given me unstinted encouragement in ensuring the book's completion and who both deployed their fine skills in detecting linguistic and other errors that draft manuscripts invariably contain.

Leslie Stein
Sydney, Australia

ACKNOWLEDGEMENTS

All photographs in the body of this book are reproduced with permission. Plates 1, 2, 3, 4, 5, 9 and 10 are from the Israeli Government Press Office; plates 7 and 8 are from Associated Press; and plate 6, photographed by Michael Curtis, is from Agence France Press.

INTRODUCTION

After ruling Palestine for over twenty-eight years, in accordance with a League of Nations Mandate for facilitating the creation of a Jewish national home in Palestine, Britain, on February 18, 1947, decided to place that country's future in the hands of the United Nations (UN). It arrived at that decision after finding itself incapable of resolving the conflicting demands of Arab and Jewish nationalists. On accepting the Palestinian brief, the UN on May 15, 1947, established a United Nations Special Commission on Palestine (UNSCOP) to examine "the problem of Palestine and all matters associated with it." At the end of an exhaustive inquiry, the majority of the eleven members of UNSCOP proposed that Palestine be partitioned into a Jewish and Arab state, with Jerusalem maintaining an international status. The commission felt that a unitary state would not be viable because the interests of the Arabs and Jews were so irreconcilable that an internecine civil war would be an inevitable outcome. What impressed the investigators was the fact that the Jews had over the years created a self-contained enclave in which Hebrew was the lingua franca. They had managed their own economic, welfare and cultural affairs and had settled on land for which every square metre had been bought and fully paid. Not only that, but the proposed area to be allotted to the Jews was one in which they had already constituted a majority. Meeting on November 29, 1947, over two-thirds of the UN General Assembly gave its blessing to the division of Palestine in the spirit of the UNSCOP recommendation. While the Jews accepted that decision with alacrity, the Arabs rejected it forthwith, and on the following day, by killing seven Jews, they inaugurated a campaign of violence against the Yishuv (Jewish Community in Palestine). In the meantime, the British authorities, while preparing for their departure (scheduled for no later than midnight May 14, 1948), abrogated their responsibility for the maintenance of law and order, which meant that the internal fighting remained unchecked.

Then on May 14, 1948, at a simple ceremony in the Tel Aviv Art Museum, David Ben-Gurion, as head of the Yishuv, declared Israel's independence. The declaration was issued despite George Marshall, the US secretary of state, warning that, in the event of the Jews claiming full sovereignty, US military assistance would not be assured.[1] Even within Zionist ranks the wisdom of undertaking such a step was subject to doubt. Of the ten Yishuv leaders who met to decide their people's fate, only six voted in favour of immediate independence. The reticence of the four dissenters was hardly surprising, considering that Yigael Yadin, Israel's de facto chief of staff, had put the odds of a Jewish State prevailing over its enemies at no more than 50 percent.[2] On the morning of the second day of its existence, Israel, whose Jewish population numbered 650,000, found itself pitted against the regular Arab armies of Syria, Iraq, Transjordan and Egypt.

In the early stages of the war Israel was extremely vulnerable. Unlike its adversaries, who were largely starting afresh, Israel's troops were fatigued. They had just undergone five and a half months of combating local Palestinian as well as bands of foreign volunteers and in the process had lost 753 soldiers, including many seasoned officers. What is more, the arms at Israel's immediate disposal were vastly inferior to those possessed by the Arabs in terms of both quantity and quality. Apart from a limited stock of mortars and PIATS (projector infantry anti-tank weapons, a type of crude bazooka), the Israelis had no field guns to speak of and, barring some Hispano Suiza guns, virtually no anti-aircraft weapons. Their armour consisted of a handful of iron-plated vehicles and two Cromwell tanks acquired from a couple of British deserters. Having no fighter planes, their air force consisted of a few Piper Cubs and Austers, two transport planes and three improvised "bombers." Rifles and machine guns, coming as they did from a variety of sources, lacked standardization. Only 60 percent of Israeli soldiers bore arms.[3] Ammunition was in such short supply that merely 50 bullets per rifle and 700 per machine gun were available.[4] The Arabs by contrast were believed to have been equipped with something of the order of 152 field guns, 140 to 159 armoured cars, 20 to 40 tanks and 55 to 59 fighter aircraft.[5]

Israel's perilous plight was impressed upon members of Kibbutz Degania A when they approached Ben-Gurion, now Israel's prime minister and minister of defence, with an urgent appeal for additional manpower. Ben-Gurion had the unpleasant task of informing them that "there are not enough guns, not enough planes; men are lacking on all fronts. The situation is very severe in the Negev, is difficult in Jerusalem, in Upper Galilee. The whole country is a front line. We cannot send reinforcements."[6]

Yet, in spite of it all, Israel largely held its ground. By mid-June, when the first truce took effect, the Arabs had notched up few successes. An Egyptian column moving in the direction of Tel Aviv was checked, the Transjordanians had mainly contented themselves with seizing what has now become known as the West Bank, Iraqi troops were garrisoned in Arab towns beyond Israel's territory, and the Syrians had laid claim to but a single Israeli settlement. This is not to suggest that the Jewish defenders were not hard pressed. Kibbutz Yad Mordehai and Kibbutz Nitzanim in the southern region, both outmanned and outgunned by the Egyptian army, fell. Just a few kilometres south of Jerusalem, Kibbutz Ramat Rahel with considerable difficulty headed off one attack after another. In Jerusalem itself, the Transjordanians overran the Old Jewish Quarter. As a consequence, the Jews no longer had access to their hallowed Western Wall. Not content with their gains in the Old City, the Transjordanians besieged the new Jewish residential area, pounding it with over 10,500 shells and causing the death of 316 and the wounding of 1,422 others.[7]

The June–July truce provided Israel with a golden opportunity to take delivery of crucial arms shipments from Czechoslovakia with Russia's full backing. It was the hope of the Soviet Union that an Israeli victory over the Arabs would damage Britain's standing in the Middle East, thereby weakening the so-called forces of colonialism.

(Transjordan's Arab Legion, it should be noted, was both financed and officered by the UK.) Not only did Israel receive reasonable quantities of military equipment (including tanks and fighter planes) but, with its gates now wide open, it welcomed Jewish volunteer soldiers from mainly Western countries as well as young migrants able and willing to play a part in their new country's defence. From that point of time onwards, the strategic balance shifted in favour of the Israelis, who by the year's end controlled somewhat more territory than had originally been designated to them by the UN.

Realizing that a continuation of the war would only compound their losses, the invading Arab countries (with the exception of Iraq, which withdrew its forces), and with the inclusion of Lebanon, entered into separate armistice agreements with Israel. The armistice agreements were meant to constitute a first step on the road to a permanent settlement and explicitly committed each signatory to abstain from any form of violence, even guerrilla or non-government-organized violence, against a fellow contractual state. However, with the exception of Transjordan (which, after acquiring large swathes of the West Bank, changed its name to Jordan), no Arab state showed any serious interest in reaching a full peace accord. Even many, if not the majority, of the Jordan parliamentary members and government ministers were opposed to their King Abdullah secretly suing for peace. When, on Friday July 22, 1951, Abdullah made his way to pray in East Jerusalem's al-Aqsa Mosque, he was assassinated at point-blank range by an agent of Haj Amin al-Husseini. As a result, all hopes of Jordan coming to terms with the Jewish State vanished. Al-Husseini was in effect the Palestinians' de facto leader. He was an ardent anti-Semite who had spent time in Nazi Germany during World War II. In his meetings with top-ranking Third Reich leaders, including Hitler, he had beseeched his hosts to extend their solution of the Jewish problem to the Jews of Palestine.[8]

Israel's victory in its war of independence was a costly one. It had lost 6,000 of the flower of its youth, a loss amounting to close to 1 percent of its initial population. Allowing for Israel's small size, Van Creveld estimated that "the blood bath was more intense than that undergone by either Britain or Germany in 1914–1918."[9] In fact, the death toll in the War of Independence approached a third of all those killed in action from November 1947 until the end of the twentieth century. No other Israeli war matched it.

The Arabs likewise suffered a heavy death toll, but in addition the Palestinians experienced the trauma of a large number of their people being uprooted from within areas falling under Israel's jurisdiction. Such refugees, totalling an estimated 730,000, sought sanctuary in Jordan, the Egyptian-controlled Gaza Strip, Lebanon and Syria. With respect to the ultimate source of the refugee problem, it unquestionably arose as a by-product of the Arab–Jewish conflict culminating, on May 15, 1948, with the invasion of Israel by four regular Arab armies. As Jacob Malek, the Soviet delegate to the UN, put it: "The existence of Arab refugees in the Middle East is the result of attempts to scuttle the UN General Assembly's decision regarding Palestine. Those implicated bear direct responsibility for the refugees' plight."[10]

The Arabs have never come to terms with their own role in causing the refugee problem. Instead, they have laid full blame for that outcome on the Jews. In this regard, they have been backed to the hilt by Western radicals motivated by a deep ideological hatred for the Jewish State. Their false charges are based largely on an Israeli Defence Force (IDF) plan (Plan Dalet) which was reputedly designed to "ethnically cleanse Palestine of its Arabs"[11] but which in reality was nothing more than an operational plan for securing the IDF's rear as it faced an oncoming invasion.[12] The spuriousness of such an outrageous slur is amply demonstrated by events that occurred during the war in Haifa and Nazareth. When, in the wake of a heated battle, the Jewish forces took control of Haifa, they met with local Arab leaders to offer their people full and equal residency rights.[13] On receiving the Jewish offer, the Arabs requested a brief adjournment to consult with Arab states. Hours later they announced to everyone's amazement, including Major-General Stockwell, a senior British officer who acted as an observer, that, rather than live under Jewish control, they would leave for Lebanon. In conclusion they stated: "We do not recognise you and we shall return when you are no longer here." Stockwell, who was utterly astounded, asked them whether they had taken leave of their senses.[14] In vain, the Jewish mayor, Shabetai Levy, implored them to reconsider their decision. (Confirmation of Jewish efforts to persuade the Arabs not to flee has been provided by both American diplomats and British officials.)[15] Similarly, with regard to Nazareth, immediately after that city had fallen into Israeli hands, Ben-Gurion sent the military commander in question an urgent message stressing that no Arab was to be expelled.[16] To this day, Nazareth remains overwhelmingly an Arab city.

The irony of it all is that, rather than the Jews, it was the Arabs themselves who were seeking an "ethnic cleansing of Palestine" and, far from being coy about their objective, they made no bones about it. In March 1948, Haj Amin al-Husseini, the leader of the Palestinian Arab Higher Command, on being interviewed by *al Sarah*, a Jaffa newspaper, stated that the Arabs "would continue fighting until the Zionists were annihilated and the whole of Palestine became a purely Arab state."[17] Similarly, Abdel Qader al-Husseini, who headed the Palestinian militia in the Jerusalem region, declared that "the Palestine problem will only be solved by the sword; all Jews must leave Palestine."[18]

In practice, whenever they overran Jewish settlements, Arab forces had no compunction in razing them to the ground. That the number of such settlements was relatively small is due solely to the fact that the Arabs did not succeed in vanquishing that many. Amos Oz, an Israeli writer who had empathized with the Arab refugees, fittingly summarized the difference between Israel and its foes by observing that

> the Arabs implemented a more complete 'ethnic cleansing' in the territories they conquered than the Jews did. Hundreds of thousands of Arabs fled or were driven out from the territory of the State of Israel in the war, but a hundred thousand remained. Whereas there were no Jews at all in the West Bank (including the Jewish quarter of the Old City of Jerusalem) or the Gaza Strip that came under Jordanian and Egyptian rule. Not one.[19]

As already suggested, the Arab refugee phenomenon emanated primarily from the dynamics of the in-fighting between Palestinian Arabs and Jews that the Arabs themselves initiated. It was then exacerbated by the pan-Arab invasion and by the IDF's attempts to repel it. Before Israel was established some 300,000 refugees had already fled.[20] The first to depart were Arab notables and their families, who may have recalled previous temporary migrations such as occurred during World

War I and during the 1936–9 Arab rebellion, when 40,000 Arabs left the country.[21] The full extent of the exodus of the Arab elite can be inferred from Majid al-Haj, an Arab-Israeli academic, who reported that, after the war, *"nearly all* members of the Palestinian Arab middle and upper classes – the urban landowning mercantile, professional and religious elite – were no longer present in Israel."[22] Whatever factors drove them, the Arab elite set a standard of desertion that was readily emulated by the broad uneducated masses.[23]

The Arab elite's growing absence led to the closure of schools, hospitals and business enterprises. General municipal and social services, which had previously been delivered by the British bureaucracy, collapsed. Unlike the Jews, the Palestinians failed to create a self-contained state in the making and were unable to take over as the British withdrew. This resulted in increased unemployment and welfare losses, all of which had a demoralizing effect.[24] To make matters worse, the unruly behaviour of extraneous Arab militias caused people endless misery. As one leading Arab citizen in Haifa recalled, "Robber gangs terrorized the residents. Food prices became inflated. A panic exodus began."[25]

One cannot of course deny that the IDF had also been instrumental in adding to the refugee flight by virtue of its destruction of numerous Arab villages judged to be actively hostile to it and which stood ready to provide material assistance to the invading forces. However, such displacements were undertaken out of strategic considerations and not out of any official antipathy to the Arabs per se. In this respect, on March 23, *after more than 100,000 Arabs had already fled*, General Ismail Safwat, the overall commander of the Arab Liberation Army, wrote that the Jews "have not attacked a single Arab village unless provoked by it."[26] Abdul Azzam, the Arab League secretary general, appreciated the strategic merit, from Israel's point of view, in expelling specific Arab villagers. He lamented that, by "driving out the inhabitants [from areas] on or near roads by which regular forces could enter the country," the Jews were providing the Arab armies with the "greatest difficulty in even entering Palestine after May 15."[27] Sir Allan Cunningham, the British high commissioner in Palestine, agreed that "the Jews for their part can hardly be blamed if, in the face of past Arab irregular action and the continued threat of interference by Arab regular forces, they take time by the forelock and consolidate their positions while they can."[28] Finally, Simha Flapan, whose book *The Birth of Israel: Myths and Realities*, has become a bedrock for anti-Israel propaganda, affirmed that the military benefits of razing certain Arab villages "were so evident that liberal and socialist commanders and their troops were able to overcome any qualms."[29]

By the end of 1949 the UN Relief and Works Agency for Palestinian Refugees (UNRWA) was formed and assumed responsibility for the care of Palestinian refugees. The establishment of UNRWA was an anomaly in that all other refugees throughout the world at large fall under the jurisdiction of the UN High Commissioner for Refugees (UNHCR). Only the Palestinians have a UN body of their own. Just as irregular, Palestinians are able to retain their refugee status even on acquiring the citizenship of another country. Perhaps most astonishing of all, Palestinian refugees are able to transfer their refugee status to succeeding generations. Partly as a result of UNRWA's interminable largesse, but mainly on account of Arabs wishing to perpetuate the existence of Palestinian refugees, the problem has become quite intractable.

As far as the Arabs are concerned, their perpetual demands for the return of the refugees have been submitted not as an alternative for the destruction of Israel but as the means to effect it.[30] For example, in October 1949, Muhammad Saleh ed-Din, Egypt's foreign minister, stated that, "in demanding the restoration of the refugees to Palestine, the Arabs intend that they shall return as the masters of the homeland, and not as slaves. More explicitly: they intend to annihilate the state of Israel."[31] As recently as 2000, a fatwa, specifically requested by Yasser Arafat, leader of the Palestine Liberation Organization (PLO), ruled that "any arrangement calling for the refugees to be compensated for their right to return or their settlement outside their homeland (that is all of Israel) is, from the point of view of the Sharia, null and void."[32] By ensuring that no alternative other than the full repatriation of all refugees to Israel is enshrined in religious doctrine, Arafat effectively put paid to any peaceful resolution of the Arab–Israeli conflict. Unless the Palestinians undergo a genuine change of heart and come to terms with the existence of Israel as a sovereign Jewish State, such a state of affairs is doomed to continue ad infinitum.

Meanwhile, with the War of Liberation behind them, the Israelis turned their minds to the mass absorption of Jews from European and Arab countries. Within a matter of only four years, an influx of migrants led to a doubling of the size of the Jewish population. Israel's newcomers did not stream into a consolidated, tranquil and ordered country but, as Ben-Gurion stressed, into "a tender and young one that had arisen in the midst of confusion, anarchy and the tribulations of war."[33] The ability of the state to rise to the challenge that the uncoordinated and unregulated arrival of destitute Jews posed was quite amazing. As many as 10 percent of all immigrants were either chronically ill or were suffering from diseases, such as polio, tuberculosis, trachoma and syphilis.[34] So pervasive were migrant medical disorders that one observer warned that the state faced the danger of becoming one big hospital for the Jewish people.[35] Those from Yemen in particular were in a most wretched condition. On a visit to an army hospital, Ben-Gurion reported seeing "children and babies who were more like skeletons than living human beings, too weak to cry, many of them unable to absorb food."[36]

Receiving and integrating such a large number of immigrants over a matter of a few years imposed tremendous strains on the country. This was especially so in view of the cascading nature of the migratory influx. Just as Israel was being inundated by the sudden arrival of thousands upon thousands of immigrants from one source, it would suddenly and unexpectedly be confronted by the arrival of a multitude of others from yet another country. The first large-scale aliyah (immigration to Israel) began in October 1948, with the appearance of the Bulgarian Jews accompanied by former inmates of displaced persons camps in Germany, Austria and Italy. Three months later, the airlift of Jews from Yemen got under way, and in February 1949 – that is, one month thereafter – as the country was buckling under the weight of dealing with them all, Jews from Turkey turned up. In November 1949, well before the immigrants in place were adequately housed, the Jews of Poland began arriving, to be followed in May 1950 by a massive number of new entrants from both Iraq and Romania. Government officials were beside themselves. Civil servants and social workers required for the task at hand greatly exceeded those available, both in absolute and in qualitative terms. Personnel with insufficient training and experience had to improvise within newly formed bureaucratic structures. Lines of demarcation were indistinct and communications between those formulating and executing policy often went awry.

At first, for many immigrants, their introduction to Israel occurred within a reception camp (and later at a more permanent transition camp) where they slept in asbestos huts or in surplus British army tents. Sometimes, thousands of incoming Jews would be transferred to a particular camp within a single day. For example, on April 11, 1949, a total of 5,340 were deposited at the main camp, Sha'ar Ha'aliyah, where the harried staff was hard pressed in arranging for their food and bedding. In general, the reception camps left much to be desired. Although they provided free food and board, living conditions were sub-optimal. Frequently, groups of fifty or more men, women and children slept in a common hall. Residents had to wait for hours at a stretch to access showers. Electrical power was sporadic and non-existent at night. The camps "swarmed with mosquitoes, flies, mice and rats. The cesspools of the toilets overflowed and the dining hall was thick with grime."[37] Unsatisfactory hygienic conditions gave rise to an increase in infant mortality, which was already adversely affected by malnourished mothers arriving in Israel in an undermined state of health. During the summer of 1949, intestinal disorders were widespread. Due to a critical shortage of hospital beds and medical supplies as many as half of afflicted camp children died.[38]

To enable immigrants to earn a living, employment was offered in the context of miscellaneous projects, of which many served no practical purpose other than to provide a pretext for doling out welfare payments. The government hesitated to support immigrants directly on an ongoing basis lest they be discouraged from entering the workforce, and with that in mind it insisted that all able-bodied men below the age of forty-five seek paid employment. Those failing to do so were subject to the withdrawal of free access to food and shelter. Obtaining work frequently entailed adapting one's calling in accordance with local labour market conditions. This applied to 60 percent of all immigrants.[39] For breadwinners who had previously been shopkeepers and petty traders and who then had to become farmers or general workers, the transformation was both physically and psychologically challenging.

Eventually, migrants found a niche for themselves within new agricultural settlements or the country's urban areas. The integration of

Israel's disparate Jewish population was not easily accomplished. Even to this day, the country is riven by differences in ethnic origins. Few Mizrahis (Jews from Arab countries) are represented in the top echelon of Israeli society, such as among cabinet ministers, army officers, high-court judges, university presidents, and so on. However, among operative unifying forces, the feeling that all Jews are kinsmen sharing the same religion and destiny has proved to be a powerful one. The very realities of life in Israel have given rise to the melding of people from vastly different backgrounds into a homogeneous national body. With Israel constantly at war with its neighbours, external threats tend to draw its Jewish citizens closer together. In that respect, the army has played a key role. By requiring most able-bodied men and women from different backgrounds and walks of life to serve within its ranks, it has subjected them to a common experience and mission.

The flood of penurious and displaced Jews seeking a haven in Israel came at a time when the state's threadbare economy was already stretched to the limit. Foreign reserves had fallen to such a low level that the continued importation of products such as wheat, flour and oil was put in doubt.[40] Internally, an abrupt exodus of Arab farmers, the mobilization of Jewish ones and war damage led to a serious shortfall in agricultural output.[41] As a result, elementary necessities (including clothes) had to be strictly rationed. But, by March 1953, Israel managed to secure a commitment from West Germany to provide it with nearly a billion dollars' worth of reparations. That, plus a combination of newly sourced funds from the USA and World Jewry and a ready availability of entrepreneurs and experts in important fields of economic endeavour, paved the way for a steady and rapid rise in national income.[42] Furthermore, the establishment of a number of new development towns in various parts of the country afforded employment for the recent immigrants and ensured a more balanced geographic dispersal of the Jewish population.

As Israel came to grips with its internal problems it had also to confront threatening challenges in the international arena. First and foremost was the continued hostility of the entire Arab World, which adamantly refused to accept Israel's very existence and which freely put about threats of a forthcoming "second round." To add substance to their comminatory remarks, in the spring of 1950 the Arab League imposed a trade and investment embargo on the Jewish State. Enlisting the support of non-Arab Muslim countries, the League threatened to boycott any company, including shipping and general transport ones, that maintained commercial ties with Israel. Extending their campaign further afield, the Arabs sought and obtained the uncritical support of the Third World bloc, which, in April 1955 at its inaugural conference in Bandung, Indonesia, adopted a pro-Arab resolution proposed by Egypt's president, Abdul Nasser. Although the conference was ostensibly a meeting of "non-aligned states," Israel was pointedly excluded, even though, unlike Turkey, Pakistan and Iraq, it had not entered into a military alliance with a Great Power.

Co-opting the UN General Assembly, and with the automatic support of the Soviet Union within the Security Council, the Arabs and their allies soon turned the entire UN into an anti-Israel organization. As an example, when in May 1956 a report on the Israeli–Arab conflict drafted by the UN Secretary General, Dag Hammarskjold, was submitted to the Security Council, Ahmed Shukeiri, Syria's representative and later chairman of the PLO, objected to the use of the term "peaceful settlement on a mutually acceptable basis." Deferring to Arab, Iranian and Soviet opposition, the offending text was duly deleted![43] To all intents and purposes, Israel has been treated within the UN as a state with less than full rights. It has never once been considered as a candidate for a temporary seat in the Security Council. In 1950, on encountering obstacles in attending a UN Food and Agriculture Organization Conference, Israel proposed that the UN guarantee all members ready access to such gatherings. Much to Israel's mortification, its resolution was overwhelmingly rejected. Only four of the forty states that participated voted in its favour.[44]

Not only did Israel have to contend with a wall of antagonism from the Arabs, the Soviet Union and the Third World, but it was also subject to baleful Western intrigues. The notion propagated by radical European and American intellectuals that Israel has always been cuddled under the caring wing of the USA is entirely belied by the facts. For one, during Israel's War of Independence, when its future was very much in the balance, the United States refused to supply it with arms. Thereafter, in April 1955, Israel informally learnt from Herbert Morrison, a British member of parliament, that Britain and the USA had reached a joint understanding, embodied in a document named Project Alpha. The two powers agreed that, in the interest of warding off war between Israel and the Arabs, Israel ought to cede parts of the Negev. In exchange Israel was to receive the Gaza Strip, along with all its Palestinians.[45] In September 1955, in a speech delivered at the Guildhall, London, Anthony Eden, Britain's foreign minister, gave some indication of the contours of the Alpha plan. He declared that the solution to the Arab–Israeli conflict required a compromise that would ultimately necessitate Israel's borders falling somewhere between the present armistice lines and the positions suggested in the UN 1947 partition resolution.[46] Such a generous British offer of Israel's territory would still have left the Arabs dissatisfied. An internal report of the secretary general of the Arab League maintained that the Arabs not only expected Israel to withdraw to the *proposed UN 1947 boundaries* and to permit the return of all refugees, but that they also required of Israel that it relinquish part of its attenuated land for refugees who might choose not to live there.[47]

By November 1955, the US secretary of state, John Dulles, provided Israel with full details of Project Alpha. In Dulles's version, there was to be a transfer of a large area of the Negev to Jordan and Egypt to enable them to maintain a territorial link with each other. Israel, if it so wished, could obtain the Gaza Strip *in exchange for transferring to Jordan compensating territory*.[48] The essence of the US–UK understanding is summed up in a joint unpublished memorandum which stated that "Israel must make concessions. The Arabs will not reconcile themselves to reaching a settlement with Israel with the present boundaries."[49] Such a conclusion was rather extraordinary, considering that both Egypt and Jordan, because of their war of aggression against Israel, were already holding large amounts of Palestinian land to which they had neither legal nor moral claims. Project Alpha never stipulated the word "peace"; rather, it alluded to an Arab "acceptance of Israel's existence."[50]

Efforts to erode Israeli gains as a means of currying favour with the Arabs extended to other areas. On a visit to Israel in May 1952, Henry Byroade, the US assistant secretary of state for Near Eastern affairs, suggested to Ben-Gurion, Israel's prime minister, that he limit Jewish immigration to permit the wholesale return of Arab refugees.[51] This call was repeated by Byroade two years later in an address to a Jewish audience in Chicago, where he added the proviso that Israel should abandon its Zionist mission by ceasing to consider itself the centre of World Jewry.[52] Byroade's demand was couched in language that would have delighted the Arab League, for he described the Jews as sharing only a commonality of religion and not of nationhood.

With regard to Jerusalem, in November 1949 Herbert Evatt, the Australian foreign minister, proposed in the UN General Assembly that the city be granted international status, in keeping with the November 1947 UN partition resolution (it came to light that Evatt had done so in order to obtain Catholic support for the Australian Labor Party in a forthcoming general election).[53] Evatt's resolution, approved by a large majority on December 10, had the backing of a host of Catholic states, communist countries, and the Arab and Muslim bloc. As had subsequently become par for the course with many UN General Assembly resolutions, this one was based on rank prejudice and pure hypocrisy. When Jewish-held Jerusalem was systematically and repetitively bombed by the Arab Legion in 1948, the UN stood by with its hands folded doing nothing to assist the beleaguered Jews, who were supposed to have received the protection of an international governor and police force. For four hundred years (1517–1917) the Christian World was reconciled to Turkish Muslim control of the city, and when in 1948 the UN intermediary, Count Folke Bernadotte, favoured handing it over to Transjordan, it raised no outcry. Only when the Jews, who had constituted a majority in Jerusalem since 1874, claimed sovereignty to the western part, where there was not one of the seven major holy sites,[54] did Western diplomats once more press for its internationalization. In the words of Monsignor Oesterreicher (a Catholic priest and scholar),

> during Jordanian rule, 34 out of the Old City's 35 synagogues were dynamited. Some were turned into stables, others into chicken coops. There appeared to be no limit to the sacrilege. Many thousands of tombstones were taken from the ancient cemetery on the Mount of Olives to serve as building material and paving stones. A few were also used to surface a footpath leading to a latrine in a Jordanian army camp.[55]

Not once did the UN General Assembly issue Jordan with merely the mildest of rebukes. Evidently, the UN's declared zeal for the protection of the holy sites in Jerusalem did not apply to Jewish ones.

On the home front, Israel began to be subject to regular acts of depredation, murder and sabotage by Arab groups or individuals infiltrating into its territory from surrounding countries. With Israel's borders being lengthy, tortuous, largely unmarked, situated for the most part in desolate areas and generally not associated with natural barriers, they were relatively easily traversed. Over the years 1951–6, Israel lost hundreds of its citizens as a result of acts of terror perpetrated by Arab intruders and the need to combat them. The sheer brazenness of the saboteurs caused Israelis to fear for their safety and to question whether their state was capable of providing them with a reasonable measure of protection and security.[56] Settlements populated by newly arrived immigrants lacking military experience were most at risk, particularly those without fencing, lighting, shelters, telephones and internal means of communication.[57] In some instances, entire villages were abandoned.

Because of general economic constraints, the army's budget was cut to the bone. Serviceable weapons were in short supply; soldiers were scantily clothed and fed, and their state of morale was abysmal.[58] Lack of discipline and absenteeism without leave was rife and, what is more, drug addicts and criminals were present among the new recruits.[59] The state of the Golani Brigade which "guarded" the north of Israel typi-fied the chaotic state of the IDF in those days. Most of its commanders had never been under fire, only 10 percent of its soldiers were native-born Israelis or immigrants from Western countries, 17 percent knew no Hebrew, 50 percent knew it partially and 30 percent had no formal education. In Uri Milstein's opinion, the "Golani was not a combat bri-gade but rather a kind of immigrant absorption centre."[60] Insufficiently trained and poorly motivated conscripts sent on missions either failed to reach their targets or disengaged on meeting token resistance.[61]

To remedy the situation, a special retaliatory unit under Ariel Sharon's command, known as Unit 101, was formed. The unit undertook an intensive commander training program that included the conveying of skills in hand-to-hand combat, weapons use, sabotage and field craft. Its recruits, who were all carefully selected, earned a reputation for bravery and daring and set an exacting standard that was gradually emulated by the rest of the IDF. Amalgamating with a parachute brigade, Sharon's men were exclusively assigned responsibility for all of the IDF's punitive raids. These invariably occurred in the wake of Arab-perpetrated atrocities such as when, in March 1954, an Israeli bus was waylaid while ascending Maale Akravim (Scorpions' Pass), a desolate Negev elevation on the road to Eilat. With the driver meeting death instantly, the bus veered backwards until it struck an embankment. The attackers then boarded the bus and fired at all passengers, including women and children, killing eleven of them and wounding three.

At first the Arab marauders were almost all freelance operators, but by April 1955 the Egyptians had formed their own official detachment of armed infiltrators, known as Fedayeen (literally, "those who sacrifice themselves"). The move was formally proclaimed in a government communiqué that made it clear that "there will be no peace on Israel's border because we demand vengeance, and vengeance is Israel's death."[62] Elaborating, Hassan el Bakuri, an Egyptian minister, declared that "there is no reason why the Fedayeen filled with hatred of their enemies should not penetrate deeply into Israel and turn the lives of its people into hell."[63] By establishing a paramilitary organization to create havoc in Israel, Egypt deliberately flouted a key clause of the Israeli–Egyptian armistice agreement. The clause in question read: "No element of the land, sea or air, military or paramilitary forces of either Party, including non-regular forces, shall commit any warlike or hostile act against the military or paramilitary forces of the other Party, or against civilians in territory under the control of that Party."[64]

An ominous aspect of the training of Arab terrorists and the general dissemination of anti-Israel sentiment within the Arab World, and within Egypt in particular, was the widespread recruitment of ex-Nazi war criminals and collaborators. Although the Arabs were infatuated with Hitler and were more than willing to draw on support from his surviving henchmen, they did not for a moment flinch at depicting both Israel and Zionism as being Nazi-inspired. In the early 1950s many ex-Nazis settled in Egypt, where they adopted Arab noms de plume. The director of the Cairo-based Institute for the Study of Zionism, Alfred Zingler, styled himself Mahmoud Saleh.[65] His assistant, Dr Johannes von Leers, who had served on the staff of Goebbels's ministry, became known as Omar Amin. In 1957, according to the German newspaper

Frankfurter Illustrierte, Egypt had welcomed more than 2,000 ex-Nazis. Two in particular, Erich Altern (Ali Bella), who was a high-ranking member of the Gestapo, and Hans Baumann (Ali Ben Khader), who had participated in the extermination of Jews in the Warsaw Ghetto, became military instructors in Palestinian refugee camps. The significant ex-Nazi presence in Egypt did not in the slightest degree detract from its popularly perceived image as a "progressive anti-imperialist state." Syria likewise became a beneficiary of German military advice.[66]

Towards the middle of 1956, after numerous rounds of Arab strikes and Israeli responses, Moshe Dayan, as Israel's chief of staff, concluded that the usefulness of reprisal attacks had run its course. The Arabs had begun to anticipate the modus operandi of Israeli actions and had taken steps either to frustrate them or to impose heavy IDF losses. What especially strengthened Dayan's assessment that the IDF had to change tack was the news on September 27, 1955, that Egypt had secured an arms agreement with Czechoslovakia (or, to be more exact, with Russia) which stood to tilt the strategic Israel–Egypt balance decisively in Egypt's favour. Within no time, the Soviets began to provide Egypt with a prodigious amount of modern weapons, of a type and calibre that had hitherto not been available to any Middle Eastern combatant, including tanks, artillery, planes and submarines. Payment, to be deferred, was to be made in Egyptian cotton. Dayan's biggest nightmare was that, on integrating and mastering its newly acquired weapons, Egypt would challenge Israel in a "second round" at a time of its own choosing. That being the case, Israel had perforce to initiate a preventive war while it still had the facility to do so.

Israel's most pressing need was somehow to augment its modest stock of weapons so as to offset Egypt's growing strategic advantage. But both the USA and the UK rejected its requests. As the US secretary of state, John Dulles, briefed President Dwight Eisenhower, the USA had to turn down Israel's appeal for arms "not on its own merits" but so as not to appear to be too pro-Israel.[67] Similarly, Dulles and Harold Macmillan, the UK foreign secretary, jointly concluded that they ought to "avoid being pushed by the Russians into a position of opposition to Arab interests . . . Our guiding principle is that we should not be moving in to supply Israel with arms on a large scale to offset those supplied by the Iron Curtain."[68] Dulles even invented a disingenuous rationale for denying Israel the means to defend itself. He held that, since the Arabs were considerably more numerous than the Israelis, Israel in the long run could never attain the ability to absorb armaments to the extent that they could. Therefore it was pointless, if not self-defeating, for the US to supply Israel with military hardware.[69] In desperation, Israel turned to France. There it had better luck, for at the time the French were beset by an uprising in Algeria, which they regarded as an integral part of their mainland. Since Nasser was providing material and moral support to the rebels, the French looked upon Israel as a natural ally. Accordingly, they more than willingly agreed to furnish it with a wide array of armaments, and by mid-1956, without seeking any military quid pro quo, they began delivering them in earnest.

Then, on July 26, 1956, Egypt unexpectedly nationalized the Suez Canal Company. This led Britain and France (whose citizens had jointly owned and managed the company) to plan to reverse that decision by force of arms. Affronted by what they regarded as Nasser's audacity, and already furious with him for meddling in Algeria and Jordan's internal affairs, not to mention his irksome anti-Western posturing, the two newfound allies were determined to bring him down a peg or two. In the course of their deliberations, the French suggested enlisting the support of the Israelis, not so much for their military usefulness as for a means of providing them with a cover or pretext to seize the general Suez Canal area. After some hesitation, Ben-Gurion acceded to their request, and on October 25, at a meeting in Sèvres (a Paris suburb), Britain, France and Israel agreed to collude in an attack on Egypt.

The Sèvres Agreement stipulated that the campaign against Egypt would open with an Israeli "raid" involving a parachute drop at the far end of the Mitla Pass, some 50 kilometres east of the Suez Canal and out of the immediate reach of major Egyptian forces. Simultaneously, an Israeli armoured column would enter the southern portion of Sinai, destroy two Egyptian positions and then proceed to link up with the paratroopers at the pass. The parachute drop and an ensuing Israeli general offensive was meant to provide Britain and France with suf-ficient cause to secure the canal from the warring parties. On the morning after the outbreak of fighting, Britain and France were to issue an ultimatum (termed "appeal" in the Sèvres Agreement) to the two protagonists to stay clear of the canal. It was anticipated that Egypt would not comply, especially since it was also to be asked to accept a "temporary" French and British presence in the Canal Zone. In that event, both Britain and France would then intercede (thirty-six hours after the Israeli parachute drop) as protectors of a vital international waterway.

As far as Israel was concerned, it was essentially pursuing its own interests, which were to free itself from the threat of an Egyptian invasion. Had its bellicose neighbour honoured the Israeli–Egyptian armistice agreement by not dispatching armed Fedayeen to Israel to wreak havoc on its population, and had it not so assiduously striven to acquire sufficient means to fulfil its publicly declared objective of destroying Israel, it is highly unlikely that Israel would have been complicit with Britain and France, who were essentially seeking to assert their mastery over a recalcitrant Third World country. When, in July 1952, Major-General Muhammad Naguib overthrew King Farouk, Ben-Gurion made it clear that "Israel wishes to see Egypt free, independent, and progressive . . . We have no enmity against Egypt." [70] The alliance with Britain and France furnished Israel with vital practical support from two European powers at a time when Egypt was being unconditionally propped up by the Soviet Union and when the USA exhibited a marked measure of aloofness towards the Jewish State.

The Sinai Campaign opened on October 29, 1956, by Israel carrying out military operations exactly as outlined in the Sèvres Agreement. Thanks in part to France undertaking to assist in the defence of Israel's skies and Nasser withdrawing forces to reinforce the Canal Zone in anticipation of a British–French invasion, Israel, in just over six and a half days, and what seemed like a practice run for the later Six-Day War, thoroughly routed the Egyptian army in Sinai. While Israel's performance was well executed, the same cannot be said for its allies, who, because of inordinate delays, were slow in getting off the mark. By the time they eventually arrived in Egypt and made some tentative inroads, American and Soviet opposition to their project was becoming so shrill and threatening that they were soon forced to back down and withdraw in ignominy. A combination of Russian hints of raining down atomic bombs on London and Paris, an American determination to withhold vital economic assistance and a growing groundswell of internal opposition in the UK persuaded the British government to change course. When Britain did so, France had no option other than to follow suit.

With the Israelis becoming the only ones occupying Egyptian terri-tory, the full weight of international opinion told against them. Apart from the usual diet of Soviet threats, which the Israelis took quite seri-ously, the USA was most adamant that Israel had to withdraw fully. In a message authorized by President Eisenhower, Herbert Hoover, Jr (the US acting secretary of state), informed Israel that, should it not do so, the USA would deprive it of all forms of aid, enforce UN sanc-tions against it and have it expelled from the UN.[71] The harshness of Hoover's communication reflected the United States' need to counter-act the spread of Soviet influence in the Middle East, which capitalized on the Anglo-French debacle and on growing anti-Western sentiments within Arab and Third World countries.

Although Israel had no alternative but to comply, it did its utmost to delay matters in order to use the time available to persuade the USA of the justice of its cause and of the need for international recognition of its natural rights, as a littoral state (denied by Egypt), to sail the Gulf of Eilat. Slowly but surely, with the US media and Congress coming round to the view that Israel indeed harbored legitimate grievances, Eisenhower mellowed somewhat and began to show a more sympa-thetic appreciation of Israel's predicament. On February 20, 1957, in a nationwide radio and television broadcast, he publicly conceded that Israeli military action against Egypt resulted from grave and repeated provocations. Although he went on to state that "military force to solve international disputes cannot be reconciled with the principles and purposes of the United Nations," he also mentioned that no nation has the right to hinder free and innocent passage in the Gulf.[72] Taking up Eisenhower on the latter point, Israel requested that the USA use its good offices to persuade other nations to deliver similar pronounce-ments. In a meeting with Dulles, Abba Eban, Israel's foreign minister, was told that the United States was predisposed to a French suggestion for resolving the deadlock. It entailed the issuing of a manifesto by the USA, France, Britain, Canada, Australia, Norway and other countries recognizing Israel's claim to free navigation in the Bay of Eilat. Should such a right be denied, Israel would be entitled to assert it by force. With that understanding, and with the UN committed to the stationing of an Emergency Force (UNEF) in Egyptian territory along the Israel–Egypt border, Israel, on March 8, 1957, finally evacuated the entire area it had conquered.

Shortly after the Sinai Campaign, the Australian prime minister, Sir Robert Menzies, observed that "the United Nations made Israel a victim of a double standard of belligerent rights." It accepted Egypt's assertion that it could deny Israel access to the Suez Canal because Israel and Egypt were in a state of war with each other, but at the same time it compelled Israel to withdraw from Egyptian territory, including the Gaza Strip, which Egypt had illegally conquered. Menzies avowed: "I cannot believe this kind of thing is a triumph of international justice."[73] Paul-Henri Spaak, one-time foreign minister of Belgium and acting president of the UN General Assembly, arrived at a similar conclusion. He wrote (in *Foreign Affairs*) that, confronted with regular Egyptian violations of the armistice agreement, the UN could not bring itself to intervene, but as soon as Israel sent its troops into Sinai there was an uproar. "All who stood by with folded arms in the face of the terrible suppression of the Hungarian uprising were beside themselves in reprimanding Israel. Justice of this sort is nothing but a travesty."[74]

Critics of Israel's Sinai Campaign have likened it to a "war of choice," implying that it was not strategically imperative and that it was motivated by a desire to acquire more land. Yet, as far as the Israeli defence establishment was concerned, Israel's "choices" were limited to biding its time until the Arabs attacked it at their leisure or foreclosing such an option by means of a pre-emptive strike. Israeli generals were not alone in assuming that Nasser was intent on going to war. In April 1956, George Kennedy Young, the deputy director of MI6, confided to the CIA that, according to their sources, Nasser aimed at nothing other than the total destruction of Israel.[75]

Israel's achievements from the Sinai Campaign were not negligible. Between March 1957 and May 1967, there was not a single Egyptian violation of the armistice agreement. Ships freely sailed to and from Eilat, a UN peacekeeping force was stationed in the Gaza Strip and Sinai, and the general state of military tension between Israel and Egypt abated. Since the Egyptian army did not immediately reoccupy its Sinai bases, for a few years the peninsula effectively became demilitarized.[76] Within the international arena there was a relaxation of tension, for proposals by Western powers to revise Israel's frontiers so as to curry Arab favour (such as Project Alpha) were finally put to rest.

While, for the time being, Egypt refrained from violating the border, it never desisted from scheming to undermine Israel. A critical step was taken in January 1964 at an Arab summit held in Cairo, when Nasser suggested that a Palestine Liberation Organization (PLO) be set up under Arab League auspices. His suggestion was readily approved and finance was budgeted for that purpose. Nasser then nominated Ahmad Shukeiry, a former Palestinian who had served successively as the Saudi Arabian and Syrian ambassador to the UN, to be the PLO's first president. Once again the summit concurred. Shukeiri then personally selected the delegates for the PLO's founding conference, which opened in May 1964 in East Jerusalem. Off his own bat, Shukeiry drafted a National Charter and a Fundamental Law for the nascent organization. At that time both the Gaza Strip and the West Bank were firmly in Arab hands. If to those regions one adds the eastern part of Jordan, then 82 percent of the original mandated Palestine was Arab held. Within those confines, the Palestinians constituted a distinct majority (even within Jordan alone, where the Bedouin were a rather small minority).[77] Not being content with such a situation, the PLO dedicated itself to the total elimination of the Jewish State. Only then, it declared, would Palestine be liberated. Interestingly, while one of the resolutions adopted at the PLO's founding conference held that the Palestinian body would assume sovereignty over Palestine, it was also agreed that such sovereignty would not abrogate Jordan's annexation of the West Bank.[78] The abnegation of Jewish national rights was but one plank in the PLO's platform. It was officially intended that all Jews bar those that had lived in Palestine before 1918 be expelled. At least that was touted as the preferred benign outcome. In reality, many PLO members and adherents expected the Jews to be massacred en masse. As one "militant" confessed, he was among those who thought "that we must slaughter the Jews."[79]

Not to be outdone by Egypt's pretensions to be the leading sponsor of Palestinian rights, the Syrians in the latter half of 1964 sought to form a rival body to the PLO under their direct control.[80] Their army intelligence agents scoured refugee camps in Lebanon in search of volunteers to be trained as Palestinian Fedayeen. One of the Syrian agents was approached by Yasser Arafat and seven of his comrades. (Yasser's first name was originally Rahman. He was given the name Yasser by a teacher in memory of a myrmidon of the Nazi collaborator Haj Amin al-Husseini, a cousin of Arafat's mother. The eponymous Yasser was killed by the British while smuggling German arms into Palestine.)[81] Arafat explained that he headed a band dubbed the Movement for the Liberation of Palestine. He and his men had opposed the formation of the PLO for not being sufficiently revolutionary and were hindered by it in that it attracted Algerian funds and facilities that they had previously enjoyed. To the great satisfaction of the recruiting agent, they agreed to cooperate with the Syrians.

Their first task was to draft a communiqué announcing the inaugural military action of their group, which they named Fatah, derived by reversing the first Arabic letters of the Movement for the Liberation of Palestine (Harakat-Tahrir Falastin). "Fatah" means "conquest through Jihad." The communiqué opens by referring to the group's dependence on God and their belief in the duty of Jihad,[82] thus making nonsense of Arafat's subsequent protestations that he was striving for a secular democratic state. The heralding of military action in January 1965 turned out to be somewhat premature, for the explosive charges meant to sabotage Israel's national water carrier failed to detonate. No matter, news of the "event" was widely disseminated, and instantly Arafat and his associates acquired celebrity status. Orchestrated by Syria, further Fatah raids got off the ground. Many were staged from Jordan in order to complicate matters for King Hussein, but a large number also originated from Syria. The Fatah raids were masterminded by the Syrian Military Intelligence organization (the Deuxième Bureau). They were plainly meant to demoralize the Israelis, and the Syrians were by no means reticent in expressing such views. Senior government officials explicitly informed Hall Saunders, a member of the US National Security Council, that the Fatah had been given free rein to endanger Israeli lives to such an extent that many, if not most, would leave for the safety of foreign shores.[83]

It was only a matter of time before Israel retaliated. For the most part it attacked bases in Jordan, but in March 1967 Prime Minister Eshkol decided to exact a punishing toll from the guerrillas' Syrian sponsors. The plan was to send tractors into the demilitarized regions (near Syria) to draw Syrian fire, to which the IDF would immediately respond. True to form, on April 7 the Syrians fired at an Israeli tractor ploughing a field near Kibbutz Ha-On, southeast of Lake Kinneret (Sea of Galilee), and at two other settlements in the same vicinity. Israel replied with an artillery barrage that in turn was met in kind. The IDF then activated its armour, but since it was unable to advance to within range of all relevant enemy positions the air force, with Eshkol's approval, was summoned. Scores of fighters took off (some allege that as many as 130 planes were involved).[84] As the Israeli planes drew near, they encountered Syrian MiGs. A furious dogfight ensued which spread deep into Syrian airspace. Six Syrian planes were downed without any Israeli losses. In full view of thousands of Syrian citizens, two of their planes fell on the outskirts of Damascus. With its prestige badly tarnished, Syria looked to Egypt to redeem it in accordance with a mutual defence treaty signed in November 1966. However, Nasser maintained that, if he were to muster his forces in response to Syrian–Israeli border skirmishes, all that Israel needed to do was to "smash a Syrian tractor to draw us in. That is not satisfactory. Only we ourselves will set the deadline."[85] Therefore, unless Syria was invaded by a large ground force, Egypt would retain its own freedom of action.

By early May 1967, the Russians stirred the pot by disclosing to both Syria and Egypt that they had "discovered" that Israel was massing eleven to thirteen brigades on its northern frontiers in preparation for a general onslaught against Syria. The Egyptians, who trusted the Russians implicitly, took the latest invasion report very seriously, especially since it was issued on at least two occasions. They soon found that the Russian report was a complete fabrication, for on May 14 Egypt's chief of staff, Muhammad Fawzi, flew to Syria, where he observed from the air that there were no signs of any unusual military activity in the area in question. In fact, Syria's army was not even placed on a war footing. As Fawzi told Nasser, "There is nothing there. No massing of forces. Nothing."[86] Nevertheless Nasser was in a bind. Considering that Syria was supposedly endangered, any attempt to disavow the Soviet alert would probably have been seen as an Egyptian ruse not to honour its defence treaty obligations. Having already been shamed by King Hussein for not aiding Jordan when, during the previous November, it was subjected to a harsh Israel military reprisal, he may well have felt that his hands were tied and that he simply was compelled to demonstrate that he was prepared to stand by his "imperilled" ally. This meant that Nasser, with much fanfare, dispatched two infantry divisions into the Sinai peninsula to augment the one already there.[87] Then suddenly King Hussein of Jordan raised the stakes by reminding everyone of an occasion when Nasser had left him in the lurch and by accusing the Egyptian army of shielding itself in a cowardly manner behind the United Nations Emergency Force (UNEF). Rising to the bait, on May 16 Egypt instructed UNEF to withdraw its forces stationed between Rafiah and the Gulf of Eilat and to reposition them in Gaza. On learning of Egypt's request to UNEF, U Thant, the UN Secretary General, ruled that there was no provision for a partial evacuation. Egypt could either continue to accept the current arrangement or it could instruct the Secretary General to withdraw the force in its entirety. Faced with such a choice, Nasser, on May 17, opted for the latter alternative, thereby seriously undermining the informal post-Sinai Campaign accords. All this caused the Israelis great concern. As a defensive measure, they began mobilizing some of their reserves.

On May 22, Eshkol addressed the Knesset. He stated that "Israel is prepared to participate in an effort to strengthen stability and the advancement of peace in our region."[88] But discreetly, through the medium of the UN Secretary General, U Thant, Eshkol cautioned that, should Egypt close the Straits of Tiran, Israel would view such a move as a *casus belli*. That very evening, while U Thant was en route to deliver Eshkol's message, Nasser upped the ante. Visiting the Abu Suweir airbase at Bir Gafgafa in Sinai, he became emboldened by the supreme confidence exuded by his pilots. As they spoke of their ability to destroy the entire Israeli air force within a matter of hours, he in turn informed them that henceforth all ships bearing Israeli flags would be barred from entering the Straits of Tiran. Not only were Israeli ships to be disallowed but so too were ships of any nationality conveying "strategic" goods to Eilat. Inspired by his own rising and uninhibited bellicosity, Nasser added: "If the Jews threaten to fight, my reply is 'ahlan wasahlan' [you are welcome], we are ready for war."[89] Elated by the grand challenge he had set himself, and beholden to events that he no longer controlled, Nasser delivered one fiery speech after another.[90] The net result was that the general Arab populace was whipped up into a delirious frenzy, sending chills down the spines of the Israelis. As Dayan noted, there was an interesting twist to the way things were panning out. Rather than Israel actually threatening to go war against Syria, as the Soviets falsely claimed, Egypt presented Israel with an enormous concentration of troops and threat of force.[91] Already the Egyptians had placed 80,000 troops and 800 tanks in Sinai, with more to follow.[92]

Concluding that war was inevitable, the IDF's general staff wanted to take up the cudgels without further delay to deprive Egypt of the advantages of a first strike. However, the government decided that it would not activate the IDF until a non-violent solution had exhaustively been pursued. With that in mind, Eban was sent on a mission to sound out the views of France, Britain and the United States. Eban's first port of call on May 24 was Paris, where he conferred with President de Gaulle. De Gaulle both insisted that, despite all Egyptian violations of the status quo, Israel should never fire the first shot, and arrogated to himself the role of *primus inter pares* (first among equals) of the four great powers (USA, UK, France and Russia) which, under his sagacious counsel, would resolve the Middle East impasse by diplomatic means. De Gaulle was prepared neither to reaffirm France's commitment to Israel's security nor to censure Egypt for its hostile posturing. When Eban reminded him of the statement issued by France in 1957 reaffirming its support of Israel's right of free passage through the Straits of Tiran, de Gaulle, with a shrug, dismissed it as no longer having any relevance. "Besides," he added, "I wasn't President then."[93] Israel was beginning to learn the hard way that the shelf life of one state's commitment to another could be short indeed. By contrast, Harold Wilson, the British prime minister, indicated that he appreciated and supported the need for ensuring complete freedom of shipping in the Straits of Tiran. But he stressed that it was up to the United States to assume the lead in securing such an outcome. This meant that all efforts to arrive at a peaceful resolution of the ongoing crisis hinged on the USA. On meeting with President Johnson, Eban did at least secure a promise that the United States would do all in its power to open the Straits of Tiran to Israeli shipping, but Johnson insisted that efforts had first to be expended within the UN. This of course meant that, for the time being, nothing of consequence would be decided.

Shortly after Eban returned to Israel without any heartening news, Hussein (on May 30) flew to Cairo to sign a defence pact with Nasser that entailed placing his army under the command of an Egyptian general and agreeing to the entry into his kingdom of both Egyptian and Iraqi troops. As an iron grip around Israel's borders was being tightened, its Arab foes made no bones about their intentions. On May 28 Nasser explained to a gathering of journalists that it was not the closure of the Straits of Tiran that was the problem but rather the very existence of Israel. Egypt would not abide coexisting with it.[94] Similarly, Hussein declared that he was looking forward to treading the "road leading to the erasure of our shame and the liberation of Palestine."[95] The Cairo-based radio station "Voice of the Arabs" made it clear that a total war would be waged against Israel "which will result in the final extermination of Zionist existence."[96] Mullahs called for a Jihad, and one of Radio Cairo's hit songs exhorted the Arabs to smite, kill, burn and destroy the Israelis. "*Itbah, itbah, itbah*" – that is, "massacre, massacre, massacre" – ran its refrain.[97] On being asked in a French television interview just what plans he had for Jews born in Israel, Shukeiry, the head of the PLO, simply drew a finger across his throat.[98] On another occasion, in answer to the same question, Shukeiri responded: "Those who survive will remain in Palestine, but I estimate that none of them will survive."[99]

Such pronouncements made a deep impression within all levels of Israeli society, as did both the relentless build-up of hostile Arab forces and the lack of any meaningful diplomatic backing. Against that sorrowful background, and after waiting for three weeks in the forlorn hope that the crisis would be peacefully resolved, the cabinet on June 4 at long last voted to give the IDF the go-ahead at a time of its own choosing. (The IDF's D-day of June 5 was essentially dictated to it by the fact that the main body of the Iraqi forces was expected to enter Jordan on the night of June 6.)[100] With the die now cast, Israel adopted rather modest war aims. It sought to extricate itself from the threat of extinction, to reassert its right to navigate through the Straits of Tiran, and to restore the status quo ante.[101] No Arab land was coveted.[102]

The long-expected war opened with an early-morning surprise air attack on Egypt's grounded air force. Within a matter of hours, 286 of Egypt's 420 warplanes were destroyed and nearly a third of its pilots were killed.[103] The IDF's armoured forces then went on the offensive, demolishing one Egyptian stronghold after another. By June 8 virtually the entire Sinai peninsula was Israeli held. Nasser's army had been humiliatingly routed. It was not Israel's intention to widen the scope of hostilities to include both Jordan and Syria. In that light Jordan was reassured that, if it refrained from becoming actively involved, it would come to no harm. However, Hussein threw caution to the wind, and within next to no time West Jerusalem was bombarded. Six thousand shells were fired into it and, as a consequence, over a thousand people were injured, 150 seriously; twenty subsequently died. Damage to property was extensive. More than 900 buildings were struck, including the Hadassah Hospital at Ein Kerem, where the famous Marc Chagall stained-glass windows were damaged.[104] Israel was left with no choice other than to strike back, with the unfortunate consequences for Hussein of forfeiting all territory west of the River Jordan. As Avi Shlaim (an historian often critical of Israeli policies) observed: "Had King Hussein heeded Eshkol's warning, he would have kept the Old City of Jerusalem and the West Bank. No one in the cabinet or the General Staff proposed the capture of the Old City before the Jordanian bombardment began."[105] Syria likewise tempted fate by raining down shells on Jewish settlements on the plain beneath the Golan Heights, damaging some 205 houses and forty-five vehicles.[106] Having neutralized the Egyptian and Jordanian forces, Israel decided against a passive response to the unprovoked and wanton Syrian acts of belligerency. The IDF, after redirecting much of its armour to its northern frontier, stormed the Golan Heights, and by June 10 the Syrian forces there were well and truly beaten. As with Jordan, had Syria stood aloof, it would have remained intact.

The immediate reaction of Israelis was not to gloat over their sweeping victories. They were simply thankful that the horrendous fate that the Arabs had wished upon them did not eventuate. There were certainly no celebratory parades or victory balls. As the writer Shabtai Teveth recalled, "People did not dance in the streets, public houses did not give free drinks to the masses and lovely young girls did not climb on tanks to kiss the soldiers." Rather, "the very first event was a three days' mourning period."[107] In a speech delivered at the Hebrew University on receiving an honorary doctorate, Rabin, the IDF chief of staff, remarked that the Jewish people were not habituated to experiencing the joy of conquest and victory. He noted that, in addition to the sorrow his men felt at losing their comrades, the terrible price that the enemy paid also touched many of them.[108] What has never been sufficiently appreciated is that, in contrast to the Arabs, who avidly craved for Jewish blood, there was a complete absence within Israel of any *public* or *official* articulation of hatred or contempt towards the Arabs. In all the popular songs sung during the war and in all those that afterwards rejoiced in Israel's victory, *not a single one* cast any slurs on the country's enemies.[109] The mood of the day was also exemplified by Prime Minister Levi Eshkol, who, in January 1968 on a visit to the USA addressed President Johnson as follows: "Mr President. I have no sense of boastful triumph nor have I entered the struggle for peace in the role of victor. My feeling is one of relief that we were saved from disaster in June and for this I thank God. All my thoughts now are turned toward getting peace with our neighbours – a peace of honour between equals."[110]

1

THE EARLY AFTERMATH OF THE
SIX-DAY WAR

No sooner had the guns of the Six-Day War fallen silent than thousands of Israelis poured into the Old City of Jerusalem and the West Bank, where they were enchanted by the landscape of the Judean hills, the "authentic Land of Israel." The human traffic flowed in both directions, since Dayan had removed all travel restrictions on Arabs in the conquered territories, allowing them to wander freely throughout Israel. Many went to gaze at their former homes and districts. Others delighted in savouring Israeli delicacies. On June 9, Teddy Kollek, the mayor of West Jerusalem, who had previously expressed qualms about the wisdom of permitting unrestricted movements of both Arabs and Jews, sent Dayan a telegraph, saying "You were right. Well done. There is a festive air in the city. All the Arabs are in Zion Square and all the Jews are in the bazaars."[1] At that stage a commingling of the two populations was seen in a positive light. Only after many years of increasing Arab violence did the Israeli authorities reluctantly embark on the construction of a security barrier to protect their citizens from deadly terrorist attacks.

In Jerusalem on the night of June 10, around 135 houses adjacent to the Western Wall were summarily bulldozed. Without consulting either Dayan or Rabin, Uzi Narkiss, commander of the central front, directed demolitions that allowed for the establishment of a large plaza facing the Western Wall in which a multitude of people could congregate during Jewish festivals and national holidays. Narkiss felt that the clearance had to be effected as rapidly as possible in anticipation of international pressures preventing Israel from undertaking structural modifications within the Old City. The Arab residents in the houses in question were allowed no more than an hour or two to vacate their homes and to remove whatever possessions they could carry. An IDF officer promised them that they would ultimately be rehoused.[2] Four days later, the cabinet authorized the eviction of the Arabs who had moved into the Jewish Quarter in 1948 after all the original Jewish residents had been expelled (about 300 Arab families were involved).[3]

Israelis were virtually unanimous that Jerusalem was to be reunited and to remain under Israeli sovereignty in perpetuity. Accordingly, its municipal boundaries were redrawn to incorporate the Old City, Mount Scopus, Sheikh Jarrah and the suburb of Shuafat up to the airport at Atarot (Kalandia), and on June 28 the Knesset essentially annexed East Jerusalem (in the actual legislation, the word "annexation" was avoided). All dividing walls were razed to the ground, mines and barbed wire fences were cleared from what was previously no-man's-land, municipal services were integrated and telephone lines were fully interconnected.

Away from Jerusalem four villages in the vicinity of Latrun were flattened to ensure unhindered and safe traffic along the Jerusalem–Tel Aviv highway. Two other villages in the region of Hebron were also demolished, and, in Kalkilya, IDF officers acting on their own account expelled the inhabitants and dynamited their houses. The mayor of Kalkilya had been ordered onto a jeep from which he was forced to call upon his townsfolk to take leave of their homes. Fearing for the worst, most fled.[4] A little later, Dayan and General Ezer Weizman visited the scene. They were appalled. All the stores were broken into and looted,[5] and some 800 housing units were badly damaged.[6] Upset by the sight of Kalkilya's residents squatting in the open air in nearby olive groves, Dayan, at the next cabinet meeting, successfully recommended that their homes be restored and that they be allowed to return to them. Similarly, the Arabs from the two destroyed villages near Hebron were provided with finance and building materials to assist them in rehabilitating their dwellings.[7]

In Israeli government circles, conflicting views relating to the appropriate management of the country's new wards and territory were bitterly contested, thus impeding effective and decisive policy-making. Had Gahal (led by Menachem Begin) and Rafi (in which Moshe Dayan was a leading light) not entered a government of national unity just before the Six-Day War, it is quite possible, yet by no means certain, that a moderate consensus under Mapai's dominance would have emerged. (See Glossary for explanations of the above-mentioned terms.) On June 19, the cabinet did at least resolve, by a vote of eleven to ten,[8] to convey to both Egypt and Syria that, in the framework of a peace agreement, Israel was prepared to withdraw to recognized international frontiers – that is, it would vacate all of Sinai (but not the Gaza Strip, which was originally within Mandated Palestine) and the Golan Heights. The only preconditions were unrestricted use of the Suez Canal and the Straits of Tiran, the demilitarization of Sinai and the Golan Heights, and no Syrian tampering with Israel's water sources. The offer was transmitted to the US government to be forwarded to the two states in question. Within a matter of days, Egypt and Syria rejected it, demanding instead an unconditional withdrawal.[9] Having been so curtly rebuffed, Israel began to entertain second thoughts about the disposition of its forces in conquered Syrian territory. By mid-July, heeding military advice that some long-term presence was required for security purposes, the government began endorsing plans for the establishment of Jewish settlements on the Golan Heights. Gradually Israel's prerequisites for peace began to harden. By December 1969, Eban, as Israel's foreign minister, enunciated that Israel would never agree to terms that did not include a permanent Israeli presence at Sharm el Sheikh with a land link to Eilat, the full incorporation of the Golan Heights into Israeli sovereignty, a united Jerusalem and an eastern defence line along the River Jordan.[10]

Missing from the Israeli overture of June 19 was any mention of the West Bank, the heartland of ancient Jewish kingdoms. In that regard, the government was deadlocked, leaving matters in abeyance. If Ben-Gurion had had any say in the matter, Israel would have ceded the entire West Bank save for East Jerusalem, so as not to become entangled with a hostile Arab population. In April 1968 he explained his position in an interview with Tom Segev (then a contributor to a student newspaper) thus: "If I have to choose between a small Israel, without territories, but with peace, and a greater Israel without peace, I prefer a small Israel."[11] On another occasion he outlined his way of thinking somewhat more forthrightly, by affirming that "historically this country [Palestine] belongs to two races . . . the Arabs drastically outbreed us . . . a Jewish state must at all times maintain within her own borders an unassailable Jewish majority . . . the logic of all this is that to get peace, we *must* return in principle to the pre-1967 borders."[12] Although Ben-Gurion's views were seen by a very small following as being eminently sensible, they were widely ridiculed. His detractors claimed that they reflected either jealousy at Prime Minister Eshkol's successes or signs of senility.[13] With so many ministers opposing an outright withdrawal from the occupied territories, the likelihood of returning to the pre-1967 borders remained a moot point. At one extreme, Begin was wedded to the "solution" of simply retaining the entire West Bank, arguing that any autonomy there would lead to an undesirable establishment of a Palestinian State,[14] whereas two divergent mainstream proposals were propagated by Yigal Allon, minister of immigration, and Dayan, minister of defence.

Allon formulated a scheme that became known as the Allon Plan, according to which Israel would indicate a willingness to sue for peace in exchange for returning sections of the West Bank to the local Palestinians – and, when that soon proved to be unattainable, to Jordan. What Allon would not surrender was a large strip of land in the Jordan Valley (to serve as a defence buffer along the Jordan River), a very much extended Jerusalem municipal region and a widened Jerusalem corridor that would include Latrun. The area to be relinquished was to enjoy semi-autonomy and to be economically integrated with Israel. Realizing that his plan was somewhat contentious, Allon never formally presented it to cabinet for fear of precipitating a coalition crisis leading to a general election, in which Dayan, with his newly acquired status as national saviour, would have substantially boosted Rafi's electoral prospects. Dayan's approach is outlined a little further below.

Three weeks after the war Ya'akov Herzog, the director general of the Prime Minister's Office, met with King Hussein in the consulting room of Dr Emmanuel Herbert, the king's London physician. That meeting, like a previous one in 1963, was conducted in utmost secrecy.

Speaking man to man and with mutual respect, Herzog asked of Hussein whether, after all that had happened, and in view of the grave consequences of not resolving the ongoing conflict, he was now ready to enter into formal negotiations with Israel. Much to Herzog's regret, even in the seclusion of a private and confidential conversation, the king refused to commit himself.[15] A similar stance was manifested by Palestinian notables. After consulting them, in conjunction with other high-ranking Israelis and with Eshkol's endorsement, Herzog discovered that they were in no frame of mind to countenance any offer that would have gone a long way towards meeting their national aspirations. During a series of talks with such dignitaries, trial balloons were floated. These included the formation of an independent Palestinian State with its capital in the greater Jerusalem area and a secure passage between Gaza and the West Bank. (The state was to have been demilitarized and defended by the IDF.) At first, a number of Palestinians seemed to be receptive to at least some of the ideas submitted, but they soon had misgivings. Bearing in mind Israel's full withdrawal after the 1956 Sinai Campaign, they wondered how long Israel would remain in the newly conquered territories and were therefore fearful of being branded as collaborators.[16]

Also of note, within the IDF a solution pertaining to the West Bank was formulated by Rehavam Ze'evi, then assistant to the head of the IDF's operations branch. The plan envisaged that, apart from East Jerusalem, the Hebron region, the Jordan Rift Valley and the Latrun enclave, the rest of the West Bank would be set aside for an independent Arab state. The state was to be demilitarized, it would have free access to an Israeli port, and residents of both sides would enjoy mutual freedom of entry, save that those from the Arab state would not be able to acquire permanent residence in Israel. Since the plan never surfaced beyond army circles, it remained a dead letter.[17]

After the Arabs had failed to defeat Israel on the battlefield, the Soviet Union tried to recoup their losses both through the medium of the UN and through big power machinations. The first shot in the diplomatic war was registered on June 14 in the UN Security Council. Russia called for the condemnation of Israel as an aggressor and for it to withdraw unconditionally to the 1949 armistice lines. Much to Israel's surprise, the Soviet resolution was rejected. Unfazed,

Russia arranged for the General Assembly to convene on June 19 in a continuous special emergency session. An hour before its opening, President Johnson publicly announced America's newly found principles on resolving the Arab–Israeli conflict. They were encapsulated by five points, embracing the recognition of each country's right to full sovereignty, the resolution of the Palestinian refugee problem, unfettered passage in all international waterways, limits to the arms race and territorial integrity. In his address, Johnson mentioned that peace could not be obtained by restoring the "fragile and often violated armistice."[18] Johnson's position set the stage for the UN to adjudicate with a measure of uncharacteristic even-handedness. That is not to say that Soviet and other delegates did not refrain from denigrating Israel. Alexei Kosygin, the Russian prime minister, accused the Jewish State of "acting in a Hitlerist [sic] manner." In response to that grotesque comparison, Abba Eban, Israel's foreign minister, reminded the General Assembly that "Our nation never compromised with Hitler's Germany. Our nation never signed a pact with it as did the USSR in 1939."[19] On July 4, after an endless debate, a resolution sponsored by Yugoslavia was tabled calling for the total withdrawal of Israeli forces without any Arab concessions. Although it was supported by, among others, the Arabs, the communists, Muslim states and France, it failed to secure the necessary two-thirds majority. The Soviet Union then proposed a resolution of its own which was even more censorious of Israel and which demanded the payment of reparations by Israel to the Arabs. It too was rejected. The genocidal ambitions of the Arab World that were openly broadcast on the eve of the war yielded a welcome albeit fleeting groundswell of sympathy and support for Israel. By July 21, the special session of the General Assembly had run its course.

Backed by the Soviet Union and by the promise of subsidized oil from Saudi Arabia, both Egypt and Jordan, at an Arab summit held between August 28 and September 2 in Khartoum, endorsed a resolution ruling out any recognition, negotiation and peace with Israel.[20] Whatever moderate views were supposedly held behind the scenes,[21] – the Israelis were not aware of any – the Khartoum pronouncement was taken as an official indication that there were no medium- to long-term prospects of resolving the Arab–Israeli conflict. The realization of this induced Eshkol to inform the Knesset that "Israel will maintain the situation fixed by the ceasefire agreements and reinforce its position by taking into account its security and development needs."[22] Having forced Israel into a war from which they emerged as the vanquished, the Arabs short-sightedly continued on a path that compounded their losses.

Nearly three months later, on November 22 1967, after interminable haggling, the UN Security Council adopted Resolution 242, drafted in the main by Lord Caradon of the UK. Concentrating the minds of both the UK and the USA were civil and guerrilla disturbances within the West Bank as well as Israel–Egypt skirmishes along the Suez Canal (described in the following chapter). By its own definition, the two most important clauses of the resolution included "withdrawal of Israel armed forces from territories occupied in the recent conflict" and "the termination of all claims or states of belligerency and respect for and acknowledgment of the sovereignty, territorial integrity and political independence of every state in the area and their right to live in peace within secure and recognized boundaries free from threats or acts of force."[23] The resolution called upon the UN Secretary General to appoint a Special Representative to proceed to the Middle East to further its compliance. The representative chosen was Gunnar Jarring, a distinguished Swedish diplomat.

It is no accident that the first clause of Resolution 242 refers to a withdrawal "from territories," rather than "from *the* territories." The USA in particular as well as other Western members realized that the 1949 armistice lines had posed a strategic nightmare to Israel. That being the case, it would have been unconscionable to insist on a complete withdrawal to the pre-Six-Day War boundaries. For that reason "the armistice lines," or "the lines of June 4, 1967," were not included in the text.[24] The US position was clearly expressed by its ambassador to the UN, Arthur Goldberg, who in addressing the Security Council on November 15 stated that the final boundaries "would have to be established by the parties themselves as part of the peacemaking process."[25]

Nevertheless, the USSR and others still insisted on interpreting the resolution as if it called for the withdrawal of "all the territories," and France and Russia translated the text of the resolution into French and Russian in accordance with such viewpoints. This prompted Lord Caradon to remark that their interpretations were invalid, for "the resolution meant what it said and not a word more."[26] In like vein, on December 9, 1969, William Rogers, the US secretary of state, reaffirmed that "the Security Council resolution neither endorses nor precludes the armistice lines as the definitive political boundaries."[27] To allay any further confusion, both the USA and the UK affirmed that, since the resolution was a British-sponsored one, the English-language text prevailed over all others.[28]

The communists and the Arabs had sanctimoniously proclaimed that no country had a right to territory taken by force and therefore Israel had to withdraw to the armistice lines. Leaving aside the hypocrisy of the Soviet Union, whose empire was based on conquest, an Israeli retreat to the 1949 armistice lines would have legitimized the 1948 land grabs in Palestine of Jordan, Egypt and even Syria, whose reach had extended beyond the original international Palestine–Syria frontier. More to the point, the phrase (in clause 2) "their right to live in peace within secure and recognized boundaries" implied that final Israeli–Arab frontiers were to be subject to negotiation.

Initially, neither Israel nor the Arabs were willing to bind themselves outright to the resolution. Israel was reluctant to commit itself to territorial withdrawals, fearing that they might be accomplished without any serious quid pro quo, whereas the Arabs looked askance at clauses calling for a termination of the state of belligerency and respect for the sovereignty of all Middle East states. In January 1968, Eban announced that, in accordance with the spirit of Resolution 242, his government was willing to confine the IDF to within secure and recognized frontiers determined by direct negotiations with Israel's neighbours. Then a few months later – that is, in May 1968 – Eban instructed Yosef Tekoah, Israel's ambassador to the UN, to announce that Israel, in terms of its own interpretation, had finally accepted Resolution 242. This led to a furore with Gahal ministers who complained that Tekoah's statement had not attained the seal of cabinet approval. In trying to deflect their wrath, Eshkol suggested that it was merely a tactical decision, leaving open the question as to whether or not Israel had in fact endorsed the resolution.[29] But, even if Israel had unconditionally agreed to a complete withdrawal to the 1949 armistice lines, as far as both Egypt and Syria were concerned it would have been beside the point. The day after the resolution was passed Nasser decreed that "all that taken from us by force can *only* be retrieved by force," whereas Nureddin al-Attasi, president of Syria, declared that "a popular war is the *only* way to resolve the struggle with Israel and *there is no room for a political solution*."[30] Pronouncements of that kind strengthened internal pressures within Israel not to return to the pre-war frontiers.

In January 1968, Mapai, Ahdut Ha'avodah and Rafi, by merging to form the Israel Labour Party, brought an end to Mapai's existence as a distinct entity. Since the state was founded in 1948, Mapai (composed of moderate social democrats), without interruption, had been the country's ruling party. Never having gained a parliamentary majority in its own right, it always governed by means of coalition cabinets in which religious parties were included to counter the influence of secular rivals. Once the religious parties' basic theocratic goals were met, they were usually compliant supporters of Mapai's social, economic, military and diplomatic policies. At an earlier stage of Mapai's history – that is, in 1944 – a faction withdrew to resurrect Ahdut Ha'avodah (a socialist pioneering party with a more hard-line approach to the Arabs), which before 1930 had existed in its own right. Then in 1965, Ben-Gurion, who had for years been at the helm of Mapai and who was now at odds with his senior colleagues, formed a breakaway party named Rafi. It was hoped that, by virtue of Ben-Gurion's long-standing reputation as the major founding father of Israel, and with the backing of Dayan, Rafi would sweep to power in the 1965 general election. But that was not to be, for Rafi secured only ten seats. When in January 1968 it became a component of the new Israel Labour Party, Ben-Gurion, on refusing to fall in line with the other nine Rafi Knesset members, found himself isolated and politically impotent as a one-member Knesset faction.

Eshkol, who on February 26, 1969, died of a heart attack, was succeeded by Golda Meir. Partly on account of her chronic ill health, she was regarded as a temporary compromise candidate needed to forestall the appointment, on the one hand, of Dayan, who was generally not trusted, and, on the other, of Allon, who was unacceptable to Dayan, Shimon Peres and other ex-Rafi members. Pinhas Sapir canvassed support for Meir by assuring those favouring one or the other of her rivals that, at the utmost, she would not serve for more than six months.[31] In many ways, Meir, who had been a strong labour Zionist stalwart since her arrival in the country in 1921, was an unlikely choice. She lacked any serious rapport with the public, of whom, if the opinion polls are to be believed, no more than 3 percent had favoured her as prime minister.[32]

Yet in March 1969 Meir assembled a new government, in which Eban remained as foreign minister, Dayan as minister of defence and Allon as deputy prime minister, while Peres became a minister without portfolio. A distinctive feature of her leadership style was her running of an informal "kitchen cabinet" that met on Saturday evenings at her apartment. Usually consisting of Yisrael Galili, Allon, Dayan, Eban and Sapir, all exclusively members of the Labour Alignment, it functioned as a secretive executive committee to set the cabinet agenda and to determine the ruling party's approach to vital issues of the day.[33]

Whereas, under Eshkol, most cabinet ministers were dovish, under Meir the forces of doves and hawks were equally balanced.[34] Meir herself became a staunch hawk, and in the process her stock with the electorate rose. Although the foreign affairs portfolio remained in Eban's moderate hands, she assumed a proactive role in formulating Israel's external policies. As a result, Eban's input was marginalized while Dayan's then uncompromising views, shared by Peres, began to receive Labour Party favour. Fearful of Dayan bolting before a general election scheduled for the end of October 1969, the party caved in to his demands – chief among which was an acceptance of a so-called oral doctrine that was not to be explicitly included in the party's election manifesto. The doctrine involved an understanding that the River Jordan was to constitute the country's eastern security border, that the Golan Heights and the Gaza Strip were to remain under Israeli control, and that freedom of navigation in the Straits of Tiran was to be assured by IDF forces stationed in Sharm el Sheikh linked by a continuous strip of territory to the Israeli mainland. The last point was encapsulated by Dayan when he asserted that "Sharm el Sheikh without peace is preferable to peace without Sharm el Sheikh."[35] At the insistence of Dayan and Peres, implicit in the Labour Party's oral doctrine was the understanding that Jewish settlements in the occupied territories would be furthered.[36] The hardening of the Labour Party's line on the conquered territories helped pave the way for the eventual ascendancy of Gahal. Before the Six-Day War, the views of Begin, Gahal's leader, were widely regarded as being beyond the pale, but, with senior Labour Party cabinet ministers such as Meir,

Dayan and Yisrael Galili now freely articulating similar notions, Begin's credibility was inadvertently enhanced. The October 1969 election (see Appendix) led to Meir retaining a government of national unity with the continued inclusion of Gahal.

In the face of continued Arab hostility, Dayan argued that there was no point in trying to entice the Arabs with generous peace offers. Dayan believed that the best that could be attained was a reduction in inter-state military tensions and social unrest among the population of the conquered territories. To strengthen Israel's grip on the West Bank, which he regarded as a strategic asset, Dayan advocated that the IDF maintain a permanent military presence on commanding hilltops near densely populated Arab centres. As early as August 20, 1967, the cabinet had approved the establishment of five such bases. Dayan was not concerned exclusively with enhancing security in the occupied territories, for he also had other objectives in mind. Prime among these was the forging of an economic integration of Gaza and the West Bank with Israel. Such a process was seen by Sapir, the Labour Party's secretary, as jeopardizing Israel's long-term existence. As far as he was concerned, the sooner Israel divested itself of the occupied territories the better, since the continuation of Israel as an essentially Jewish State would be undermined by having Palestinians intricately linked to it. However, Sapir's articulated forebodings essentially fell on deaf ears. Dayan's view prevailed, and by 1970 Gaza was connected to Israel's electrical and water grids, a development that many Israelis later came to regret.

With regard to the conquered territories, Dayan was prepared to see its Arab inhabitants only as individuals, never as a collective entity.[37] That did not prevent him from promoting the alleviation of their living conditions. To a large degree, the Arabs were allowed to conduct their affairs with minimal interference. Their freedom also extended to their being able to travel and transport goods across the Jordan River in terms of the much vaunted "open bridges policy." In the summer of 1967, Palestinian farmers reaped bumper crops; had they not been able to dispose of their goods in Jordan they would have suffered substantial losses of income. Because all bridges over the Jordan had been destroyed, vehicles had to be hauled across shallow stretches of the river (it was the dry summer season). To facilitate easier passage, Israel approached Jordan to arrange for the reconstruction of the bridges. Jordan was amenable to the idea provided it undertook the job itself. Israel agreed, and thus, towards winter, two Bailey bridges were installed, one alongside the old Allenby Bridge and the other at Damiya. In addition, Dayan authorized residents in the rest of the Arab World to pay summer visits to their relatives in the West Bank and Gaza. Within the first seven years after the Six-Day War, some 1,800,000 such visits were made.[38]

After some time, the question of Resolution 242 was once again brought to the fore, on this occasion by the Americans. On December 9, 1969, the USA issued the "Rogers Plan," named after William Rogers, its secretary of state. The plan spelt out in some detail the route by which an amicable settlement between Israel and its neighbours could be attained. In the framework of an agreement negotiated under the auspices of Jarring, Israel was to withdraw (with minor adjustments) to its 1967 frontiers. Jerusalem was to remain united, but its eastern sections would not fall under Israeli sovereignty. Taking Israel's security concerns into account, the Rogers Plan allowed for the demilitarization of specific areas and for guaranteed free Israeli navigation in the Straits of Tiran and the Suez Canal. The very next day, Israel rejected the plan, primarily on the grounds that it did not posit a full peace agreement but rather some form of non-belligerence. The Israelis also took umbrage at what they regarded as the plan's retreat from Resolution 242, for, by contrast with the UN resolution, which deliberately left open the extent of any Israeli withdrawal, the USA now seemed to have adopted the Arab position of calling for a full return to the pre-Six-Day War borders.[39] In his capacity as Israel's ambassador to the USA, Yitzhak Rabin complained that the Rogers Plan implied that Israel was required to make maximal concessions while the Arabs needed to make only minimal ones.[40]

Egypt too rejected the Rogers Plan, described by its foreign minister, Mahmoud Riad, as being "worse than the old ones,"[41] and, with the Soviet Union following suit, the Rogers Plan in its entirety was laid to rest. According to Anatoly Dobrynin, the Soviet Union's ambassador to the USA, there was no way in which Nasser would negotiate with Israel about anything, and certainly not general security arrangements, demilitarization or free maritime passage.[42]

The United States soon made one more stab at an agreement, this time involving only Israel and Jordan. It was outlined in late December 1969 in the UN by Charles Yost, the American ambassador. Yost proposed that, apart from certain minor areas, Israel should vacate most of the West Bank. A united Jerusalem would prevail in which Israel would administer the Jewish neighbourhoods and Jordan the Arab ones. Although Yost referred to the establishment of peaceful Israeli–Jordanian relations, there was no mention of direct negotiations, a signed peace treaty, open borders or an exchange of diplomats. While Jordan expressed a willingness to accept Yost's terms, Israel rejected them out of hand.[43] One may well speculate whether or not on Israel's part that was a wise move. Would acceding to Yost's suggestions have resulted in freeing Israel of the burden and demographic threat of maintaining what seems to have amounted to an endless control of the West Bank Arabs? Would Hussein have risen to the occasion by crushing the PLO in his kingdom, thereby minimizing Palestinian terror? He certainly was prepared to throw down the gauntlet nearly a year later in a violent showdown with Arafat's militia. On the other hand, even had Golda Meir wanted to do so, by once again incorporating Gahal in her government (after the October 1969 elections), and having Dayan, Allon and other Labour hawks breathing down her neck, it is most improbable that she would have been able to sway the cabinet to be more yielding. Israel was no longer as disinterested in acquiring additional land as it sincerely purported to be on the eve of the Six-Day War.

Meanwhile the economy had emerged from the torpor of its 1966 recession. To a large extent this resulted from a marked increase in state expenditures, involving the construction of a network of roads in the conquered territories, an Israel air force (IAF) base in Sinai and various other building projects, including a revamped Hebrew University campus on Mount Scopus. In the three-year period between 1967 and 1970, overall defence outlays more than doubled. Whereas, in the period between the 1956 Sinai Campaign and the 1967 Six-Day War, yearly average defence outlays were 9.7 percent of GDP, from 1967 until the Yom Kippur War they rose to an average of 21 percent.[44] Much of this increase fed through to increases in local purchasing power. An excess supply of workers was superseded by manpower scarcities, particularly in the building sector, restaurants, municipal cleaning services and various branches within agriculture. The shortfalls were made up by utilizing thousands of Arabs from the conquered territories. While such an expedient provided some immediate relief to Israeli employers, not to mention benefits to the new Arab wage-earners, it made Israel more dependent on outside labour. However, it did allow for Israelis on the lowest levels of the employment ladder to move up several rungs, thereby enjoying improved living standards. Another source of growth can be traced to a big influx of immigrants. In the first two years after the Six-Day War, some 50,000 arrived, mostly from the USA and other advanced countries.[45] The new migrants in turn gave rise to a greater demand for apartments, thus stimulating a housing construction boom.

Israel's economic growth was partly facilitated by donations from Western Jewry, which helped to ease the country's balance of payments constraint, thus allowing for reductions in import duties. A combination of readier access to imports and increases in incomes was reflected in a durable consumer goods buying spree. Apart from washing machines and refrigerators, television sets sold like hot cakes. Although regular local television transmissions commenced only in the spring of 1968, by mid-1970 there was on average one television set per household.[46]

After some slowdown in the pace of economic growth in 1969–70, an upward trend in economic activity recurred. In 1971 Israel recorded an annual rate of change of GDP of 11.1 percent; a year later this rose to 12.6 percent. A partial relaxation of the Soviet Union's emigration policy was a big factor accounting for such a startling performance. From 1971 to 1973 some 100,000 Soviet immigrants provided an extra boost to the building industry and to other aspects of the Israeli economy. While the specific qualifications of many of the newcomers reflected Russian requirements (for example, engineers in mining technology), there were still more than enough others with skills and technical expertise that readily met domestic needs. One area in which progress was particularly striking was the field of armaments. Conscious of its acute dependence on foreign sources for its material defence needs, Israel stepped up the production of locally made goods. The field of its endeavours was extensive, encompassing the manufacturing of highly sophisticated weaponry such as the Kfir fighter aircraft and state-of-the-art missile boats. Over time, as its capacity and reputation for turning out top-notch military equipment grew, so too did the export of such products. Of no less significance, the process of expanding the required human technological base for Israel's armaments industry yielded valuable spill-over effects for knowledge-intensive enterprises based, for example, on electro-optics or information processing.

Typically, when sustained spurts of economic activity occur, relative gaps between those in the top and those in the bottom income deciles tend to widen. In this respect, Israel was no exception. The general gains recorded in the period under review accrued disproportionately to highly educated Ashkenazi Jews, giving rise to feelings of resentment among less well-placed Mizrahim. What heightened their sense of deprivation was the fact that, whereas they (now second-generation Israelis) were living largely in substandard and overcrowded housing estates, new migrants from Russia moved into far better apartments. What is more, unlike them, the Russian Jews enjoyed the benefits of being able to purchase consumer durables (including cars) duty free. Organized around a movement calling itself the Israeli Black Panthers, the Mizrahim conducted a series of demonstrations in Jerusalem that resulted in clashes between them and the authorities. Although Meir was very dismissive of them and their cause, she appointed a special commission, the Prime Minister's Committee Concerning Children and Youth in Distress, to make recommendations for streamlining Israel's response to poverty. In its report, issued in June 1973, it recommended the institution of a negative income tax and improvements in the fields of child allowances, old-age pensions and the education system, as well as the introduction of measures to alleviate the housing shortage.

Combating the PLO

As early as June 20, 1967, the PLO announced that it was transferring its operational command to the conquered territories. More specifically, on June 12, just two days after the end of the Six-Day War, Fatah leaders assembling in Damascus pledged to renew terrorist activity within Israel "to free our stolen homeland from the hands of the Zionists."[47] Clearly, soul searching in the wake of a failed Arab attempt to wipe Israel off the map was not something PLO leaders indulged in, either then or now. Leaving aside the platitudinous bromides that PLO "moderates" peddle among Westerners, to this day not even the most irenic among them has ever come to terms with the fact that Israel has a legitimate right to exist as an independent and sovereign Jewish state.

In October 1967, a viewer at the Zion cinema in Jerusalem noticed that two dark-skinned women, after having placed a bag in the seat in front of him, left prematurely. An alerted usher found that the bag contained a time bomb, which was defused before causing any damage. As a result, it soon became the norm for handbags to be checked at the entrances of most public places.[48] The IDF responded by blowing up houses providing shelter to known terrorists and by exiling their leaders. The Israeli general security service succeeded in establishing a widespread network of Arab informers, and by so doing was able to nip in the bud most underground terror units before they were able to undertake any action. By the end of the year, PLO efforts to wage a "popular war of liberation" based on cadres in the occupied areas had basically petered out. Nearly a thousand PLO members were arrested and some 200 were killed.[49]

In tandem with the acts of terror, a campaign of non-violent opposition to Israeli rule began to get underway. In essence it amounted to Arabs in various West Bank towns not opening their schools after the summer recess. An Israeli insistence that texts inciting anti-Jewish hatred and opposition to Israel be expunged from the curriculum was taken as the pretext for the closures. As a means of encouraging teacher defiance, Jordan promised all those on strike or subject to dismissal that their salaries would be paid in full. The school closures were soon followed by a declaration, on October 19, of a general economic shutdown to coincide with the opening of the annual convening of the UN General Assembly. While the general response to down tools was solid in Jenin, it was far less so in other West Bank cities. The willingness of Jenin residents to continue with their strike was eroded by the military authorities threatening to withdraw trading and transport licences and by non-striking areas picking up the slack left by Jenin's self-imposed inactivity. In a matter of weeks, strikes and school closures became a thing of the past.

Being unable to conduct a popular resistance campaign based in the occupied territories, the PLO shifted the centre of gravity of its activities to Jordan. From there it shelled Israeli settlements along the border and directed armed groups to pursue sabotage missions, not only in the West Bank but also in Israel proper. During the first year after the Six-Day War the PLO and its allies carried out 687 acts of terror causing 175 Israelis to be killed.[50] On March 21, 1968, with punitive IAF air attacks proving to be ineffectual, three reduced-sized IDF brigades (two infantry and one of armour) crossed the River Jordan to punish the PLO. The final provocation that induced that IDF operation was the mining, on March 18, of a school bus which caused the death of the driver and guide and injuries to twenty-eight children. The Israeli raid was meant to deal Fatah a crushing blow in the town of Karameh, where about 900 Fatah militia were stationed. It was not Israel's intention to take on the Arab Legion, but the latter's determination to stand by the beleaguered Palestinians forced its hand.[51] After a raging battle, in which 232 Arabs were killed and 132 taken prisoner, the IDF withdrew.[52] (Among those eluding the IDF was Yasser Arafat, who bolted while the going was good.) From Israel's point of the view, the military operation in Karameh was not a resounding success. Twenty-eight of its soldiers fell and some ninety were wounded.[53] In addition, four tanks and four armoured vehicles were abandoned and one airplane was downed by the Jordanians.[54] Although there was some decline in the number of incidences of armed Palestinians crossing the Jordanian border (due more to increased border patrols and electronically equipped fences than to anything else), there was little by way of reduced cross-frontier gunfire exchanges. Above all, both the Palestinians and the Jordanians wallowed in their claims to victory over the IDF. Despite the fact that their losses vastly exceeded those of the Israelis, by merely firmly resisting them, the Arabs felt that they had broken the post-Six-Day War spell of Israel's invincibility. Fatah in particular reaped dividends from a newly enhanced image that its credible performance in Karameh yielded. Thousands of young Palestinians rallied to its ranks and Arab states opened their coffers to it. The real loser was Hussein, since within his realm Fatah began to constitute itself as a state within a state. With overweening arrogance, its members, shouldering AK-47 rifles, strutted about the country's towns and villages as if they were the lords of the land.[55]

Almost four months later – that is, during July1–17, 1968 – at a conference of the PLO's Palestine National Council, the PLO's National

Charter was redrawn.[56] Its first article proclaims that "Palestine is the homeland of the Arab Palestinian people: it is an indivisible part of the Arab homeland and the Palestinian people are an integral part of the Arab nation." Article 6 indicates that only those Jews who had normally resided in Palestine until the beginning of what it called "the Zionist invasion" (generally taken to date from 1919) will be considered Palestinians. The charter (in article 19) refers to the establishment of Israel as having no legal basis. Jews are explicitly not recognized as having any national status, and "claims of historical or religious ties of Jews with Palestine are incompatible with the facts of history" (article 20). Setting the tone for many years of futile acts of violence, article 9 placed the armed struggle as "the only way to liberate Palestine."

As a program of national liberation, the PLO's charter is very exclusive. It denies citizen rights to all Jews who had immigrated into Palestine after 1919 as well as to their offspring born in the country. Unlike Jews, non-Palestinian Arabs who during the 1920s and 1930s migrated to Palestine were accepted by the PLO as Palestinians. Israel, by contrast, was not so discriminatory. Its Declaration of Independence includes the following paragraph: "We appeal, in the very midst of the onslaught launched against us, to the Arab inhabitants of the State of Israel to preserve peace and participate in the up-building of the State on the basis of full and equal citizenship and due representation in all its provisional and permanent institutions." In deference to its Arab minority, Arabic was granted the status of an official language with that of Hebrew. While the PLO charter calls for the realization of the national rights of the Palestinians, it is totally impervious and disdainful of Jewish ones. Ironically, unlike the Arabs, it is the so-called Jewish interlopers who speak the country's ancient language and who can readily read sections of the Dead Sea Scrolls and inscriptions on local coins minted in biblical times. The continued refusal of PLO leaders to concede that Palestine is the cradle of the Jewish nation is well illustrated by Yasser Arafat's assertion in 2000 that the Jewish Holy Temples in Jerusalem never existed and therefore the Palestinians need not share the Temple Mount (which could well be a metaphor for Palestine) with the Jews.[57]

With the new PLO charter well enshrined, Palestinian terrorists continued to reap havoc in Israel. Since they adhered to various factions of the PLO, it is worth digressing at this point to list the factions in question. Pride of place was of course assumed by Arafat's Fatah organization, already described. Coming on Fatah's heels was the Popular Front for the Liberation of Palestine (PFLP), founded in December 1967 by George Habash and Wadi Haddad, both medical practitioners. Independent of the PLO until 1970, the PFLP had the pretensions of being a Marxist body. A few months after its inception, Ahmed Jibril in April 1968 broke away to set up a group of his own, dubbed the PFLP-General Command, which was distinguished by an even greater propensity for violence. Then in 1969, with the PFLP not living up to the revolutionary hopes of Naif Hawatmeh, a Jordanian, a splinter organization called the Democratic Front for the Liberation of Palestine (DFLP) was formed. Under Hawatmeh's guidance, the DFLP targeted not only Israel but also Arab regimes in the hope of replacing them with communist "people's democracies."[58] Finally, there was al-Saiqa, established by the Syrian government in 1966, but which only saw action in 1968. Despite being a Syrian instrument, al-Saiqa became an affiliate of the PLO.

Returning to the course of PLO activities, in September 1968 a bomb planted in the Tel Aviv central bus station took three lives, then in November that year a car packed with explosives and parked adjacent to the Mahane Yehuda Market in Jerusalem blew up, killing twelve passers-by. Similar incendiary devices were planted in supermarkets, the Hebrew University cafeteria and other public places.[59] Significantly, as Dayan pointed out, on no occasion in the wake of grisly PLO acts of violence in Jerusalem and Tel Aviv did the Jewish population "turn on the Arab workers and visitors in their midst."[60] By the end of 1968, after the continued harassing of Jewish settlements in Israel's Jordan Valley, the PLO began to turn their attention to the south of Lebanon, where they set up bases from which they could cross into Israel. In next to no time, they controlled a fairly large swathe of land in which they ruled as they saw fit. The resulting conflict with the Lebanese government was "resolved" through pressure by Arab League countries, which culminated at the end of 1969 with the so-called Cairo Agreement. In terms of that agreement, provided the PLO confined its activities to the area in which it was situated and did not clash with the central government, it was given a free hand.[61] Given such an arrangement, on May

22, 1970, members of al-Saiqa attacked, with bazookas, an Israeli school bus ferrying children in the vicinity of the border farming village of Moshav Avivim. The attack led to the death of twelve innocent people, including nine children, and the wounding of twenty-five others.[62] Israel generally reacted to such provocations by undertaking punitive raids and by conducting armed patrols within Lebanese territory. While meeting with occasional success in limiting cross-border violations or the firing of the odd volley of Katyusha rockets, Israel's military reprisals were unable to put a complete stop to such incidents.

Realizing that the deployment of terror within Israel would not in itself further their overall objectives, the Palestinians decided to project their struggle onto the international arena. They selected operations that would both attract world public attention and sow fear into the hearts of innocent bystanders, thereby hoping to intimidate Westerners in support of their cause. Their preferred tactic was the hijacking of commercial aircraft, an activity that they turned into an art form. Between 1968 and 1977 the PLO attacked twenty-nine civilian passenger airliners,[63] a feat that no other terrorist umbrella organization has ever matched.

In late July 1968 the PLO commenced its new course of action by seizing control of an El Al plane en route from Rome to Lod Airport (later renamed Ben-Gurion Airport). The plane was diverted to Algeria, where all the Israelis aboard were held for five weeks, until they were released in exchange for Palestinians detained in Israel. On December 26, 1968, PFLP terrorists fired at a grounded El Al plane in Athens, killing a passenger and wounding a member of the flight crew. Two days later, Israeli commandos raided Beirut Airport, where they destroyed thirteen civilian Arab-owned planes. This induced the PLO to concentrate mainly but not exclusively on non-Israeli aircraft. The first was a Swiss passenger aircraft, which in February 1970 was blown up in mid-flight by the PFLP-General Command. As a result, forty-seven people met their death.

Rising to a crescendo, between 6 and 9 September, 1970, the PFLP hijacked four Western civilian passenger planes and forced three of them to land at the Jordanian hamlet of Zerqa (also known as Dawson's Field), some 48 kilometres east of Amman, and the fourth (thought to be too large for the Zerqa runway) in Cairo. Around that period, there was also a failed attempt to capture an El Al plane en route to London. El Al security personnel overpowered the two hijackers on board, killing one of them. The other, a woman by the name of Leila Khaled, was handed over to the British authorities, who in turn refused requests to have her extradited to Israel. Now holding some 315 hostages, the PFLP demanded the release of Khaled, some 200 of its comrades-in-arms imprisoned in Israel, terrorists detained in Britain, Germany and Switzerland and, finally, Sirhan Bishara Sirhan, the assassin of US Senator Robert Kennedy.[64] The terrorists declared that, should their demands not be met within a specified deadline, all three grounded aircraft in Jordan with their passengers and crew would be dynamited. Fortunately, just before the ultimatum expired, the planes were emptied and only then blown up. Most hostages were put up at a hotel in Amman, but forty Jews (Israelis and others holding both Israeli and US passports) were taken to a Palestinian refugee camp to be held as "prisoners of war."[65]

The PFLP's operation constituted the final straw for the Jordanian government, which had already encountered a series of PLO acts of subversion. Because Hussein along with Nasser had during 1970 agreed to talks with Israel under a UN umbrella (as elaborated in the following chapter), the PLO decided to assassinate him in accordance with a public Fatah commitment to murder any Arab head of state seeking to reach a peaceful settlement with Israel.[66] On June 9, in an attempt to make good on their word, PLO gunmen fired at Hussein's motor cavalcade as it neared his summer palace. Hussein escaped unscathed but his driver was wounded. That incident, which did little to endear Hussein to the fractious Palestinians, had followed two days of bitter clashes in and around Amman, where as many as 400 people may have been killed.[67] After another botched attempt to assassinate him on the first day of September, and in the wake of the PFLP's multiple plane hijackings, Hussein realized that, if he did not act quickly and decisively, the PLO would assume control over his entire reign. The writing was clearly on the wall. Palestinians made up the majority of the population. The refugee camps had become no-go areas for the central authorities. Thousands of armed foreigners roamed about the kingdom without let or hindrance. On September 5, after gaining a hold of large parts of northern Jordan, including the town of Irbid, a Fatah commander designated the area as the "First Arab Soviet."[68] To reassert full and unquestioned authority, Hussein appreciated that he had no choice other than to bite the bullet and deal harshly with the PLO marauders. Deploying large numbers of tanks and artillery, the Jordanian Arab Legion set upon them ferociously. The exact number of deaths that followed has never been officially released, but Yitzhak Rabin held that it was believed to have reached many thousands.[69]

Given the ensuing bedlam, on September 20 President Hafiz al-Assad of Syria, who long wished to annex his neighbour's territory, invaded the northern regions of Jordan. (It ought to be noted that the UN Security Council did not censure Syria for its infringement of Jordanian sovereignty.) Syria was by no means the only Arab country posing a threat to Jordan. Stationed in that troubled kingdom were 17,000 Iraqi troops left over from the Six-Day War.[70] Affecting a show of solidarity with the terrorists, the Iraqi regime warned that, unless the Jordanian army ceased its bombardment of PLO camps, Iraq would forcefully impose a ceasefire. But, after having paid due lip service to the PLO cause, nothing further was heard from the Iraqis. That still left Jordan having to contend with the invading Syrians. With his forces locked in combat with large remnants of Palestinian resistance, Hussein appealed to the United States to help repel the Syrians, making it clear that assistance would be welcome from any source. The USA responded by asking Israel to strafe the intruding Syrian armoured columns. Israel was quite prepared to oblige, but the IDF's general staff thought that air attacks would not in themselves suffice. Therefore, with US approval,[71] IDF armoured forces began assembling near the Jordanian border with the intention of meeting the Syrians on the ground. However, the Jordanian army soon found that it was capable of handling both the Syrians and the PLO, and by September 23, having incurred the loss of at least 120 tanks, the Syrians withdrew.

Meanwhile, intermittent fighting continued against the PLO until, in a massive showdown, the Arab Legion finally eradicated the entire PLO apparatus in Jordan. Terrorists not killed or captured fled. So merciless were the Jordanians (the PLO claimed that over 4,000 Palestinians were slain)[72] that about 100 PLO foot soldiers sought refuge in Israel, where they readily gave themselves up and handed over their weapons.[73] Most of the other PLO survivors fled, via Syria, to Southern Lebanon. As for the detained aircraft passengers held as hostages, they had all been rescued.

So demoralized were the Palestinians that they subsequently referred to events in that period as "Black September." Of more note, a PLO organization of that same name, and under Fatah's control, came into existence. It specialized in acts of terror with which Fatah did not officially wish to be associated. One of its first deeds was the assassination in a Cairo hotel on November 28 of the Jordanian prime minister, Wasfi Tel. On gunning him down, one of his killers, in full view of horrified onlookers, bent down to lick Tel's blood spilt onto the hotel lobby's marble floor.[74]

During 1971 the PLO suffered another grievous setback. After the Six-Day War, the PLO confined its activities largely to the West Bank, to which it had relatively free access from Jordan. That meant that, within the Gaza Strip, Palestinians were for the first two post-war years mostly quiescent. Only in 1969 did they show serious signs of offering violent resistance, not all of which incidentally was directed against Israelis. For, as the historian Benny Morris reports, "dozens of local residents, suspected of collaborating with the Israelis or *merely working in Israel*, were murdered."[75] By January 1971, in the wake of increasing anti-Israel operations that culminated in the killing of two Israeli children, Sharon, who was then CO of the Southern Command, was authorized to eradicate the Gaza terrorist infrastructure. Deploying regular patrols, including units posing as Arab civilians, PLO members were ruthlessly hunted down and shot. After around 100 were killed and 700 captured, resistance in Gaza was essentially crushed. To enhance its security further, Israel enclosed the Gaza Strip with barbed-wire fencing and segmented refugee camps by an interlaced road network that facilitated the movement of military convoys. It was also in this period that Jewish settlements were established in the area – the first one being Kfar Darom, replacing the original kibbutz by that name which was razed in 1948 by the Egyptians.

On May 8, 1972, a Sabena aircraft en route from Vienna to Tel Aviv was hijacked by four Black September members. The plane was allowed to land in Lod (Israel's civilian airport), where the terrorists threatened that, unless 315 of their comrades imprisoned in Israel were released, they would blow up the plane with all its passengers. The next day, sixteen members of Israel's elite commando unit, Sayeret Matkal (General Staff Patrol), dressed as airport maintenance workers and led by Ehud Barak (a future prime minister), stormed the aircraft, killing two of the Palestinians and overpowering the other two. Three passengers were wounded (one fatally) and an Israeli commando, Benjamin Netanyahu (another future prime minister), was injured by friendly fire.

At the end of the same month – that is, on May 30 – three members of the Japanese Red Army, acting on behalf of the PFLP, arrived at Lod Airport on an Air France flight from Paris. Dressed conventionally, they aroused little suspicion. Once inside the baggage hall, they opened their luggage to retrieve rifles and hand grenades and then commenced firing indiscriminately. By the time that two of the terrorists had been killed (one by suicide) and the third one captured, twenty-four people, including sixteen Puerto Rican pilgrims, had been slain and around eighty were wounded. (Years later, in 2008, when the leader of the terrorist organization responsible for such gruesome acts, Dr George Habash, died, Mahmoud Abbas, the president of the Palestinian National Authority, declared three days of official mourning, entailing the flying of Palestinian flags at half-mast. In Abbas's view, Habash was an "historic leader.")[76]

The Lod massacre was soon followed by Black September's most notorious act of infamy, the Munich Olympics massacre. In the early hours of September 5, 1972, during the second week of the Munich Olympic Games, eight Black September members, having donned tracksuits and carrying duffel bags containing assault rifles, pistols and hand grenades, scrambled over a 2-metre fence into the grounds of the Olympic village. With the aid of stolen keys they entered a building in which most of the Israeli team were sleeping. The building in question was located close to the fence in a fairly isolated part of the village. This made it particularly vulnerable, especially since armed guards were conspicuous by their absence. Once inside the building the terrorists captured eleven of the twenty-three-member Israeli team. Two of the Israeli athletes, a wrestling coach and a weightlifter, attacked the gunmen, injuring three of them before being shot dead. The rest were then securely bound and totally immobilized. The attackers then demanded the release and safe passage to Egypt of 234 of their comrades held in Israel as well as the two founders of a kindred terrorist group, the German Red Army Faction (aka the Baader–Meinhof Gang).[77] Feigning agreement, the German authorities ferried both the hostages and the captors by helicopter to a NATO airbase, where they were ostensibly to be transferred onto a Boeing 727. At the base ill-trained marksmen began taking pot shots at the hijackers, who then slaughtered the nine Israelis. In the general exchange of fire, five Palestinians and a German policeman were killed, while three Palestinians were wounded and captured. All the while, the games carried on as normal. Only in the wake of mounting pressure did the International Olympic Committee (IOC) agree to a temporary suspension. The next day a memorial service was held at the Olympic Stadium, but the IOC president, Avery Brundage, barely referred to the murdered sportsmen, preferring instead to concentrate on the merits of the Olympic spirit. Less than three months later the three detained terrorists were released after Black September hijacked a Lufthansa jetliner en route to Beirut. The Munich Games massacre, like the slaughter of arrival passengers at Lod Airport, was not a PLO aberration, as evidenced by indiscriminate murderous acts that the organization orchestrated in Athens Airport, in hotels and in other public places. On September 15, 1972, Meir approved a Mossad brief to hunt down and assassinate the Olympic Games terrorists. Years later, on January 24, 2000, the official newspaper of the Palestinian Authority (*al-Hayat al-Jadida*) urged Arab regimes to boycott the summer Olympic Games in Australia, because a moment of silence was planned at the start of the games in memory of the eleven Israeli athletes murdered by the PLO functionaries.

In an effort to curb the PLO's penchant for gratuitous violence, the IDF's Sayeret Matkal organized a raiding party to enter Beirut on the night of April 1973. Led by Barak, the commandos arrived on Lebanon's shores in inflatable motor boats launched from Israeli naval craft out at sea. They were met by Mossad agents, who drove them in rented cars to the prestigious Beirut suburb of Verdun. There, disguised as ordinary civilians (Barak as a female), they entered the residences of PLO leaders and killed three of them. During the encounters two bystanders and two policemen were also shot dead. While this was going on, an IDF paratrooper unit led by Amnon Lipkin-Shahak blasted a building, causing the deaths of dozens of PFLP men.[78] All told, the Israelis lost two of their own men.

It had in fact become standard practice for Israel to eliminate leading Black September agents wherever found. Under an ongoing Mossad project called Finger of God, they were either killed through direct contact or by remote means, such as activating explosives telephonically, dispatching letter bombs or priming cars to blow up when opened or started. On July 21, 1973, in the Norwegian town of Lillehammer, after notching up a series of spectacular successes, Mossad agents came a cropper when they shot a Moroccan waiter, whom they mistook for a senior Black September official. Swiftly moving in, the Norwegian police netted five Israelis, who were subsequently tried and convicted. The Norwegian mishap seemed to have led to a simultaneous cessation of Operation Finger of God and the existence of Black September. Future Palestinian acts of terror would openly be touted by respective PLO bodies initiating them. As with Israel's retaliation raids conducted in the 1950s, it is difficult to assess the effectiveness of such methods, but it seems that they did at least boost the Israeli public's morale somewhat.[79] Meanwhile, the PLO, still smarting from its futile September 1970 collision with Jordan's Arab League, sounded out the possibility of rallying the USA to its side in its quest to unseat King Hussein. In mid-1973, a close associate of Arafat made overtures on his behalf to US diplomats. The gist of Arafat's supposed new approach was that he was prepared to live with the state of Israel provided that Jordan, sans King Hussein, be deemed the homeland of the Palestinians. According to Arafat, a Palestinian State in the West Bank and Gaza would not do, and therefore the solution lay in replacing the Hashemite dynasty so as to provide the necessary space for such a state.[80] Looking even closer at the PLO démarche, it became evident that the seeming preparedness to accept Israel was illusory. Pressed to clarify the PLO position vis-à-vis Israel, Arafat's associate explained that what they had in mind was a secular state, which, as Kissinger noted, was a "code word for the destruction of Israel."[81]

The Settlement Movement

Compared with the pre-Six-Day War years, when the international frontier was never more than a short drive away, Israelis now began to relish their enhanced territorial space. Just as the world came to recognize Israel's post-1949 borders, many assumed that eventually its post-1967 ones would also be so accepted.[82] Overnight, as it were, the previously moderate and pacifist religious Mafdal Party began to sanctify the acquisition of territory.[83] Rabbi Zvi Yehuda Kook, head of the Merkaz Harav Yeshiva (seminary) and the spiritual guide of Mafdal's youth movement, Bnei Akiva, intoned that the Jews had returned under divine injunction to their homeland (in the West Bank) from where they would never budge.[84] Many socialist secular Israelis also manifested strong emotional attachments to the West Bank. Under the initiative of Tzvi Shiloah from the Rafi Party in September 1967 was founded a body called the Movement for the Complete Land of Israel. Its manifesto declared that, just as Jews may not forego the state of Israel, so may they not forego the entire Land of Israel. More specifically, it stated: "The borders of our land as they stand today represent a guarantee for security and peace – in addition they present unprecedented horizons for the strengthening of the nation both in the material and spiritual realm."[85] Among the seventy-two signatories inaugurating the movement were Labour stalwarts such as Iser Harel, the first head of the Mossad, Yaakov Dori, Israel's first chief of staff, the poet Nathan Alterman, the Nobel Laureate S. Y. Agnon, and Rachel Ben Zvi, the widow of Israel's second president.

Settlement in the conquered territories, known in those days simply as "the territories," rapidly got off the mark. As early as August 1967 the government authorized the cultivation of land in the Golan Heights, and in next to no time a kibbutz, ultimately named Merom Golan, took root there. By the following June it had a membership of 169 people.[86] On the heels of the founding kibbutz came a number of other "holdings." The legal adviser of the Israeli Foreign Office, Theodore Meron, determined that settlements in the Golan Heights (on which Israel never had any prior claims) violated Article 49, paragraph 6, of the Geneva Convention.[87] The Convention explicitly forbade a conqueror to transfer or allow the transfer of its own citizens onto occupied land. With that in mind, some settlements were first formed in the guise of army bases. Nevertheless, by June 1968 there were already six settlements in the Golan Heights. They were populated mostly by members of the Kibbutz Hameuhad Federation, linked to Ahdut Ha'avodah, which, as already mentioned, in January 1968 had merged with Mapai and Rafi to form the Israel Labour Party. In other words, at that early stage, *a very large contingent of settlers emanated from the ranks of the labour movement.* Attempts were made to reconcile their growing presence in occupied territory with Israel's ostensible policy of being willing to trade land for peace by assuring the public and themselves that they were confining their settlements to areas that would not be relinquished under any circumstances. Parts of the Golan and the Jordan Valley were what they had uppermost in mind. The trouble is that no such areas had been officially demarcated. To add to the general justification of settlement activity, it had been suggested that the colonization process would very likely encourage the Arabs to lose little time in suing for peace lest their land be irrevocably lost. The problem is that such an argument cuts both ways, for, as more and more land becomes integrally connected to the Jewish state, so the growing settler community becomes a powerful lobby for minimizing territorial concessions.

Within the West Bank the onset of Jewish settlements occurred at the end of September 1967, when a band of young adults left Jerusalem in a motorized convoy to re-establish Kfar Etzion. Kfar Etzion was one of a group of four religious kibbutzim that, on the eve of the War of Independence, were overrun and destroyed by the Arab Legion. A large percentage of the original settlers were massacred. The restoration of Kfar Etzion, which had full public support, was launched with a festive fanfare.

Then in April 1968, Yigal Allon, as minister of labour, permitted Rabbi Moshe Levinger and his followers to stay in the Park Hotel (formerly the Hahar al-Khalid Hotel) in Hebron for the duration of Pesah (Passover). Their stopover in Hebron was subject to the condition that they were to leave at the conclusion of the festival. But Rabbi Levinger reneged on the agreement. He hoisted an Israeli flag over the hotel and announced that he and his party had come to stay there permanently. As with the Gush Etzion bloc, there had in the past been a Jewish presence in Hebron, which with Jerusalem, Safed and Tiberias had from time immemorial constituted one of Judaism's four holy cities. (In 1929 the non-Zionist pious Jews of Hebron were subjected to a murderous pogrom. As a result they evacuated the city.) Not wishing to dislodge the recalcitrant "visitors," Allon secured Eshkol's agreement to leave them in peace until such time as the government formulated a policy on

Jewish settlement there. In addition, Allon provided them with firearms derived from Ahdut Ha'avodah kibbutzim. His interest in supporting Levinger's group arose from his seeing them as a possible bridgehead in planting Jews in the Hebron region – a region which in terms of his plan was to be annexed to Israel.[88] Indeed, a few months later, some tentative groundwork commenced for the settlement of Kiryat Arba, lying less than 5 kilometres to Hebron's east. The project was officially sanctioned in March 1970 by a large Knesset majority, and by late 1971 the first fifty families took possession of specially built homes in the new township.

2

THE WAR OF ATTRITION AND THE
PRELUDE TO THE YOM KIPPUR WAR

In the days immediately after the Six-Day War, Israelis fervently believed that the longed-for era, if not of formal peace then at least an absence of war, had finally arrived. They assumed that, having been decisively routed, the Arabs would finally forego their dreams of defeating the IDF. Not only were the Arabs not expected to wage war but it was thought that they would henceforth refrain from pursuing miscellaneous acts of violence for fear of igniting another full-blown confrontation. Israel's excessive self-confidence was derived in part from its new borders. Previously, when Israel was far more attenuated, its tortuous frontiers were 985 kilometres in length. Now spanning a far greater land area, they were straighter and, as a result, were only 650 kilometres long. The frontier with Jordan presented a natural obstacle, the River Jordan. Damascus was now less than an hour's drive from the new Israeli–Syrian ceasefire line, and the whole of southern Syria could be scanned from IDF observation posts.[1] On the southern front, the Egyptians were driven back hundreds of kilometres to the Suez Canal, regarded as the "biggest anti-tank ditch in the world." With tremendous self-satisfaction, former air forces chief Ezer Weizman affirmed: "We are now strutting about as if each of us were three metres tall, like giants among grasshoppers."[2]

The Israelis were so mesmerized by the devastating blows that they had administered that they became blinded to the rising Egyptian and Syrian military phoenixes. As early as June 1967, a high-level Soviet delegation headed by the Russian chief of staff arrived in Cairo for an urgent assessment of Egypt's war needs. By the end of the year, the Soviets, at no cost to Egypt, had replenished between 60 and 80 percent of lost Egyptian weaponry.[3] The equipment supplied, which included planes, tanks and artillery, was superior in quality to previous issues. Accompanying such replacements were around 10,000 Russian technicians and advisors.

During the Six-Day War Israel lost forty-five combat airplanes out of a total of around 200, and a large proportion of its remaining stock was outdated.[4] Unlike the Arabs, Israel did not have the full and unconditional support of any superpower. France continued to impose its arms embargo, denying Israel delivery of the fifty Mirage fighter jets that it had earlier promised, and, although it stood by a previous decision to provide Israel with Skyhawks, the United States refused to supplement their numbers or to make any other advanced aircraft available. Only on the eve of the US presidential elections in November 1968 did President Johnson authorize the sale to Israel of the first fifty of a new fleet of Phantom jets.

The realization that the Arabs stood to regain a distinct upper edge in the quantity of weapons available to them persuaded the Israelis that a former decision to moderate their research efforts in the quest for a nuclear weapon had to be reconsidered. Although the details of Israel's nuclear program remain clouded in secrecy, by July 1970 the head of the CIA informed the US Senate Committee on Foreign Affairs that, in his evaluation, Israel had already acquired the necessary means to produce an atomic bomb.[5]

By early July 1967, armed clashes between Egyptian and Israeli forces resumed. In the closing hours of the war, the IDF had inadvertently permitted a small Egyptian force to remain on the east bank of the Suez Canal a few kilometres south of Port Fuad. Dayan, as minister of defence, was unperturbed, for in his view the Egyptians there posed no serious threat. However, he deferred to Chief of Staff Rabin, who insisted on dislodging them. The attempt to do so met with unexpected Egyptian resistance, particularly from tank and artillery fire emanating from the west bank of the canal. In the end a UN-brokered ceasefire allowed for the continued presence of Egyptian forces within the area in question. Shortly thereafter, both the Egyptians and the Israelis began to sail along their respective shores of the canal in an effort to assert their authority there. This culminated in a widespread exchange of tank and artillery fire involving casualties on both sides, with the Egyptians absorbing most of the losses. The refinery in Suez was badly damaged and petrol storage tanks in Ismailia went up in flames. As the fighting continued there was a mass flight of residents from Suez, Ismailia, Kantara and Port Said. To some extent, Israel responded ever so fiercely as a reprisal for the sinking on October 21, 1967, outside Egypt's territorial waters of its destroyer *Eilat* by an Egyptian missile boat that led to the loss of forty-seven of its sailors. Eventually a stalemate was reached, with both sides desisting from further attempts to ply even small vessels along the canal's waters. The general flare-up ought to have signalled to the Israelis that, despite their recent defeat, the Egyptians were not prepared to accept the new status quo, nor were they cowed. But that was something that the Israelis were yet to grasp.

By early September 1968, clashes recommenced as Egyptian artillery batteries fired salvos along the entire length of the Suez Canal. Although IDF units were relatively well dug in, their cover was insufficient and, as a result, they lost ten men and suffered eighteen injuries. A few weeks later, an additional round of bombardments claimed the lives of another fifteen IDF soldiers. The exchanges of fire that continued on a daily basis reflected a marked change in the constellation of opposing forces at the Suez front. While the Israeli deployment had barely altered, the Egyptian one had grown immensely. On the Israeli side there was but one solitary tank brigade, eight mobile artillery pieces and just over 2,000 men. Across the water there were some 100,000 soldiers of the Second Army in the north and the Third Army in the south.[6] Given the futility of escalating the frontal fighting, the Israeli cabinet approved the dispatch of elite commando units to the rear of Egyptian lines in order to sabotage bridges, dams and power cables.[7] One such operation involved the penetration of Israeli paratroopers into the desert town of Nag Hammadi, some 200 kilometres west of the canal, where they blew up installations supplying electricity to Cairo. It appeared that the Israeli initiatives resulted in a measure of calm that persisted over a six-month period.

To provide IDF troops with better protection against possible future shelling, measures were taken to establish a line of thirty-one small fortifications along 180 kilometres of the canal. Although known as the Bar Lev Line (after Haim Bar Lev, who had replaced Rabin as chief of staff) the concept was devised by General Avraham Adan (nicknamed Bren). Adan conceived that the handful of soldiers manning each stronghold would conduct motorized patrols, monitor Egyptian movements across the waterway and direct the fire of IDF artillery situated further inland.[8] A short distance to their rear, additional armoured forces could rapidly be deployed in the event of a serious Egyptian attack. Built to withstand the force of 1,000-pound bombs, the forts were protected by surrounding barbed-wire entanglements and minefields. Attached to each stronghold was a courtyard enclosed by a stone wall that could contain a few tanks. As an extra precaution against possible enemy infantry incursions, earthen ramparts over 20 metres high and with a 45 degree slope facing the canal were constructed. In the interest of facilitating inter-fort communications and access to the tank concentrations, a few kilometres to the east a network of roads was laid where eleven other strongholds (somewhat larger than those along the canal) were also assembled.

A massive effort was made to complete the entire project in the shortest possible time. Vast amounts of stone and concrete were hauled to the area, where innumerable bulldozers and earth-moving machines were employed. With an emphasis on speed, budgetary controls and practices were, to say the least, less than satisfactory. Nonetheless, when open hostilities once again flared up, IDF units were not as exposed as in the past. Israeli soldiers may have had more fortifications in which to take shelter, but that did not assure them complete safety in the face of the unrelenting downpouring of Egyptian shells and bullets. As it happened, in the four-month period to July 1969, twenty-nine Israeli lives were lost.[9]

Although Bar Lev believed that the line of fortified strongholds offered a reliable and economic means of guarding the Suez front, other high-ranking officers begged to differ. Prominent among the dissenters was General Israel Tal, who advocated that, instead of maintaining strongholds that could readily be bombarded, the IDF should simply concentrate armoured forces further east, out of Egyptian artillery

Plate 1   *Briefing of soldiers in a Bar Lev Line bunker*

range. Should the Egyptians cross the canal, Israeli tanks could then sally forth to crush them. Their capacity to do so would be enhanced by the inability of the Egyptians to call upon covering shell fire. Tal argued that, by contrast, the Bar Lev Line would constrain the IDF to engage in static warfare, for which it was ill-suited.[10] Both generals Ariel Sharon and Raful Eitan were essentially of the same opinion,[11] and when Sharon served as head of the Southern Command (between 1969 to August 1973) he let many of the strongholds fall into disuse. The verdict of Mohamed Heikal, a leading Egyptian journalist, that the "building of the Bar Lev Line was a victory for politics over strategy,"[12] was not far off the mark. As far as Meir and many of her associates were concerned, a continued presence of Israeli soldiers along the eastern bank of the canal was a non-negotiable necessity.

On March 8, 1969, the Egyptians embarked on a war of attrition along the entire Suez Canal line. As General Fawzi, the chief commander of Egypt's forces, explained, the Egyptians aimed to "kill the largest number of enemy personnel," since Israel valued its human resources far above anything else.[13] With Israel's intolerance of a cumulative casualty rate not being mirrored on the Egyptian side, Fawzi believed that his forces would gain the upper hand. In addition to the incessant shelling of IDF fortifications and transport facilities on and near the front, Egyptian commando units periodically crossed the canal to harass the Israelis.

Having not allocated sufficient artillery to the Suez Canal front, the IDF hoped to compensate for that shortfall by means of its air force. Between July 20 and July 28, 1969, the IAF flew 500 bombing sorties, which exacted the deaths of some 300 Egyptian soldiers.[14] In addition, the IAF bombed and strafed targets ranging from Kantara to Port Said. In one action five Egyptian planes were downed at a cost of two Israeli ones, but in another Egypt lost twelve aircraft without inflicting any damage on Israeli ones. By July 22 the IAF had destroyed all enemy surface-to-air missile batteries in the Suez Canal area. In addition, IDF commando raids were undertaken. Some involved deep penetration raids and attacks on fortified islands in the southern approaches to the canal. In an operation on September 9, IDF troops led by Baruch Harel, equipped with six tanks and three armoured troop carriers, were dropped off by the Israel navy on the western coast of the Gulf of Suez at Abu Darag.[15] From there they headed to Ras Zafarna, where a moderately small number of Egyptian troops were taken by surprise. In the ensuing battle the Egyptians absorbed 200 to 300 casualties, while Israeli losses amounted to the downing of an accompanying aircraft and the wounding of one soldier. All others returned safely to base along with a captured Soviet T-62 tank, the latest and most advanced of Egypt's armour.[16] So outraged was Nasser by the failure of his forces to nip Harel's raid in the bud that he relieved both his chief of staff, General Ahmad Ismaili, and the commander of the navy, Admiral Fouad Zaki, of their posts. In return, on September 11, Egypt launched scores of air fighters in an offensive against Israeli positions on the canal. The attacking aircraft were met by the IAF, and in the course of dogfights during that day and the next the Egyptians lost eighteen planes to only one of Israel's. To cap it all, towards the end of December, an Israeli raiding party organized by Eitan landed on a beach in Egyptian territory on the Gulf of Suez. It then crept up to a well-concealed radar installation used to track low-flying aircraft. After overcoming the few Egyptians at the site, the Israelis dismounted the radar from its base so that one of their helicopters could remove it.[17]

With the P-12 radar being a new and highly sophisticated product of Soviet technical ingenuity, the seizing of it intact was a remarkable coup. However, successful daring missions were not the sole preserve of the IAF. During the night of November 15, Egyptian frogmen swam from the Jordanian port of Aqaba to attach limpet mines to two Israeli civilian vessels.[18]

Israeli precision bombing of the Canal Zone plus dramatic ground incursions gave rise to highly inflated appraisals of the IDF's operational successes. Moshe Carmel, Israel's minister of transport, vaunted that the IDF's actions had demonstrated that Israel could well sap Egypt's military strength. In similar vein, Dayan declared that Egypt had lost the battle of the Suez Canal and that a resumption of heavy fighting in the near to medium future was not to be expected.[19] Unquestionably, Egypt had been paying a high price. Over 400,000 citizens displaced from Port Said, Ismailia, Suez and other canal localities were now housed in makeshift living quarters in and around Cairo.[20]

At the beginning of 1970, Meir's "kitchen cabinet" decided to widen the conflict by initiating in-depth aerial bombing up to the outskirts of Cairo. The idea emanated from Rabin with support from Allon. Dayan was unenthusiastic while Eban was opposed to the idea, fearing that it might jeopardize Israel's arms supplies from America.[21] The rationale for such actions was that, by destroying vital Egyptian installations, the IAF would lessen Egypt's inclination to engage in military adventures along the Canal Zone, and that would lead to its acceptance of a cease-fire.[22] As an added bonus it was hoped that, once the IAF appeared over densely populated areas, not only would the Egyptian army find itself in the embarrassing situation of not having a ready answer to Israel's new sorties, but Nasser's reputation and that of his entire regime would be seriously impaired. Accordingly, in January 1970, recently acquired Israeli Phantom bombers began pounding away. The new aerial bombardment strategy was adopted on the assumption that, provided the IAF avoided attacking Alexandria and other areas where Soviet naval and air personnel were present, there was no reason to fear any serious Russian response.[23] Nevertheless, some within the cabinet, such as Moshe Kol, Dayan and Eban, had serious misgivings.[24]

With the Egyptians determined to find a way to match Israel's superior air force, Nasser, on January 22, 1970, flew to Moscow. Much to his satisfaction, the Russians agreed to supply him with a new batch of surface-to-air missiles – SAM 3s with a 20-kilometre range and capable of hitting both high- and low-flying planes – against which the USA lacked countermeasures. Never before had the Soviets provided SAM 3s to another country, not even to North Vietnam.[25] Added to that, they supplied Egypt with four 15-B radars, embodying cutting-edge technology in tracking oncoming aircraft.[26] Shipments began arriving in Egypt in March, and by midsummer fifty-five SAM 3 batteries were in place, to be largely operated and under the complete control of Soviet military crews. In addition, 120 MiG 21s, the most up-to-date planes in the Soviet arsenal, were delivered. To meet the shortage of trained Egyptian pilots capable of flying them, Russian pilots were made available. That marked the beginning of the first deployment, since World War II, of Soviet air combat personnel beyond the Iron Curtain.[27] Soon 200 Soviet airmen and 15,000 other Soviet servicemen were present in Egypt.[28] Effectively, Israel was now facing not only Arab forces but also the Arabs' big power sponsor. On July 30, that became evident when, in a dogfight, the IAF downed five MiGs piloted by Russians.[29]

Considering that most Israeli government and military leaders had previously discounted the possibility of Soviet intervention, its actualization caught them off balance. Rather than acknowledging that it arose as a direct result of their in-depth bombing, they tended to offer alternative explanations. One such theory held that the Soviets had decided to intervene well before the IAF's new strategy took effect.[30] Playing down the seriousness of the Soviet arms shipments, Allon, Galili and Weizman argued for the continued adherence to Israel's misguided military strategy.

Sadly, the in-depth bombing missions had other unintended consequences. On February 12, 1970, as the IAF was en route to el-Khanka, the Abu Zaabal metalworks plant, mistaken for an Egyptian air force depot, was attacked. That target identification error resulted in some seventy civilian deaths and led to an outpouring of public wrath directed against Israel. The condemnation soon became worldwide, to be shared even by the USA.[31] Two months later, when an Egyptian installation at Salahiya was bombed, some forty-seven children were killed.[32] In their ignorance, the Israelis were unaware that the complex housed an elementary school.

By April, once the Soviet SAM missiles were stationed well behind the Canal Zone, the IAF had little choice other than to abandon its in-depth raids. But that was not the end of the matter. Within a short while, SAM missiles, including advanced SA-3 and SA-2 models, began in stages to creep up towards the Canal Zone, thus making it next to impossible for the IAF to act as an alternative for the IDF's inadequate disposal of artillery. The repositioning of missile batteries was accompanied by a frenetic Egyptian effort to construct the emplacements, fortifications and roads needed for an integrated missile defence system. The amount of labour and material resources expended induced Heikal to liken the project to a construction of a second "High Dam."[33] Egyptian determination to install an impregnable wall of missile defences paid off. Within less than three weeks, Israel lost five of its top-flight aircraft, despite the fact that they were newly equipped with updated US electronic countermeasures reputed to be capable of warding off the Soviet missiles. Although they were effective with respect to SA-2s, they were ineffectual in terms of SA-3s, thus sapping somewhat the IAF pilots' self-confidence.[34]

On June 24, the Syrians, after raining down shells over the entire Golan front, mounted an armoured attack on two Israeli positions. This gave rise to three days of battle involving Israeli artillery, tanks and airplanes. In the process, the Syrians may have lost up to 350 men, while Israeli losses amounted to ten fatalities and the destruction of an IAF Phantom jet, leading to the capture of its two-man crew.[35] Having come off worse for wear, Syria refrained, for the time being, from pursuing further actions.

A month later, Russians piloting Egyptian MiGs engaged the IAF within the Canal Zone. On July 25, an Israeli Skyhawk was damaged by an air-to-air missile fired by one of the Russians. On July 30, as an act of retribution, the Israelis lured the Russians into a trap by appearing to send four Phantom bombers accompanied by four Mirage fighters on a mission to destroy an Egyptian radar station near the Egyptian shoreline of the Gulf of Suez. Russian pilots, after scrambling in MiGs to meet them, found themselves in the midst of a furious air battle that culminated in the loss of five of their aircraft in less than two minutes. The rest scurried back to base. To some extent the Russians had their revenge on August 3, when they induced the IAF to attack dummy missile sites. As the Israelis approached them they were met with a wall of missiles that destroyed two of their planes. The Soviet air defence system had turned the scales against the IAF. According to the military historian Dan Schueftan, arrayed against a single Israeli plane were as many surface-to-air missiles as were normally stocked by a medium-sized country.[36]

Apart from making good all Israeli losses, the United States decided to withhold assurances that it would furnish Israel with additional Phantoms and Skyhawks. Elsewhere, Israel had ordered and paid for fifty new French Mirage jets, but President Georges Pompidou had refused to release them, even though he approved the sale of 100 such aircraft to Libya, knowing full well that they would in all probability land up in Egypt. Taking stock of the changed circumstances, the IDF general staff began airing the possibility of shifting its front-line forces slightly eastward so as to be beyond the reach of Egyptian missiles. While Dayan was inclined to favour such a move, Meir was adamantly opposed to the idea on the grounds that it would encourage the Arabs to demand a full Israeli withdrawal to the 1949 boundaries without any prior direct negotiations.

All the while Israel was sustaining mounting casualties, causing the country's general morale to begin to falter.[37] Among those distressed was Jonathan Netanyahu, the brother of the future prime minister Benjamin (Bibi) Netanyahu and a distinguished IDF officer. In August 1969, writing to his parents in the USA, he expressed his anguish at constantly hearing the national radio's daily reports of the "toll of dead and wounded, acts of murder and mine laying, exchanges of fire along the front lines and shelling of settlements."[38] Over six months later, a group of high-school students about to be conscripted wrote an open letter to the government seeking to be reassured that it was leaving no stone unturned in pursuing peace.[39] The students were particularly upset by the refusal of the cabinet (on April 6 1970) to sanction a proposed trip by Nahum Goldmann, the president of the World Jewish Congress, to meet with Nasser in Cairo. Taking cognizance of Goldmann's oft-repeated views that Israel ought to withdraw from all occupied territories, Meir and most of her colleagues did not welcome his entering into talks with the Egyptians as a leading Jewish dignitary. For that they were subject to scathing media criticism. But what really affronted Meir and her colleagues was the satirical and irreverent play *The Queen of the Bathtub* by Hanoch Levin, which opened in April 1970 in a Haifa theatre. The play's season was prematurely concluded on account of disruptive audiences: viewers with a high regard for members of the establishment found the script more than they could bear. In one scene Meir is depicted as telling her cabinet colleagues that, try as she might, she could not identify any defect in herself. In the playwright's words, she proclaims: "For seventy-one years [Meir's then age] I look at myself and I find only perfection such as God should preserve. Every day it amazes me anew."[40] The irony of the putative Goldmann–Nasser talks is that, contrary to the impression given by Goldmann that the Egyptians suggested that he meet with Nasser in Cairo, Mahmoud Riad, the Egyptian foreign minister, both flatly denied the issuing of any such invitation and made it clear that under no circumstances would he have done so.[41]

Meir's reluctance to countenance any Israeli withdrawal was manifest in early May 1970 in her talks with Joseph Sisco, the US assistant secretary of state. Urged by Sisco to assert publicly that Israel would be willing to cede land in exchange for peace, the most that Meir was prepared to offer was a promise to convene a special committee to consider such a proposal.[42] Some days later, bowing to internal public opinion, Meir was more upfront. On May 26, in an address to the Knesset, she made it clear that Israel had in fact accepted UN Resolution 242 entailing a withdrawal from conquered territories. Meir's speech so affronted Menachem Begin of Gahal that he warned her that, if she ever repeated such an assertion, Gahal would leave the government.

The intensification of the war of attrition, plus the growing risk of an unwanted and dangerous collision between the two superpowers, induced US Secretary of State William Rogers and Anatoly Dobrynin, the Soviet ambassador, to meet in early June. Agreeing that the status quo was untenable, they arrived a joint understanding that formed the basis for a new version of the original Rogers Plan.[43] Publicized by the end of the month, it called for a ninety-day ceasefire during which Jarring's mission was to be renewed. Jarring then drafted a one-page document calling upon Israel, Egypt and Jordan to accept UN Resolution 242, to nominate delegates to talks to be held under his auspices, and to abide by a ninety-day ceasefire. The aim of the talks was to bring about the establishment of a just peace, mutual recognition and an Israeli withdrawal. Once the above-requested assurances were received, Jarring would resume functioning as an intermediary. Both the Israeli cabinet and the IDF looked askance at Jarring's document. Despite the explicit inclusion of a reference to peace, Meir and most of her colleagues regarded the proposal as a tawdry ploy to resurrect the original Rogers Plan, which they had already rejected. As for the IDF general staff, it had serious reservations about a ceasefire of limited duration, during which time Egypt was more than likely to utilize the lull in fighting to prepare for further hostilities.

After both Egypt and Jordan had by the end of July indicated that they were prepared to go along with Rogers Mark II, US President Richard Nixon coaxed Israel into cooperating by providing assurances that final borders would be determined only on the basis of mutual agreements and that no Israeli soldier need withdraw until a stable and permanent peace had first been secured. Israel, wrote Nixon, would not be pressed to accept a solution to the refugee problem that would fundamentally alter its Jewish character.[44] Finally, as an added incentive, Nixon promised that the USA would ensure that a balance of arms would be maintained and that Israel would receive increased economic aid.[45] On July 31, the Israeli cabinet met and decided by a vote of 17 against 6 to respond positively to Nixon's request. This paved the way for a ceasefire that went into effect on August 7. One of the terms of the ceasefire (clause 3) stipulated that neither side would introduce or construct any new military installations within 50 kilometres of the Suez Canal. The next day Gahal left the cabinet in protest against Israel's acceptance of UN Resolution 242. Gahal's exit was not at first supported by all its ministers, and Begin had to use the full force of his authority as leader of the bloc to bring them into line. Be all that as it may, the war of attrition had come to an end.

Many if not most Israelis believed that the war of attrition terminated in an Israeli victory. But that turned out to be a fateful illusion. The war plus a host of other "incidents" cost Israel 727 lives, not far short of the number the country lost in the Six-Day War.[46] As for non-human material costs, Israel's defence budget was spiralling out of control, rising from 17.7 percent of GDP in 1967 to 26.3 percent by 1971.[47] Egypt too paid a heavy price. Its canal cities became ghost towns, its industrial complexes in the region were shattered, and the continued closure of the waterway deprived it of a large amount of foreign revenue.

Israeli reservists who had been stationed along the canal felt that they had borne more than their fair share in defending their country. Between April 19 and April 26, Egyptian commandos crossed the canal on a nightly basis. On one occasion, an Israeli stronghold just south of Ismailia was almost overrun. The attackers, who had reached the fort's outer emplacements and who had approached its firing embrasures, were, at the eleventh hour, driven off by the timely intervention of tanks. Throughout the month of April alone, twenty-one Israelis manning the Bar Lev Line were killed.[48] Although the defenders were not meant to remain at the canal front for longer than three months at a stretch, many were there for far longer. Rarely, if ever, being visited by a high-ranking officer, saturated with dust, overcome with heat and discomfort, and constantly in fear for their lives, their morale hit rock bottom.[49] On the odd occasion when they took leave, troops were dismayed to find that, in Israel itself, life went on as normal, with no apparent awareness or concern for those manning the Bar Lev Line. On returning to their posts some conscripts became completely apathetic, caring neither for themselves nor for their weapons.[50] During the summer of 1970, when the canal strongholds became subject to round-the-clock shelling, it became difficult, and at times nearly impossible, to evacuate the wounded.

With regard to the negotiations that Jarring was meant to sponsor, Israel had taken exception to a creeping Egyptian repositioning of SAM launching units towards the Canal Zone, which they regarded as an infringement of the ceasefire. According to the writer David Korn, Nasser accepted the US-proposed ceasefire "in bad faith" to use the respite "to push his antiaircraft missiles up to the Suez line and gird again for war."[51] He certainly wasted no time, for, on the very day that the ceasefire went into effect, Israeli pilots spotted convoys of vehicles bearing missiles heading towards the canal. The following day films taken by Israeli reconnaissance planes showed that work on new missile sites had commenced. Although US spy planes confirmed the Israeli observations, Rogers simply refused to believe that Nasser would so blatantly hoodwink him. Even after Sisco had persuaded Rogers to accompany him to National Security headquarters to examine the

evidence, he was not inclined to issue any public statement confirming Israel's complaints. His pigheadedness deeply troubled Meir, who
was now subject to searing criticism from Gahal. In a Knesset address,
Begin warned that, given the constant approach of Egyptian missiles
towards the canal, "whenever Egypt decides to reopen fire and knowing the realities we have to assume that such a day shall surely come,
it will have a decisive advantage over us."[52] Eventually, on September
3, the US State Department censored Egypt for violating the terms of
the ceasefire. With Egypt refusing to backtrack, Israel suspended its
participation in Jarring's round of talks, promising to return only when
all SAMs were returned to their pre-truce positions.[53] Far from Egypt
obliging, its transfer and consolidation of such missile networks continued unabated. By the end of October Egypt had accumulated an array
of missile batteries that, in the estimation of Aharon Yariv, Israel's chief
of military intelligence, was "one of the most advanced in the world."[54]
Both Dayan and Bar Lev pressed for decisive military action to extir-
pate the offending missile sites, but they were overruled by the majority
of the cabinet, who had no stomach for a renewal of hostilities that
could well have pitted the IDF against Soviet forces.[55] Other reasons
for not resorting to force included the hope that Israel's restraint would
bear fruit in persuading the USA to supply it with more sophisticated
weapons and electronic devices and also the fact that Israel wished to
take advantage of the ceasefire to add finishing touches to the fortification of its Bar Lev strongholds.[56]

On September 28, 1970, Nasser, who had died of a sudden heart
attack, was succeeded by Anwar Sadat. The change in Egyptian leadership was seized upon by many Israeli cabinet members as an additional
reason for not attending the talks (they argued that they needed time
to assess Sadat's intentions) but, ironically, Dayan, who had previously
advocated boycotting them, now thought differently. He favoured
Israel's participation in order to be able to effect, in an orderly way,
a scheme he was proposing to Meir. In essence he proposed, as a first
stage, a 30-kilometre mutual withdrawal from the canal, based on an
Egyptian acceptance of the termination of the state of war. Infantry
units would initially stay put but would soon be replaced by Egyptian
civilians on both sides of the waterway to prepare for the resumption of naval passage in the canal. Finally, talks would commence to

establish a permanent solution.[57] The basis for this proposition lay in Dayan's growing fear of Israel being becoming ensnared in a direct military conflict with the Soviet Union. Dayan believed that such a withdrawal would result in a general reduction of tension in the area. The opening of the canal would both yield an effective separation of forces and diminish Sadat's interest in provoking a war with Israel.[58] From Israel's perspective, thought Dayan, there was also the strategic advantage in abandoning the not readily defensible Bar Lev Line by adopting eastern positions within Sinai lying beyond the range of Soviet SAMs and Egyptian artillery. Whether or not all this would have been true remains academic. With Meir vehemently rejecting Dayan's ideas, the matter was not brought before the cabinet. Eventually, by the end of December, after being subject to continued US pressure and persuasion – which included a willingness to provide Israel with more arms – Israel agreed to return to the bargaining table. When the Jarring talks resumed at the beginning of January 1971, Israel wasted little time in clarifying its approach. It was prepared to strive for the attainment of mutually agreeable borders, but under no circumstances would it commit itself unless these were determined in the framework of direct negotiations. (The Jarring talks were indirect ones, with Jarring acting as a conduit between the parties.) Within a week both Egypt and Jordan rejected Israel's conditions, and once again the talks were frozen.

Then, at the beginning of February, Sadat publicly aired a proposal somewhat akin to Dayan's way of thinking, except that only Israel would withdraw. He favoured an interim arrangement by which Israel, on the firm understanding that the pre-Six-Day War boundaries would ultimately prevail, would withdraw to a distance of 40 kilometres from the canal. In return, Egypt would reopen the canal and extend the cease-fire.[59] Writing from Washington, where he was now Israel's ambassador, Rabin stressed that Sadat's overture merited serious consideration.[60] But Meir, still fixated on remaining at the edge of the canal, felt that the most that Israel could offer was a 10-kilometre pullback without holding out any prospects of further adjustments, especially since Sadat did not, in her view, sufficiently express any willingness to recognize Israel and conclude a peace treaty with it.

Disappointed with Israel's unwillingness to agree to Sadat's interim proposal, the Egyptians had reluctantly accepted a continuation of the ceasefire, even if only for one more month. This provided Jarring with some breathing space to explore ways of ending the stalemate. What he did was to come up with a renewed version of the original Rogers Plan. There would be a full withdrawal of Israeli forces in exchange for Egypt agreeing to the establishment of demilitarized zones and permitting Israel free and unhindered access to the Suez Canal and the Straits of Tiran. The state of war would be terminated and there would be mutual recognition of all states in the area. Egypt essentially agreed to Jarring's terms but with two reservations. Demilitarization was to occur in equal dimensions on both sides of the Egyptian–Israeli border and a just settlement had to be arranged for the Palestinian refugees.[61]

Israel's reply effectively scuttled Jarring's new initiative. While it reiterated its desire for secure and recognized borders sanctioned by a peace treaty, gone were the days of its immediate post-Six-Day War magnanimity. Not only would Israel under no circumstances withdraw to the 1967 boundaries but, as Meir began repeating ad nauseam, if ever it wished to reach an agreement with Israel, Egypt had to be prepared to concede large portions of its territory.[62] Despite Jarring's efforts coming to naught, Sadat persisted in pursuing an interim arrangement. By March he fine-tuned his proposal. In addition to a 40-kilometre Israeli withdrawal, the area between Israel's new position and the canal was to be demilitarized. Egyptian civilians (including small forces needed to protect them) were to be permitted to enter a strip along the canal 10 kilometres wide in order to ensure its clearance and reopening for international shipping. Six months after an interim accord had been secured, with the premise that it was but a prelude to further Israeli withdrawals, Israeli vessels would be permitted to use the canal. After rebuking Dayan for informing Joseph Sisco that he essentially agreed with Sadat's proposal, Meir once again galvanized the majority of her cabinet to reject Sadat's overtures in their entirety. The negative Israeli response disappointed not only the Egyptians but also those in the US administration who felt that Israel was passing up a golden opportunity for peace.[63]

Korn ascribes the major responsibility for Israel's failing to rise to the occasion to Meir, "whose certainty in her beliefs instilled in her the conviction that by refusing any compromise she was saving Israel." [64] On December 5, 1973, in the aftermath of the tragic Yom Kippur War,

Meir, no longer so self-assured and somewhat contrite, admitted that she had failed to grasp the essence of Dayan's 1971 withdrawal proposal, thinking that it amounted to a needless retreat.[65] Meir's previous insistence on maintaining Egyptian territory did not emanate from any allure of increasing Israel's land mass as such. In particular this applied to the West Bank. In an interview on September 1972, she mentioned that the borders of Judea and Samaria (the West Bank) that she would seek would be those "that contain as few Arabs as possible."[66]

Whether peace was indeed theoretically attainable is another matter. There is no way of knowing whether a continued state of non-belligerency offered by Sadat would, in due course, have led to a full peace agreement. In US Secretary of State Henry Kissinger's judgment, Egypt had actually "agreed to a peace agreement, rather than a mere declaration of non-belligerency, if Israel returned to the 1967 borders."[67] While this was affirmed by Sadat years later,[68] in February 1973 Sadat's emissary to the United States, Hafiz Ismail, explained that what was actually envisaged was an Israeli return to the 1967 borders with respect to *all* of its Arab neighbours, and that at the very most Egypt was prepared to discuss the modus vivendi for ensuring mutual security.[69] As Ismail saw things, if Israel wanted peace, it would have to put an end to immigration and cut its links with world Zionism.[70] In a retrospective assessment, Jehan, Sadat's widow, maintained that peace would not have been possible until Egypt had first, by means of war, redeemed its self-esteem.[71] Jehan's views reflected those of her late husband, who on October 24, 1972, told his military leaders that he would never negotiate with Israel until Egypt had first proved to its enemies and friends alike that it was both capable of making and willing to make necessary sacrifices in war to alter the status quo.[72] Sadat was well aware that, without first resorting to war, any peaceful overture to the Israelis would have been universally perceived as being nothing less than an abject Egyptian surrender.

Although all tentative probes for a final settlement had reached a dead end and the formal ceasefire had long since expired, Sadat did not resume hostilities. With quiet reigning along the canal, Israelis mistakenly concluded that Egypt had finally appreciated that it was simply too weak to take them on and that the status quo would endure for years to come.

Nearly a year later – that is, in February 1972 – the president of Romania informed Meir that he was authorized to pass on a message from Sadat to the effect that Egypt was willing to enter into direct discussions with Israel. These were to be conducted by senior officials after some preparatory talks at a more junior level had cleared the way and Israel had provided some basic prior commitments. Since Meir replied that Israel was prepared to enter into a dialogue only with no strings attached, nothing further materialized.[73] Unbeknown to the Israelis, Sadat had reached the conclusion that there was only one way left for Egypt to retrieve its lost territory, and that was through the application of force. He devoted his entire efforts to that purpose, never once wavering or troubled by doubts. In July 1972 he unexpectedly ordered all Soviet military experts to leave Egypt. The Soviet mission in Egypt then included around 21,000 Russian advisors.[74] The installations that they had helped set up and the equipment brought over from Russia became Egyptian property. The move to expel the Soviet personnel was by no means based on any Egyptian grievance towards Russia but, as Sadat later revealed, was taken as a necessary step to clear the decks for war. In order for Egypt to regain its self-esteem by liberating its land, it was necessary for it to be seen by the world at large as in no way being directly dependent on any external power.

However, the Israeli government and many others interpreted the expulsion of Soviet personnel both as indicating a serious rift with Russia and as a step that lessened Egypt's ability to throw down the gauntlet of a military challenge. As far as the Israelis were concerned, with no obvious threat on the horizon, they were more than content to sit back and savour the status quo, which did not require of them any costly concessions. The same applied to Jordan, where internal order prevailed after the PLO had been routed in September 1970. In 1972 Hussein made an offer to Israel to negotiate a peace treaty whereby the West Bank and Gaza would combine with Jordan in a federation in which the Palestinians would enjoy a limited measure of autonomy. Hussein was prepared to accept minor border adjustments and even the presence of isolated IDF military outposts and Jewish settlements along the Jordan Rift Valley once it was fully restored to Jordanian rule.[75] Currently many Israelis would welcome such an arrangement, but in those days, when there was little threat to life and limb emanating from the occupied areas, Meir disdainfully dismissed Hussein's suggestion by questioning his right to tender solutions for land that was not his.[76]

The year 1973 began with a tragic air incident. On February 21, a 727 Libyan passenger plane accidently flew into Israeli-held airspace in Sinai. It was intercepted by two Israeli Phantoms, whose pilots, suspecting that it was on a terrorist mission, observed that curtains were drawn across all its windows so that none of its passengers was visible. The pilots signalled to the captain of the intruding aircraft to follow them. At first the pilot seemed to be complying. His plane was losing altitude and releasing its landing gear. But suddenly it veered westward at top speed. After a quick consultation with IAF headquarters, the Israeli pilots shot it down. One hundred and five people were killed and only seven survived. From the airliner's black box it was revealed that the pilot at first thought that he was being escorted by Egyptian planes towards Cairo Airport; only when he discovered his error did he attempt to escape.[77] No civilian planes had flown over Sinai since the Six-Day War, and after a series of terrorist attacks the Israelis had considered various sabotage scenarios employing commercial airlines. Israel was severely reprimanded in international forums, but its actions were not unique. On July 27, 1955, an El Al Constellation accidently strayed over Bulgaria to be struck down by two Bulgarian MiGs, and fifty-eight people were killed. On April 20, 1978, Soviet Sukhoi jets rocketed a South Korean civilian airliner, and on July 3, 1988, an Iranian commercial plane flying in Iranian airspace was destroyed by a guided missile fired by a US missile cruiser, killing 290 passengers.

In July 1973, Sharon relinquished his post as head of the Southern Command to retire from the army in order to play a leading role in Likud. Likud was founded in 1973 as a result of the merging of Gahal with Laam (a party made up of the Free Center, an offshoot of Herut), the right-wing State List and the Movement for Greater Israel. The replacement of Sharon by Shmuel Gonen (widely known as Gorodish) soon proved to be disastrous, both for Gonen personally and for the IDF as a whole. While Gonen had an exemplary fighting record and was decorated for bravery, he was not cut out to be a front commander, for his personality and behaviour towards his subordinates left much to be desired. He treated them poorly, identifying (sometimes falsely) petty infractions for which severe punishments were meted out. Having an uncontrollable temper, he dressed down subordinates harshly. Once when a reservist lieutenant-colonel, an economics professor in civilian life, arrived late for a meeting, Gonen hurled a microphone at him, hitting the poor man in his face.[78] All too often his men requested transfers to other units. On observing that, during a field exercise, Gonen's officers were reticent to report candidly to him, Adan told David Elazar, the chief of staff, that "Gorodish has no place in the IDF."[79] Unfortunately for the IDF, that did not impede Gonen's promotion.

By late 1973, three years after the end of the war of attrition, Israel attributed the ongoing lull in border clashes to a general Arab inability to alter the status quo by means of force. Eminently satisfied with such a state of affairs, and oblivious to Egypt's long-term resolve to retrieve its lost territories, the Labour Party submitted an uncompromising platform for the forthcoming October election. It included support to private contractors to widen settlement activity in the West Bank and, of all things, prospective plans for the development of a deep-sea port, as well as a new urban area in Northern Sinai just south of Rafiah.[80]

The widespread belief that, with regard to the management of the occupied land, Israel could do as it pleased was reinforced by its army intelligence unit. Such a situation was to no small extent cultivated by the appointment in October 1972 of Eli Zeira as the army's chief intelligence officer. By all accounts, Zeira, gifted with an analytical mind, was so suffused with conceit and arrogance that he generally could not bring himself to consider points of view at variance with his own. Breaking with previous practice, he ceased forwarding raw intelligence material for the chief of staff's perusal, making the latter entirely dependent on Zeira's own assessments.[81] Worse still, Zeira became fixated on a hypothesis that emanated from a reliable Egyptian source, and that subsequently became known as "the concept," that Sadat would never go to war unless or until he received from the Soviet Union both fighter-bombers capable of attacking IAF bases within Israel and Scud missiles that could reach Tel Aviv. (Much later it came to light that the reliable Egyptian source was none other than Ashraf Marwan, Nasser's son-in-law, who had in 1969 offered his services to the Mossad in return for a large sum of money.)[82] Placing complete faith in the Egyptian informant, Zeira remained adamant that, no matter what, as long as the above two preconditions were not met, Israel could confidently rule out an Arab invasion. The irony of it all is that, although the "concept" was once valid, in the very month that Zeira assumed office it had already become defunct. On October 24, 1972, Sadat informed his military hierarchy that he no longer intended to wait until his country obtained long-range aircraft and Scud missiles and that he would proceed to wage war, albeit a more limited one, without them.[83] That decision, according to the writer Bar-Joseph, effectively "paved the way for the October 1973 war."[84] Moving to a more limited operation, entailing the capturing of a small stretch of Sinai east of the canal, meant that Egyptian military objectives were fully compatible with Egypt's existing military means. Its interlocking system of SAM batteries enabled it to cross the canal without severe hindrance from the IAF. Such an outcome had previously been envisaged by Aharon Yariv, Zeira's predecessor, who upheld that the IDF should "take into account the possibility that the Egyptians might in a big way attempt to ford the Canal."[85] By February 1973, Egypt and Syria were already coordinating plans for a joint inva-sion. Yet, as will become apparent further below, through a stubborn refusal to reappraise the validity of the "concept," Zeira and his chief subordinates (as was the case with presidents Kennedy and Johnson's "best and brightest") demonstrated the ability of men of high intellect to become beholden to notions confuted by the evidence.

On April 18, 1973, after receiving a tip-off from the "reliable source" that war was scheduled to take place on May 19, Meir, at a "kitchen cab-inet," was reassured by Zeira that the likelihood of fighting occurring was very low. After declaring that he did not think it possible that Egypt could surprise Israel with a canal crossing, Zeira guaranteed that he would be able to detect such a move well beforehand.[86] Questioned by Meir as to just how he would be able to do so, Zeira replied that he would take into account the forward movement of enemy forces, reinforced aerial defences, additions to existing anti-aircraft batter-ies, the refurbishment of neglected trenches along the canal, and so on[87] (all of which he later dismissed as being irrelevant). While Meir seemed to have been reassured, Chief of Staff David Elazar was far less sanguine, and on the following day he ordered a high IDF alert, code named Blue-White. Tank depots containing emergency supplies were relocated closer to the front lines, roads were improved, the formation of new units was expedited, and bridging equipment for possible use in the canal was readied.[88] No reserves were called up, since Elazar had complete confidence in his military intelligence's ability to issue a warning at least two days, and possibly even more, before the advent of any war. The process of retaining the IDF in a high state of alert lasted over a few summer months of calm. Soon there were grumblings about the $45 million economic cost of the IDF crying wolf.[89] The seeming vindication of Zeira's even-headedness raised both the measure of his influence and his own self-confidence. As for Elazar, he would think twice before adopting measures not in keeping with that of his army intelligence chief. What neither Zeira nor Elazar had appreciated was that the suspected war preparations of both Syria and Egypt were genuine ones, and that the reason why war did not eventuate then was because of last-minute Syrian appraisals that they were not quite ready.[90]

Dayan, who had indeed earlier thought that the Egyptians might resort to war, began to write off the Arabs as credible foes. In early July he had concluded that the IDF's April/May state of alert was excessive,[91] and towards the end of the month, in an interview with *Time* magazine (published on July 30, 1973), he predicted that over the next ten years there would be no border changes and no major war.[92] In August 1973, Dayan spoke of inherent Arab military weaknesses that he believed would continue into the foreseeable future. Poor educational standards, limited technological knowledge, a general lack of integrity and Arab disunity were, in his assessment, responsible for the Arabs not being able to pose any serious threat to Israel.[93] Long before Dayan had made his facile pronouncements, the Egyptian armed forces were being thoroughly revamped. New appointments were being made on the basis of competence and not cronyism. Illiterates in the armoured corps were being replaced by educated conscripts, and university graduates were no longer exempt from the draft.[94]

Dayan was not alone in breeding public complacency. As a part of its campaign for the scheduled general elections in October, the Labour Party put out a placard suggesting that "on the banks of Suez quiet reigns as it does in Sinai, Gaza, the West Bank and the Golan Heights. The borders are secure, the bridges are open, Jerusalem is united, settlement construction is proceeding and our national position is solid."[95] Not to be outdone, Sharon, in soliciting support for the Likud Party, described Israel's military situation in idyllic terms. As far as he was concerned, "Israel is now facing years of quiet . . . we have in effect no problems of security."[96]

By the end of August, Sadat and Assad of Syria had already finally agreed to attack Israel jointly at the beginning of the following October.[97] In keeping with such intentions, both Syria and Egypt began increasing the concentration of their forces along their respective fronts. In the process, the Syrians, with full knowledge of IDF intelligence, brought forward a number of SAM batteries. As it happened, on September 13, in an air battle between Israel and Syria off the Syrian coast that raged as a result of the interception of an Israeli reconnaissance flight, the Syrians lost twelve planes to one Israeli plane.[98] That encounter strengthened the IDF in its conviction that a general Arab attack would be tantamount to suicide. As a corollary, the IDF concluded that the Syrian build-up reflected nothing more than fears of the likelihood of an emboldened IDF launching a more devastating operation.

During that period Israeli army intelligence secured extensive information detailing a gargantuan concentration of enemy power along the ceasefire lines. On the Syrian side the anti-aircraft missile system installed "was so dense and so sophisticated" that it covered both the Syrian positions and "most of the Israeli territory on the Golan Heights."[99] That meant that, on the northern front, the IAF no longer possessed unimpeded access. The same applied to the Canal Zone. Such a turn of events made nonsense of a prevailing presumption that Israel could reasonably deploy only a rather limited number of front-line forces that could hold the enemy at bay while reservists were being mobilized.[100]

The IDF's general preparations for a possible conflict with the Arabs were grounded in a total misreading of enemy intentions. In the southern zone, plans were prepared for either a renewed war of attrition or a limited Egyptian land grab. To meet such contingencies, Operation Shovah Yonim (Dovecote) was formulated. It rested on the assumed ability of some 300 Sinai-based tanks and the IAF to neutralize such actions. Taking into account what was regarded as a remote possibility – that is, a full-scale invasion – Operation Sela (Rock) allowed for the deployment of two reserve armoured divisions. But the snag was that

that deployment was to take place *before* war broke out. So confident was the IDF that it would receive adequate forewarnings, the flaw in Operation Sela did not trouble anyone. Finally, even in what was regarded as a scenario with an almost zero probability of unfolding – that is, an invasion without any prior warning whatsoever – the regular army alone was expected to hold its ground until reserve forces were mobilized and brought to the front. On a later admission by Elazar, the general staff neither took into account nor planned for the possibility of war breaking out without any prior warning.[101] Nor was any allowance made for the accumulation by Egypt of advanced anti-tank weapons. The belief shared by many high-ranking officers that the regular army could stave off a surprise massive Arab offensive while the reserves were being mobilized downplayed the sense of urgency of ensuring that IDF military intelligence was up to the mark.[102]

Yitzhak Hofi (generally known as Haka), the head of the Northern Command, was one of the few who did not believe that, in the event of an unexpected onslaught, one could rely on the standing army alone. On September 24, at a meeting of the general staff, he voiced concerns relating to the security of the Golan. The heavy concentration of Syrians could, in his opinion, launch a full-scale attack at a moment's notice. Should that occur, they could readily overpower the sparse Israeli forces confronting them who would be unable to rely on the IAF to protect them because of the near presence of sophisticated and overlapping Syrian anti-air missile batteries. Elazar tried to mollify Hofi's fears by assuring him that, even though army intelligence could not always determine whether or not some limited form of fighting would occur, standing IDF forces could readily hold their own. In Elazar's estimation, "the Syrian deployment of anti-air missile batteries did not impinge on the IAF's ability to eliminate them within a half a day."[103] Hofi's presentiments influenced Dayan, who began to fear not for a full-scale war, but for an unforeseen Syrian armoured corps raid that might succeed in bursting into one or two Golan Heights settlements either to kidnap or to slaughter their inhabitants. Should that occur, it would, as Dayan asserted, amount to "a catastrophe, the likes of which we have yet never encountered."[104]

On the night of the next day (September 25) King Hussein of Jordan secretly landed by helicopter at a secure Mossad site on the outskirts of

Tel Aviv. There, accompanied by Zeid Rifai, his prime minister, Hussein, at his own request, met with Meir in the presence of Mordechai Gazit, the premier's office director, and Lou Kedar, Meir's secretary and friend. The conversation was monitored from another room by Zussia Keniezer, the IDF's intelligence officer overseeing Jordanian affairs. After a bout of small talk, Hussein, whom Lou Kedar described as looking rather nervous,[105] let it be known that Syria was poised for an attack on Israel (Hussein had received that information from a spy in the Syrian army).[106] On being asked by Meir whether Syria was planning to go it alone, Hussein replied that he did not think so, for in all probability Syria and Egypt would act in unison.[107] Keniezer took Hussein's message very seriously. He was well aware of the fact that the king had consulted with Sadat and Assad in Alexandria just two weeks beforehand and felt that it was more than likely that Hussein had been given a strong hint that war was imminent. But Keniezer's assessment was not shared by his superiors. One might well ask what drove Hussein to take his Israeli adversaries into his confidence. The answer lies in his wishing to avoid potential pan-Arab pressure embroiling him in a war not of his own making and in which his army and kingdom might be seriously jeopardized. When later he succumbed to the importuning call to arms, he did so without opening an additional front on the Jordan–Israel border.

The following morning, at a meeting of the general staff, Elazar simply reported that a credible source had indicated that Syria was on the verge of launching a full-scale war. For some reason, Elazar went on to state that it was not clear whether or not Syria was acting in conjunction with Egypt. After concluding that the mysterious source added nothing new to what was already known, the meeting went on to consider strengthening the IDF on the Golan front lest the Syrians launch a limited kidnapping raid in revenge for their heavy loss of planes in mid-September. To meet such a contingency the number of tanks stationed in the Golan Heights was brought up to 100, an additional artillery battery was posted in the region, and both air and ground forces were alerted. As far as Elazar was concerned, 100 tanks facing a conjectured total of 800 Syrian ones "ought to be enough."[108] A little later Dayan joined the meeting, to be assured by Elazar that Syria would not act alone and, since there was no question of both Syria and

Egypt acting jointly, that he saw no reason to place the Golan Heights on a war footing. Nevertheless, Dayan, troubled by Hofi's apprehensions, decided to visit the northern front to see things for himself. Accompanied by Elazar and Zeira, Dayan was briefed by Major Shmuel Askarov, who thought that war was imminent. At that point Dayan turned to Zeira for comment. Zeira in turn asserted that "there will not be another war for ten years."[109]

Hussein not only cautioned Israel but did the same for the USA. Unlike the Israelis, the Americans took Hussein seriously, even taking the trouble to advise Israel (on September 28) that they were in receipt of a reliable report that Syria was on the verge of attacking Israel in order to retrieve the Golan Heights. Correctly concluding that both the American and the Israeli report were derived from Hussein, the IDF general staff on September 30 (with the notable exception of Israel Tal, the deputy chief of staff) deemed the prospect of a looming invasion as being virtually non-existent. The IDF assessment was relayed to the Americans. To his credit, Tal tried to persuade both Elazar and Zeira to give the US communication the benefit of the doubt. Tal was convinced that the Syrians were about to initiate a general assault, and in that light he called for an extra armoured brigade and an artillery battalion to be stationed on the Golan Heights and for the mobilization of reservists necessary to man them.[110] But Elazar, having already been once bitten by issuing a false alarm during the previous months of April and May, abided by Zeira's appraisal, which, as it turned out, was based on nothing more than wishful thinking. First Zeira summarized the gist of information just received, which indicated that, after moving the bulk of its fighter planes right up to the front line along with large quantities of its armour, Syria was now capable of waging war at a moment's notice. Contrary to what might have been expected, that caused Zeira no undue alarm, for he held that Syria would never open hostilities unless Egypt did so, and even then Syria would hold back until the Egyptians had made significant advances. But since Egypt had nothing to gain from entering the fray, Zeira concluded that a Syrian attack could safely be ruled out. As far as he was concerned, the unprecedented mobilization of Syrian forces ought to be seen as an outcome of their growing fears of an Israeli attack or, more absurdly, as a means of producing some momentum within the army by way of "full gas in neutral."[111] When Tal proposed to Zeira that he reconsider his assessment, Zeira haughtily snapped that he and not Tal had the necessary expertise to gauge enemy intentions. An exasperated Tal responded that, as an expert on tank warfare, he could inform Zeira that, should the Syrians launch a surprise attack, the limited deployment of IDF forces facing them would be wiped out.[112] The meeting did at least result in a decision to place some more tanks on the Golan Heights, bringing their number up to 146.

As it happened, the US concerns relayed to Israel were not based solely on a message received by Hussein, for the CIA had itself observed that the Egyptians were amassing far more men and materiel and a far larger communication network than any manoeuvre could possibly warrant. But once Israel had so adamantly asserted that there was no basis for assuming that the Egyptians were involved in anything other than large-scale military exercises, the CIA, the US State Department's intelligence bureau and the Defence Intelligence Agency all adopted Israel's position.[113] To make matters worse, Israel later provided the Americans with an updated version of its assessment, stressing not only that the massing of Arab troops was related to the undertaking of manoeuvres but that it had also arisen in part due to Arab fears of Israel launching a military offensive.

While the situation on the ground in the Middle East was becoming increasingly portentous, Meir was distracted by a PLO incident in Europe. Following a partial relaxation of Soviet emigration restrictions in relation to Jews wishing to leave for Israel, some formal travel arrangements were concluded. The migrants were to journey by train to Austria (via Czechoslovakia) to be processed by Israeli officials at Vienna's Schonau Castle. On September 28, two PLO members carrying luggage containing automatic rifles boarded one of the trains at Bratislava. As the train entered Austria the Palestinians captured five Jewish passengers (two of whom escaped) and an Austrian customs official. In return for the release of their captives they insisted that the Schonau reception centre be closed. Much to Meir's chagrin, the Austrian chancellor, Bruno Kreisky, who was himself a Jew, readily acceded to their demands. Worried about the possible adverse effects on the continued flow of Soviet Jewish migrants, Meir flew to Austria, where she tried in vain to persuade Kreisky to alter his decision.

Kreisky, no warm friend of Israel, was a most ungracious host. Not only did he not want to meet her in the first place but he did not even offer her as much as a glass of water.[114] Only by October 3 did Meir return home. In the interim, public attention was riveted on her futile efforts.

At 2 a.m. on October 1, while Meir was occupied with Kreisky, IDF intelligence received tidings that there was a strong chance of both Syria and Egypt going to war within the next twenty-four hours. The agent who was the source of that disclosure also highlighted recent Egyptian military developments that tended to corroborate his forecast. Among the points listed were that the examinations for officers seeking promotion scheduled for early October were postponed; a large-scale mobilization of reservists was in train, including the recall of those released in July; and motorized divisions, bridging units, parachutists and airborne forces were situated at full strength along the canal. Finally, Cairo International Airport had closed without any explanation.[115] The agent could just as well have added what the Israelis had already noted – that is, the removal of canal mines. True to form, Zeira and his senior aides dismissed the report as being groundless, but in this case they did not even bother to inform Dayan. Zeira would later justify not expeditiously passing on the alert to Dayan because he did not wish to disturb his sleep.

Later that morning, at a general staff meeting where, paradoxically, most of the discussion centred around the IDF's needs for the next five years,[116] Zeira explained that, while some intelligence sources pointed to war, he and his team were sceptical; there was nothing untoward and therefore an outbreak of war was not to be expected.[117] What Zeira did not tell his fellow generals is that there were high-ranking analysts who were open to the view that war was indeed probable.[118] Colonel Yoel Ben-Porat, head of signal intelligence, was one of them. Not buying into the notion that the unprecedented Egyptian build-up merely reflected a military exercise, he requested permission to call up 200 intelligence reservists. When Zeira declined, Ben-Porat suggested that the IDF activate its special electronic listening devices. Again Zeira answered in the negative. Highly disconcerted, Ben-Porat wondered: "What do these sources exist for, if not for situations like the one we're facing?" Zeira's rejoinder, "The situations you see are not the ones I see," typified his general stance.[119] Zeira then continued: "Listen Yoel, the function of intelligence is to preserve the state's nerves, not to unsettle the population and not to undermine the economy."[120] That same day, Benjamin Telem, the head of the Israeli navy, also requested and received an audience with Zeira. Telem was alarmed by the fact that, while Zeira held that nothing more than an Egyptian military exercise was in hand, the navy's intelligence officer had determined that in fact Israel stood on the threshold of war. Zeira curtly dismissed Telem's concerns by claiming simply: "I have better information than your intelligence officer."[121]

The next day (October 2) military intelligence, in perusing dispatches received within the past twenty-four hours that detailed the dismantling by the Egyptians of sand mounds for ease of access to the waters of the canal, as well as the transportation by them of rafts and bridging equipment, blithely concluded that the Egyptian "manoeuvres" were on their projected course.[122] Then some hours later information came to hand that did not square with the notion that nothing more than Egyptian manoeuvres were in play. That is, 1,500 tons of live ammunition was being shipped by 300 trucks from emergency stores near Cairo to the front and, by contrast with normal procedure, inspection points along the route had not been notified.[123] At the same time, the Egyptian forces' general radio signal traffic was down to less than 5 percent of the average attained in previous exercises, which in itself should have indicated that something was amiss. On the northern front, the Syrians' amassing of weaponry was far in excess of what had been attained in the past. In the general area were 750 to 850 tanks, 550 artillery pieces and 31 anti-air missile batteries, compared with 250, 180 and 2, respectively, in May.[124]

There were many reasons why the IDF was blasé in the face of evident and massive Egyptian transfers to the canal front of men and equipment. Apart from Zeira being beholden to preconceptions that discounted the relevance of such transfers, other factors tended, in Israeli eyes, to minimize their significance. First of all, since 1968 the Egyptians had openly undertaken numerous exercises in gearing their men to cross the canal, and as a result the IDF had become inured to such procedures. Then between the beginning of 1973 and October the Egyptians had on twenty-two separate occasions mobilized their reserves, to release them fairly shortly thereafter.[125] A full-blown "manoeuvre," Tahrir 41, was officially and publicly scheduled to be completed by October 7, by which time most of the men were to be sent home. A few days into October, by way of deception, a group of Egyptian soldiers was authorized to undertake a pilgrimage to Mecca on the expiration of the month of Ramadan. Finally, to provide an air of normalcy, Egyptian soldiers on the canal's west bank swam, fished and nonchalantly walked about, peeling and eating fruit. Civilians in the potential war zone were not evacuated and the flame torches in the Morgan oil field remained ablaze. Given the generally rather unsophisticated manner in which the Egyptians tried to mislead the Israelis, General Saad El-Shazly, the man who conceived his country's war plans, was dumbfounded that even at that late hour Israel had not read Egyptian intentions correctly.[126] As the Israeli writer Hanoch Bartov summarized the situation: "The facts continued to move steadily in one direction but through the lenses of the men who assessed them they appeared to be pointing to a dramatically opposite conclusion."[127]

Dayan's tour at the northern front had heightened his sense of unease, and on Meir's return from Austria he requested an urgent meeting with her, Zeira, Elazar, Allon, Galili and the air force commander, Binyamin Peled. Since Zeira was ill in bed, Aryeh Shalev, the head of the IDF's military research branch, deputized for him. At the meeting, held on October 3, Shalev conceded that the Syrians and Egyptians were capable of mounting an immediate offensive. Nevertheless, in his considered judgment (shared of course by Zeira), the Egyptians being involved in manoeuvres and the Syrians preoccupied with preparing for an expected Israeli onslaught, they were unlikely to do so. As the author Abraham Rabinovich perceptively observed, by the "discounting a priori of any unusual movements by the Egyptian army as part of a military exercise, Israel's early warning system was effectively shut down."[128] What was not accorded sufficient attention at the meeting was the fact that the Syrians had not gathered their missiles in defence of Damascus but had instead concentrated them opposite the Golan Heights. Even though Dayan noted that that was "not a normal defence deployment,"[129] none of the participants at the meeting favoured the IDF taking far-reaching significant steps to strengthen its position on the Golan Heights.[130] Elazar, in summarizing possible military options, recommended the maintenance, with minor reinforcements, of the IDF's existing deployment of forces.[131] His seeming insouciance reflected his belief that, should the worst come to the worst, the IDF would be notified in good time. Paradoxically, he failed to take into account the fact that, if, technically speaking, the Arabs could switch from a defensive to an aggressive posture at a moment's notice, military intelligence could not therefore be assured of being in a position to provide adequate forewarnings. At the end of the session Meir, in shaking Shalev's hand, thanked him for his calming review and concluded that the security situation did not merit attention at the following day's full cabinet meeting. Accordingly, the government remained in the dark about the possibility of war.[132] Had Meir known that some high-ranking members of army intelligence not party to the organization's dominant consensus were, on the basis of incoming information, convinced that war was inevitable, she would almost certainly have felt that she had serious cause for concern. But at no time did Zeira even hint that there were within his ranks officers with divergent views. The very day (October 3) that Shalev so facilely assured Meir that war was not in the offing, Egyptian generals Ismail and Nofal met in Damascus with their Syrian counterparts, Tlas and Shakur, where details for the date and timing of the war were conclusively settled.[133] Egypt dubbed its forthcoming campaign "Badr," in commemoration of a battle in which the Prophet Muhammad smote his enemies and by so doing advanced on Mecca.

By October 4, news came to hand that the families of remaining Russian advisers in Syria and Egypt were all being airlifted to the Soviet Union. What is more, the Soviet ships anchored in the ports of Alexandria and Mersa Matruh had set sail. If ever there was a clear-cut omen that war was on the horizon, this was it. That afternoon the Israeli signal intelligence unit intercepted a message which revealed that the Soviets were evacuating their civilians precisely because Egypt and Syria were about to go to war. When Zeira was apprised of it, he demanded that, for the time being, the information be suppressed. Elazar was later to claim that, had he been party to that information, he would have without any further ado authorized a comprehensive mobilization.

At a general staff meeting on October 5, Zeira once again opined that nothing had changed to make him think that there was anything other than a very low probability of war. Then a little later, at a meeting convened by Dayan, he asserted: "All indications show that the Syrians and Egyptians are not preparing to attack. On the contrary, they are gripped by a state of fear of us."[134] Such an appraisal was, to say the least, preposterous. That very morning the results of an aerial photo survey of an extensive area of the western Canal Zone revealed that the Egyptian army was in a state of readiness far surpassing all past deployments.[135] In his effort to explain just why the Russians were withdrawing their civilians in such haste, Zeira ingenuously submitted: "Maybe the Russians think the Arabs are going to attack because they don't understand them well."[136] In point of fact, the Russians not only had certain knowledge that war was imminent, they even knew at exactly what time it would commence.[137] Their airlift involving large transport airplanes disconcerted Sadat, since it conveyed a clear signal of true Egyptian intentions.[138] Zeira had even known that Zvi Zamir, the Mossad director, had the night before been urgently summoned by the "reliable" Egyptian source to meet with him in London. Realizing, through the inclusion of a coded term in the informant's request, that he was likely to receive alarming news, Zamir had already left for the UK. But Zeira did not think it important to convey such information immediately either to Dayan or to Elazar; when he eventually made mention of it, it was in the form of an aside.

Despite Zeira's apparent sangfroid, Elazar was beginning to experience some serious qualms. Given the unprecedented concentration of enemy forces at the northern and southern front lines, he concluded not only that the Arabs were capable of launching an offensive forthwith but that there was no evidence that they would not do so.[139] With that in mind, Elazar cancelled the leave of strategic regular units, the air force was put on full alert, some extra measures were taken to reinforce front-line troops and the IDF's mobilization mechanism was activated. But, still relying on Zeira to alert him in the hour of need, Elazar did not press for the mobilization of the reservists.

Later that morning, farcically convinced that the Egyptian and Syrian moves were motivated by considerations of defence, a hastily convened cabinet decided to ask of Kissinger to pass on a message to the Russians and to the Arabs stressing that Israel harboured no aggressive intent and was not planning any military adventure. (The Israeli belief that Egypt was bracing itself for an Israeli attack was derived from nothing more than reports in the Egyptian press.)[140] Attached to the message and in effect cancelling out its purpose, which was to forestall any pre-emptive Arab strike based on fear, was a note appended by IDF intelligence reaffirming that the odds of an Arab-waged war occurring were rather low. For that reason, Kissinger did not regard the communication as necessitating urgent attention, and as a result he approached the Soviets only on the following day, just over an hour before the outbreak of war.[141] Despite Zeira's habitual words of balm, an element of uncertainty gripped most participants, who authorized Meir and Dayan to mobilize reservists on the following day, Yom Kippur, should the need arise. Before the meeting dispersed, Galili praised Zeira and Elazar for their assessments, saying that in his opinion Israel was blessed with excellent intelligence services. But on that occasion Meir was rather uneasy. She noted that the Egyptian and Syrian media were beginning to behave as they did on the eve of the Six-Day War and thought that the massive enemy build-up could surely not be a prelude to only a minor action. Thinking aloud, she remarked: "Who knows? We don't sit with them and we don't know what they want to do."[142]

By the evening of October 5, high-ranking officials within IDF intelligence received information confirming that the swift evacuation of Soviet personnel and ships from Egypt and Syria was brought about by a definite Soviet realization that an outbreak of war was a foregone conclusion. That critical information was tardily passed on to Zeira, who in turn was in no hurry to share it with Elazar. During a session in a post-war commission of inquiry, when asked why he waited until the next morning to contact the chief of staff, Zeira, claiming that he had no confidence in the source of the information and that he was certain that the IDF was on a maximum state of alert, replied: "I did not think it appropriate to trouble Elazar at eleven at night."[143] From Elazar's testimony, we learn that, had he been alerted the night before, he would have ordered the immediate mobilization of the reservists and that in his judgment the outcome of the war would have been entirely different.[144]

All the while Israeli troops posted along the Bar Lev Line watched events over the waterway with utter dismay. Before their very eyes, convoys were arriving at night, ramparts overlooking their positions were being raised, and at numerous points ready vehicle access to the canal was being prepared by bulldozers forging passageways through the ramparts. Among the men newly assigned to the canal strongholds were mature-aged reservists. They included new immigrants who had undergone only rudimentary military training and were, as a group, not regarded as front-line material. Many strongholds were undermanned, ranging from seven to twenty-four soldiers. In most there was only one officer and few included a medical doctor.[145]

When Captain Motti Ashkenazi took possession of the stronghold named Budapest, he found it in disrepair. Fences were submerged in the desert sand, trenches were collapsing, firing positions lacked sandbags and there was insufficient ammunition. With commendable responsibility, Ashkenazi refused to sign confirming that everything was in order. Since that forestalled the departure of the troops being replaced, his irritated battalion commander took it upon himself to certify that all was by the book.[146] Both the decrepit conditions at the fort and the cavalier attitude of the battalion commander reflected a flagrant disregard for correct procedures. Such an attitude not only characterized Israeli society then but continues to the present day. It was much the same in the other strongholds, where, according to Dayan, "communications equipment and vehicles were generally not properly maintained and weapons and ammunition were below acceptable levels and in some they were even below the essential minimum."[147] On being asked by a more senior-aged sergeant about to be posted to the canal front what would become of him and the others should the Egyptians suddenly attack, his battalion commander flippantly replied: "When someone breaks wind in Cairo, we hear it in Tel Aviv. We'll have plenty of time to replace you with regular units if and when we think something is about to happen."[148] In the end, during the Yom Kippur War, Budapest under Ashkenazi's watch was the only canal stronghold to hold out. But before all that, on October 5, the Israeli public were lulled into a false sense of security by leading newspapers such as *Haaretz* and *Yediot Ahronot*, which informed their readers that all was well. Quoting Dayan, *Haaretz* reported that "the Egyptians will not go to war within the next few years," whereas *Yediot Ahronot*'s military correspondent, Eitan Haber, claimed that the army "had adopted full measures to deprive Egypt of the possibility of surprise."[149]

3

THE YOM KIPPUR WAR

On Yom Kippur 1973 the watchman noticed the sword but failed to raise the alarm. The sword subsequently claimed many lives. The watchman did not raise the alarm because for days on end, close to a year in fact, he slept on his watch.[1]

At 4 in the morning of October 6, when Yom Kippur, the Jewish Day of Atonement fell, Golda Meir was awakened by a call from Yisrael Lior, her military attaché, to hear him say: "War is going to break out today." After a moment's pause, she replied "I thought as much."[2] The Egyptian undercover source from whom those grim tidings were derived was judged to be impeccable. As already mentioned, Zvi Zamir, the director of Mossad, Israel's intelligence agency, had especially flown to London to meet with him. Around midnight, soon after the meeting, Zamir decided to phone through the startling information in language that could readily be deciphered. Unfortunately, as it was the eve of Yom Kippur, telephone calls to Israel were not easily placed and only by 2.45 a.m. did he succeed in contacting Freddy Eini, his most senior subordinate. It then took another hour for the news to be passed on to Lior, who in turn aroused Meir. A general consensus rapidly emerged that the forthcoming Arab assault was timed to commence at exactly 6 p.m. However, the source of that information cannot be traced. In retrospect

Meir recalled that, as she understood things, war was to break out "late in the afternoon."[3]

Elazar was alerted at 4.30 a.m. After summoning his general staff, he spoke to Benny Peled, head of the IAF, who recommended a pre-emptive airstrike. Elazar concurred, anticipating both Dayan and Meir's support. What is more, he wished to activate a full-scale mobilization of the reserves. At a cursory general staff meeting held at 5.30 a.m., Zeira still could not bring himself to accept that he had misread Arab intentions. Sticking to his guns, he stressed that the likelihood of a war occurring was not simply low but "even lower than low."[4] Dayan, like Zeira, was not convinced of the full seriousness of the situation. Being adamantly opposed to a large-scale mobilization, he told Elazar in his office at 6 a.m.: "We don't order full mobilization just on the basis of a report by Zvika" (Zamir's nickname).[5] Yet, in his subsequent memoirs describing that fateful morning, he wrote: "It was clear that we had to operate on the assumption that both Egypt and Syria were about to wage war."[6] Whatever the case, he was willing to accept only a small-scale call-up in his anticipation of a possible Arab raid of one kind or another. His reluctance to comply with Elazar's demand stemmed not only from his disbelief that Israel stood on the verge of total war but, being preoccupied with a forthcoming general election (on October 31), he was also wary of upsetting voters by perhaps needlessly summoning a multitude of reservists on Yom Kippur. Probably for that reason he exclaimed: "It would be a great scandal if we mobilized all the reservists."[7] Dayan then reasoned that a full mobilization on Israel's part would be seen by the world at large as an Israeli decision to wage war[8] – a non sequitur, considering that the Arabs had already amassed forces on Israel's front lines that far exceeded anything Israel was capable of matching. Initially Dayan contemplated drafting 30,000 reservists exclusively for the Golan Heights. But, in the face of Elazar's insistence, he expressed a willingness to raise the number to between 50,000 and 60,000 men, to be divided equally between the northern and southern fronts. Nor was Dayan amenable to a pre-emptive airstrike. As far as he was concerned, the issue of a pre-emptive strike was not to be raised unless it was known for certain that the country stood on the threshold of, say, an attack on Tel Aviv.[9] Dayan did at least allow Elazar to put his case to Meir. But according to Elazar the discussion ended "without the defence minister's approval for any call-up whatsoever."[10]

As to the encounter with Meir, Dayan at first suggested that it be held between 10 and 11 a.m. but then begrudgingly agreed to attend at 8 a.m.[11] At the meeting, at which Dayan, Elazar, Zeira, Galili, Allon and Bar Lev were present, Meir emphatically ruled out a pre-emptive strike. Considering that (as mentioned in the previous chapter) Israel had only recently convinced the United States that no war was imminent, she feared that such a move would be seen as an Israeli act of aggression and that the Americans would therefore not respond favourably to subsequent Israeli requests for military assistance. In many respects her judgment may well have been sound, for when Henry Kissinger, the US secretary of state, was aroused at 6.15 a.m. by Joseph Sisco, the assistant secretary of state, to inform him that news at hand suggested that Egypt and Syria were about to attack Israel, Kissinger recalled that, on the basis of previous Israeli reports, he was convinced that "such an attack was nearly impossible."[12] In the past, Kissinger had stressed both to the Israeli ambassador, Simcha Dinitz, and to his predecessor, Yitzhak Rabin, that "America's ability to help Israel in any war would be impaired if Israel struck first."[13]

The pre-emptive strike that Elazar sought was intended to be directed only against Syria. Targets suggested were (because of adverse weather) deep within Syrian territory, so that the massive alignment of Syrian tanks, artillery, infantry and anti-aircraft weapons concentrated near the border would have escaped unscathed. What is more, the operation could not commence before 12 noon. Taking all these points into account, Dayan later concluded that, even had such a pre-emptive strike been authorized, it would hardly have affected the course of the war.[14] On the other hand, on another occasion, Dayan was reported as saying, "Had I known for certain that war was on the horizon, I would have called for a strike."[15] Such an admission accords with a statement made by Dayan in the previous June to Peled, which was as follows: "My dear Benny, do you really think if we were ever confronted with even a minuscule amount of fear that we were about to be attacked the air force would not receive an order to attack first?"[16]

In terms of bracing the IDF to meet the expected onslaught, Elazar sought authorization to call up to 200,000 reservists. Dayan, who once again expressed scepticism that war was certain, argued for a more limited mobilization, claiming that, if by nightfall hostilities did occur, the remainder of the reservists could be summoned. In the end, Meir, never for a moment doubting the seriousness of the situation, tilted towards Elazar's side, authorizing the drafting of up to 120,000 reservists. Unlike Dayan, political considerations did not seem to impinge on her decision-making. As she reasoned: "If we issue a large call up and war does not materialize that would impact on the economy but that's no disaster. On the other hand, if a war was to occur we could never forgive ourselves for dithering."[17] At 9.20 a.m., after a meeting that commenced at 8 a.m., and just about five and a half hours since Meir was jolted from her sleep, Elazar was finally able to order his deputy, Israel Tal, to activate the mobilization process. But it took until 11 a.m. for it to get into top gear.[18] Lior, who was present at the meeting, could not understand why Dayan quibbled over the mobilization. In his memoirs he wrote: "Couldn't the minister of defence order a mobilization immediately on receiving the advance notice of war? Couldn't he at 4 a.m., at 5 a.m., request permission from the prime minister to do so in order to derive the benefit of four, five or six hours (extra) of mobilization on such a hard pressed, urgent and dreadful day?"[19]

As the meeting with Meir turned to the evacuation of women and children from the Golan Heights settlements, Dayan thought that it would be better to handle that task just before the onset of hostilities. After Meir insisted that the evacuation be undertaken immediately, Dayan replied, "If you want to remove the children now, take them down now. Tomorrow let them complain to you."[20] An hour after the meeting, still smarting from its outcome, Dayan snarled: "The chief of staff wants to mobilize troops for a counterattack in a war that hasn't even begun."[21]

The launching of war on Yom Kippur appeared to place the Arabs in an advantageous position. A large number of IDF personnel would have been on leave and, like everything else, radio and television transmissions as well as public transport would have been suspended. On the other hand, it was relatively easy to locate servicemen, for they were either at home or at a synagogue and, with all roads deserted, the IDF could move men and equipment with relative ease. As army couriers scoured synagogues, services were interrupted so that reservists' names could be called out. Rabbis announced that the conscripted could break their fast and ride. In one house of prayer a tearful father wrapped his arms tightly around his son. Only on his rabbi interceding did he relax his grasp. The rabbi then placed his hands upon the young man's head and blessed him.[22] In Haifa, Moshe Waks, an architectural student, took leave of his young wife, his seventeen-month-old daughter and one-week-old son. Departing in good spirits and laughingly waving goodbye, Waks was to meet his death within the next twenty-four hours.[23] Reservists who were abroad at the time hurried home. On landing in Israel, tank crew members were swiftly processed at the airport and then sent directly to the fronts. Some died in battle without their families being aware of their return.[24] Yossi Ben Hanan's experience encapsulates that of many reservists overseas at the time. He was on honeymoon in the Himalayas, but as soon as he learnt that Israel was at war, without a second thought he secured flights via Delhi and Bombay to Athens, whence an El Al airliner took him to Israel. As prearranged, his parents met him at the airport with all his military gear, and within two hours he reported for duty at command headquarters on the northern front. With minimum delay, and with only eleven tanks under his direction, he secured a crucial hill contested by a Syrian force made up of sixty to seventy tanks. In a heated exchange of fire, Ben Hanan repelled the enemy. Some days later, in a broad Israeli countersweep within Syrian territory, his tank was struck by a rocket, and he found himself lying beside it with a shattered hip, bones protruding outwards and the remains of his left leg dangling before him. Thanks to the devoted care of his driver, his haemorrhage was largely staunched during the three-hour wait until he was retrieved and flown in a helicopter to a hospital in Haifa. In recounting the story, Dayan wrote that, on being wheeled into the operating theatre Ben Hanan was met by his newly-wed bride, whom he assured: "It's nothing. You have nothing to worry about, I have checked myself over and I have only lost a leg."[25]

If war was indeed to break out at 6 p.m. on that Yom Kippur day, from an Arab perspective the time would have been optimal. It would have meant that Israeli pilots facing a setting sun would have been hindered in their efforts to identify and attack Egyptian targets. With night approaching, darkness would soon envelop the battleground, enabling Egyptian forces to ferry the canal in relative security. Because the expected timing made perfect sense, Israel was twice taken by surprise, for in fact fighting erupted at 2 p.m. That of course meant that Israel had even less time to reinforce its endangered fronts.[26]

At the moment of truth, Israel on the Syrian front deployed 5,000 men, 177 tanks and 44 field guns, and on the Egyptian front 290 tanks and 48 pieces of artillery. Apart from the tank and artillery crews, 450 men manned the sixteen remaining canal strongholds (the other fifteen having over time fallen into disuse). Facing the Israelis were 45,000 Syrians with 1,400 tanks and 690 field guns and 100,000 Egyptians equipped with 2,200 tanks and 690 field guns.[27] In terms of the total number of forces available to the protagonists, the Egyptian army had mustered 650,000 troops and the Syrians 150,000, and, in addition, 100,000 men were eventually thrown into the battle by Jordan, Iraq and other Arab states. Israel, by contrast, had total recourse to only 375,000 men.[28] As for war materiel, Israel's stock of tanks and first-line planes amounted to 2,100 and 359 respectively, whereas the Arabs were equipped with a total of 4,500 tanks and 680 planes.[29]

At 12 noon on October 6, the Israeli cabinet assembled for an emergency session which dragged on for a couple of hours. A debate ensued as to whether Israel should attack Syria if only Egypt opened hostilities. Holding the floor, Meir was suggesting that it was by no means certain that war would erupt at 6 p.m. Perhaps it would occur even sooner. As she was speaking, sirens began shrieking, inducing Meir to ask "What's that?" Her stenographer sitting beside her replied, "It seems that the war has started," to which Meir in Yiddish exclaimed: "Nohr dos felt mir [That's all I need]."[30] Two hours later, on being asked by Israeli newspaper editors whether he was optimistic, Dayan replied: "Do you want the truth? Very ... I am assuming that the Egyptians have undertaken a great adventure without forethought. We will proceed until tomorrow afternoon. After that I would not like to be in any of their shoes."[31]

Before Dayan so frivolously held court, on both the northern and southern fronts a thunderous Arab artillery barrage heralded the war's outbreak. Shells poured down incessantly on the strongholds of the Bar Lev Line along the canal and on forward IDF positions in the Golan Heights, while Egyptian and Syrian planes raced across the length of both fronts. Confronted with a pall of black smoke billowing across the horizon, Uri Shimhoni, like many another IDF defender, grasped that a moment of reckoning had arrived: "that the state was imperilled, all those who had soothed us, all those know-alls, knew nothing."[32] To confound US and world assessments, half an hour before the war actually commenced, Egyptian radio broadcasts were interrupted by the announcement of a news flash: "It has been reported that elements of Israel's armed forces have attacked our positions in Zafarana [a small village on the Red Sea Coast]. This represents a most serious breach of the ceasefire and the Security Council has been so informed."[33]

On the southern front, 8,000 Egyptians moving behind smoke screens and chanting "Allahu akbar" (God is the greatest) crossed along the entire length of the canal in rubber dinghies.[34] Using over 400 high-pressure hydraulic hoses, they sprayed the large defensive sand barriers erected by the IDF. Like sandcastles subject to poured buckets of water, the barriers rapidly disintegrated. By 10.30 p.m. twelve bridges were laid, and within the first twenty-four hours of the war 100,000 Egyptian soldiers, 1,000 tanks and 13,500 other vehicles were transferred to the east bank.[35] For the most part, the sixteen manned strongholds of the Bar Lev Line were bypassed. Egyptian infantry had been clearly instructed not to expend their resources in challenging them.[36]

Israeli tanks were in the main not within immediate reach of the canal. In fact, many were as far away as 70 kilometres from the front.[37] Ignoring explicit instructions from Elazar, Gonen, who was unacquainted with Egyptian war plans long since gathered by army intelligence, had, without Elazar's knowledge, decided to wait until 5 p.m. before ordering the forward movements of his armoured forces.[38] Only after General Albert Mendler appealed to him to be allowed to set out earlier did Gonen concede an hour.[39] When Mendler's forces drew up to the front, awaiting them were Egyptian ground troops equipped not only with lethal rocket-propelled anti-tank grenades but also with the latest Soviet Saggers, small anti-tank missiles with up to a 3-kilometre range. Compounding their deadly effect, the Saggers were issued in incredible numbers. Heikal later related that it was intended that the first 8,000 Egyptian shock troops and the infantry divisions that followed them would be equipped with such weapons "on a scale far in excess of anything previously contemplated."[40] Despite military intelligence having knowledge of the Saggers, most Israeli tank crews had never heard of them. General Avraham Adan (Bren) admitted that he had taken them into account before the war but then dismissed them as not amounting to any serious threat.[41]

Controlled by the manipulation of joy sticks that could, by means of thin wire strands, transmit signals to alter their trajectory, the light-weight Saggers were easily handled by individual soldiers. By the day's end, they had played a decisive role in knocking out two-thirds of the IDF's tanks in Sinai and rendering many surviving Israeli soldiers in what Sharon described as being "in a state of shock."[42] Nor were Israeli tank crew members the only ones to be stunned. Uri Ben Ari, Gonen's adjunct, recalled that, on arrival at the Sinai-based war room, Gonen tended to lose his self-control and that the atmosphere pervading there was "one of fear and terror."[43] However, Gonen soon pulled himself together after having regained the confidence that he could engineer a turning point in Israel's favour.[44]

Aside from the potency of Egyptian Saggers and other anti-tank weapons, because the Egyptians crossed the canal over a very wide front, IDF tanks could not zero in on the main points of enemy con-centration. Nor did the IAF fare any better. With its pilots soon dazzled by the setting sun, adequate support could not be provided to the IDF's ground forces. The IAF succeeded in damaging only two canal bridges, which were soon made good. Egyptian troops arriving on the east side of the canal enjoyed the protection of overlapping batteries of surface-to-air missiles (SAMS) stationed at their rear. What is more, they possessed hand-held Soviet anti-aircraft rockets capable of hitting low-flying planes attempting to strafe them. Consequently, thirty-five IAF planes were downed within the war's opening twenty-four hours.[45] The IAF could at least claim one significant achievement. At around 2 p.m., two Egyptian Topolev bombers flying over the Mediterranean some 80 to 90 kilometres from Israel discharged two lethal air-to-surface missiles directed towards Tel Aviv. One of the missiles developed a tech-nical mishap and fell into the sea. The other was spotted by an Israeli pilot whose Mirage could outpace it. That enabled him to keep abreast with the missile, fire at it and cause it to plummet into the ocean.[46]

With two full Egyptian armies having crossed over to Sinai, the Egyptian situation could not have been better. Their losses in both human and material terms were far lighter than anticipated. In their planning stages the Egyptians had allowed for the possibility of incurring 30,000 casualties during the early phase of the war, yet in practice they lost only 208 soldiers, twenty tanks and five planes.[47] Moreover, they demonstrated that they were capable of matching the Israelis both in daring and in their newly acquired ability to handle technologically advanced weapons.[48] Efforts to mobilize well-educated officer material,[49] meticulous attention to detailed planning, and endless drilling and manoeuvres had transformed the Egyptian army into a formidable fighting force. In cutting the IDF down to size it had redeemed its lost honour.

As grim as things were for Israel along the Suez Canal, they were far more precarious on the Golan Heights, where at first some of the IDF personnel imagined that they were facing the prospect merely of a day's engagement.[50] In the first hours of the war, airborne Syrian troops stormed an IDF intelligence base on Mount Hermon manned by fifty-seven defenders in order quickly to overrun it. Thirteen of the defenders were killed, thirty-one were taken prisoner, ten escaped, and for the next six days three remained within one of the bunkers.[51] The fall of the base deprived the IDF of a crucial facility for monitoring enemy air and ground traffic. At the same time, 500 Syrian tanks sought to enter the main body of the heights, concentrating their efforts both north and south of Kuneitra. The Israelis were able to keep the Syrians at bay only until the early hours of the morning of October 7, when a force of 300 Syrian tanks broke through IDF lines in the region of Hushniyah, nearly 13 kilometres south of Kuneitra. Opposing them were fewer than thirty IDF tanks. To all intents and purposes, Israel's defence in the entire southern section of the Golan Heights had collapsed.[52]

The Syrians were able to break through Israeli lines with relative ease partly as a consequence of Hofi, the regional commander, insisting on defending them at all points, causing the sparse IDF forces on hand to be far too thinly spread. By mistakenly assuming that the Syrians had no taste for nocturnal fighting, the Israeli tank crews lacked night-sighting devices, whereas their foes were more than adequately provisioned. Furthermore, the focal point of the Syrian thrust was incorrectly anticipated. Three battalions of the Seventh Armoured Brigade, headed by Avigdor Ben Gal (known as Yanosh), were posted in the north, while only two battalions of the Barak Brigade, under Yitzhak Ben Shoham, were placed in the south where the fighting was more intense.

Shortly before daybreak, Dayan arrived by helicopter at the Northern Command to ascertain how the IDF was faring. Briefing him, Hofi mentioned that the Israeli forces at his immediate disposal would probably be incapable of retaining the heights, while Dan Laner, one of Hofi's reserve divisional commanders, quietly reported: "Fighting in the south of the heights is over and we have lost. We are without the means to stop them."[53] Utterly astounded, Dayan, after trying in vain to contact Elazar by phone, got through to Peled to instruct him to commit the entire IAF to the northern front. When Peled replied that Elazar had already prioritized an attack on Egyptian anti-air missile batteries, Dayan answered that the Third Temple (a metonym for Israel) was in grave danger and that, unless the IAF appeared en masse over the Golan Heights no later than noon, nothing would prevent the Syrians from pouring into the Jordan Valley.[54] A little later, and without being aware of Dayan's irregular intercession, Elazar also charged Peled to go for the heights.[55] The IAF needed extra time to fulfil its new mission, for its planes were all primed for action on the southern front. Weapons intended for the Egyptian missile batteries had to be unloaded and then replaced by others more suitable for destroying tanks. Even when the full might of the IAF bore down on the Syrians it was not able to turn the tide. Electronic equipment used to neutralize enemy radar could not readily be relocated from Sinai to the Golan Heights and up-to-date aerial photographs pinpointing Syrian SAM positions were not on hand. Of the thirty-one Syrian missile sites attacked, only one was effectively destroyed and another partly damaged.[56]

Just after noon, Syrian tanks began to approach the village of El Al, not far from the reaches of the River Jordan. At much the same time other Syrian forces progressed towards Camp Nafeh, where Eitan coordinated the overall defence of the Golan Heights. The haste in which reservists were rushed to the front exacerbated the task of containing the enemy. Units arrived under strength because they could not afford to wait for their numbers to be brought up to par. Tanks broke down en route, maps, goggles and machine guns were insufficiently available, and in many cases tank guns were not bore sighted – that is, the sights were not aligned with the barrels of the guns.[57] Commander Amnon Sharon, on taking possession of ten tanks with which he was to race up to the front, found that they were low on fuel, without sufficient repair tool kits and, more critically, provided with only twelve shells per tank instead of a standard complement of seventy-two.[58]

In a desperate effort to stem the Syrian advance, the handful of tanks remaining in the 188th Barak battalion stood their ground, but not without critical losses, including that of Ben Shoham, its commander, and his deputy, David Yisraeli. Finally, following the arrival of a reservist armoured brigade plus (despite its losses) IAF aerial harassment, the IDF managed to stem the Syrian advance.

By then Hofi began to manifest signs of exhaustion as well as a growing incapacity to think and act coherently. He was reported to have been seen lying on his cot like a "broken man, lacking in spirit and muttering 'all is lost, all is lost.'"[59] After considering replacing him, Elazar decided to ask Bar Lev to proceed to northern front headquarters with powers to intervene wherever necessary. Under Bar Lev's soothing influence, a measure of order and level-headedness prevailed. In a call to Meir, Bar Lev reported that, although the situation in the north was critical, it was not quite desperate.[60]

Meanwhile, at 10 p.m. (on October 7), the Syrians launched an assault on a sector of the Golan Heights not too far south of Mount Hermon, in an area that was to become known as "the Valley of Tears," where they pitted 500 tanks against forty IDF ones commanded by Avigdor Kahalani. Despite the odds against them, the Israelis blocked the Syrian advance, if only by pure grit. A gruesome aspect of the violent clash of armour that occurred there and elsewhere was that Israeli tank commanders were occasionally decapitated while standing upright in their turrets. The sight of headless torsos collapsing into the main compartments of the tanks was thoroughly unsettling, causing some of the surviving crews to abandon their vehicles.[61]

On the southern front on October 7 there was little that the IDF could do by way of assuming any of its own initiatives. A significant quantity of additional tanks could not be rushed to the Canal Zone until at least the third day of the war, for it took time to assemble and transport an adequate number of reservists. On flying by helicopter to Southern Command's headquarters, Dayan appeared to be a broken man. As he edged away from the helicopter, the pilot called out to him to run for shelter, since Egyptian planes were priming to attack them. But he continued listlessly like one detached from reality and oblivious to the dangers about him.[62] Dayan subsequently wrote that risks to his own personal security had never daunted him. What did fill him with dread were "the dangers hovering over Israel."[63]

Later, on imparting his deep disquiet to Meir (accompanied by Galili and Allon and later joined by Elazar), Dayan suggested that strenuous efforts be made to obtain additional planes and tanks from the USA, since Israel's limited stocks were dwindling at a rapid rate. He feared that Israel was on the verge of being left without sufficient planes, tanks and trained personnel to ward off its enemies.[64] Shaken by Dayan's uncharacteristic demeanour, Meir briefly left the meeting to inform her friend and assistant, Lou Kedar, that she thought that Dayan was contemplating surrender.[65] As Meir was later to confide to another friend, Yaacov Hazan, for the next day or so, tormented by a series of woeful tidings, she was on the verge of committing suicide.[66]

In reality Dayan had merely recommended surrendering some territory,[67] for both he and Elazar had concluded that all attempts to reach the Bar Lev forts ought to be abandoned and that a second line of defence should be formed. The Bar Lev forts, far from playing any meaningful role in rebutting the enemy, turned out to be a grave liability requiring the use of scarce human resources to rescue their defenders. Elazar and Dayan differed on how far back the IDF ought to redeploy. Dayan thought in terms of quite a substantial withdrawal, to the Mitla and Gidi passes, where the IDF would be far better placed to defend itself. But Dayan's concept was fraught with danger. It would potentially have amounted to handing Egypt a victory on a silver platter. Egypt could simply have sat tight in the area vacated and awaited a UN Security Council demand for a complete cessation of fighting, with the demarcation lines determined by the forces in place. Elazar objected to Dayan's recommendation. Similarly, Galili described Dayan's proposal as pregnant with fatal consequences.[68] After the meeting, a dejected Dayan told Meir that he was prepared to resign, but Meir would not hear of it.

Foreign sources have alleged that, on the night of October 8, the Israeli government, overcome by forebodings, decided to prepare its nuclear weapons for use if and when it became patently clear that the country was about to be overrun. *Time* magazine claimed that it had learnt that Israel had assembled thirteen atomic bombs "at a secret underground tunnel." The journal maintained that, "what is certain" is that, on October 13, Russia dispatched nuclear warheads "to Alexandria, to be fitted on Russian Scud missiles based in Egypt."[69] Neither assertion was backed by any available evidence. Some writers suspect that a prospective use of nuclear weapons was arranged to induce the USA to rearm Israel promptly[70] but, like all else, that remained purely speculative. What is known is that Dayan had discounted Egyptian use of chemical weapons because, as he saw things, the Egyptians realized "that Israel has a nuclear capacity and that they know that we are not Yemen."[71]

Elazar was confident that the IDF could assume the offensive on October 8 by way of a broad sweep against Egyptian forces east of the canal. After conferring with Gonen and other high-ranking Southern Command officers – other than Sharon, who was absent – Elazar ordered such an operation, emphasizing that it was to be a limited one.[72] The IDF was to approach no closer than 3 kilometres from the canal and only one division was to move at a time. Every effort was to be made to avoid areas swarming with Egyptian infantry bearing anti-tank weapons, and on no account was any unit to approach the Bar Lev strongholds. As he took his leave, Elazar made it known that his scheme was open to refinement and that he expected later to receive a final version from Gonen. Assuming he had sufficient leeway, Gonen devised a far more ambitious plan that included a rescue attempt of the canal forts and preparations for a canal crossing. Elazar, without scrutinizing Gonen's modifications in detail, and not grasping the extent to which it varied from his original directive, endorsed it.[73]

At first, Gonen's hopes appeared to be warranted. Word was received that the Egyptian Third Army had come to grief and that some IDF units were in the process of crossing to the west bank of the canal. When Elazar conveyed such news to members of the cabinet, they were ecstatic.[74] To newspaper editors, Elazar reported that, from early morning, successful counter-attacks had been pursued on the two fronts. "We have managed to repel the Syrians from the Golan Heights . . . we have commenced the destruction of the Egyptian army." [75]

But by the morning of October 9, when the full facts came to light, it turned out not only that the Israeli euphoria was premature but that the IDF had suffered its worst setback ever. In no small part, that debacle resulted from a misunderstanding as to what was expected of the various participating units. Elazar thought that Adan would first engage his armoured division against Egypt's Second Army at Kantara and then sweep southwards to the Bitter Lake. As he did so, Sharon and Mendler's divisions were to be on hand should Adan require additional support. Only after Adan had completed his primary mission were Sharon's forces to go on the offensive in the southern canal sector, with the assurance that Adan and Mendler's men would ward off any Egyptian counter-attack. No crossing of the canal was planned, but such a contingency was not firmly ruled out.

The campaign commenced at 8 a.m. (on October 8) with Adan's undermanned brigade moving southwards parallel to the canal yet out of range of infantry missiles. Backing them was only a small amount of artillery, as the rest was still en route.[76] Air support was totally lacking. If Adan had had his way, the operation would have been postponed until all necessary IDF firepower had arrived.[77] An hour later, Adan was instructed to veer westwards to rescue an IDF canal stronghold under intense pressure. As he did so, his forces met with a wall of anti-tank fire emanating from Egyptian infantry in well-entrenched positions. Under the illusion that all was well with Adan, Gonen gave Sharon the green light to move south. Sharon was reluctant to do so. Having from high ground observed the lack of progress that Adan had made, and not being willing to abandon the crucial ridges that he was holding, Sharon told Gonen in no uncertain terms that his order simply did not make sense. In the heated exchange that followed, Gonen repetitively threatened Sharon with immediate dismissal, which led Sharon, against his better judgment, to comply. Then by 2 p.m., after learning that the Egyptians were about to launch a counter-attack along the entire length of the canal and of the battered state of Adan's division, Gonen ordered Sharon to return to his starting position to assist Adan. That was easier said than done, for, while Sharon's forces had initially been able to move southwards unhindered, as they reversed direction they encountered strong Egyptian fire.

The upshot of it all was that, at the day's end, the IDF, minus another eighty of its tanks, was in part further away from the canal than had been the case early that morning.[78] Dayan despairingly concluded that, on October 8, the effort of deploying three divisions and scores of aircraft "had been wasted, frittered away, all for nothing."[79] By now around 400 of Israel's tanks were either totally destroyed or disabled. The Second and Third Egyptian armies were barely dented and the IDF canal strongholds remained marooned as small islands in a sea of Egyptian forces. Although the part of each stronghold below ground, where the men slept, provided reasonable protection against shelling, firing positions and communication trenches were extremely vulnerable. The IDF was in no position to link up and rescue its beleaguered troops. An opportunity to do so on the first night of the war was squandered by Gonen, who was confident that, if necessary, they could readily be extricated later. While some of the soldiers posted in the forts ultimately succeeded in infiltrating through enemy lines to join up with Israeli units further to the east, others were either killed or taken prisoner. In one of the besieged forts, Yaakov Ben Nahum, a Yemenite Jew from Jerusalem, had established radio contact with Southern Command headquarters. Ben Nahum, who talked incessantly, appealed for artillery fire to be directed against the attacking Egyptians, but all attempts to alleviate his situation failed. Eventually, after requesting that his mother be told that he had fought courageously, he reported that bazooka rockets were blasting open his bunker door. His listeners sat in horror as they heard the noise of the explosions until suddenly all was quiet.[80]

Setbacks on October 8 were not confined to the southern front. In the northern zone, units of the Golani Brigade had ventured out in an attempt to recapture the Mount Hermon stronghold. At first Hofi was reluctant to authorize the operation but, on hearing that some IDF troops were still holding out there, he gave the go-ahead. On ascending the slopes the Golani units unexpectedly encountered the Syrians in forward positions away from the fortress. With the slopes shrouded in mist ruling out any reliance on artillery and the IAF for air cover, the Israelis were severely handicapped. Not being able to make headway, they withdrew after twenty-eight of their men were killed and another fifty-seven wounded.[81]

That afternoon Dayan imparted the grim tidings to newspaper editors, and Aharon Yariv, the former head of the IDF information branch, appeared on television to give a toned-down account of Israel's setbacks. Although he tried to put a favourable gloss on recent events, the public's confidence in its armed forces was shaken. Given the earlier dissemination of glowing battle accounts, the proverbial person in the street began to feel that the Arabs had learnt from the Israelis just how to fight while the Israelis had learnt from the Arabs just how to lie.[82]

Within the upper ranks of the general staff as well as within the defence ministry, there was a growing consensus that Gonen was simply not up to the task of commanding the southern front. His ability as a brigade commander, as exhibited in the Six-Day War, was beyond reproach, but Elazar had come to the conclusion that he was incapable of thinking and operating as a front commander. On October 10 he was replaced by Bar Lev, who had to relinquish his cabinet position of trade and industry minister to be reinducted into the IDF. As a face-saving device, Bar Lev was posted "alongside" Gonen, who retained the title of Officer in Command of the Southern Front, but everyone was made to understand that ultimately it was Bar Lev who was in charge. Ever the perfect gentleman, Bar Lev did all he could not to humiliate Gonen; whenever he discussed matters with him, he did so behind closed doors, away from the prying ears of others.[83] Needless to say, Gonen was mortified by such a turn of events.

Turning to the northern front, where, after having fought without let-up for three solid days against superior forces, Ben Gal's Seventh Armoured Brigade, or more notably the battalion commanded by Avigdor Kahalani, had reached the point where its remaining men were totally enfeebled by exhaustion. On the fourth day of the war, October 9, they had to contend with a renewed Syrian assault that was, in Dayan's words, "the heaviest ever."[84] It opened with a thunderous artillery barrage, followed by the advance of 160 Syrian tanks accompanied by motorized infantry.[85] The battle raged over a narrow front in which the opposing forces were tightly massed. In the process Syrian tanks edged up to within 50 to 100 metres of the Israeli ones to duel in a "cauldron of smoke and flames laced with the reek of burning cordite."[86] By midday many IDF tanks were put out of action, and the seven remaining were each left with only four to five shells. Having fought for four days and three nights, Ben Gal informed Eitan that his men could no longer hold out. But at that very moment Eitan received a communiqué that a unit led by Yossi Ben Hanan had taken a nearby strategic ridge northwest of Kuneitra and was reaping havoc on Syrian armour, causing them to retreat. That information was duly relayed to

Kahalani, who with his fellow fighters were inspired to draw upon their near depleted mental and physical reserves in a final effort to see the back of the Syrians.

The next morning (October 10) the IDF launched a concerted Israeli counter-attack. On that occasion the IDF truly made headway. The Syrians, ejected from the Golan Heights, abandoned hundreds upon hundreds of damaged tanks, some of which were later repaired and utilized by the Israelis. By the following day, the IDF had chalked up inroads into Syria proper, approaching within 40 kilometres of Damascus. Eventually they would be within artillery range of the Syrian capital. Commander Rafiq Helwai, a member of the Druze community, was summoned to Damascus, where after a brief sham trial he was executed for ordering his forces to retreat.[87] Helwai's putative panic aside, most Syrian units continued to function with commendable fortitude, and even by October 15 there was no indication that Syrian forces were on the verge of disintegration.[88] From a general strategic point of view, Israel would have liked to deliver the Syrians a *coup de grâce*, but its troops were fatigued to the point of falling asleep in every lull in fighting and, more to the point, critical shortages of certain types of ammunition emerged. The continuation of pressing problems at the southern front meant that reinforcements were being diverted there, and, finally, there was a serious risk that, if Israel further pressed its advantage over the Syrians, the Russians might intervene.[89] Also forestalling further Israeli advances was the unexpected arrival on October 11 of an Iraqi expeditionary force. Although the Iraqis were not an insurmountable threat, they were, by virtue of their large numbers, somewhat threatening. Nonetheless, their forward contingent was surrounded and easily overcome. Similarly, on October 12, Jordan, feeling compelled to rally to the Arab cause, provided two armoured brigades consisting of 170 tanks and 100 armoured personnel carriers (APCs) that saw action four days later.[90] Jordan would have preferred to have dispatched its forces to Syria as a token of support without actually committing them to any serious action, but that option was not realistically available.[91] After a half-hearted effort and the loss of twenty-two of its tanks, it withdrew.

Nor were the Iraqis and Jordanians the only ones who lent active support to Egypt and Syria. Two Algerian brigades plus one from Libya assisted Egypt, while at the northern front a number of men, tanks and aircraft arrived from Morocco, Kuwait and Saudi Arabia. On the financial side, rich Arab oil producers promised to provide many millions of dollars to help cover the general cost of the war effort.[92] Libya alone doled out just over a billion dollars.[93] It might also be added that, apart from Soviet support through its massive shipments of arms, a token team of twenty North Korean pilots, air controllers and other support personnel played a role in defensive operations.[94] Finally, to add insult to injury, Mirage Vs were sent to Egypt by courtesy of Libya. As already mentioned, the planes in question were originally manufactured in France on order from Israel according to Israeli specifications, but they were not delivered on account of a newly imposed French arms embargo.[95]

Meanwhile, at the southern front, the Egyptians rested content with their territorial gains and made no significant effort to push further ahead. They neither planned to penetrate deeply into the Sinai peninsula nor, for that matter, intended to encroach upon any part of Israel.[96] To attempt to do so would have entailed its army moving away from its protective anti-aircraft cover, providing the IAF with scope to bomb and strafe it. As far as Sadat was concerned, the initial Egyptian attack was meant to break the diplomatic deadlock in order to create the necessary momentum for the return to Egypt of its lost land. From his perspective he had already attained the essence of what he had been seeking. While the Egyptian army busied itself with reinforcing its bridgehead, the Israelis repaired damaged tanks and consolidated their arms and men with the intention of lying low to await further developments.

Soon Sadat found himself subject to inexorable pressure from Hafez al-Assad, Syria's president, to extend his campaign to relieve the pressure put upon his beleaguered men. Assad's proposal was vehemently opposed by the Egyptian chief of staff, Saad El-Shazly, who argued that, by moving beyond the range of their protective anti-aircraft shield, his forces would be imperilled by the Israeli armoured brigades awaiting them.[97] El-Shazly's objections were overruled by Sadat, who on October 13 authorized an extensive sweep into the Sinai heartland. For that purpose around 1,000 tanks and hundreds of armoured personnel carriers were arrayed.

Unfortunately for the Egyptians, the Israelis, with 750 tanks at the ready, were brimming with renewed self-confidence. The resulting battle commenced at dawn on October 14 and lasted throughout that day and the next. At its conclusion Egypt had lost 250 tanks compared with the IDF's loss of only twenty-five.[98] Realizing that they had made a grievous error in running ahead of their anti-aircraft shield, the Egyptians withdrew in an orderly manner. Their setback was not attributable only to their impulsive advance, for other mistakes were made in the execution of their offensive. Their forces were far too dispersed and too haphazard, and in many cases they undertook ill-advised frontal assaults.

From the initial opening of the war, Israel sought from the USA the delivery of urgently needed tanks and Phantom jet fighters. Dayan believed that Israel's request was submitted with clean hands. Israel had heeded US admonitions not to act precipitously and, by not exercising the option of a preventive air strike, inadvertently found itself militarily weakened.[99] By the end of the first week of fighting, the IDF was running low on critically needed armaments, as no prior allowance had been made for hostilities to continue beyond a ten-day period.[100] Israel's ability to defend itself was fast eroding. What followed is subject to different interpretations and accounts. One has it that Israel's appeals met with receptive ears by both Henry Kissinger and President Richard Nixon. But functionaries in the State and Defence departments, who were wary of the United States being too closely associated with Israel's war effort, thwarted aid transfers. James Schlesinger, the secretary of defence, is supposed to have recommended that a distinction be made between ensuring Israel's survival (believed not to be in jeopardy) and helping Israel to retain its grip on Arab territory.[101] As a result, efforts to fulfil Israel's pressing needs got off to a tardy start. However, through the intervention of Kissinger and with the strong support of Nixon, a massive airlift was eventually organized.

Another version of events suggests that the bureaucracies of the State and Defence departments were not the ultimate source of the hold-ups. Schlesinger was subsequently to assert that he had received specific orders not to forward military equipment to Israel in excess of what Israeli transport planes could convey.[102] In answer to Admiral Elmo Zumwalt's enquiry as to why arms shipments to Israel were not flowing freely, Schlesinger replied that it was national policy (formulated by Kissinger with Nixon's compliance) to retain a low profile in aiding Israel and that his hands were tied.[103] By contrast, in a conversation with the Israeli ambassador, Simcha Dinitz, Kissinger claimed that things were the other way round, that it was the Pentagon that kept throwing a spanner in the works.[104]

In all probability the true course of events was as follows. The US was not intent on callously leaving Israel in the lurch. Based on information previously obtained from the IDF, the Americans were under the impression that, in a matter of days, Israel would decisively rout both the Egyptian and the Syrian forces. After all, at a meeting with the US ambassador, Kenneth Keating, at 9.30 on Yom Kippur morning, Meir had asserted: "Should the Arabs resort to war, they will confront a State of Israel fully prepared. We will respond in a most aggressive and forceful manner and they will pay dearly for it."[105]

Given that the Soviets seemed to be behaving with some restraint, the United States was reluctant to be seen as the only superpower rallying to one of the belligerents. A secondary consideration may have been an unwillingness to risk the "goodwill" between the USA and the USSR emanating from a newly formed détente. But when on October 10 the Soviets began restocking the Arabs on an inordinate scale, the Americans felt impelled to do likewise for Israel. Confronted with the full extent of the Soviet arms shipments, Kissinger applied himself to facilitate a swift transfer of military equipment to Israel. He brushed aside one technical or administrative hitch after another, ensuring that, by October 14, a massive US arms airlift, including fighter aircraft, was under way. Convoys of Galaxies in direct flights from the American mainland began arriving in Israel. The flights continued until November 14 – that is, for a full month – and the sum of deliveries exceeded those that were executed in the 1948 US airlift to West Berlin. Notwithstanding the bounteous nature of the convoys, no tanks were transferred. But on one occasion a US Hercules aircraft landed at an Israeli airfield to be greeted by an assembly of journalists. From the bowels of the plane emerged a tank. After the journalists duly photographed it and departed, the tank was reloaded onto the plane to be flown back to its base in Germany.[106] The Americans were loath to draw upon their stocks of tanks stationed in Europe.

The USA would have preferred to refuel its convoys in Europe but, fearful of an Arab oil embargo, no country other than Portugal would permit that. Britain, outbidding its European neighbours in Arab appeasement, even delayed the shipment to Israel of medical supplies donated by UK Jewry.[107] However, secure in the knowledge that its arms supply was indeed being generously refurbished, the IDF felt that, in formulating its battle plans, weapon losses could now largely be discounted.[108]

The Israelis realized that they would be unable to dislodge the two Egyptian armies still well secured on the east bank of the canal on account of the fifty or so SAM batteries at the Egyptians' immediate rear. A solution lay in somehow or other crossing over to the west bank, where IDF tanks and other forces could then chip away at the SAM batteries. The timing was propitious in that, by transferring a large quantity of forces to the east bank of the canal in preparation for its botched October 14 assault, Egypt had left the west bank in a far weaker state.

Of all possible sites for the potential Israeli crossing, the most promising seemed to be at Deversoir, on the northern tip of the Great Bitter Lake. Further north lay the Second Egyptian Army and on the lake's south the Third Egyptian Army. This meant that only one Egyptian land force, albeit a very large one, was more or less on hand to challenge the crossing. Sharon's division was chosen to carve out a path 4 kilometres wide up to the canal and then to transfer some of his men to the west bank, where they were to secure a bridgehead. Following that, pre-constructed bridges were to be assembled so that IDF armour could traverse the waterway. Once the IDF had entered into what the Israelis liked to call "Africa," Adan was to direct his division southwards on a mission to capture airfields, eliminate SAM batteries and isolate the Third Army from its home base.

The operation, which began on the evening of October 15, met with many setbacks. Approaches to the designated area were under enemy control and, as a result, the acquired passage to the canal was far narrower than desired. Later, in what was dubbed "the war of the generals," Sharon was censored for not adhering to his brief. Instead of committing most of his men to ensure that the passage was adequate – that is, both sufficiently broad and defensible – he focused his efforts on the canal crossing, leaving Adan's men to undertake what should have been his primary task.

All the while, the roads leading to the canal were congested, which meant that the prefabricated bridges could not be delivered on schedule. In his defence, Sharon claimed that his seniors sought to dissipate his resources in a futile attempt to dislodge the Second Army because of exaggerated fears that it would disrupt IDF movements. It was far better for him, he argued, to attend to the task of crossing the canal. What further soured the atmosphere was Sharon's penchant for self-promotion. Ever the politician (he was a senior figure in the Likud Party), he played to press reporters that were only too willing to support him.[109] Gonen, Dayan and Elazar continued to encounter, with growing exasperation, Sharon's many acts of outright disobedience and his customary offhand reports. Elazar complained that Sharon's dispatches were arrogant, non-informative and imprecise.[110] After the war, Sharon told a group of Israeli news editors that, if he had been given free rein, far fewer casualties would have been incurred in crossing the canal and in sweeping up Egyptian concentrations on the west bank.[111]

On the night of October 15, a paratrooper unit of Sharon's division commanded by Danny Matt crossed the canal on rubber dinghies, to be followed at dawn by twenty-seven tanks brought over on self-propelled rafts. No Egyptians were present at the point where the Israelis reached the west bank.[112] Because of fears that, in the absence of fixed bridges, contact with IDF forces on the west bank might easily be severed, the main bulk of the tanks available were initially retained on the east bank. In tactlessly informing the Knesset that the IDF had crossed the canal, Meir put at further risk the few tanks on the west bank. Until then Sadat was unaware of any crossing, and his immediate reaction was to dismiss Meir's pronouncement as mere bluff.[113]

Most of Sharon's men were left to confront the Egyptian Second Army, still in control of an area from which it could hinder, if not prevent, the movement of goods and men to the IDF's budding bridgehead. To help redress the problem, an airborne paratrooper brigade commanded by Uzi Yairi was assigned the mission of subduing the well-fortified Egyptian infantry. Clearing the general area proved to be exceedingly taxing. Heavy fighting took place in what was erroneously termed the "Chinese Farm" on account of lettering found on agricultural equipment (the language in question was actually Japanese). But the IDF paratroopers were no match for their opponents, who

were far more numerous, well dug in and equipped with a large spec-
trum of anti-tank weapons, machine guns and mortars. The Israelis,
who absorbed fire from all sides, began to accumulate casualties at
an alarming rate. With no chance of prevailing, and with the cost of
remaining on hand becoming increasingly untenable, they appealed to
Adan to send in an armoured battalion to retrieve them. Adan's forces,
after having repelled advancing Egyptian tanks, had then to contend
with infantry bearing anti-tank weapons. They met that challenge by
driving roughshod over the Egyptian troops. Having seemingly completed their rescue mission, Adan's men withdrew. But, on discovering
that a small group had been overlooked, Adan's men, under the protective cover of smoke screens, returned to the battleground, where after
several hours of fighting they finally extricated the stranded Israelis.
All in all, it basically took the IDF some three and a half days to subdue
the opposition (bar small enemy pockets) at the Chinese Farm. In the
aftermath of those battles, Dayan visited the area and came across
fifty-six destroyed Israeli tanks, together with 118 Egyptian ones (apart
from another fifteen abandoned intact), and the wrecks of hundreds of
armoured personnel carriers and other vehicles. The eerie spectacle
that greeted him testified to the ferociousness of the battles that had
taken place. As Sharon reported: "Here and there Israeli and Egyptian
tanks had destroyed each other at a distance of a few meters barrel to
barrel . . . Inside those tanks and next to them lay their dead crews . . .
No picture could capture the horror of the scene."[114] The seemingly
futile operation did at least have the effect of disrupting Egyptian
preparations for an onslaught on Israel's slowly consolidating bridgehead.[115] This meant that, by 6.30 a.m. on October 17, pontoons for
further canal crossings had finally arrived. They could not have come
soon enough for, in the course of the previous day, Dayan, who was
becoming anxious about mounting Israeli casualties, toyed with the
idea of cancelling the entire operation. Expressing his thoughts as "a
suggestion," he was opposed by both Gonen and Bar Lev.[116] All efforts
to consummate the project continued unabated. Under an intense
artillery bombardment and nerve-wracking aerial attacks, IDF engineers frantically worked to assemble a sectional raft bridge, which was
completed by late afternoon – but not without encountering deadly
Egyptian shelling that at one point struck a ferry transporting two

Plate 2   *Israeli soldiers crossing the Suez Canal*

tanks. As the stricken ferry became submerged, both the tanks and the men within them disappeared into the water.[117]

By early morning on October 18, Adan, along with two tank brigades, crossed the bridge. After the corridor to the bridgehead was widened and regular access to it was secured, additional tanks followed. Egyptian MiGs and helicopters kept targeting the Israeli bridge, hoping to set it ablaze through the use of napalm. But all such efforts proved to be in vain, for Israeli anti-aircraft gunners and pilots obliterated them. Just before midnight a second bridge was installed, as was a third two days later. All three bridges were within 500 yards of one another. Once over the waterway, Adan's men fanned out southwards to eliminate locally placed SAM batteries. In their wake came units of another division headed by Kalman Magen, who had taken over from Albert Mendler after he was killed by an Egyptian shell. Within a few days the two formations had disposed of thirty-four SAM batteries that had been protecting Egypt's Third Army.

When the IDF first appeared on the west bank of the canal the Egyptians misjudged their intentions. They regarded the crossing, which in their assessment numbered no more than seven to ten tanks, as being a hit-and-run raid along the lines of those that occurred during the war of attrition. A reserve armoured force of the Second Army stationed near Cairo was therefore not immediately summoned to dislodge the Israelis. Only by October 18, after they had received photographs taken from a Soviet satellite, did the Egyptians realize that over 100 Israeli tanks were already west of the canal. So incensed was Sadat that he promptly dismissed his chief of staff, General Saad El-Shazly, to replace him with Abd al-Ghan al-Gamazi. But it was already too late, for by October 19 Adan and Magen were to move their divisions southwards to encircle the Third Army, while Sharon's forces were to proceed north along the west bank to destroy, in as much as was possible, the artillery and SAM batteries of the Egyptian Second Army. While Adan and Magen's divisions made rapid gains, covering 40 kilometres of the Egyptian mainland, Sharon's division faced stiff resistance from Egyptian paratrooper and commando battalions. As a result, Sharon's men advanced no further northwards than 3 kilometres. Meanwhile, Egyptian fighter planes appeared in wave after wave over the Israeli bridgehead, to be met by the IAF, which downed them one after the other until twenty-five were disposed of; there were no Israeli air losses.[118] Nonetheless, IDF land forces suffered 400 casualties, including 100 fatalities.[119] Not having succeeded in denting the bridges through aerial attacks, the Egyptians dispatched a unit of 200 paratroopers to do the job, but half of them were killed and the other half fled.[120]

That very day (October 19) Sadat, now fully conscious of the serious threat that the IDF forces west of the canal were posing, finally accepted the notion of a ceasefire. From the war's early days there was indeed a diplomatic search for an acceptable ceasefire. In a UN Security Council session convened on October 8, Israel requested one based on the premise that all combatants would return to positions held before the outbreak of hostilities. Since that would have negated the Syrian and Egyptian war gains, the Arabs, along with their Soviet sponsor, not only opposed such a proposal but insisted that Israel withdraw to the pre-Six-Day War borders. The Americans for their part were in no hurry to endorse any hastily concocted resolution. Convinced that within a matter of days things would pan out in Israel's favour, the USA, wishing to avail Israel of sufficient time, managed to bring the session to an inconclusive close. When a subsequent Security Council meeting was held on October 12, the situation on the ground had changed somewhat. Israel had ejected the Syrians from the Golan Heights and had made inroads into Syrian territory. Now, with Egyptian and Soviet connivance, the Syrians were amenable to putting a ceasefire in place, which of course meant a temporary acceptance of the new reality, but Israel still baulked at agreeing to a continued presence of Egyptian forces east of the canal. Once again, with the USA wishing to provide Israel with sufficient leeway to dislodge the Egyptians, the meeting adjourned without any decision. All that changed once the Third Army was about to be surrounded, making, as already indicated, Sadat amenable to an immediate ceasefire. In this respect, he was also swayed by a promise given by Kissinger that, once hostilities ceased, the United States would employ its good offices to promote a just and lasting peace. Sadat's preparedness to accept a ceasefire based on existing lines contrasted markedly with previous Egyptian terms which had linked the closure of hostilities to an Israeli commitment to withdraw to the 1967 borders. It also violated an understanding with Syria that neither ally would end the war without the consent of the other. In vain, an aggrieved Assad adjured Sadat to change his mind.

At a Soviet request, Kissinger arrived in Moscow on October 20 to confer with Leonid Brezhnev, the general secretary of the Soviet Communist Party. An agreement on the terms for a ceasefire to be submitted to the UN Security Council was reached. If the Soviets had had their way, the Americans would have acquiesced in insisting upon an Israeli return to the pre-Six-Day War boundaries, but Kissinger made it clear that he was open only to the idea of effecting the termination of hostilities.[121] He then flew to Israel to brief Meir, who endorsed the proposal. Kissinger could of course have forwarded the details by telephone or telegraph, but he preferred to stop over in Israel to allow the IDF a little more time to consolidate its gains. On October 22 the Security Council unanimously passed Resolution 338, calling for an immediate ceasefire and for the opening of negotiations for a just and stable peace. At first both sides breached the ceasefire, and it took two more days of fighting until it was finally and firmly held. In the interim, Israel made further headway. It completed its encirclement of Egypt's Third Army, with its 45,000 men and 250 tanks,[122] and captured both the port lying to the south of Suez City and a ridge that overlooked the northwest Gulf of Suez coastline. Fearful for the Egyptians, the Soviet minister of defence, Andrei Grechko, who had yearned for Israel's destruction, ordered the discharge of Scud medium-range missiles manned by Russians at a site near Cairo. Fortunately for Israel, the Scuds failed to find their target of IDF troop concentrations near the canal.[123]

Reassured by a growing confidence in its regained prowess, in the early hours of October 24 the IDF recklessly made a bid for Suez City. Despite foreknowledge of the presence there of three Egyptian battalions as well as an anti-tank missile company, Adan, whose men were to take the city, was convinced that it was ripe for the picking and that all that was required was for his troops to enter and take possession of it. After initially approaching the city centre without incident, and with the commanders of the twenty Israeli tanks involved standing erect in their turrets, the Israelis suddenly encountered heavy gunfire as well as a multitude of rocket-propelled grenades. Within seconds almost all the tank commanders were either killed or wounded. A similar fate awaited a paratrooper column travelling in fifteen armoured personnel carriers, forcing the occupants to take cover in adjacent buildings. By nightfall, all the armoured IDF vehicles had withdrawn, leaving two paratrooper units to their own devices. One soon escaped with relative ease, but the other was trapped further within the city centre. The ninety-odd men in question, hoping in vain for the armoured forces to rescue them, were reluctant to abandon the relative safety of the building in which they had taken refuge. But, on learning that no help would be forthcoming, they were left with no option other than to walk away under cover of darkness. In a radio conversation Gonen tried to indicate an appropriate exit route. Considering that his instructions were both convoluted and misguided (the pathway suggested was riddled with Egyptian soldiers), the men, under Lieutenant David Amit's leadership, opted for an alternative approach. It too was fraught with danger. When they trod on broken glass, their whereabouts could be revealed by crackling noises, and as Rabinovich pointed out, "Egyptian troops passed close, sometimes even emerging from side streets and cutting through gaps in the (IDF) column."[124] For some reason the Israelis were never challenged and just before dawn, after a few nerve-wracking experiences, they made contact with an IDF tank force on the city's outskirts. The misadventure in Suez City cost the lives of eighty men and the infliction of wounds on 120 others – an unnecessarily high and pointless cost considering that Adan was later to admit that the city's capture would not have altered Israel's strategic situation.[125]

On the northern front an IDF attack on Mount Hermon commencing on October 21 culminated the following day with Israel regaining not only its lost observation site but also both a pre-war Syrian-held position and Syria's Mount Hermon peak. An Israeli force consisting of paratroopers and soldiers of the Golani Brigade took part, with the latter just about absorbing all the casualties, amounting to fifty deaths and more than 100 wounded.[126] Finally, in the late afternoon of October 24, the ceasefire came into effect.

Although the IDF was able to retain the areas it had secured between the time the ceasefire was supposed to be enforced and when it actually came into effect, Israel had to contend with stringent diplomatic efforts to compel it to forego such gains. Israel ignored a UN Security Council resolution adopted on October 24 calling for it to withdraw to the positions it had held on October 22, on the grounds that it was impossible to ascertain just where they were. To some extent, Israel was fortified by a confidential remark Kissinger had made to its ambassador, Simcha Dinitz, that, if only the IDF would see fit to withdraw by, say, 200 to 300 yards to an area without any importance or military significance, the USA on its part would not press it further.[127] Even so, the IDF refused to undertake as much as a symbolic withdrawal. Faced with Israel's resoluteness, the Soviets suggested that the USA and Russia jointly impose force on Israel to obtain compliance with the UN Security Council decision. Since the last thing the Americans desired was an armoured Soviet entry into the Middle East under the guise of furthering UN objectives, it rejected that proposal. Increasingly dismayed by Israel's military advances, and being particularly concerned with the entrapment of Egypt's Third Army, the Soviet Union now intended to launch a unilateral military intervention to save its Egyptian client from an impending disaster. The Soviet threat, backed by hasty preparations to airlift troops to Egypt, met with a decisive American reaction. Its forces were put on a very high state of general and nuclear alert and additional naval craft were directed to the eastern Mediterranean.

Bearing down the full weight of its influence on Israel, the USA sought to persuade it to permit the passage of convoys delivering food, water and medicine to the Third Army. As Kissinger made clear, the destruction of the Third Army "is an option that does not exist."[128] At first Israel was reluctant to acquiesce but, once Sadat unexpectedly agreed to the holding of direct talks between high-ranking Egyptian and Israeli officers, it fell into line, thus defusing a grave international crisis.[129] On October 26, the Security Council authorized the dispatch of UN observers to monitor the ceasefire and to arrange for a separation of the combatant forces. In the interest of furthering the latter objective, direct negotiations between high-ranking Israeli and Egyptian officers began to take place at kilometre 101 on the road to Cairo. Generals Aharon Yariv and Mohamed Abol al-Ghan al-Gamazi, respectively, headed the Israeli and Egyptian delegations. The opening of the talks represented a historic breakthrough. Never before, not even in the War of Independence armistice talks held in Cyprus in 1949, had the two parties to the conflict conversed face to face. By November 11, with no small prompting from Kissinger, agreement was reached to preserve the ceasefire, to negotiate a return to the October 22 demarcation lines, to guarantee the continued flow of non-military provisions to the Third Army as well as to residents and military personnel in Suez City, and to arrange for an exchange of prisoners, which was to commence once Israel handed over to the UN its control point on the Suez–Cairo road (that occurred on November 15). Furthermore, access to Israel's port of Eilat was to be assured and deliberations for a return to the October 22 lines were to be undertaken under UN auspices.

On January 18, thanks to Kissinger's intermediation, a disengagement agreement between Egypt and Israel was reached. In accordance with that agreement, Israel was to withdraw all its forces some distance east of the canal but not as far as the Gidi and Mitla passes, whereas Egyptian forces would remain in place along a strip of land 6 miles wide east of the canal, separated from the IDF by a UN buffer zone. Eighteen months later – that is, on June 5, 1975 – the Suez Canal reopened to international shipping. By September 4 Israel and Egypt had reached agreement on and signed what became known as "Sinai II." In terms of that agreement, the two sides were bound to forswear either the use or the threat of force and to resolve outstanding issues by peaceful means. The UN buffer zone was expanded eastwards and Israeli forces were to withdraw to the eastern side of the Gidi and Mitla passes. Finally, Egypt resumed control of the Abu Rodeis oilfields, now within the UN buffer zone.

As for the Syrians, who had at no time assented to direct negotiations with the Israelis, in early 1974 there were clear signs that they were on the verge of renewing hostilities, and only after Kissinger's personal intervention, in May 1974, entailing thirty-two shuttle flights between Syria and Israel, was a Syrian–Israeli disengagement agreement concluded. Its signing on June 5, 1974, in Geneva marked the official termination of the war. According to the agreement, Israel was to withdraw from all land beyond the pre-war frontier as well as from the deserted town of Kuneitra, the Syrian summit on Mount Hermon and small patches of territory elsewhere. In turn the Syrians were committed to a POW exchange, a limitation of forces near the front lines and a UN observer force between the two foes. There was also an unwritten understanding that Syria would prevent guerrilla incursions into Israel from within its borders, an undertaking that Syria honoured throughout all subsequent years. Nevertheless, that did not hinder Syria from becoming a major sponsor of anti-Israel terror and of housing and financing various Palestinian terror organizations and their wanton leaders.

While all branches of the IDF fought with vigour and fortitude, the navy deserves to be singled out, not for its overall importance in stemming the Egyptian–Syrian invasion, which was small, but for its clockwork execution of the tasks assigned to it. The few naval battles that took place were historic ones in which, for the first time in modern warfare, guided missiles were on hand. In that regard the Arabs had a theoretical advantage, since their Russian-supplied Styx missiles, with a 500-kilogram payload and a 50-kilometre range, were superior to those of the Israeli Gabriel missiles, with only a 400-kilogram payload and a 22-kilometre range. This meant that, to get the better of the enemy, Israeli naval craft had swiftly to encroach upon enemy vessels before giving them a chance to activate their missiles.[130] The first engagement occurred as early as the first night of the war, when Israeli naval boats 400 kilometres away from their home base in Haifa encountered five Syrian warships southwest of the Syrian port of Lattakia. All five were sunk without any Israeli losses. On the Egyptian front, three enemy vessels were destroyed near port Dumyat, while further south, in the region of the Bay of Suez and the Red Sea, the Israeli navy bombarded Egyptian ports and destroyed a number of Egyptian vessels. Although all its craft survived intact, Israel suffered the loss of four sailors and another twenty-seven wounded.[131]

In many respects the Yom Kippur War and the circumstances leading up to it reflected Israel's perpetual dilemma. Simply put, the war occurred because Egypt and Syria refused to accept a peaceful alternative.[132] Such a stand was in line with the general Arab consensus that Israel was a hostile foreign transplant within the Arab nation whose territorial expanse stretched from the Persian Gulf to the Atlantic Ocean. Israel has always found itself surrounded and out-populated by Arab regimes. In 2002, for example, the Arab World numbered some 300 million souls,[133] in contrast to 6.3 million Israelis.[134] Not only is the Arab World exceedingly numerous in human terms but it is richly endowed with oil resources, making it the cynosure for both Western and non-Western regimes, all of which avidly compete for its favour. This has resulted in the Arabs being amply supplied with the latest in sophisticated weaponry and being accorded an unmerited status in international organizations and forums. All the while, Israel has essentially remained alone. Even though the the Americans have been well disposed toward it, the United States has often come to Israel's aid reluctantly, fearing that it might offend its Arab allies.

Although taken by surprise and suffering severe setbacks, Israel at the war's end emerged with significant gains by holding more enemy territory than it did at the beginning. Nevertheless, it incurred a high toll, losing 2,656 men, almost half of whom were in the armed corps. As one Israeli historian noted, on a per capita basis, Israel lost as many men as did the USA in Vietnam.[135] In addition to those that were killed, 7,250 were wounded, of whom many were permanently disabled. Arab losses were estimated to be of the order of 15,600 dead, 35,000 wounded and 8,700 taken prisoner.[136]

Shortly after the war Elazar left his office in search of a document in the general secretaries' bureau, where his attention was drawn to a transistor radio broadcasting Naomi Shemer's song "May it be." The song spoke of a prayer of the narrator-singer who at summer's end asked for nothing more than for the men to return home safely and for loved ones to be strong and tranquil. Up to then Elazar had never heard it. He stood transfixed by its haunting refrain and then withdrew, leaving the document behind. One of the secretaries picked it up to give it to him. After finding him at his desk with his face buried in his hands and weeping with what she described as "a choking cry," she quietly slipped away.[137] Elazar's anguish, which reflected a mixture of remorse and an unwarranted sense of personal responsibility, symbolized the nation in mourning.

For the first time in Israel's history, fathers and sons fought along-side one another in the same war, often at the same front. There are numerous accounts of fathers, who were usually officers, seeking out their sons, and vice versa. In a ditch near the Egyptian Third Army, Major-General Amos Horev retrieved the body of his son-in-law.[138] On October 18, Lieutenant Shevi Zarhaya was in command of a tank that, along with one other, was crossing the canal on a motorized ferry. At one point the ferry was hit by a shell and began slowly to submerge. At Shevi's bidding, two of his crew swam away. Shevi still had time to join them but then realized that his gunner had been asleep and was unaware of what had transpired. While he was trying to awaken him the ferry capsized, forming a covering over the sinking tanks and making it impossible for the two men to save themselves. Seven days later, Shevi's father, Lieutenant-Colonel David Zarhaya, sat on the canal's east bank while IDF divers sought to extract his son's body. In recalling the events he stated: "The diver emerged on the shore, Shevi was in his hands. Thereafter I can remember nothing. Perhaps I fainted ... The next morning I arrived home at Kiryat Haim. My wife opened the door and then I told her 'Liza, our Shevi no longer exists.'"[139]

Virtually nothing could surpass the extreme anguish of learning that one's loved one had fallen in battle. Even so, some Israelis reacted with incredible stoicism. Take the case of Michal Amdur. As she arrived home one Sunday from the school in which she taught, a taxi pulled up beside her gate. It contained army messengers bringing tidings of her husband's death as he crossed the canal. She had only been married for a short while and was still childless. In her shocked state she begged them not to approach her late husband's parents or anyone else for that matter until the following Thursday. Her sister was getting married on the Wednesday and above all she wanted the occasion to be a joyous one. During the remaining days before the wedding she kept to herself, crying inconsolably. Then, on the Wednesday, she pulled herself together, applied her make-up and with a cheerful countenance attended the wedding. The next day she told her father that she was pleased that he had a son-in-law and, to his reply that he now had two, she sobbed "You only have one." Eight months later, she gave birth to a son.[140]

The ordeal of the late Moshe Karasenti's parents was particularly poignant. Moshe was caught and killed by the Syrians. He was later buried in Migdal, his home village. Beforehand one of his friends who had stumbled across his body removed his dog tags and other personal effects, meaning to pass them on to his folks. But before he could do so he was transferred to the southern front, and in the turmoil of war the matter had temporarily slipped his mind. A month later, the friend passed on the items to an officer, who in turn forwarded them to a military office in the region of Migdal. That resulted in the dispatch of an army messenger, a doctor and a psychologist to inform the family that Moshe had died in Sinai. The bewildered parents had his body exhumed, but the results were indeterminate. Moshe's father then pinned high hopes on his son having been taken prisoner. When the final batch of POWs returned Moshe's father waited in vain at the airport until all had disembarked from the plane. Stricken by despair, he returned home to shoot himself over his son's grave.[141]

Mention needs also to be made of the 314 IDF soldiers taken prisoner. In the aftermath of the war, the IDF came into possession of a written communication from Saad El-Shazly, the Egyptian chief of staff, who exhorted his men to "kill them [the Israelis] wherever you find them ... kill them without any kindness and mercy."[142] Sergeant Strolovitz of the stronghold Hizayon recalled that, as he and his comrades were led away by the Egyptians, they spotted the bodies of eleven other IDF soldiers whose hands had been bound behind their backs.[143] At another stronghold, after expressing a willingness to surrender, Israeli soldiers emerged to find that five of their number had been mowed down by machine-gun fire. Those who survived, according to Zeev Schiff, an Israeli military analyst, "were transferred, amid blows and insults, to a military prison near Cairo, for interrogation punctuated by torture." Avi Wiess describes his experiences as a prisoner of war in Egypt as being constantly subject to brutal beatings and deprivation of water and not having access to a toilet.[144] When Sorin Coblio was taken prisoner by the Syrians he caught sight of one of his fellow soldiers hanging by a rope with his eyes gouged out.[145] On October 24 a cluster of Israeli bodies were found in the Golan Heights, all shot with their hands tied. Not too far away, under the guidance of Syrian prisoners, other IDF corpses were exhumed. All exhibited signs of having been mutilated.[146] Five surviving Israeli soldiers from the Syrian attack on Mount Hermon were, on surrendering, looked over by an angry Syrian commander, who then ordered their execution. Elsewhere wounded Israeli prisoners unable to keep pace in a march with their fellow captives were summarily shot.[147] A graphic portrayal of the sadistic nature of the Syrian captors has been provided by Amnon Sharon. Below are a few excerpts of his account.

> The jailers added kicks, punches over my entire body, beatings with iron rods, and whippings with rubber hoses and sticks ... A hefty soldier jumped on my chest and I heard my ribs cracking ... someone threw me up into the air, jammed me into the tire dangling from the ceiling, and whirled it around while the soldiers stood on all sides and beat me with iron rods ... The interrogator took a metal bar and inserted it under my toenails until they popped off.[148]

Only by January 27, 1974, did the Syrians deign to release the names of the sixty-five Israeli POWs that they were holding.

How did Israel care for its captives? In an incident that occurred on October 22, hundreds of Egyptian soldiers sought the shelter of Israeli-built ramparts on the Sinai side of the canal. Lying along the western side of the ramparts with their backs exposed to IDF forces from the west bank, they could readily be slaughtered. Sharon, appreciating their predicament, ordered his men to hold their fire so that they could be taken prisoner.[149] In captivity, the Arabs were, more often than not, humanely treated; never were they subject to extreme physical brutality. For example, on October 10, a few dozen Egyptian prisoners were rounded up into an improvised holding pen in Sinai. Issued with only one blanket per person, they keenly felt the night desert cold.

Identifying with their plight, a compassionate guard did the rounds, covering each one with an additional rug.[150] Yonatan Paz, an IDF jeep driver, noticed an Israeli officer approaching his vehicle accompanying two Syrian prisoners. To his surprise the officer was none other than Moshe Agozi, his battalion commander. Anxious to ensure that his captives were out of harm's way, he personally undertook the task. Ironically, Agozi met his death a few hours later, when a shell struck his caterpillar track vehicle.[151] In the present day, in a world that Melanie Phillips, a British writer, described as having been turned upside down,[152] high-ranking IDF officers had faced the prospect of arrest on arrival in Britain for alleged war crimes, yet their Egyptian and Syrian counterparts could freely come and go.

Israeli losses in military hardware included 102 airplanes and around 400 tanks, not to mention the economic costs caused by the mass mobilization. Some 600 other tanks were at one stage or another put out of action, but they were later repaired and overhauled. The general mauling of Israel's armour reflected the fact that more tanks were involved in battles on the Golan and in Sinai than any World War II battle bar the battle of Kursk and the Allied breakout from Normandy.[153] Weapons deployed were far more lethal, leading to the destruction of entire tank battalions within a matter of hours. Arab materiel losses amounted to 370 planes and 2,150 tanks.[154] To put this into perspective, during World War II, in the six months of conflict in North Africa between Montgomery and Rommel, no more than 650 tanks were destroyed.[155] Although the USA through its airlift munificently refurbished Israel with a good deal of its lost armour, sending it almost 100,000 tons of weapons and ammunition, the shipments in no way matched the resupplied stock obtained by Egypt and Syria. It has been estimated that the latter two countries received 300,000 tons from the Soviet Union, which included far more planes and tanks than Israel received from America.[156]

As far as Egypt was concerned, the Yom Kippur War was a huge success. From June 1967 until October 1973, Egyptians were reeling from the effect of their devastating defeat in the Six-Day War. Their national self-confidence was deeply sapped, their entire world seemed to be locked in endless defeats, their regime had lost its gloss, and their people felt utterly rudderless and thoroughly humiliated. Apart from anything else, Egypt had foregone substantial revenue on account of the closure of the Suez Canal and of the loss of its Sinai oilfields. By crossing the canal and inflicting serious damage on the IDF, the Egyptian army restored national honour and morale. In effect, Egypt had achieved the very military goals that it had chosen – namely, the seizing of a strip 12 miles wide along the east bank of the canal. It had no serious intention of heading any further eastwards, as expected by Israel, even though it gave Syria to understand, both verbally and in writing, *that at a minimum* it would retake the Sinai passes.[157] Only very reluctantly did it ultimately make an unsuccessful bid for them in response to Syria's desperate pleas to help reduce the inordinate pressure that the IDF had put upon it. From Egypt's point of view the sacrifices made in the war were not in vain, for they resulted in Israeli withdrawals both from the west bank of the canal and further inland as a prelude to the ultimate return of all of Egypt's lost land. To no small extent, the concessions it later extracted from the Israelis were derived from the fact that, in the Yom Kippur War, Egypt had demonstrated its ability unduly to harm the IDF, and, in so doing, it regained its self-confidence and respect.

As part of their contribution to the Egyptian–Syrian war effort, Arab oil producers imposed an oil embargo on Western countries. France was exempted, thanks to its foreign minister, Michel Jobert, declaring at the outset of the war that the Arabs had not engaged in aggression.[158] The effectiveness of the embargo was manifested by a rise in the price of oil, from $6 per barrel before the outbreak of the war to $20 and, as the embargo continued, to as much as $30 and more. With fuel shortages beginning to play havoc with the world economy, there was a universal desire to bring the armed conflict to a close. Hoping to ingratiate themselves with Arab oil suppliers, almost all African countries severed their diplomatic ties with Israel.

The IDF learnt a number of valuable lessons from that tragic episode. Its doctrine that the extension of a land barrier between Israel and its enemies could effectively offset the number of troops required to stave off an invasion was put in question. Given the rapid rate in which its armaments were depleted, a far greater stockpile was needed. In certain areas IDF personnel had not been issued with equipment fitting to the occasion. The infantry had outdated bazooka rocket launchers, and their semi-automatic rifles manufactured in the 1950s were no match for the latest Egyptian-held AK-47 automatic assault rifles, not to mention the Saggers and RPG-7s borne by Egyptian infantry. Fortunately, the Israelis fought heroically and their officer corps was able to draw upon its reservoir of initiatives and resourcefulness that compensated for the above-mentioned shortcomings. The fact remains that, by any standards, the IDF's final achievements were remarkable. Having been taken by complete surprise, and being confronted with forces far superior in numbers and equipment, it ultimately succeeded in recovering the Golan Heights and crossing the Suez Canal to entrap the Egyptian Third Army.

4

MAJOR EVENTS OVER THE YEARS

1974–1979

A general election was to be held in Israel in October 1973 but, follow-ing the onset of the Yom Kippur War, it was postponed until December 31. The Maarah (an alignment of socialist parties led by the Labour Party) once more emerged with the largest single number of seats. It was able to retain power because many of its traditional supporters, captivated by ongoing direct talks between high-ranking Israeli and Egyptian army officers and by the inauguration on December 21 of the Geneva Peace Conference, believed that at last there were promis-ing prospects of attaining a comprehensive settlement. The Geneva Conference had opened with a flourish. It was attended by the foreign ministers of Israel, Egypt and Jordan as well as those of the USA and USSR and was chaired by the Secretary General of the UN. Watching the proceedings on their television sets, Israeli viewers were awed by the occasion. Nonetheless, the Maarah's Knesset representation fell from 56 to 51, while that of the Likud, headed by Begin, rose sharply from 32 to 39 (for detailed election results, see Appendix). More to the point, a poll of young voters revealed that support for both parties had been more or less even, with the possibility of the Likud having edged slightly ahead of the Maarah.[1] Bar Lev attributed the Maarah's decline both to the war and to internal social issues, encompassing an erosion of wages, a shortage of housing and crippling taxes.[2]

The process of assembling a new government involved two months of wheeling and dealing. The National Religious Party (Mafdal), edged on by a new breed of more religiously outspoken members, and sensing a weakening in the bargaining power of the Maarah, made the passing of a Knesset resolution of "who is a Jew" its prerequisite for joining the coalition. If Mafdal had had its way, the law of return granting the right of Jews to immigrate to Israel would have been amended to define a Jew as someone born to a Jewish mother or as one who had undergone an orthodox Jewish conversion. Resisting such demands, primarily because they would antagonize American non-orthodox Jewry, Meir determined that she would recommend to the president a minority government without Mafdal's participation. She did have the option of forming a government with a slender majority through the incorporation of the Independent Liberals, three Arab Knesset members and Ratz (the Movement for Civil Rights and Peace), but Meir emphatically ruled out Ratz's participation. Ratz, established in 1973, had opposed all settlement activity in the West Bank and Gaza and had favoured a rapprochement with the PLO. Meir had thoroughly detested its leader, Shulamit Aloni, and had sworn that only over her dead body would Aloni ever enter her government.[3]

One of her big bones of contention in assembling a government related to Dayan, who, after learning that Meir had sat passively at a conference while a senior military officer had excoriated him, indicated that he would not serve in the next administration.[4] Meir, shaken by his decision, began to feel the combined effects of the constant and enervating political haggling, her lymphatic cancer and her advanced years (she was seventy-seven). With reluctant perseverance, she secured the makings of a minority government without the inclusion of Mafdal and Dayan's faction (Rafi). Meir offered Dayan's post of minister of defence to Rabin, who accepted it. At first glance it might seem odd that Meir considered Rabin for the job. He had only just been elevated to the Knesset as a novice and was not au fait with political machinations. But to his credit he was not associated with the debacle of the Yom Kippur War, he had established a reputation as an outstanding chief of staff both before and during the Six-Day War, and he had completed a very successful term as Israel's ambassador to the USA. Rabin was highly intelligent and well admired. Even Sharon, as a member of the Likud opposition party, considered him the obvious choice.[5]

As the central committee of the Maarah met to ratify Meir's prospective arrangements, some members began venting their displeasure. As one old timer after another railed against her proposal (some preferring a broad cabinet of national unity), Meir, who affected a sense of being betrayed, announced that she would inform the president that she had been unable to form a government. A few days later – that is, on March 5 – the Maarah central committee members gathered in a show of contrition to implore Meir to reconsider. During the proceedings Dayan was called away. On arriving at his office he was confronted with intelligence reports (that were not subsequently verified) indicating that Syria was on the verge of resuming hostilities.

That night, during an emergency meeting of the caretaker cabinet, Dayan withdrew his refusal to serve in the next administration. All differences with an ecstatic Meir were patched up, and it was resolved that he would continue as minister of defence, bringing Rabin's prospective tenure to a sudden halt. Similarly, Mafdal returned to the fold, with the Independent Liberals also joining in. Meir retained the premiership and Dayan and Eban the defence and foreign affairs portfolios, respectively. Rabin was allocated the ministry of labour. The new government received the endorsement of the Knesset on March 10, 1974. In his memoirs, Rabin describes how he saw events unravelling: "I was not versed in political intrigue. My appointment was merely intended to constitute a red rag to be waved in front of Dayan to induce him to backtrack. Golda had cautioned me that Dayan was really her preferred candidate."[6]

Soon after the Yom Kippur War the public manifested a growing groundswell of discontent at Dayan's handling of the defence portfolio both in the lead up to the war and during hostilities. Dayan was not the exclusive object of resentment, for there was a widespread feeling that the entire Maarah leadership had somehow been remiss. Responding to the general public's disquiet with the abysmal performance of the IDF's intelligence unit and the army's inadequate preparation for a looming war, the government, on November 17, 1973, appointed a five-man commission of inquiry chaired by the chief justice of the Supreme Court, Shimon Agranat. The other members were Yigael Yadin, Haim Laskov (both former chiefs of staff), Supreme Court Justice Moshe Landau and the state comptroller, Itzhak Nebenzahl.

On a general note of interest, a major intelligence failure was not unique to the IDF. The US National Security Agency, like its Israeli counterpart, also did not anticipate the Yom Kippur War. It too harvested a wealth of detailed information that was not thoroughly and correctly analyzed. Nor was that the first time that the USA was caught unawares, for it did not foresee the Soviet placement of nuclear missiles in Cuba, the erection of the Berlin Wall or the Soviet invasion of Czechoslovakia.[7] Stalin did not expect Hitler to invade Russia and nor did the Dutch and Belgian governments realize that their countries were about to encounter a German attack.

The Agranat Commission was charged with investigating all aspects of army intelligence as well as the IDF's overall performance both before and during the war. On April 2, 1974, Justice Agranat released the commission's preliminary findings. Six high-ranking IDF officers were singled out. They included Elazar for his poor assessment of the situation and for the IDF's initial inability to rise to the occasion, as well as Zeira and his deputy, Shalev, both for "grave errors." All three were recommended for dismissal. Transfers were recommended for Yona Bandman, chief of the Egyptian IDF intelligence desk, and for David Gedalia, chief intelligence officer of Southern Command. Finally the commission proposed that Gonen be relieved of duty pending its final conclusion.

Although Elazar had foolishly brushed aside Hussein's warning of war, he did place the IDF on a high state of alert a day before October 6, even though his intelligence chief considered such a move unnecessary. On October 6 his wish for a pre-emptive IAF strike was overruled, as was his request for the complete mobilization of the reservists. During the war, he kept his nerve and composure, sustained the morale of his staff and weighed all options with consummate professionalism. His contribution to Israel ultimately gaining the upper hand was considerable. Meir described him as being "like a rock," one who never faltered under the inordinate strains and stresses of his command. As far as she was concerned, history would record Elazar as a great and much extolled commander. Rabin likened Elazar to a firm cliff on which rested the entire system of defence. It would seem that singling him out for severe censure was harsh and entirely misplaced. On the morning of April 1, 1974, Meir sent for him, and when he arrived at her office he was presented with Agranat's provisional report, which Meir had just received and which was to be released the following day. On reading it he was astonished to learn that he was faulted for negligence and was therefore obliged to resign.

According to the Israeli law relating to investigative committees, a person liable to be stigmatized ought to be advised of such a contingency and was entitled to appear before the committee in question to present arguments in his or her defence. No such dispensation was given to any of those that the Agranat Committee censured. Elazar and Gonen were seriously psychologically wounded by the hurt Agranat and his associates caused them. Elazar complained to Rabin that he had been living with an unremitting depression that he could not slough off.[8] Gonen withdrew from life in Israel to secrete himself in the jungles of the Central African Republic in search of diamonds. Both died young from heart attacks, Elazar in 1976 at the age of fifty-one and Gonen in 1991 at the age of sixty-one.

With respect to Meir and Dayan, the Agranat Commission found no cause for admonishment. In exculpating Dayan, the commission determined that he had no independent means of securing his own intelligence and that he was certainly not a "super chief of staff" expected to intervene in operative military decisions. However, being an ex-chief of staff, Dayan ought to have been able to have read the many signs known to be available to him, including the sudden evacuation of Russian advisers and their families from both Egypt and Syria, the departure of Russian vessels from their Egyptian bases, the manifold information relating to the unrelenting build-up of enemy forces on both fronts, and the fact that the Syrians had moved most of their air support away from Damascus to forward positions. As for not being a "super chief of staff," Dayan could not resist taking a hands-on approach whenever he felt the need to do so. Even on that fateful morning of October 6, when he was presented with news that, within a matter of hours, war was to break out, he opposed a large-scale mobilization. Then, when on the following day he realized that Israel's situation in the Golan Heights was calamitous, he personally instructed the air force to concentrate all its forces on that specific front. On October 9, after an unprecedented defeat of an IDF armoured attack on the Egyptians, Dayan pressed for a significant eastward withdrawal. Fortunately, the general staff ignored him, for, had they not done so, the IDF would have later faced even greater difficulties in mounting a canal crossing. Throughout the war Dayan continued on innumerable occasions to act as if he were chief of staff. Finally, on October 20, Elazar's patience snapped. After Gonen reported that Dayan had given him operational instructions, Elazar replied: "What the minister has said to you is very interesting but I would like you to take orders from me alone."[9]

There were among government members differences of opinion in evaluating the Agranat Commission's provisional report. Rabin wanted to know why it could not be rejected on the grounds that the commission had not fully adhered to its brief. As Rabin saw things, in establishing the commission, the government intended that the management of security affairs by *both* the IDF and relevant ministers would be scrutinized. After all, argued Rabin, since both the IDF and the government took credit for Israel's subsequent successes, why was it only the IDF that was singled out for its setbacks?[10] However, Peres, as Dayan's sidekick, hinted that, unless the report was unhesitatingly accepted, Rafi would withdraw from the coalition.[11]

Rabin's reservations relating to the Agranat Commission extended to its composition. He believed that Haim Laskov, on account of his still serving in the Defence Ministry (as the IDF's ombudsman) and answerable to Dayan, should have automatically been recused. In addition, thought Rabin, Yigael Yadin should not have been appointed considering that he publicly prided himself on ensuring that Dayan was appointed as minister of defence in the first place.[12]

By absolving Meir and Dayan of responsibility for the IDF's set-backs, the Agranat Commission fuelled public resentment. Faced with a deafening clamour for her and Dayan's removal, Meir, on April 11, a week after the commission's initial report was released, finally and ultimately tendered her resignation. The Labour Party's choice to succeed Meir was Pinhas Sapir, an accomplished minister of finance. But he firmly declined. Explaining his unwillingness, Sapir asserted that the premiership was simply beyond his personal capabilities and temperament. Many suspected that the true reason for rejecting his friends' entreaties lay in Meir's complete detachment and lack of overt support, interpreted by him as reflecting her opposition to his candidature.[13] With Sapir not available, Haim Tzadok and Yosef Almogi were then unsuccessfully canvassed. That left the field open to Rabin and Peres. But before the votes were cast Ezer Weizman, a stalwart of Likud but a firm friend of Peres, publicly revealed that Rabin had suffered from a nervous breakdown on the eve of the Six-Day War. Even so, with Sapir's backing, Rabin prevailed, receiving 298 votes against 254 for Peres.[14] In Rabin's government Allon became foreign minister and Peres minister of defence. Meir, Dayan, Eban and Sapir were all excluded. Eban had been offered a post as a minister responsible for propagating Israel's case in the international arena. Affronted by such an offer, deemed by him to be beneath his dignity and sense of self-importance, he declined.

Rabin's administration heralded a fresh start in that, of its nineteen cabinet ministers, only seven had held ministerial posts during the Yom Kippur War. It was initially made up of the Maarah, Independent Liberals, Ratz (the Civil Rights Movement) and two Arab groups sympathetic to the Maarah. When the Mafdal eventually joined the cabinet in October 1974, Ratz, subscribing to a policy of the separation of state and religion, withdrew. Rabin had in fact tried to attract the Mafdal into the coalition in the first place, but their insistence on altering the law defining a Jew rendered that impossible. Only then did Rabin turn to Ratz. The moment Ratz's inclusion was approved at a Maarah conclave, Meir demonstrably walked out, slamming the door behind her.[15]

Before the Maarah leadership vote, Peres proposed a "friendly pact" with Rabin whereby the loser would serve in the cabinet in a post of his choosing. That subsequently tied Rabin's hands. Rabin would have liked to have appointed Yigal Allon, who headed the Palmah (strike forces) in the War of Independence, as minister of defence. Instead he felt compelled to defer to Peres, even though he considered that Peres, as someone who had never served in the IDF, lacked the moral authority to make life or death decisions. What is more, Rabin was convinced that, had Peres been chosen as prime minister, he himself would not have been given the same consideration.[16] In his memoirs, Rabin wrote: "For some time I have known Peres, his nature and characteristics and I have not believed a single word of his . . . I saw the possibility of Peres serving as prime minister as a very grievous one."[17] That judgment was not idiosyncratic. Years beforehand, Moshe Sharett, Israel's prime minister in the period 1953–5, entered the following into his personal diary: "I have stated that I totally and utterly reject Peres and consider his rise to prominence a malignant, immoral disgrace."[18] Similarly, Meir's biographer recorded her view of Peres as being "the one party figure she longest despised."[19] Nearly two months expired between Meir's resignation on April 11, 1974, and June 3, when Rabin officially replaced her. During that interim period Meir's government continued to function in a caretaker role.

Just two weeks after Rabin's government was formed, the country hosted Richard Nixon, the first US president to visit Israel. Rabin expressed appreciation for all that Nixon had done for Israel during and after the Yom Kippur War. In his view, Nixon ranked as the most well-disposed US president toward Israel. Nixon, as a Republican, enjoyed scant support among American Jewry, and he was by no means indebted to them for his decisive victory in the 1972 election. Nevertheless, as Rabin noted, Nixon remained a staunch supporter of the Jewish State.[20] However, the denouement of the Watergate Scandal, in which he was threatened with impeachment, led to Nixon's resignation from office on August 9, 1974. He was succeeded by Gerald Ford, who proved to be less of friend to Israel than Nixon had been.

Among other issues facing Rabin's administration was the possibility of arriving at some understanding with Jordan. As Rabin recounted to Ford and Kissinger while visiting the United States in September, Israel had submitted four distinct proposals to Jordan at a secret meeting in August between King Hussein and Rabin, Peres and Allon. The first proposal entailed exploring the possibility of negotiating a final comprehensive agreement involving some territorial compromise, with the proviso that Israel would not return to the June 1967 lines. Second, the parties would implement mutually agreed upon commitments in stages until a general state of peace was attained. Third, some mechanism could be created for shared control of the West Bank and Gaza. Jordan would administer to the general civil needs of the Arab community while Israel would assume responsibility for the region's defence. Fourth and finally, an Israeli–Jordanian Condominium was suggested. The contested territory would be jointly managed by Israel and Jordan. Arabs would be granted Jordanian citizenship and Israelis would be entitled to live in the area in question.[21] Absent from Israel's proposals was any possibility of setting up an independent Palestinian State west of the River Jordan. Given the overt determination of the

PLO to eliminate Israel, such a state would have posed a serious threat to Israel's continued existence.

All four options were rejected by Jordan on the grounds that its standing in the Arab World would become intolerable should it be seen to be assisting the continuation of an Israeli presence in the conquered areas. Jordan hoped to emulate the Israeli–Egyptian disengagement agreement resulting in a separation of forces. But, since Israel and Jordan had not recently been at war, the notion had no appeal for the Israelis. Even had Israel and Jordan made headway, they would have been foiled by the Arab League. For in late October, at an historic conference in Rabat, the Arab League recognized the PLO as the sole representative of the Palestinians and supported it in its striving to secure an independent Palestinian State. As a result, Jordan had no option other than to fall in line with its Arab brethren and to refrain from undertaking any initiatives affecting the future of the Arab inhabitants in the disputed territories. The lessons of the Rabat conference were not lost on the Israelis. They correctly understood that, for the foreseeable future, Hussein's room for manoeuvre was negligible and that it was pointless pursuing further talks with him.

In May 1976, following a period of violent clashes between the PLO, which was beginning to constitute a state within a state in Southern Lebanon, and the mainly Christian Phalangists, Syria, at the invitation of the Maronite Lebanese president, Suleiman Franjieh, decided to intervene. Such a decision reflected Syria's long-standing goal of creating a "Greater Syrian State" incorporating both Lebanon and Palestine. Given its rivalry with the PLO for leadership of the Palestinian movement, it chose to side with the Christians. Like the Syrians, Israel too made common cause with the Christian militia by providing it with arms, training and general economic aid. As a result, for a limited time Syria and Israel were both propping up Lebanon's major Christian community.

At first Syria commissioned, as a proxy force, members of the terror group al-Saiqa, headed by Zuhayr Muhsin. Al-Saiqa is a Baathist Palestinian organization founded in September 1966 by the Syrian regime as an alternative to Fatah. To all intents and purposes, it has served as a tool of the Syrian government. Before May 1976, al-Saiqa worked hand in glove with the PLO in the massacre of Damour, where over 500 Christians were senselessly slaughtered. Now on Syrian instructions it was turning its guns against fellow Palestinians. Once it became clear that al-Saiqa was not fully up to the task, elements of the Syrian army entered Lebanon. By August 13, 1976, under Syrian protection, the Christian Phalangists attacked the Tel al-Za'atar refugee camp northeast of Beirut, disposing of as many as 2,000 to 3,000 Palestinians.[22] (For its role in the massacre, Syria was not subject to any international outcry. Yet when, in September 1982, this time under Israeli protection, Christian forces went on a rampage in the Palestinian "camps"[23] of Sabra and Shatila, killing fewer than the number at Tel al-Za'atar, the UN denounced the acts as "genocide," and Israel was universally condemned.)

Alarmed by the Syrian intrusion into Lebanon, Israel warned that it would not tolerate the presence of any Syrian forces within 25 kilometres north of the Litani River. But, even without crossing Israel's "red line," the Syrians were able to kill more Palestinians than were killed in all their previous Palestinian engagements with Israel.[24] Soon thousands of Palestinians sought haven in the Syrian free zone declared by Israel, with the unexpected consequence of Israel inadvertently and momentarily becoming a Palestinian protector.

The next general Israeli election was scheduled for the fall of 1977, but an unforeseen dispute with the religious ministers brought it forward to May 17. In December 1976 an official welcoming ceremony was laid on for the arrival at Tel Nof Airbase of the first three of twenty-five F-15 fighter aircraft supplied to Israel by the USA. Since the planes landed close to the time of the commencement of the Sabbath, Mafdal was offended by what it regarded as a desecration of the day of rest. Except for Yosef Burg, who voted against, Mafdal abstained in a Knesset vote of censure against the government introduced by the ultra-orthodox Agudat Yisrael. With his cabinet in crisis, Rabin resigned, thus advancing the general election date.

While serving as head of a now caretaker government, Rabin was challenged by Peres for the Maarah's leadership. Although Peres made a great fanfare of recent corruption scandals (outlined below), he was defeated by a very narrow margin. Peres's bid for office unsettled Rabin, who later wrote that the former's "ardour knew no boundaries, his drive did not recognize any limits. Everything was permissible, including leaks and the constant undermining of the prime minister and that of the government according to well-known Bolshevik doctrine."[25] It was a harsh judgment and, to be fair to Peres, it did not seem to be shared by nearly half of his Maarah colleagues who had voted for him. In his own memoirs, Peres upholds that he had always acted honourably and that he was mystified by Rabin's aspersions.[26]

In early March 1977, in response to an invitation from the newly installed US president, Jimmy Carter, to meet with him, Rabin flew to Washington. He described his first impression of Carter as "a president the likes of which I have not previously known, one imbued with arrogance."[27] What particularly aroused Rabin's ire was Carter's proposal for attaining an Israeli–Arab peace settlement. In contrast with previous US interpretations of UN Resolution 242, it entailed Israel withdrawing to the June 5, 1967, borders, allowing for the possibility of some minor adjustments along the West Bank. In addition, Carter asked of Israel to express its readiness to negotiate with the PLO provided it accepted and recognized the Jewish State. Some days later, Carter further declared that he favoured the formation of a Palestinian State – a concept that was then anathema to most Israelis, given the PLO's violent record and its charter calling for Israel's elimination. Rabin sensed that not only was there a crisis in the making concerning US–Israeli relations but that Carter's brusque statements provided grist to the mill to the opposition parties canvassing for Israel's forthcoming elections.

Finally, by early April, a comparatively minor scandal drove Rabin from office. In March 1977 Dan Margalit, a journalist for the Israeli newspaper *Haaretz*, went to a bank in Washington where Rabin had previously established a joint account with his wife, Leah, while serving as Israel's ambassador to the United States. As a means of ascertaining whether, contrary to Israeli law, the account was still open, Margalit informed a teller that he wished to deposit a small sum in favour of Rabin but that he had mislaid the account number. Soon he was provided with sufficient details to write a scoop. It seemed that the amount held by Rabin and his wife was in the region of $20,000. Despite Leah claiming that she alone continued to operate the account, Rabin accepted full responsibility for the failure to disclose it (for which he was fined approximately $2,140) and declared his willingness to step down, which he was not legally required to do. Since he could not formally resign as head of a caretaker government, he took leave of absence, enabling Peres to take his place as "chairperson of cabinet sessions."

The May election resulted in a sea change in Israeli politics (see Appendix for detailed results). For the first time in its history, a non-Labour party swept into power. Likud secured 43 seats while Maarah, its main rival, obtained only 32, down from a commanding height of 51 in the previous election. Maarah's standing was rocked by a series of corruption scandals, by a lingering dissatisfaction with its handling of the Yom Kippur War, by ongoing Palestinian terrorism and by growing social rifts within Israeli society. The brief rise of the Democratic Movement for Change, which gained fifteen Knesset seats, played a major part in Likud's success. Many disaffected Maarah supporters who could not bring themselves to vote for Likud turned to the Democratic Movement for Change instead. Even some traditional Revisionists such as Shmuel Tamir joined its ranks, as did prominent liberals, a contingent of ex-generals and some well-known non-political figures. The party was headed by Yigael Yadin, who had served as Israel's acting chief of staff in the War of Independence and who was a noted archaeologist. It held out the promise of a break with the past and a return to core Zionist values, including the reduction of growing social and economic disparities. But, riven by internal dissent, the party dissolved within two years, proving to be a flash in the pan, as it were.

Sharon's own party, Shlomzion, represents some of the quirks to which Israel's system of proportionate representation gives rise. Electors vote for a party list in which candidates are ranked in order of preference. If for example, a particular party secures, say, 10 percent of the total votes cast, it would be entitled to twelve Knesset seats allocated to the twelve candidates heading its list (there are 120 members in the Knesset). There is nothing preventing individuals or tiny groups submitting lists of their own. Shlomzion arose as a result of unsuccessful bids by Sharon to be included in mainstream party listings. Previously he had not only been an original member of Likud but had played a major role in its founding. After briefly serving as a Likud Knesset member in 1974, Sharon resigned. Then, as the 1977 elections loomed, he tried to re-enter the political arena as head of the Likud (that is, by displacing Begin) and, after that failed, made futile efforts to be accepted in a leading position first by the Maarah and then by the Democratic

Movement for Change. Finally he resorted to forming Shlomzion as a means of entering parliament. In that same election there was, technically speaking, a similar anomaly. Shmuel Flatto-Sharon, sought by the French authorities for embezzling $60 million, fled to Israel in 1975 and by 1977 had formed his own party, "Flatto-Sharon," to avoid, as a Knesset member, extradition to France. He succeeded beyond expectations, winning enough votes to obtain two seats, but only he was listed. The absurdity of his elevation to parliament was underscored by his need to have his maiden speech first translated into Hebrew and then transcribed into Latin letters so that he could read it.[28]

On June 5, Begin formed a government consisting of the Likud, Mafdal, Agudat Yisrael and Shlomzion. Within a month Shlomzion merged into Likud, and on October 24 the Democratic Movement for Change also entered the coalition. On the face of it, the Democratic Movement for Change would have naturally been allied with the Maarah, since it also favoured some sort of territorial disengagement from the Arab-populated heartlands of the West Bank and Gaza, but that was not to be. A Maarah-led government was simply no longer a feasible option, while Begin, impressed by the movement's high-flying generals, and hoping that its inclusion would soften his hard-line image as well as strengthening the government's majority, was able to offer it amenable and sufficient inducements. On assuming office Begin modified his behaviour to present himself to the Israeli public as a moderate and reasonable premier. He reined in his sarcastic barbs and maintained a friendly smiling countenance. Soon many electors who had voted against him began to view him in a more favourable light.[29]

Key portfolios in Begin's regime were initially held by Dayan as foreign minister, Ezer Weizman as minister of defence, and Simha Erlich as minister of finance. Sharon became minister of agriculture. More significantly, Sharon was also appointed as chairperson of the ministerial committee of settlement affairs, which he soon used to good effect to promote widespread settlement construction in the occupied territories. When the Democratic Movement for Change eventually joined the fold, Yadin was appointed deputy prime minister. The prospect of attaining such an appointment acted as a catalyst in clinching the deal. In September Begin was stricken and hospitalized with meningitis, and the prospect of Yadin serving as temporary prime minister presented his party with a golden opportunity for maximizing its influence, even if only temporarily.

It is relatively easy to understand why Dayan joined Begin's cabinet. Although re-elected to the Knesset on a Maarah ticket, Dayan did not feel unduly indebted to it, for, in furthering his political career, considerations of party loyalty were relegated to a low level of priority. That did not mean to say that Dayan was an outright opportunist. He conditioned his entry into the new government on an assurance that it would not annex the West Bank while negotiating peace with the Arabs. What is not so easy to understand is why Begin would have wanted a man tainted with the ignominy of the Yom Kippur War disaster. The answer provided by Robert Slater is that Begin appreciated Dayan's international standing as a symbol of Israeli intrepidness and as one who would make his regime more "palatable to world leaders."[30]

Peace with Egypt

As already mentioned, on December 21, 1973, a peace congress was convened in Geneva. Under the joint auspices of the United States and the Soviet Union, it was attended by the foreign ministers of Egypt, Israel and Jordan. Syria was invited, but it did not appear in protest at the exclusion of a Palestinian delegation. Little of substance was achieved and after a few days the congress adjourned. Deliberations resumed on January 2, 1974, only to close on January 9 without any date being set for a future gathering. Meanwhile, to reiterate what was recorded in the previous chapter, thanks to Kissinger's indefatigable shuttle diplomacy involving his mediating between the belligerents, by February 18, 1974, Egypt and Israel had signed a separation of forces agreement. Israel undertook to withdraw all its forces west of the Suez Canal. On the immediate east side of the canal up to a depth of 30 kilometres, three separate strips were formed. In the one alongside the waterway, the Egyptians could retain a military presence of no more than 7,000 soldiers, 30 tanks and 36 artillery barrels. The middle strip was designated for UN forces and, in the one furthest east, the Israelis could be deployed in a strength not exceeding that maintained by the Egyptians in their sector. Elsewhere, neither country was subject to any restriction.[31] As the Israeli historian David Shaham observed, the irony of it was that Israel had now agreed to undertake a far greater commitment both in terms of the distance of the pullback of its forces from the canal and in terms of the size of the Egyptian contingent that could occupy the east bank than it refused to do before the war. For, in 1971, Israel rejected Sadat's suggestion of a partial Israeli evacuation to be followed by the disposition of only 700 Egyptian "soldiers." Furthermore, the 1974 separation agreement was not predicated on any Egyptian declaration of a state of non-belligerency. Effecting a Syrian–Israeli separation agreement proved to be far more taxing, entailing Kissinger's presence in the region for thirty-two consecutive days. Finally, on May 31, one was attained. It involved an Israeli withdrawal from all Syrian land taken in the Yom Kippur War. The deserted and largely destroyed town of Kuneitra captured in the Six-Day War was also to be returned to Syria, but it was attached to a small demilitarized area that UN forces patrolled for a six-month period subject to renewal. Over a short distance on either side of the demilitarized zone, Syrian and Israeli forces were subject to some limitations.

In due course, renewed efforts were undertaken in bringing about an enhanced Israel–Egypt disengagement agreement. But the Egyptians demanded a larger measure of Israeli concessions than the Israelis were then prepared to concede, while the Egyptians were not willing to satisfy Israel's demands for clear-cut political gestures in return. If Egypt was not yet ready to sue for peace, Israel wanted, at the very least, a formal declaration of an end to hostilities. The US administration, whose term of office was drawing to a close, wished to leave the stage with some notable success. With an eye on its Arab interests as well as on its own general strategic considerations, it began to pressure Israel for more far-reaching compromises involving substantial withdrawals from the Mitla and Gidi passes and for some accord with the PLO once it accepted UN Resolution 242. When these demands were rejected, Kissinger in March 1975 abandoned his efforts of trying to conciliate between the Israelis and Egyptians. On taking leave from Israel at Ben-Gurion Airport, he was visibly upset. Some observers noticed that his voice was quavering and that he seemed to be on the verge of tears.[32] President Ford, who was highly disappointed, announced that the USA was reassessing its Middle East policies. The practical effects of that "reassessment" resulted in a US refusal to enter into further arms transhipment agreements with Israel.

With a serious rupture in US–Israeli relations seemingly in the offing, Israel eventually adopted a more flexible stance, allowing Kissinger in the second half of 1975 confidently to resume his shuttle diplomacy. Since the United States was counting on Israel to forego significant amounts of Sinai real estate, Kissinger aroused the wrath of the pro-settler movement Gush Emunim. Its members constantly hounded him. Among other things, they likened him to Count Bernadotte, who was assassinated by Jewish terrorists for jeopardizing Israel's interests; they called him "Jew Boy," in a manner redolent of traditional anti-Semites, and mocked him for marrying a Christian. Rabin found it utterly disgraceful.[33] Little did he know that the outpouring of such bile that began to poison the political discourse in Israel was to reach a crescendo in November 1995, when he would be assassinated by a Jewish religious fanatic.

Nonetheless, Kissinger's efforts reached fruition. A second and far more extensive Israel–Egypt disengagement agreement was concluded on September 4, 1975. It entailed an Israeli withdrawal to the east end of the Sinai passes with the Egyptians moving up to the western entrances. The area vacated by Israel was to be demilitarized in varying degrees. Within the region of the passes themselves there were to be two monitoring stations, formally controlled by the United States but in practice manned respectively by Israeli and Egyptian technicians. One station was to keep track of events occurring in the Israeli zone and the other to monitor the Egyptian one. Instead of Egypt agreeing to declare an end to hostilities, the Israelis settled for a statement accepting the principle of the non-use of force. The oil fields along the Gulf of Suez were to be returned to Egypt and were to be patrolled by UN forces. As a reward for Israel agreeing to go beyond the bounds of what it considered to be prudent, the USA secretly undertook to fulfil various commitments. These included guaranteeing Israel's access to oil; ensuring, through the use of its veto, that UN Resolution 242 would remain unchanged; and refusing to negotiate with the PLO unless it accepted Resolution 242 and forsook terror.[34] To shore up Israel's defence capability, it agreed to supply state-of-the-art jet fighters, complemented during 1975–6 with a grant of $235 million to help finance such transactions.

Tentative moves towards a general Egypt–Israel accord began to take effect after Dayan, as Israel's foreign minister, received an invitation in early September 1977 to visit secretly with King Hassan of Morocco. During his discussions with the king, Dayan proposed a face-to-face meeting between either Begin or himself with Sadat or Hosni Mubarak, Egypt's vice-president. At first the Egyptians were amenable to the idea but they soon began to harbour reservations.[35] As a means of averting any further deadlocks, the Israelis drafted a provisional Egyptian–Israeli peace contract, forwarding copies to US President Carter and Sadat. After perusing the document, Carter approached Sadat to agree to a reconvening of the Geneva Peace Conference. Responding to Carter's suggestion, Sadat authorized a secret meeting on September 16 in Morocco between his deputy prime minister, Dr Hassan Tuhami, and Dayan. In a sense the ice was broken, in that a very high-ranking Egyptian government official was finally conversing face to face with an Israeli one. However, Tuhami conveyed terms of conditions that, while they did not appear to be insurmountable to Dayan, proved to be unacceptable to Begin. Essentially, the Egyptian position was that Sadat would enter into an open dialogue with Begin only provided the Israelis first agreed in principle to a total withdrawal from Sinai. For the time being, that brought direct high-level Egyptian–Israeli contacts to an end.

On September 19, Dayan, without disclosing any of his talks in Morocco, met with President Carter, who presented him with demands that not only should the Palestinians be represented in their own right at a prospective Geneva Conference but that Israel should be prepared to accept the formation of a Palestinian homeland in the West Bank and Gaza. In furthering that demand the USA cooperated with Russia in drafting a joint statement on Middle East policy that explicitly called for the participation of Palestinians at the Geneva Conference, to be convened no later than December 1977. An incensed Dayan told a gathering of US Jewish leaders that Israel would never accept or talk with the PLO and that it would attend the Geneva Conference only if the joint US–USSR statement was non-binding.[36] Sensing the strength of a growing and unexpected negative reaction on the part of American Jewry, Carter reluctantly modified his stand and, at a further meeting with Dayan on October 4, agreed that, while only existing states could send delegations to Geneva, Palestinian individuals could be included within an Arab one. Peace treaties would be concluded by existing states only, and the future of the West Bank and Gaza would be discussed by a working group made up of Israeli, Jordanian and Egyptian delegates as well as acceptable Palestinians.

Realizing that the Geneva Conference would not progress beyond the issuing of irreconcilable demands, thereby thwarting Egyptian hopes for reclaiming Sinai, Sadat on November 9 broke a long-standing Arab taboo by announcing to the Egyptian parliament that, in pursuit of peace, he was prepared to go to the end of the earth to prevent another war, even to the extent of going to the Israeli Knesset. At one fell swoop, Sadat swept away his precondition for direct talks – namely, that Israel should accept in principle its complete withdrawal from Sinai. Begin responded positively by extending an official invitation to Sadat to visit Israel and to address the Knesset. Sadat's volte-face was not without cost to him. At the very best, fellow Arab states regarded his actions with extreme misgivings, suspecting that he was about to strike a deal pursuing only Egyptian interests at the expense of the general Arab cause. Internally there were also some rumblings, exemplified by the resignation of Ismail Fahmi, his foreign minister, who thought that Sadat's new moves were fraught with danger. While not doubting Sadat's sincere desire for peace for its own sake, Benny Morris suggests that there were probably also other meaningful considerations. It is likely that Sadat had concluded that, due to the strength of Israel's armed forces, backed up by ready access to non-conventional weapons, a military solution favourable to the Arabs was not feasible. Furthermore, a peace treaty with Israel held out prospects of Egypt receiving a generous allocation of US economic aid that would help alleviate the country's chronic economic problems.[37]

So extraordinary was Sadat's historic breakthrough that for some Israelis it was simply beyond belief. Motta Gur, the IDF chief of staff, remarked that Sadat's peace initiative was more likely than not a cover for another Egyptian surprise attack.[38] Heeding Gur's concern, Yadin, as acting minister of defence while Weizman was recovering from a road accident, proposed a partial mobilization of the reserves. One Israeli newspaper published a far-fetched account of so-called experts who, on analyzing a vocal recording of Sadat as he spoke at the Egyptian parliament, determined that they detected tension in his voice, indicating that he was lying. Horrified by all that inanity, Weizman, temporarily confined to a wheelchair, promptly reassumed office and admonished Gur for his rash pronouncements.[39]

On November 19, Sadat's plane landed at Ben-Gurion Airport. Greeting him with an effusive welcome were Israel's leading political and military figures. Sadat responded with good grace, exchanging a brief word of friendship or witticism with each and every one of them. To Gur he joked, "It seems that I am not lying this time, hey?" And to Meir he exclaimed: "I have been meaning to talk with you for a long time."[40] When Meir asked: "What took you [so long]?," Sadat replied, "Up to now the time was not right." After the official airport reception Sadat was driven to Jerusalem, where streams of Israelis, crowding along the footpaths and with some brandishing Egyptian flags, delightedly cheered him. For Sadat it was a moving experience, as it was also for the entire Jewish populace watching on television. Only in their wildest dreams could they have imagined an Arab head of state visiting their country. The next day Sadat made history by appearing before a hushed Knesset. He told his listeners that he had come to Israel in search of a real peace based on Israel relinquishing all the land conquered in the Six-Day War and the establishment of a Palestinian State. Not only was Sadat as an Arab head of state speaking to Israelis for the first time but, equally remarkably, he formally acknowledged that he appreciated that Israel had legitimate reasons to be concerned with its security. To no small extent, such an acknowledgment ultimately paved the way for Israel fully conceding all of Sinai. In reply Begin assured Sadat that Israel sought peace with all its neighbours and that everything was negotiable.[41] Later, after a state banquet, Begin and Sadat met privately. Key differences between them were not resolved but, as they afterwards stated in their joint declaration, they were adamant that there would be no more war, no more bloodshed. As Sadat was about to depart, the two exchanged words of encouragement and mutual respect, but as yet no date had been set for Begin in turn to visit Egypt.

Sadat's visit did not yield any immediate tangible results. On December 2, Dayan once again secretly met Tuhami in Morocco, but the two failed to find common ground. One of the sticking points was Israel's unwillingness to relinquish specific parts of Sinai, including its new settlement of Yamit.[42] On December 25 Begin met Sadat at Ismailia. Begin had finally decided to forego all of Sinai except for the Israeli settlements there under the proposed protection of Israeli and UN troops.[43] Such a proposal was taken by Sadat as a serious breach of the trust that he believed had been forged with Begin during their Jerusalem tête-à-tête. After a general and at times acrimonious exchange of views, it was patently clear that serious differences remained. What was resolved was the creation of two committees, one to deal with military matters and the other with political issues. But, since nothing of substance emerged, the peace process effectively fell into limbo.

At the beginning of February, 1978, Sadat visited the United States, where he impressed both the president and the wider public that he was earnest in his quest for peace. Much to the chagrin of Begin, in endorsing Sadat's efforts, Carter, determined that UN Resolution 242 calling for Israeli withdrawal applied to all fronts of the Six-Day War and not exclusively to the Egyptian–Israeli one. Even more affronting to the Israeli administration, Carter depicted Jewish settlements in the occupied territory as being contrary to international law and as constituting a serious obstacle to peace. Towards the end of March it was Begin's turn to meet with Carter, but the two did not strike up a rapport. Not only was Carter critical of the extent of Israel's retaliatory strike into Lebanon (see section below dealing with terrorism) but he felt that Begin was not bargaining in good faith in relation to the granting of Palestinian autonomy.

Carter's misgivings began to be shared by a growing number of Israelis. In the very same month of March, 348 IDF reserve officers sent an open letter to Begin expressing their concern that his obsession with retaining the occupied territories threatened to jeopardize Israel's unique prospects for peace. Not only that, but in their words: "A government policy that will cause a continuation of control over a million Arabs will hurt the Jewish-democratic character of the state, and will make it difficult for us to identify with the path of the State of Israel."[44] The officers' letter struck a responsive chord among thousands of other Israelis, culminating in the foundation of Peace Now, a movement supporting efforts in bringing the Israeli–Egyptian dialogue to a swift and mutually satisfying conclusion. Although Peace Now adherents were drawn largely from left-leaning parties, Begin could not dismiss them out of hand, since many of them had distinguished themselves in battle, demonstrating that their patriotism was beyond reproach.

On July 17, a two-day meeting of the foreign ministers of Israel and Egypt, presided over by the US secretary of state, Cyrus Vance, was convened at Leeds Castle in the UK. In an effort to break the logjam, Dayan, at his own initiative, indicated that, at the expiration of a Palestinian autonomy transition period, Israel would deliberate on the issue of sovereignty. On learning of Dayan's overture Begin was furious, but he nonetheless had the good grace to support his foreign minister. But at the end of the day the Leeds Conference closed inconclusively.

Realizing that fitful Israeli–Egyptian talks were getting nowhere, Carter in August 1978 invited both Begin and Sadat along with their advisors to join him on September 5 for an extended period at the presidential Camp David retreat in Maryland. On the eve of Begin's departure, Peace Now drew nearly 100,000 protesters to a rally in Tel Aviv, marking the occasion as, at that point, the largest political gathering in Israel's history. The participants demanded of Begin that he return home with a peace agreement. It is difficult to assess the extent to which Peace Now influenced Begin. The historian Benny Morris reports that both Weizman and Moshe Arens, Israel's ambassador to the USA, who both accompanied Begin, thought that the rally bore some weight in inducing Israeli negotiators to be more flexible.[45]

Carter, a man of strong religious beliefs, felt that he had a divine mission to bring peace to the Middle East. Driven by that conviction, he was prepared to set aside, wherever feasible, all other issues requiring his immediate attention to allocate time to sit together with Begin and Sadat, to mediate between them and to counsel them. An attempt was made to create an easy-going relaxed atmosphere. The dress code was casual and the participants were invited to enjoy the leisurely activities that the site provided, such as ambling forest walks, table tennis, court tennis, football or even a quiet game of chess.

Sadat soon realized that, in order to conclude a peace agreement with Israel, he would have to pursue Egypt's narrow interests exclusively, which meant foregoing demands for Israel's evacuation of the Golan Heights, the West Bank and the Gaza Strip. This he reluctantly accepted. But, as attention began to be focused on the details of an Israel withdrawal from Sinai, an Israeli refusal to dismantle their Sinai settlements proved to be a critical stumbling block. With Sadat insisting that he would not conclude a peace treaty with Israel unless the settlements were removed, and with Begin obdurately refusing, the exchanges between the two became quite heated and interspersed with farcical outbursts. Carter later recalled that Begin complained to Sadat that he was addressing the Israelis as if they were a routed nation. Sadat, mistakenly thinking that Begin was calling the Egyptians a routed nation, angrily retorted: "We are not routed. We are not routed." At that point, as Carter wrote, "All restraint was now gone. Their faces were flushed and the niceties of diplomatic language and protocol were stripped away."[46] The talks seemed doomed to fail.

Dejectedly, Carter indicated that he would wrap up the proceedings on Sunday September 17 and on the following day would inform Congress and the media that all his efforts had come to naught. Meanwhile Sharon had telephoned Begin to reassure him that, if peace was at stake, he personally would not object to sacrificing the Sinai settlements (Sharon was one of the government's leading settlement advocates). Furthermore, with Dayan's assertion that the settlements had to go, and realizing that unless he backed down Israel would forego a unique opportunity for obtaining peace, Begin became more malleable. Not bearing any emotional national attachment to Sinai as he had to the West Bank, Begin, on the evening of Saturday September 16, bowed to Sadat's demands, subject to the Knesset's endorsement. In the process, he pulled back the Camp David talks from the brink of disaster. It was not only Begin who had made concessions. Sadat, at Carter's prodding, had reluctantly agreed not to press Israel for an explicit commitment to withdraw from Gaza and the West Bank and promised that Egyptian and Israeli relations would be completely normalized.

An agreement, known as the Camp David Accords, was signed by Sadat and Begin on September 17. It entailed a commitment on the part of Israel to vacate the entire Sinai peninsula. However, for the first three years following the ratification of a peace treaty, the IDF would retain a presence from El Arish to Ras Muhammad. A fully returned Sinai was to contain a demilitarized zone and one where Egyptian forces would be strictly limited. Nine months after the signing of the peace treaty, Egypt was to normalize relations with the Jewish State. There was to be an exchange of ambassadors, the opening up of frontiers, and

Plate 3   *Left to right: Sadat, Carter and Begin at the Israel–Egypt Peace Treaty signing ceremony*

the fostering of trade and cultural relations. As a gesture to Sadat, Israel, without foregoing any claim to sovereignty to the West Bank and Gaza, undertook to grant the Palestinians full autonomy, valid for five years.

While Begin can justly be credited for ultimately rising to the historic occasion by doing what was necessary in the interest of peace, the critical role of Dayan and Weizman in edging him on merits mention. Both men had in the past established their credentials as dyed-in-the-wool hawks who under no circumstances would countenance a total withdrawal from Sinai. Yet they both underwent a complete change of heart. Dayan, ever the pragmatist, could readily segue from one viewpoint to another. For Weizman, Sadat's visit to Jerusalem was an epiphany. Since then, he never doubted Sadat's desire for peace. Both Dayan and Weizman worked tirelessly to soften Begin's resistance to formulations that concerned him and to help him interpret them in a more positive light.[47]

On September 25, the Knesset voted in favour of withdrawing its settlements from the Sinai peninsula. The vote was 84 for and 19 against, with 17 abstentions.[48] A formal peace treaty was to be signed within three months, but unanticipated hitches caused both further delays and some caustic disputes. The Egyptians demanded liaison officers between Egypt and Gaza in setting up Palestinian autonomy. They were willing to sell oil to Israel only via prior sales to the USA, so it would seem as if Egypt still adhered to the Arab economic embargo of Israel. Finally, they insisted that the peace treaty with Israel would not supersede Egypt's defence treaty obligations to other Arab states. Only after hectic negotiations involving Carter's personal intervention was everything resolved. Carter had summoned Begin to visit him in Washington on March 4, 1979. Then, on March 7, he flew to Cairo to consult with Sadat. That was followed by a short stay in Jerusalem commencing on March 10 and a return visit on March 18 to Cairo, from where Carter was finally able to telephone Begin that all outstanding issues had been ironed out. The Egyptian demand for liaison officers was dropped, the USA secured a guarantee for Israel that it would obtain oil from Egypt for fifteen years, and the issue of Egypt's conflicting treaty obligations was resolved in favour of the spirit of the peace accords.[49] On March 20, the amended agreement received the Knesset's blessing in a vote of 95 for and 18 against, with 2 abstentions. Finally, on March 26, 1979, Carter, Sadat and Begin met on the front lawn of the White House to sign the peace treaty. It represented an unprecedented milestone in Egyptian–Israeli relations.

Evacuating the Sinai settlements turned out to be quite traumatic. With the settlers and their supporters resisting attempts to remove them, a large body of soldiers had to be deployed to drag them out kicking and screaming. Weizman, who had appeared on the scene, was met with derision. He was called a traitor and was spat at in the face. The settlers of Naot Sinai, who had been members of the youth movement Betar that was affiliated with Herut (now part of Likud), were particularly incensed with Begin, since he had once expressed a heartfelt desire to live among them upon his retirement.[50]

Egypt bore an even heavier toll for concluding peace. It was condemned and excluded from the Arab League. Arab ambassadors were recalled from Cairo and the country was threatened with punitive economic sanctions. From being the acknowledged leading player in the Arab world, Egypt found itself perceived as a pariah state. Opposition within Egypt to the peace treaty was wide-ranging. It was condemned not only by the communists and the Muslim Brothers but also by mainstream members of the Egyptian establishment, such as Mohamed Heikal, the former editor of the influential *al-Ahram*, and some of Sadat's ministers, as well as by university professors and general Islamic preachers. Their main grievances were that the Palestinian cause was betrayed and that, by acquiescing to the stationing of international forces in parts of Sinai and by allowing a section of it to be demilitarized, Egypt in essence did not regain complete sovereignty of that territory. To the present day, those issues still rankle with many Egyptians.

In terms of setting up Palestinian autonomy, Israel and Egypt, with the participation of Jordan and Palestinian representatives, were expected to negotiate an agreement within a year. Topics to be covered included the organization of elections and the authority of those elected. Within three years of the founding of an autonomous Palestinian entity, negotiations determining the final status of the West Bank and Gaza were to commence. Both Jordan and the Palestinians expressed their unwillingness to be involved, but in any case Begin had not the slightest intention of fulfilling Israel's Palestine autonomy commitments. As far as he was concerned the notion of Israeli withdrawals did not apply to the West Bank and to Gaza. Instead of appointing Dayan to represent Israel in the autonomy talks, Begin handed the task to Yosef Burg, minister of internal affairs and a leading light in Mafdal. Unlike Dayan, who actually wished the talks to succeed, Burg was cautious by nature and more amenable to Begin's views. With him at the helm, the talks never amounted to anything. That Burg was minister of internal affairs was not incidental to his appointment, for Begin meant to signal that Palestinian autonomy was exclusively a matter of Israel's internal affairs.

Realizing that his control over foreign policy was ebbing away, Dayan resigned as foreign minister on October 21, 1979. The straw that broke the proverbial camel's back was a government decision to fortify settlement activity in the West Bank. Now no longer in the government, Dayan as a newly converted peace-maker advocated that Israel unilaterally dismantle its military establishment in the occupied territories, a proposal that Begin dismissed as being a recipe for disaster.[51] Cut adrift from the leadership of both Likud and the Maarah, Dayan in the spring of 1981 formed his own political party, Telem. Hoping to secure ten to fifteen seats in the June 1981 election, he was in for a great disappointment. His party gained only two mandates, which meant that he was cast into the political wilderness. He did not have long to linger there, for on October 16, 1981, after suffering from colon cancer, he died of a heart attack at the age of sixty-six.

Right-wing opponents of the peace treaty and its application began to bedevil Begin's authority. Prominent among them was Guelah Cohen, who withdrew from Likud to form, in October 1979, a new party named Tehiya. Including such luminaries such as the renowned physicist Yuval Neeman, the party effectively represented the interests of the Gush Emunim settler movement. With some Mafdal members openly cooperating with Tehiya and with the loyalty of others in his own party falling under a cloud, Begin's hold on power was waning.

On another front, the Democratic Movement for Change, which had derived its following mainly from ex-Maarah voters seeking a clean slate in politics, began to disintegrate. Against the wishes and expectations of most of its supporters, the party had aligned itself with the Begin government. It tried to rationalize that move as one serving the national interest, but its influence was marginal, since the government was not dependent on it to survive. By September 1978 its fifteen Knesset members had divided into three factions. Seven formed a group called Shinui (Change), another seven metamorphosed into the Democratic Movement, and one founded a single-member party called Ya'ad (Objective). Only members of the Democratic Movement remained in the government.

Settlements

In September 1973, Meir's cabinet accepted amendments, drafted by Galili, of its 1969 oral settlement doctrine. It made allowances for new settlements in the Jordan Rift Valley, the Golan Heights and, of all places, Northern Sinai. Dayan had been particularly keen on the establishment of an Israeli settlement on Egyptian territory just south of Rafah. Named Yamit, the settlement was meant to serve as a port and to seal off Gaza from Egypt. Gearing up for the December 1973 general election, the Labour Party formulated a settlement policy favoured by the majority of its central leadership and tolerated by its minority. It read as follows: "Provision will be made for the continuation and fortification of settlements in accordance with government decisions made from time to time that prioritise state security concerns."[52] By so doing, it was hoped that, whenever an expansion of settlements was authorized, advancing a defence needs case would satisfy all party members. During Rabin's short tenure of office, settlement construction in the "territories," as they were then called, gathered pace. Some thirty-three new colonies were established, representing 50 per cent of all settlements founded since the conclusion of the 1967 Six-Day War. Rabin's justification for that increase is that they were all established in accordance with well-defined security considerations in areas such as the Jordan Valley, the Golan Heights, the surrounds of Jerusalem and the Etzion Block near Hebron.[53] As to locating settlements elsewhere in the territories, Rabin was adamantly opposed. He submitted that to encroach upon densely Arab populated regions would be courting disaster. It would be seen by both the Arabs and the United States purely as a provocation without serving any defensive purposes.[54]

At odds with the Labour Party consensus, Peres did little to disguise his warm feelings for the Gush Emunim (Block of the Faithful) movement, a movement regarded by Rabin as "a cancer in the body of Israeli democracy."[55] Gush Emunim was founded in March 1974 by followers of Rabbi Zvi Yehuda Kook who were motivated primarily by deeply held religious convictions impelling them to settle and assume unlimited possession of the West Bank. In their way of thinking, Judah and Samaria (the West Bank) was an inalienable God-given component of Israel. In his autobiography, Peres wrote: "I came to appreciate the strength of the Emunim movement, and I have never since disparaged the depth of their commitment or the vibrancy of their pioneering spirit."[56] Gush Emunim members likened themselves to Jewish labour pioneers who had previously tilled land in what eventually became Israel, but the analogy is flawed. For one, the *pre-state* pioneers both worked and lived on land that was purchased by the Jewish National Fund at a handsome price from its previous owners, and in many cases the land in question was at the time either fully or semi-desolate. The pioneers often broke ground in arid or non-cultivated areas where, among other things, they personally drained swamps and were plagued by malaria-bearing mosquitoes. All physical labour was borne by them alone. Above all, the overriding purpose of the pioneers was to prepare the way for the formation of Israel as a haven for diaspora Jews. The Gush Emunim "pioneers," by contrast, have usually acquired land requisitioned by the government on spurious defence pretexts. Their homes have been constructed largely by Arab labour, and the livelihoods of many, although certainly not all, of their members are derived from outside their settlements. They have been motivated less by the need to secure Jewish national independence as such and more by a drive to repossess the remnant of the ancient Jewish homeland. In the process they explicitly aimed to create a situation whereby it would become impossible to transfer any part of the West Bank to the Arabs, thereby foreclosing any future or potential peace agreement based on territorial compromise.[57] In short, the pre-state pioneers founded settlements in order to establish a homeland, whereas the Gush Emunim derive assistance from an existing Jewish State to build settlements.

In 1974 the Gush Emunim made various attempts to settle at the site of the Sebastia railway station, some 15 kilometres northwest of Nablus. After repeatedly being rebuffed by a cordon of IDF soldiers, a number of its members eventually succeeded in breaking through. Both Rabin and Allon wished to evict them forthwith, but they were opposed by Peres, who backed the settlers, and by all the ministers of Mafdal, who threatened to bolt from the government.[58] Also reluctant to confront the settlers was Chief of Staff Gur, who explained to Rabin that, given that Gush Emunim supporters would converge en masse on the site, the evacuation process would require more than 5,000 troops and would take a few days. [59] After negotiations with the settlers, a "compromise" was reached. They were given permission to transfer to camp Kadum, a nearby military base, where, by the end of 1975, they formally founded a civilian settlement named Kedumim.

On a visit to the USA on September 19, 1977, Dayan, as foreign minister, promised President Carter, who was angered by Sharon's announcement foreshadowing hundreds of thousands of Jews settling in the West Bank, that he would recommend that only IDF soldiers be quartered in designated military sites. Needless to say, Begin thought otherwise.[60] During the first half of 1978 Begin became subject to bitter recriminations from Carter for his lukewarm commitment to the notion of West Bank–Gaza autonomy. In what has become a recurring practice, Sharon proposed that Israel ought to respond to US pressure by launching a widespread surge in settlement activity as a means of upping the ante. As soon as Weizman, who was abroad at the time, learnt that Sharon had already secured the go-ahead, he threatened to resign unless the approval was rescinded. At first Begin was not unduly perturbed, but when his finance minister, Simha Erlich, informed him that he and other more moderate ministers would follow suit, Begin officially stifled the project. That is not to say that settlement expansion ground to a halt. Under the guise of expanding existing settlements, new ones came into being bearing other names.[61] From its beginning the new Likud government aspired to raise the number of settlements in the West Bank from thirty-four in 1977 to well over 100 by 1983, bringing the number of settlers up from 4,000 to 100,000.[62] In addition, the centre of gravity of the settlements was to shift from peripheral uninhabited areas to densely Arab-populated ones. As for their character, they were to change from small rural communities to urban-like townships. The spurt in settlement construction took place at the very time when, in terms of the Israeli–Egyptian peace treaty, Israel was supposed to be facilitating a measure of Palestinian autonomy in the areas in question. Under Begin, settlement activity was no longer left largely to the private initiatives of individual settler groups. Instead it had become a major government objective for which state finances and other resources were copiously mobilized.

Palestinian Terrorism and Measures to Contain it

On April 11, 1974, while Israel was preoccupied with formally concluding the Yom Kippur War by negotiating, through the auspices of Kissinger, permanent ceasefire terms with Syria, Palestinian terrorists resumed their murderous offensive. Shortly before noon, Radio Damascus announced that the Popular Front for the Liberation of Palestine General Command had taken possession of a school in Kiryat Shmona, an Israeli town near the Lebanese border. According to the announcement, schoolchildren were being held as hostages and IDF efforts to rescue them would simply endanger their lives.[63] As it turned out, Radio Damascus had read out a prepared script that did not mirror the actual course of events. The terrorists had indeed approached the school, but they found it to be empty as the pupils were away over the Passover holidays. They then entered a nearby apartment complex, passing from one unit to another and firing at anyone they encountered. Finally, on reaching the top floor, they battened down in one of the apartments at the end of a corridor. An alerted elite IDF platoon soon burst into the apartment in which the assailants were ensconced and slew all three of them, but not before they had succeeded in taking the lives of eight civilian adults, eight children and two soldiers as well as wounding another fifteen.[64]

Just over a month later, on May 15, the Israeli township of Maalot, also near the Lebanese border, was singled out for another Palestinian outrage, this time by the Democratic Front for the Liberation of Palestine. Once again only three terrorists were involved. On that occasion their slaughter was even more indiscriminate. Their first victims were Arab women workers travelling home in a small van just outside of Maalot. Discharging their Kalashnikov rifles, they killed one of the women and wounded nine others, including the male Arab driver. Next they rushed into a Maalot house, where they wiped out a family of three, and then moved on to take control of a small school, where 100 pupils and four teachers were present. Holding everyone to ransom, they demanded the release of twenty of their imprisoned comrades. Once again the IDF responded with force, killing all three, but only after the terrorists had succeeded in slaying twenty-one children and one soldier and wounding seventy others. Following on the heels of the Israeli soldiers, Dayan beheld a grisly scene. The floor was bloodsoaked. The injured students were lying pressed against a wall. As a wounded girl was placed on a stretcher she recognized Dayan and beckoned to him. As he drew near she moaned, "It was horrific, it was horrific."[65]

During the night of June 25, three members of Arafat's Fatah militia, having sailed from Lebanon on an engine-propelled inflatable boat, entered an apartment building in the coastal town of Nahariya in the north of Israel. On hearing gunfire from the apartment above him, Mr Zarkin helped his wife and two children escape through a window. But all three were struck down by one of the gunmen, who had remained outside.[66] In the brief firefight that followed, the three Palestinian terrorists were killed.

Rather than standing by a beleaguered member state, as its charter would require (article 1 declares that the UN would be committed "to take effective collective measures for the prevention and removal of threats to the peace, and for the suppression of acts of aggression or other breaches of the peace"), on November 13, 1974, the UN General Assembly enthusiastically welcomed Arafat to its podium. Basking in the glory of it all, Arafat presented the Palestinian case to his generally doting audience. He allowed for no legitimacy of any Jewish national sovereignty in Palestine no matter how attenuated. As far as he was concerned the Jews, unlike the Arabs of Palestine, who in fact acquired a sense of national identity only after the formation of Zionism, were not entitled to regard themselves as a people. In his scheme of things, Palestine was always inhabited by Arabs. They were the ones who bequeathed to the world "the most ancient cultures and civilizations."[67] Appearing to be magnanimous, Arafat offered the Jews an olive branch should they peacefully succumb to his dictates and, if not, on offer was the sword the likes of which had, as outlined above, already been revealed to the innocent Jewish civilians (including children) of Kiryat Shmona, Maalot and Nahariya. At the conclusion of his speech, as he faced them shaking his clenched hands above his head like a victorious prize fighter, Arafat was accorded a standing ovation by the General Assembly delegates.

Six days after Arafat appeared before the UN General Assembly – that is, on November 19 – four members of the Democratic Front for the Liberation of Palestine penetrated into Beit She'an, an Israeli town adjacent to the Jordan River and Jezreel Valley. Having taken possession of a family apartment, they entered into negotiations with the Israeli authorities. While that was transpiring, the IDF readied itself and after a three-hour waiting period attacked and killed the four terrorists, who had already murdered a woman by firing through her apartment door and shot both the mother of the family they were holding and a neighbour on the ground who was rendering assistance to those who, in fear of their lives, had jumped from the building. Altogether twenty Israelis were injured and, in addition, the father of the family held hostage was fatally shot during the IDF operation. In the aftermath, enraged Israelis hurled the bodies of the Palestinian perpetrators onto the street, where they were doused with petrol and set alight. Chief Rabbi Shlomo

Goren, who officiated at the funeral for the Israeli victims, reprimanded the wrathful mob for acting contrary to Jewish Law, which prohibits the violation of the remains of the dead whether they be friend or foe.

The next major incident occurred over March 4–5, 1975, when eight PLO mainstream Fatah commanders made a sea landing from two small craft just off Tel Aviv's main beach. Arriving late at night, they forced their way into the Savoy Hotel, where they held all guests hostage. Unwilling to accede to their demands, the IDF commissioned its choice unit, the Sayeret Matkal (General Staff Patrol), under the command of Uzi Yairi (mentioned in chapter 3 for his role in the battle of the Chinese Farm). The unit rapidly overpowered the terrorists, killing seven of them and capturing the sole survivor, but at a heavy price. Three hostages and three IDF fighters were killed in the exchange of fire, Uzi Yairi being among them.[68] Many years later, in April 2011, Abu Jihad, who masterminded the raid (plus a 1978 raid detailed further below), was commemorated at a memorial ceremony. The officiant was Mahmoud al-Aloul, a member of the Fatah Central Committee, in his capacity as a representative of the Palestine Authority under Mahmoud Abbas. Al-Aloul referred to Abu Jihad as "one of the greatest shaheed leaders who should be praised and emulated."[69]

During the remainder of the year there were a number of other acts of terror. The most lethal occurred on Friday July 4, when two Palestinians drove a cab truck into Zion Square in Jerusalem. There they unloaded a refrigerator and placed it against a wall adjacent to the sidewalk. The refrigerator contained a bomb assembled in Nablus which exploded within minutes of the Palestinians' getaway. Fourteen people were killed and sixty-two were injured.[70] Responsibility for the deed, which was an act of mass murder purely and simply, was assumed by Arafat's Fatah organization.

Sinking to a new low, on November 10, 1975, the UN General Assembly, by a sweeping majority of mainly communist and Third World states, passed a resolution specifying that Zionism (that is, the national movement of the Jewish people) is "a form of racism and racial discrimination." The resolution, sponsored by the Arab and Soviet blocs, was foreshadowed at the World Conference of the International Women's Year held in Mexico from June 19 to July 2, 1975. Most of the delegates represented countries that systematically deprived women of their basic human rights. No matter. Ignoring all the blatant racism and discrimination that existed in their own homelands, the conference delegates concluded that "international co-operation and peace require the elimination of" (among other things) Zionism. Similarly, a meeting of the Organization of African Unity, a body composed largely of a motley collection of tyrants, from 28 July to 1 August 1975 in of all places Kampala, the capital of Uganda (where Idi Amin's terror squads had recently killed between 100,000 to 300,000 innocent civilians),[71] sanctimoniously declared that "the racist regime in occupied Palestine ... aimed at repression of the dignity and integrity of the human being." To top it all, the "Non-Aligned" Countries, at a gathering in Lima in late August, with then such paragons of democracy as Cuba, Egypt, Libya, Saudi Arabia, Algeria, Ethiopia, Haiti, North Vietnam, North Korea, Iraq, Syria, Oman, and so on, affirmed that Zionism was a threat to world peace and security. By going along with such blatant anti-Semitism, the UN demonstrated that it was totally devoid of any semblance of decency or of any ethical underpinning. Even though the infamous "Zionism is racism" resolution was revoked in 1991 (after the collapse of the Soviet Empire), the UN continued to serve as the in-house organization of despotic anti-Israel regimes.

Perhaps the most dramatic terrorist course of events (in the period reviewed in this chapter) began on June 27, 1976, when an Air France passenger plane en route from Ben-Gurion Airport to Paris was hijacked following a stopover in Athens. The leading perpetrators were members of a faction of the Popular Front for the Liberation of Palestine. Initially the hijackers numbered four – two Palestinians and two Germans from the German "Revolutionary Cells," who purported to be against racism but who were in fact rabid anti-Semites. One of the Revolutionary Cells' adherents, Hans-Joachim Klein, in subsequently disassociating himself from the gang, asserted that his ex-comrades had even planned to assassinate the renowned Nazi hunter Simon Wiesenthal.[72]

The hijacked plane first landed at Benghazi, Libya, where it refuelled. After being denied permission to land in Sudan, it finally touched down at Entebbe Airport, Uganda, where it was joined by at least four other co-conspirators. On June 29, Radio Uganda broadcast that the hijackers demanded the release of fifty-three "freedom fighters" held in various countries, including forty in Israel, and six members of the Baader–Meinhoff Gang in West Germany. According to the captors, unless their demands were fully met by July 1 – soon extended to July 4 – they would commence killing their hostages, who had already been separated into two groups, Israelis and non-Israelis.

In the immediate absence of a realistic rescue plan, the Israeli cabinet agreed to negotiate with the hijackers. Even Begin, as the leader of the opposition, lent his support to that decision. Some of the proposed solutions to the impasse that had thus far been canvassed were somewhat hair-brained. One put forward at a cabinet session was that the pope ought to be approached to intercede with the hijackers, with a promise that Israel would release Archbishop Capucci, imprisoned for smuggling weapons to the PLO (he was but one of the forty men listed by the hijackers serving time in Israel). Another, endorsed by Peres and Gur, was that Dayan ought to be sent to Uganda to soft-soap its leader, Idi Amin.[73] Eventually, with the help of Israelis who had previously worked in Uganda and the Israeli company that had constructed Entebbe Airport, a realistic operational plan crystallized and was meticulously devised. It involved flying two large Hercules transport planes directly from Israel to Uganda. The first plane was to touch down at Entebbe Airport at night between the arrival times of two regularly scheduled commercial flights, when all landing strips would be fully illuminated. It was then to taxi as close as possible to the old terminal building where the hostages were held. On coming to a halt the plane was to disgorge the attack force, riding in jeeps and a black Mercedes automobile (to give the impression that Idi Amin was a passenger). IDF troops were to debouche from the second plane to capture the new terminal building in order to provide a haven for the first group should the need arise. According to Rabin, the plan, under the overall command of General Dan Shomron, was executed as planned. The first plane took off from Entebbe thirty minutes after landing, bearing the surviving hostages (three were killed in the battle's crossfire), five wounded soldiers, the crew of the Air France plane, some of the attack force and the body of Yonatan Natanyahu, (Bibi Natanyahu's brother). In commanding a twenty-nine-man assault force to extricate the hostages, Yonatan was shot by a Ugandan sniper.[74]

On receiving news that the two Israeli planes were homebound, the entire Israeli population felt a sense of both pride and relief. Unfortunately, one survivor was left behind. She was 75-year-old Dora Bloch, who had been hospitalized in Kampala. As an act of revenge for the three hijackers and forty-five Ugandan troops killed in the operation, Dora Bloch was murdered by Amin's soldiers, along with the doctors and nurses who had tried to protect her.

From the beginning of the saga when he was first briefed until its ultimate denouement, Rabin asserted that he had consistently done his utmost to obtain a satisfactory outcome and that, when he was ultimately presented with a well-considered plan with some realistic promise of success, he welcomed it. By contrast, Peres's spokesperson, Naftali Lavi, told a *New York Times* reporter that Rabin was strongly opposed to the Entebbe raid, and it was only through Peres's forceful intervention that he reluctantly concurred.[75] The jockeying between Rabin and Peres for the Labour Party leadership had become a public spectacle.[76]

In 1978, the PLO attempted to derail Sadat's peace initiative by means of a daring act of terror carried out by Arafat's Fatah unit and planned by Abu Jihad. On the morning of March 11, eleven Palestinians in Zodiac boats landed as a result of a navigational error on a beach near Kibbutz Maagan. They had intended to land 43 miles south at the Tel Aviv beach, where they hoped to seize a luxury hotel so as to exchange its guests for the release of their imprisoned comrades. Coming across Gail Rubin, an American photojournalist, they enquired of her as to their whereabouts and then murdered her. Upon approaching the Tel Aviv–Haifa highway, they randomly fired at passing cars and then commandeered a bus travelling to Haifa. The bus was ordered to turn around and proceed to Tel Aviv. Meanwhile, the terrorists resumed firing not only at passing traffic but also at some of the bus passengers, killing one and ditching his body. Soon, as the bus blocked the passage of an oncoming car, a terrorist alighted to machine gun its occupants, slaying a father and son.[77] Moments later another bus was seized. All passengers of the first bus were forced into the second one. The macabre journey towards Tel Aviv then continued. Eventually, at a roadblock near the Country Club just north of Tel Aviv, the bus was forced to a halt and a furious gun-fight arose between Israeli police and the hijackers. In the mayhem the bus was blown up. By the time it was all over, thirty-eight Israeli civilians, including thirteen children, had been killed and seventy-one wounded.

There was a rather unseemly aftermath years later. Towards the end of 2009 and thereafter the Palestine Authority (PA) conducted a campaign eulogizing Dalal Mughrabi, the woman who led the terrorist raid, naming after her, among things, a town square, two high schools and a summer camp. When *al-Hayat al-Jadida*, an official PA newspaper, questioned Abbas about the lavishing on Mughrabi of such praise, he replied, "Of course we want to name a square after her. We carried out a 'military action'. Can I then later renounce all that we have done? No I don't renounce it."[78]

Returning to events immediately after that terrorist attack, the Israeli government resolved to react forcibly. On March 15, in a military engagement known as Operation Litani, a large IDF contingent crossed over the border into Southern Lebanon, sweeping up to the Litani River without entering the town of Tyre, where the Palestinians had established their major base. As the fighting raged most of the PLO gunmen fled, but even so some 300 were killed. Six days later, in the face of international condemnation, the IDF withdrew, and by March 23 a United Nations Interim Force (UNIFIL) was deployed in its stead. Israel's retributive act cost it fifteen of its own soldiers.[79] A few Shiite villages that had been in strife with the Palestinians had welcomed the Israeli intrusion, but many innocent civilians incurred heavy losses as a result of clashes within villages.[80]

Some Economic and Social Facets

The Yom Kippur War not only bequeathed to Israel the loss of many soldiers' lives and the undermining of its sense of security but it also left in its wake a costly economic legacy. Taking all aspects of the management of the war into account, it has been estimated that it imposed on Israel an economic burden equivalent in value to a full year's national product.[81] In addition, the international oil price crisis that was a direct by-product of the war presented the country with a sharp rise in import prices. That, coupled with crippling expenses resulting from the need to re-equip its armoured forces, led to a sharp deterioration of Israel's balance of payments. The expenses entailed in maintaining its armed forces became increasingly prohibitive. On average, between the years 1973 and 1975, they amounted to 32.8 percent of GNP.[82] By contrast, military outlays as a percentage of GNP in the Western world ranged from 3.1 to 5.4 percent. Not computed in the Israeli data are the opportunity costs that a three-year conscription period and a month's annual reserve duty impose on the people involved.

In the first three years of the 1970s, the Israeli economy had grown rapidly, at an average rate of 9.3 percent per year.[83] By 1973, the growth rate had fallen to 5.6 percent, and by 1976 it hit rock bottom, at 0.9 percent. To a large extent the fall resulted from the government adopting strict austerity measures in the form of sharp taxation increases that caused private consumption and gross investment to fall. Contrary to expectations, there was no significant concurrent rise in unemployment rates. This may be explained partially by a decline in the labour force participation rate as a result of more people serving in the IDF, falls in net immigration and hours worked, and finally a drop in the employment of Arabs from the West Bank and Gaza.[84] In this period a managed exchange-rate float was instituted that resulted in a sharp devaluation. From a rate of 4.2 Israeli lira to the US dollar in 1971, the exchange rate fell by 1977 to 10.75 Israeli lira to the US dollar. That, plus a previously large expansion in the money supply, fuelled inflation.

On October 28, 1977, the Begin government announced its new economic policy. The exchange rate would no longer be regulated and would be allowed to float in the international currency market without buying or selling restrictions. All Israeli citizens would be permitted to hold up to US$3,000 as well as use their credit cards abroad. As a result, the Israeli lira plummeted, from 10.75 to 16 to the US dollar. In addition, the value added tax rate was raised from 8 to 12 percent while subsidies on basic commodities were reduced, leading to a surge in prices that was also aggravated by higher import costs. Much to the concern of Israel's Treasury, the inflation rate for the year 1977 was 46 percent. After that it spun out of control, reaching 116 percent in 1979. The government was caught in a dilemma. It considered cancelling subsidies on basic commodities, but that would have caused prices to rise even further. On the other hand, the continued maintenance of the subsidies meant running a budgetary deficit financed by increasing the money supply, and hence inflation.[85] On November 7, 1979, Yigal

Horowitz, on becoming the minister of finance, promised to rectify the economy by reducing subsidies, balancing the budget and unearthing undisclosed transactions. He preached consumer restraint and did his best to limit government outlays, but the public were not convinced. Confidence in the local currency nosedived, and in major transactions the practice developed of quoting prices in terms of US dollars.

In Israel there are various norms within central and local government bureaucracies as well as within semi-autonomous corporations that facilitate corruption. For one, although such bodies are theoretically regulated by set rules, in practice, Israelis as individuals manifest an outright disdain for formal structures and generally demand exceptional treatment.[86] In addition there had been a widely held attitude that one could bend the rules in service of a just cause, thus blurring the line been between idealistic and pecuniary corruption, both of which of course are illegal.[87] Within the civil service at large, formal wages did not keep abreast of those in the private sector. As a way of compensating civil servants, a blind eye was turned towards the padding of incomes by extending overtime payments and the use of generous and unmonitored allowances. Not only were internal checks and controls defective but so too were external ones. As the Israeli political scientist Simcha Werner summed up the situation: "As Israelis continue to expect their public officials to be content with a meagre salary, while they themselves become more materialistic, the double standard that is created tends to erode even further the morality of the public servants."[88]

A number of serious corruption scandals occurred in the 1970s. The first of note took place in 1974, when Yehoshua Ben-Zion, the manager of the Israel-British Bank, was arrested for embezzling $47 million, which ultimately led to the bank's collapse. In 1975 he was sentenced to twelve years' imprisonment, but by 1977 Begin, in his dual capacity as premier and acting minister of justice, pardoned Ben-Zion – ostensibly on grounds of health but not fully supported by medical evidence. Ben-Zion had been a financial backer of an ultra-nationalist movement close to Likud.[89] By pardoning Ben-Zion so prematurely, Begin did little to dispel the notion that establishment figures do not really view large-scale corruption as meriting serious punishment.

Two further corruption scandals in the late 1970s had strong political overtones. In March 1976, after pleading guilty, Asher Yadlin, head

of the Histadrut's (Trade Union Federation) Health Insurance agency
(the Kupat Holim) and governor designate of the Bank of Israel, was
sentenced to five years' imprisonment for soliciting bribes and income
tax evasion. In mitigation he submitted that he had handed over some
of the money to the Labour Party. That admission was used both by the
opposition parties and by the Rafi component of the Maarah to smear
the Labour Party, headed by Rabin, as if it were an accessory to Yadlin's
malversations.

In the wake of the Yadlin affair, Avraham Ofer, the minister of housing, came under suspicion for embezzlement in light of information
supplied by Yigal Laviv, a correspondent for a leftist weekly, *Haolam
Hazeh*. On January 3, 1977, Ofer committed suicide. His body was
found in a car next to a North Tel Aviv beach. A note left behind indicated that, although he firmly believed in his innocence, he lacked the
fortitude to endure what seemed to him a needlessly prolonged ordeal.
The public prosecutors' office under Aharon Barak let it be known that
it was considering bringing charges against Ofer but kept prolonging
its investigation without disclosing the nature of the evidence at hand.
Barak had promised Rabin that he would expedite matters, but Barak's
promise was not kept.[90] To Rabin it seemed that Barak "laboured in
accordance with public opinion pressures. He aspired to appease the
'street' and while he cultivated an appearance of a bold and impartial
authority, he had surrendered to the public mood."[91] Meanwhile, Ofer
continued to be subject to malicious media speculation – a situation
that is not uncommon as a result of Israel's peculiar judicial procedures.
The day before Ofer's suicide Barak informed Rabin that, of the thirty-
six complaints that the police were considering, thirty-two were found
to be baseless and the remaining four were still pending.[92]

5

THE DECADE OF THE 1980s

On May 26, 1980, Weizman resigned as defence minister. As a newly converted dove, he felt that he could no longer participate in an administration that was demonstrably not honouring its commitment to further an acceptable measure of autonomy for the Palestinians in the West Bank and Gaza. He was also opposed to government increases in settlement funding at a time when the national security budget was being curtailed.[1] In his stead, Begin managed the defence portfolio along with his premiership. The government's fortunes were on the decline. Sharon, smarting at not securing the defence portfolio, began to speak ill of Begin, who at the time suffered from a heart attack that put his continued leadership in doubt. Meanwhile, the economy began to teeter. Farmers confronted with external competition were experiencing difficulties in keeping their heads above water. Inflation began accelerating at a rate that was seemingly uncontrollable, for during 1980 the cost of living rose by 133 percent. The new shekel (which replaced the old shekel in October 1980) was depreciating and private consumption fell. Within the cabinet a bitter dispute erupted between the minister of finance, Yigal Horowitz, and the minister of education, Zevulun Hammer, over teachers' wages. With the teachers holding what seemed to be an endless series of work stoppages, Begin, in January 1981, cast his lot in favour of Hammer and, as a result,

Horowitz resigned to be replaced by Yoram Aridor. To the outsider, it looked as if the government was in complete disarray.[2]

With a general election set for June 30, 1981, it did not take Aridor long to pander to voters. Within the first three weeks of his new tenure, he drastically reduced import tariffs on a wide range of durable appliances and lifted the restriction on colour television transmissions, which boosted the purchase of colour television sets. Excise taxes on cigarettes were lowered and state employees were awarded wage rises and benefits pertaining to the acquisition of new apartments. Settlements were not overlooked. The government approved the establishment of ten new ones and the construction of 1,800 homes on West Bank land moderately close to the June 1967 frontier that was sold to contractors at highly discounted prices. (Terms of financial credit for the purchase of homes on settlements were far more generous than for homes in Israel proper.) Income taxes were lowered and import duties on automobiles with an engine capacity of under 1,300 cc were slashed. As one observer noted, for the first time in its history, "the roads of Israel were filled with new cars."[3]

Likud's election knockout blow was delivered on June 7, 1981, three weeks before the poll. Begin had authorized the IAF to bomb Iraq's Osirak atomic reactor, which potentially facilitated Iraq's attempt to acquire an atomic weapon. The IAF successfully accomplished its mission. It evaded Jordanian and Saudi Arabian radar detections to destroy the plant completely. Begin wasted no time in boasting of the IAF's accomplishments and in stressing how he had spared the nation from an impending holocaust.

Taking all of the above into account, the reader might well appreciate how Likud, which was earlier billed as an election loser, eventually turned into the front runner, even if only just. Despite gaining an extra five seats, bringing its total to forty-eight (see Appendix), it beat the Maarah led by Peres by only a single seat. The Maarah had made an impressive comeback, rebounding from thirty-two seats won in the previous election to forty-seven in 1981. To a large extent, the total collapse four months prior to the 1981 election of the Democratic Movement for Change enabled the Maarah to attract its disaffected members, many of whom had come from the Maarah in the first place. Another factor that might have shored up additional support for the party was a cynical manoeuvre on the part of Peres. At the opening of his election campaign, Peres released the names of those he would like to nominate for government in the event of his attaining power. A noticeable name absent from his wish list was that of Rabin, who had challenged him for the party leadership. As the campaign was drawing to a close, Peres, sensing a rise in Rabin's star while his own appeared to be waning, made a last-ditch effort to woo voters by announcing that he would appoint Rabin as defence minister.[4]

By August 5, 1981, after much horse trading, Begin successfully formed a new coalition government consisting of Likud, Mafdal, Agudat Yisrael, Tami and Telem, with Tehiya (representing the Gush Emunim) joining three weeks later. It was more solidly right wing in its composition and orientation than his previous team, which had included the moderate middle-of-the-road party the Democratic Movement for Change. Ariel Sharon became the new minister of defence and Yitzhak Shamir the foreign minister. Together, they projected a more hard-line approach in terms of Israel's foreign and self-defence policies. Adding ballast to the hardliners in cabinet were Moshe Arens (Israel's ambassador to the USA, who, like Shamir, had opposed the peace treaty with Egypt) and ex-chief of staff Rafael Eitan, a courageous uncompromising warrior who regarded the Arabs with complete disdain.

After the elections, the Israeli stock exchange rallied as share prices began to exhibit an upward trend. In particular, bank shares rose sharply, partly because banks effectively manipulated the market through the medium of especially created subsidiaries. Unaware of what caused the banks' apparent above average performance, thousands of Israelis, confident that they provided the safest and best return, invested heavily in them.[5] Meanwhile, the country's trade balance was deteriorating and the national debt was rising. Despite Aridor's now best efforts to rein in inflation by restraining public-sector wages and slashing government expenditure, by January 1982 prices were rising at the fastest rate since the year 1951.

Israel's Invasion of Lebanon

Despite Israel's 1978 Litani Operation, which was intended to eliminate armed PLO forces in Southern Lebanon and which brought about the subsequent entry of the United Nations Interim Force in Lebanon (UNIFIL), the PLO menace to Israel remained unchanged. UNIFIL's brief was to "confirm Israeli withdrawal from Lebanon, restore international peace and security and assist the Lebanese Government in restoring its effective authority in the area."[6] Only the first objective was achieved, for the PLO quickly re-established its entire military infrastructure and more. Although there was a period of relative calm on Israel's northern front, the PLO was actively entrenching its forces in Southern Lebanon where it effectively operated as an autonomous entity. It enhanced its stock of weapons to include not only numerous Katyusha rockets but also long-range artillery.

Troubled by the PLO's renewed ability to organize sorties into Israel and to hit its population centres at will, the Begin government adopted a new approach. Rather than restricting itself to retaliatory raids in response to PLO attacks, it decided to initiate a series of preventive strikes aimed at degrading the enemy's military capacity. On July 10, 1981, the IAF began attacking Palestinian positions in the south of Lebanon, and on July 17 it bombed Palestinian concentrations in Beirut, causing the deaths of over 100 people.[7] In return, the PLO rained down rockets on northern Galilee, hitting the town of Kiryat Shmona and the coastal town of Nahariya. Over a ten-day period, Israelis were subject to PLO bombardments that led to six people being killed and fifty-nine wounded.[8] With, among other things, bomb shelters being in a substandard condition, 40 percent of the residents of Kiryat Shmona fled in search of safety further afield. For those that remained, the IDF took responsibility for ensuring the delivery of essential food supplies.[9] By July 24, through the auspices of Philip Habib, US President Reagan's special advisor, a ceasefire was hammered out whereby the PLO undertook not to launch attacks on Israel from its bases in Lebanon. But, since Israel had not insisted on the PLO not refurbishing its armaments, its townships in the Galilee remained as vulnerable as ever. That induced Begin to consider the need for a large-scale IDF operation to root out the PLO's presence in Southern Lebanon once and for all.

On becoming defence minister in early August 1981, Sharon instructed Amir Drori, the commander of the northern front, to draw up a contingency plan for invading Lebanon by combining two that had previously been prepared. The first, "Little Pines," involved the conquest of Southern Lebanon to include the towns of Tyre and Sidon. The second, "Big Pines," was far more wide-ranging, envisaging the seizure of parts of central Lebanon up to a point just north of the main Beirut–Damascus highway. Sharon harboured a desire to remove the PLO and the Syrians from Lebanon and to ensure that Bachir Gemayel of the Christian Phalangists would become the country's president. Gemayel in turn was expected to sign a peace treaty with Israel and – the icing on the cake – with the PLO so irretrievably routed, a more compliant local Palestinian leadership was expected to emerge that would accept, to Israel's liking, a Palestinian autonomy agreement covering the West Bank and Gaza. The bottom line was that Sharon was planning a military campaign that would seem as if the IDF's objectives were relatively minor, whereas in reality they would be quite extensive. By December 1981, in anticipation of the realization of his schemes, Sharon ordered the IDF to concentrate reinforcements along Israel's northern frontiers.

Sharon was not unique in concocting extravagant notions regarding Lebanon. In 1955, Ben-Gurion, as minister of defence in Moshe Sharett's government, and Dayan, as chief of staff, jointly agreed that, with the cooperation of a Lebanese officer willing to declare himself the saviour of the Christian Maronites, Israel would invade Lebanon and establish a friendly Christian government in territory conquered for that purpose. However, Sharon ought to have heeded the remarks of Sharett, for in his diary he had written that the lack of seriousness exhibited by Ben-Gurion and Dayan in their "approach to the affairs of the neighbouring countries and especially toward the most complicated problem of Lebanon's internal and external situation was simply horrifying."[10]

In the same month of August as Sharon was finalizing his strategy, Arafat convened the PLO's Supreme Military Council in preparation for war. His forces already had in place three infantry brigades, several artillery and supporting units, and a fledging tank battalion.[11] What Arafat primarily had in mind was focusing PLO artillery fire on the enemy's vulnerable population "with an eye to choking off all immigration to Israel."[12] Meanwhile, the PLO began to scour Eastern Europe and North Korea for additional arms. North Korea agreed to provide Katyusha rockets with thirty launching barrels, while Hungary promised a few dozen T-34 tanks. In less than a year, the PLO's artillery capacity increased from 80 to 250 cannons and rocket launchers.[13] It was clearly becoming a growing threat to Israel's security. Nominally, UNIFIL troops were posted in Southern Lebanon to prevent a PLO fighter presence there. But, in line with the UN's generally abysmal record in preserving the peace, the very reason for which it was founded in the first place, UNIFIL not only did nothing of the kind, it even coordinated with PLO military units in the area. In one sector a Norwegian officer concluded an agreement with his PLO counterpart setting out protocols for the disposition and activities of the PLO forces that actually allowed for Palestinian militia to confiscate films taken of them.[14]

In December, by initiating a Knesset motion for Israel to annex the Golan Heights, Begin alienated the US administration, causing President Reagan to suspend military aid.[15] Responding to Reagan's new measures, Begin on December 20 summoned the US ambassador, Samuel Lewis, to his home to give him a dressing down and to tell him that Israel was no US vassal state.[16] As Lewis took his leave he noticed that Sharon, Eitan and a cluster of senior officers bearing large maps were waiting in the entrance hall. It struck Lewis that some military venture was being set in train, for, true enough, Begin had summoned the full cabinet to propose authorizing the IDF to enter Lebanon to seize territory up to the outskirts of Beirut.[17] Advancing reasons for such a venture, Begin argued that violent clashes with Syria could occur at any moment and that, in addition, the PLO had thus far not desisted from harming Israelis and Jews. But in face of a large measure of ministerial opposition, the matter was dropped. Then on January 28, 1982, when six terrorists entered the Jordan Rift Valley settlement of Mehola, Sharon suggested that Israel ought to bombard PLO objectives. Once again, the cabinet was not receptive to any military action, considering that the terrorists entered the West Bank from Jordanian territory and failed to inflict any casualties.

All the while the IDF began gearing up for a large-scale assault to commence the moment a suitable pretext materialized. Yet the PLO failed to oblige. Since the ceasefire agreement of July 1981, it had diligently refrained from initiating terrorist acts originating in Lebanese territory. In the interim, Begin remained hopeful of persuading the cabinet to authorize an immediate and forceful IDF riposte should the PLO revert to its former modus operandi. On clarifying what he intended, Begin claimed that he had only a relatively small-scale operation in mind.

On April 21, the day an IDF officer met his death in Southern Lebanon after his vehicle hit a road mine, Begin ordered the IAF to bomb PLO bases. But, since the PLO remained restrained, Israel had no immediate further choice other than to stay its hand.[18] A couple of weeks later, on May 9, the prospect of war erupting indeed loomed large. For no specific reason other than in reprisal for previously accumulated PLO acts of terror, the IAF took to bombing PLO targets. This time, the PLO reacted by rocketing Kiryat Shmona and other Israeli townships in the Upper Galilee, but as there were no Israeli injuries and a minimal amount of property damage was sustained, the cabinet refused to approve of an extended IDF offensive. However, the cabinet did agree that, should Israel encounter just one more provocation, it would be far more receptive to a vigorous IDF response.[19]

To gauge how the Americans might view an Israeli military offensive against the PLO, Sharon in late May 1982 travelled to the United States to consult with Secretary of State Alexander Haig. What he learnt was that the USA would not censure Israel provided the provocation was serious and significant, and provided that the IDF acted promptly and sharply so as to complete its mission within a short time span. After returning to Israel, Sharon led the cabinet to understand that Haig had given him a green light. In writing to Haig, Begin explained that, in line with an understanding that he believed he had reached with Habib, Israel would not distinguish between a terrorist attack on an Israeli or Jew no matter where it might occur.

Finally, an incident seemingly meeting Israel's quest for a pretext arose in London on June 3, when Shlomo Argov, the Israeli ambassador to the UK, was shot in the head by three Palestinian assailants. Although Argov survived, he was permanently disabled and spent the remaining twenty-one years of his life in hospital. Israeli intelligence agencies realized from the start that the would-be assassins were adherents of Abu Nidal's group, which was not only estranged from the PLO but actively hostile to it.[20] However, that did not trouble Begin. As far as he was concerned, all Palestinian terrorists were de facto PLO members. In the morning of June 4, the Israeli cabinet, with only Yitzhak Berman in opposition, authorized the IAF to bomb PLO positions. At first, Eitan would have liked the IAF to strike at sixteen PLO targets –nine in Beirut and seven in Southern Lebanon – but, fearful of a sharp US rebuke, the number of sites was reduced to five – two in Beirut (the football stadium, used as a PLO munitions dump, and a PLO training centre) and three PLO bases in Southern Lebanon.[21] The IAF attacks commenced just after 3 p.m., and just over two hours later the PLO responded by firing some 500 shells and rockets directed against twenty-nine Israeli settlements near the Lebanese border. Meeting the following evening at the conclusion of the Sabbath, the cabinet approved the launching of operation "Peace for Galilee," meant to free all Israeli settlements from PLO fire emanating in Lebanon. In arguing for the campaign, Begin maintained that "It is quite impossible to cope with the fact that for days on end there would be two categories of state citizens: Citizens in Tel Aviv that live quietly and tranquilly and citizens in Naharia and Kiryat Shmonah that live in bomb shelters. Such a situation cannot be allowed to endure."[22] Furthermore, as was his wont, Begin invoked the lessons of the Holocaust, claiming "The alternative to this is Treblinka and we have decided that there will not be another Treblinka."[23]

To ensure that all northern Israeli towns and settlements would be beyond the range of PLO artillery, Sharon and Eitan explicitly sought approval for the IDF to advance into Lebanese territory up to a distance of 40 kilometres. The only minister who expressed any qualms was Mordechai Zippori, a former brigadier-general. Suggesting that the notion of 40 kilometres was "too abstract," he wanted to know precisely where the finishing lines would be. In addition, he was apprehensive at the prospect of the IDF colliding with Syrian forces, for he believed that the "measures outlined here will bring us into contact with Syrians."[24] At that point another minister wanted to be reassured that Beirut would not be approached. Begin emphatically interjected, "I said we will not attack the Syrians," while Sharon insisted, "Beirut is outside the picture. Operation Peace for Galilee is designed not to capture Beirut."[25] As the meeting concluded, the cabinet members believed that they had merely given the go-ahead to a clearly defined operation of limited extent that was not expected to take more than a day or two days at the utmost. Begin exuded extreme confidence that "The matter would not get out of hand as has happened in past Israeli wars. The Cabinet will meet every day and if need be even a few times per day."[26]

Irrespective of what the cabinet thought, Sharon did not for a moment forego his intention to enter Beirut. If Sharon's intentions were not clear to the cabinet, senior IDF officers on the other hand could not help noticing that the sum of forces mobilized for the operation was far in excess of that required for the securement of a 40-kilometre thrust.[27] Since Sharon needed to maintain the illusion of merely initiating a less ambitious project, the IDF perforce had to adopt a sub-optimal means of attack. Instead of leapfrogging troops by landing them at the enemy's rear along the Beirut–Damascus highway, thus saving time and lives, the IDF had to confront the opposition face on, slowly pushing its way forward from the south to the north.[28]

Zero hour for the operation was set for 11 a.m. on the following Sunday, June 6. In the meanwhile, without Begin's full knowledge, tanks, artillery and paratroopers led by Amos Yaron were sent by sea to land at a site beyond the 40-kilometre limit between Sidon and Damour, just north of the Awali River.[29] Elsewhere, the ground forces entering Lebanon on June 6 proceeded along three principal axes. The 91st Division, commanded by Yizhak Mordechai, moved up the coastal road with the intention of linking up with Yaron and his men. The 36th Division, led by Avigdor Kahalani, entered Lebanon from the Galilee panhandle heading in a northwest direction, to join Mordechai's division as it neared Sidon from the south. Finally, the 162nd Division, under Menahem Einan's command, advanced due north with its sights on the Beirut–Damascus highway. All told, the force that the IDF amassed was considerable. It incorporated over 75,000 men, 1,240 tanks, 1,520 armoured troop carriers, and a large bulk of the IAF and navy.[30]

When the cabinet met on June 6, it was presented with plans for a thrust by Einan's division up the central axis through the Shouf Mountains to the Beirut–Damascus highway and then to veer eastwards to outflank a large proportion of Syrian troops stationed in Lebanon. The underlying assumption of the move was that, once the Syrians felt threatened, they would force the Palestinians out from the region under their control, to forestall a clash with the IDF. Mesmerized by the audacity of it all, Begin exclaimed: "It is a tactic worthy of Hannibal," and gave it his seal of approval despite the fact that it meant that the IDF would both advance beyond 40 kilometres and almost inevitably find itself engaging Syrian forces.[31]

Within half an hour of being in Lebanese territory, Mordechai's lead unit, commanded by Eli Geva, encountered a PLO ambush that it repelled. On approaching Tyre, Geva decided to bypass the town, but it took the follow-up units four days to subdue Tyre's refugee camps. The fighting was bitter and fierce, as the Israelis had to contend with determined forces armed with rifles and rocket-propelled grenades (RPGs) firing from well-prepared trenches and bunkers. Hundreds of Palestinians were slain, while the IDF lost twenty-one men and suffered the wounding of ninety-five others.[32] Eventually Geva's men reached the outskirts of Sidon, which they skirted by taking a hilly route to the east, from which, on June 9, they finally linked up with Yaron's forces awaiting them by the Awali River.

That same morning, Sidon was taken care of by a unit of para-troopers backed by armour, artillery and air support. That meant that virtually the entire coastal road, from the border with Israel to Sidon, had been cleared. The only serious remaining obstacles were the Ein al Hilwe refugee camp south of Sidon and the city's Kasbah. It took three days of horrendous fighting to capture the Kasbah and a full week to subdue the refugee camp, where IDF soldiers advanced tenta-tively from alley to alley and house to house while the camp was being pounded by artillery shells, reducing most of it to rubble. Meanwhile, Yaron's troops began edging up along the coast towards Beirut, while Geva's men took to nearby hills to the east to approach positions over-looking the capital city.

In the central sector of Lebanon, Einan's troops made headway, reaching on June 8 the town of Jezzine, to which Syria had dispatched a brigade. Intending to capture the town, a company of Israeli tanks paused at its outskirts while another proceeded to traverse its main thoroughfare. As the Israelis made headway they were assaulted from all sides by a torrent of RPGs. Nonetheless, they were able to emerge from the other end, destroying in the process three Syrian tanks. The fortunes of the other IDF company that had remained stationary were not so auspicious. Syrian commanders attacked it with Sagger rockets, taking out three of its tanks. However, the Israelis ultimately prevailed.

The Syrian forces withdrew to the Beqaa Valley, where they increased their disposition of SAM missile batteries from fourteen to nineteen. At the time, Begin had no idea that such a battle was raging and, when eventually he was informed, he was led to understand that it arose as a result of a Syrian initiative.[33]

Later the same day the Syrians succeeded in blocking Einan's advances just as his troops reached the outskirts of Ein Zahalta, some 6.5 kilometres short of the Beirut–Damascus highway. There his men remained until June 11, when an American-sponsored ceasefire, brought about by hints of a pending Russian involvement, took effect. With his tanks perched on a narrow mountain road from which they could not deviate, Einan's forces were not well placed to dent the Syrian offensive.

With respect to the existence of the Syrian SAM missile batteries in the eastern part of Lebanon, Sharon was adamant that they had to be extirpated. Knowing that the cabinet would not take kindly to such a suggestion – for, after all, Begin had previously assured his ministers that Operation Peace for Galilee would not entail clashes with Syria – he carefully chose the moment to broach the subject. That moment arose when Einan's forces were subject to a vigorous Syrian attack. Sharon spelt out the urgent need for the IAF to relieve the pressure on Einan's beleaguered men, but, in order for them to be able to do so, Syria's missile system had first to be neutralized. Not wishing to hinder the IDF's efforts to save Israeli lives, the cabinet approved an IAF strike against Syria's SAM batteries. It did so without knowing that the chief of staff and the head of the IAF were anything but enthusiastic about Sharon's proposal, for neither were they present nor were their reservations drawn to the cabinet ministers' attention.[34]

On Wednesday June 9, within a two-hour period, seventeen of the nineteen missile installations were completely destroyed. The next day the remaining two were eliminated, as were four more rushed in as replacements. To ward off the attack, the Syrian air force threw into the arena some 100 MiGs to face a similar number of Israeli planes, and the resulting air battle became one of the biggest in post-World War II history. Israel's air supremacy was startlingly evident: twenty-nine Syrian planes were downed without the IAF incurring a single loss.[35]

Shortly after the culmination of the Israeli–Syrian air battle, a large contingent led by Avigdor Ben Gal made a dash on Einan's eastern flank for the Beirut–Damascus highway. En route, it locked horns with Syria's First Division, dealing it a crippling blow, but Syrian reinforcements rushed in at the last moment to stall the Israelis. Somehow or other, a task force of Ben Gal's forces, commanded by Yossi Peled, managed to reach Kab Elias, nearly 5 kilometres from the coveted highway, but, like Einan's unit, it too was stopped dead in its tracks because of the imposed ceasefire.

Despite it all, the IDF ultimately did reach its northern objective. Yaron's men, who had taken the mountainous route east of the coast, pushed through to the Phalangist stronghold at Basaba, 13 kilometres from Beirut. From that position, ignoring the ceasefire, they pounced onto the Beirut–Damascus highway, and by June 24 they controlled a reasonable section of it.

Meanwhile, on June 10, when the IDF was already on Beirut's doorstep and was pressing in on that city, Sharon casually informed credulous cabinet ministers that the IDF had "explicit instructions not to enter or in any way operate within Beirut."[36] Sharon would have preferred leaving the routing of Beirut and the PLO command structure within it to the Phalangists, who had initially undertaken to do so; however, when it came to the crunch, Gemayel would not commit himself. By June 13, the day that Yaron's men reached Ba'abda, which housed the presidential palace and which was effectively an outer suburb of Beirut, Begin had no idea of the presence of Israeli forces there. His denial was broadcast on the Israeli state radio, and only when speaking to Habib did he discover the truth.[37] At first, Begin refused to believe Habib. He asked his military secretary, Azriel Nevo, to contact Sharon, and when he received a reassuring answer he told Habib that he was wrong. But Habib insisted that his information had been derived from a reliable source. Nevo was then asked to contact Eitan, and after speaking to a duty officer at general staff headquarters Nevo returned to confirm Habib's assertions, leaving Begin in a state of acute embarrassment.[38]

As for Arafat, when told by one of his officers that he had espied Israeli armoured personnel carriers pouring into Ba'abda, he replied, "Are you mad?"[39] But by June 14, accepting that he was indeed encircled by the Israelis, Arafat decided that, rather than negotiate a safe exit for himself and his men, he would sit out the siege. With the PLO in

Beirut amply stocked with armaments, food and medicine, the war in Lebanon had entered a new and fatal stage that was to be drawn out and costly, for, until mid-August, Beirut was routinely subject to IDF shelling and the gradual penetration of Israeli land forces.

Eventually, in light of the PLO's precarious situation and the general civilian tribulations emanating from the siege, Arafat accepted that he ought to negotiate an honourable exit. Habib served as an intermediary. At the beginning of July Habib had formulated a proposal that would facilitate a PLO withdrawal involving two stages. At first, the PLO would concentrate in refugee camps in South Beirut, where they would hand over their heavy weapons to the Lebanese army, while the IDF would remove its forces to positions between 5 to 10 kilometres from the city. Thereafter, the PLO would leave Beirut. Although the Israelis were not averse to that proposal, they deferred to the strong objections voiced both by Gemayal and the Lebanese president, Elias Sarkis, who feared that the PLO would pass on their weapons to the leftist militia in Beirut.[40]

Tiring of the negotiating process, Sharon, at a defence ministry meeting on July 11, insisted that within a week the IDF was to attack the refugee camps in the southern part of West Beirut so as not to leave "a single terrorist neighbourhood standing."[41] As the matter was deliberated upon, it became evident that not all those present were in accord with Sharon's approach. The general consensus was that there were three options on the table: negotiations could still be pursued, the area could be bombed, or a ground offensive could be launched. In choosing the last, Sharon presented it to the cabinet for its approval, avoiding mention of the other two options on the grounds that "the cabinet has enough problems to deal with."[42] Most cabinet members were inclined to go along with Sharon's proposal, but since a sizeable minority opposed it Begin withheld his authorization.[43]

A few days later, Sharon instructed Drori to draft a plan for the conquest of West Beirut. On dutifully briefing a group of brigade commanders, Drori talked in terms of having the mission completed within forty-eight hours. That met with skepticism from most of the commanders, who felt that it could not be accomplished in less than ten days and then at a needless loss of life. Then, even though the plan was aborted, Geva, who had become so disenchanted with the way

Operation Peace for the Galilee had unfolded, offered to relinquish his brigade commission while staying on as a tank commander. After being interviewed by Eitan and then Sharon, he was finally shunted to Begin, to whom he predicted that a ground offensive in West Beirut would result in a high number of casualties. For his pains, shortly after meeting with Begin, Geva was notified that his services with the IDF were no longer required.

With unrelenting determination to break the back of PLO resistance, Sharon at July's end chose to activate a combination of more intensive air-bombing runs and a gradual process of enlarging the IDF's presence within the peripheral areas of West Beirut. On August 1, the runways of Beirut Airport were captured, and by August 5 the IDF had advanced to the edge of the Palestinian neighbourhoods.[44] In a final effort to bring the war to an end, Habib on August 10 presented to the Israelis a document specifying terms for a PLO evacuation of Beirut. After the cabinet approved Habib's document in principle, Sharon used the IDF as a lever in an attempt to thwart its implementation. On August 12 he ordered the IAF to conduct a massive attack on Beirut accompanied by an equally devastating artillery bombardment. For eleven hours the residents of West Beirut went through a living hell in which an estimated 300 people were killed.[45] Cabinet members were so mortified that, at a hastily convened session, Sharon was severely censured and was no longer given authority to activate the air force on his own initiative. Furthermore, all future military operations involving artillery and the navy supposedly conducted to defend IDF soldiers were to obtain prior cabinet clearance.[46]

Ironically, the extensive carnage caused by Sharon's directive led Arafat to change his mind. On the night of August 12, he informed Habib that he was now willing, despite his earlier reservations, to agree to the PLO leaving Beirut. By August 21, with much fanfare and bursts of firing in the air in celebration of a Palestinian "victory," the PLO evacuation commenced. At the same time, an international force of US and French troops entered Beirut to guarantee security to the departing PLO personnel.[47] All told, around 14,000 fighters and their families were involved, with most leaving by sea to assume residence in various Arab countries. Of such countries, Tunisia became the host state for the PLO leadership.[48]

As already mentioned, Sharon had hoped that the war in Lebanon would result in Gemayel becoming president and then signing a peace treaty with Israel. The first part was realized. With both the IDF's heavy-handed prodding and American backing, Gemayel, on August 23, did indeed secure the presidency. He was the only candidate. However, he did not deliver on formally making peace with Israel. Meeting with Begin and Sharon in the northern Israeli coastal town of Nahariya on September 1, Gemayel refused to comply unless there was a Lebanese consensus in its favour. Given the nature of Lebanon's population, that condition was most unlikely to be met. For Gemayel to become an effective and enduring president of Lebanon, he could not afford to antagonize the country's Muslim and Druze communities, a factor that both Begin and Sharon seemed to have overlooked. Both Begin and Sharon were riled by Gemayel who, in turn, as an ardent Lebanese nationalist, took offence both at their overbearing way of addressing him and at their assertions that the IDF would remain on Lebanese soil until a peace treaty was concluded. Gemayel came away from the meeting in a depressed state of mind, hurt by the forceful tone of Begin's exhortations.[49]

Under other circumstances Begin might well have been more conciliatory, but during that encounter he was burdened by two weighty matters. First, he had just received a letter from Reagan spelling out his new initiative on the Middle East, which entailed moving rapidly to awarding full autonomy to the Palestinians of the West Bank and Gaza that could have paved the way for the eventual establishment of a sovereign Palestinian State. Begin was so incensed by it that he rejected it out of hand. Second, the war in Lebanon, having proceeded far further than envisaged, and having cost far more IDF lives and casualties than were bargained for, was being seen by a growing number of Israelis in a most critical light. In order to show that it had all been worthwhile, Begin desperately needed to be able to flourish an Israeli–Lebanese peace treaty before their eyes. Israel had provided large sums in economic and military aid to the Phalangists, had trained many of their troops, and had even come to their rescue when they were in desperate straits. All that was done after receiving firm promises from Gemayel that not only would his militia play an active role in combating the PLO, he would also, on becoming president, sue for peace. Accordingly, Begin found Gemayel's subsequent prevarications totally unacceptable.

On September 14, Gemayel was assassinated. He and twenty-six of his associates were killed by a bomb detonated by a Syrian agent at the Phalangist headquarters. In the wake of Gemayal's assassination the situation went from bad to worse. On September 15, to the surprise of cabinet ministers, who first heard about it on Israel Radio,[50] the IDF made its presence felt in the western part of Beirut, where it encountered a residue of PLO fighters firing on IDF troops from Palestinian refugee camps (the international US–French force had already withdrawn from the city). Included in their arsenal were rifles, machine guns, RPGs and bazookas. At first General Drori appealed to the Lebanese armed forces to maintain order in the camps but, on the basis of a directive from their prime minister, they refused.

The next morning, Reagan's special ambassador to the Middle East, Morris Draper, approached Sharon to demand, on the president's behalf, that the IDF withdraw its forces from Beirut. Citing a letter from Begin assuring Reagan that the IDF would not enter Beirut, Draper complained that Israel had reneged on its commitment. To that Sharon replied: "When the promise was given, the situation was different."[51] Paying little heed to US concerns, Sharon instructed Eitan to subcontract the task of pacifying the refugee camps to the Phalangists. Eitan warned Sharon that the Phalangists are "thirsting for revenge and that there could be torrents of blood."[52] But Sharon was unmoved.

There were reasons enough to suppose that the Phalangists would not conduct themselves with any moral propriety. Shortly before their entry into West Beirut, Jesse Sokar, one of their commanders, invited Ze'ev Schiff, a correspondent of *Haaretz*, to accompany him and his men as they embarked on their mission. After advising Schiff to learn how to use a knife, he went on to mention that, according to his standards, "no rape of girls under the age of twelve is allowed."[53] By mid-afternoon of September16, Yaron, who had occupied a position on the roof of a six-storey building overlooking the Shatila refugee camp, bade farewell to Elie Hobeika, a Phalangist officer, as he went off with his 150-man unit. In Yaron's departing words to Hobeika, he pleaded with him not to harm any civilians. Yaron's division intelligence officer tried to monitor their movements, but they soon dropped out of sight among Shatila's narrow alleys. As darkness fell, the Phalangists requested and received illumination from Israeli-fired flares. At 7 p.m.

Yaron's adjutant heard Hobeika on the radio network admonishing one of his subordinates for asking what he should do with the fifty women and children under his control. Hobeika's words were: "That's the last time you're going to ask me. You know what to do."[54] Sounds of raucous laughter stemming from fellow Phalangists in Hobeika's company could be heard in the background.[55]

While all this was going on, Begin, who had not yet been informed by Sharon that the IDF had delegated the Phalangists to enter the refugee camps, was reassuring his cabinet colleagues who had expressed concern about the IDF's presence in Beirut that it was necessary in the interest of safeguarding the lives of innocent civilians. Then, in the course of the meeting, Sharon, holding a bulletin he had just received, read out: "A large Phalangist unit has made its way into the Sabra and Shatila camps and is combing through them."[56] Apparently, no one in the cabinet followed through with either questions or comments. But, as the meeting was about to close, David Levy could no longer contain himself. Taking the floor, he declared: "When I hear that the Phalangists are entering a certain neighbourhood I am cognizant of the significance of revenge to them, such slaughter. No one would believe that we went in to ensure order there and the indictment would be leveled against us."[57] Levy might just as well have spoken to the wall, for no one stirred or replied.

The next day (September 17), despite the IDF's military intelligence gaining knowledge that up to 300 Palestinians had been killed in the two refugee camps, the information was not forwarded to Begin. By chance Schiff heard about the story and passed it on to the minister of communications, Mordechai Tzipori. Tzipori in turn contacted the foreign minister, Yitzhak Shamir, asking him to look into the matter through sources of his own, but Shamir was unwilling to do so. As the day wore on, the local Phalangist commander secured a tractor from Eitan, ostensibly for demolishing "unlicensed" buildings. Eitan had a shrewd idea that, in reality, the tractor was needed for no good purpose, but he chose not to press the point. By the evening he nonetheless telephoned Sharon to tell him that the Phalangists had "overdone it" and that he had issued orders to remove them from the camps.[58] On September 18, although it was a Saturday and Begin was known to be an observant Jew, he listened on the radio to the BBC news. Much to his horror, he heard that hundreds of the two refugee camp residents, including women and children, had been slaughtered. He immediately contacted Sharon, who, even though he had been told about it the night before, denied all prior knowledge. Sharon promised to secure a full report from the IDF, but the killings continued both during the rest of that day and the day after.[59]

With the ultimate death toll reaching between 700 and 800, Israel was universally pilloried. Caught off-guard, the Israeli government tried to absolve itself from any blame by issuing a statement that was less than truthful. It falsely claimed that the Phalangists had entered the camps in question without the IDF's prior approval, and as soon as it became known where they were they were swiftly evicted. Such a demonstrably misleading account exacerbated Israel's international standing, while internally a substantial number of people were appalled. On September 25, under the auspices of the Peace Now Movement, a protest rally of possibly up to 400,000 demonstrators (the largest gathering in Israel's history) assembled in Tel Aviv.[60] Strong calls were made for a commission of inquiry and, while he was opposed to the idea, faced with a potential coalition crisis, Begin relented. Three days later the government established one to be chaired by Yitzhak Kahan, the president of the Supreme Court. Its other two members were Aharon Barak, now a Supreme Court judge, and Major-General Yona Efrat, and its brief was to determine the events leading up to and giving rise to the Sabra and Shatila massacres.

Meanwhile, in Lebanon on September 23, Bachir Gemayel's brother Amin succeeded him as president. At first Amin distanced himself from the Israelis by refusing to meet with any Israeli official. But, deferring to the USA, he agreed to negotiate a peace treaty with Israel, which was concluded on May 17, 1983. Then on March 5, 1984, after the US marines had withdrawn and Israel began pulling out, Gemayal, now subject to inexorable Syrian pressures, abrogated the peace treaty.

Israel in the Wake of the Lebanese War

On February 8, 1983, the Kahan Commission's report was released. It found that the direct responsibility for the massacres rested on Phalangist forces that were "steeped in hatred for the Palestinians."[61]

The commission determined that there was no evidence of any IDF personnel being involved and that notions to that effect "are completely groundless and constitute a baseless libel."[62] Furthermore, it rejected assertions that Israeli soldiers could see or hear what was happening. As far as the commission was concerned, soldiers from the roof of the forward command post "neither saw the actions of the Phalangists nor heard any sounds indicating that a massacre was in progress." But Israel was not entirely exculpated, for the commission concluded that it had an indirect and moral responsibility for the killings on account of their being foreseeable. Apart from rebuking Begin, Shamir, Eitan, Drori and Yehoshua Saguy, head of IDF intelligence, Kahan and his colleagues singled out Sharon "for having disregarded the dangers of acts of vengeance and bloodshed by the Phalangists against the population of the refugee camps and for having failed to take this danger into account." Sharon, in their view, by not fulfilling a duty of care, was deemed unfit to continue holding the defence portfolio. As they reasoned, he ought to "draw the appropriate personal conclusions" and, failing that, the prime minister ought to remove him from office.[63] After both Sharon and Begin refused to budge, it took another Peace Now demonstration, in which one of the participants, Emil Grunzweig, was killed and ten others injured by a grenade thrown by a government supporter, to persuade them to change their minds. Sharon agreed to step down as minister of defence, to remain in the cabinet as a minister without portfolio. He was replaced by Arens, who was recalled from Washington.

When the IDF invaded Lebanon it met with passive support, if not encouragement, from Amal, then the largest Shiite militia, which was also at odds with the PLO. But, as the war progressed, the Iranian regime nurtured a more extremist Islamic rival to Amal which took the name of Hezbollah. Endowed with a never ending flow of finance and arms from its sponsor, Hezbollah, by providing its recruits with generous monthly allowances, by establishing a general welfare system for its followers, and by offering what seemed a more authentic Islamic way of life and religious piety, attracted adherents in droves. It soon overshadowed Amal and led the way in an armed guerrilla struggle to rid Lebanon of Israel. By the end of August the IDF withdrew from the Shouf Mountains to reassemble along the Awali River. In the wake of the IDF's departure, Druze militia ferociously struck at the Maronites in the Shouf, destroying sixty of their villages and killing 1,000 of them.[64]

As the above described events unfolded, the Israeli government underwent a change of leadership. At the end of August Begin announced his intention to resign. From then on, he closeted himself at home and no longer appeared in public. By not actually submitting his resignation to the state president, Begin left the cabinet in limbo. After securing the Herut party nomination to succeed him, Shamir had to wait until he was officially able to assume the premiership. Fortunately the matter was resolved by September 15, and by October 10 Shamir headed a cabinet similar in composition to the previous one.

The Israeli withdrawal from Beirut once again afforded the Syrians access to that city, and in the process their influence over the country was restored. Hezbollah cadres became increasingly aggressive. On October 23 they bombed two separate buildings housing US marines and French soldiers killing 299 of them. For both the USA and France, it was a terrible blow. As the correspondents of *Time* magazine reflected, the marines "represented an antidote to fanaticism – and fanaticism had brought them down."[65] Ten days later a Hezbollah suicide bomber succeeded in blowing up a building in Tyre used as regional headquarters by the IDF. Thirty Israelis were killed. By February 1984, a combined Druze and Shiite force moved into Beirut, causing the Lebanese army to disintegrate and leaving Amin Gemayal isolated in the presidential palace at Ba'abda.

Save for the PLO removal from Southern Lebanon and Beirut, all Sharon's grandiose schemes came to naught. Syria resumed control of key strategic Lebanese areas, the undermining of the Phalangists left no possibility of an enduring Israeli–Lebanese peace treaty ever being attained and, more ominously, the southern part of the country was in the process of becoming a Shiite springboard for attacks on Israel. As for Begin, he was overwhelmed by all the suffering resulting from the war and by the loss in November 1982 of his wife, Aliza. He lived the life of a recluse, emerging from his apartment only to visit Aliza's grave. In a Shakespearian denouement, the war in Lebanon left, in addition to Begin, all the other main players as victims. Sharon was no longer defence minister, Bachir Gemayel had been assassinated, Arafat had been deported and Haig, who had seemingly given Sharon a green light, had been dismissed. But in truth the real victims from Israel's point of view were the 368 IDF soldiers killed in the fighting up to the departure from Beirut, plus another 148 who died during the IDF's first year in occupying Lebanese territory. To that one might add the 2,800 Israelis who were wounded.[66] Putting such figures into relative perspective, if the USA had suffered the same proportionate losses, it would have encountered 32,460 dead and 168,380 wounded in what amounted to six weeks of combat and a year of occupation.[67]

The course that the war took was not one that the government intended. Rather it was orchestrated by Sharon who, by stealth, assumed the role, if not of prime minister, then prime mover. Step by step, he elicited government member support for a project that most would have regarded as anathema, by feeding them with partial information and faits accomplis and by capitalizing on the fog of war, with the irresistible but sometimes specious argument that, unless they acceded to his requests, Israeli soldiers' lives would be put in jeopardy. Misgivings among high-ranking officers were not brought to the attention of the cabinet, and the Labour opposition and the general press did not provide a serious counterweight to Sharon's wheedling, rising to the occasion only after things were patently going awry. No small part of the problem was that the cabinet had no independent means of assessing Sharon's piecemeal proposals and evaluating them in terms of possible alternatives.

The war in Lebanon was also in part responsible for the severe economic upsets plaguing Israel in 1982 and 1983. In 1982, with inflation still rampant and running at an annual rate of 132 percent, per capita GNP fell by 0.2 percent. Previously there had been only one other year when per capita GNP fell, and that was 1953. Then in 1983 per capita GNP fell even further, by another 2 percent. To shore up its growing budgetary deficit, the government raised income taxes, levies (one of which was for Operation Peace for Galilee) and loans. By early 1983, a stock market crash led to a host of bankruptcies and individual savings losses. Only the banks held out as a seemingly safe investment haven.

In August 1983 with the government incapable of warding off inflation, rumours began to circulate that plans were afoot to link the prices of all goods sold in Israel to the US dollar. Already prices for many durable products and real estate were being quoted in US dollars. That made Israelis anxious to acquire dollars or dollar accounts to hedge against shekel devaluations. To finance such acquisitions, people began divesting themselves of shares, which caused the stock market to crash. This time the banks were no longer immune, and many individual and institutional investors experienced massive capital losses. For a while stock exchange transactions were frozen. In an attempt to bolster the public's confidence in the country's banks, the government gave a guarantee to investors committing themselves to holding bank shares for a five-year period that it would stand ready to redeem such shares at the same real dollar value that they attained on the first day of the resumption of share trading, based on the exchange rate that existed before the crisis. Such a guarantee involved a government commitment of $7 billion. To amass the necessary funds, the government resorted to augmenting the money supply, which further fuelled an inflation now heading towards an annual rate of 200 percent. A 1,000 shekel note was issued, and foreign currency purchases were severely restricted. Even so, the inflationary tide gathered force, reaching 400 percent in 1984.

At the end of March 1984 Shamir, confronted with a roaring inflation rate and general monetary problems, in agreement with Peres as leader of the Maarah, arranged for a general election to be scheduled for the following July, over a year earlier than was legally mandatory. The election announcement led to the formation of new parties (or lists) and to general political realignments. Within the Maarah, the two long-standing rivals for its leadership, Peres and Rabin, reached an understanding that, in the event of the party forming a government, Peres would be prime minister and Rabin foreign minister. Eitan, no longer chief of staff, organized a group called Tzomet (Crossroads) drawn primarily from Labour veterans of the Movement for the Complete Land of Israel. Tzomet stood for the separation of religion from the state and for offering peace for peace, rather than land for peace. It entered into an electoral alliance with Tehiya, which lost a section of its settler supporters who in turn, along with deserters from Mafdal (Israel Religious Party), established the Morasha (Heritage) Party. Weizman, having left Likud, assembled his own list, named Yahad (Together). Telem changed its name to Ometz (Bravery), and, at the eleventh hour, God-fearing Jews from the Mizrahi Jewish community, who had previously been members either of Agudat Yisrael or of Tami (a Mizrahi Haredi party), created a party of their own that became known as Shas.

The detailed results of the election are listed in the Appendix. The Likud suffered heavy losses, foregoing seven seats to retain only forty-one. Maarah also performed poorly, with its Knesset representation receding from forty-seven to forty-four. Likud was in no position to head a government, and the Maarah could potentially do so only if it secured the support both of Kach, represented by the lone voice of Meir Kahane, whose extreme chauvinistic views were almost universally regarded as being abominable, and of the Progressive List for Peace, whose two Knesset members had at best an ambivalent attitude to the existence of a Jewish State. Under such circumstances, Peres was not prepared to seek a mandate from the president to govern. After lengthy negotiations, the two leading parties agreed on a formula enabling them to share power. Peres would head the unity government, while Shamir would be foreign minister for the first two years; thereafter they would switch roles for the remaining two years. Rabin by contrast would serve as defence minister for the full four-year term. To obviate any of the two major parties forcing through a decision with the support of the minor ones, it was determined that all important issues would be arrived at by an inner cabinet consisting of five members each of the Maarah and Likud. With all that settled, the new government was formally instated on September 13, 1984. A by-product of the power-sharing arrangement was that the Mapam Party withdrew from the Maarah on the grounds that it would have no truck with any partnership with Likud, given the latter's initiation of the War in Lebanon and its disastrous management of the economy.

Within a few months the new government decided to withdraw the IDF from almost all of Lebanon except for a small southern security strip, where the Christian-run Army of South Lebanon held sway with Israeli backing. The IDF withdrawal commenced at the beginning of 1985 and was essentially concluded by mid-year, by which time only a relatively small IDF contingent remained. Although that rear-guard had to cope with the occasional Hezbollah raid, it suffered relatively small casualties. In Israel there was now a general feeling that the Lebanese nightmare was finally over.[68]

However, another Israeli nightmare continued to haunt the country, and that was the nightmare of inflation. As already mentioned, by 1984 it had reached a rate of 400 percent, and in the first half of 1985 it showed no sign of diminishing. By July the government took the bull by the horns. It devalued the shekel by 20 percent and decreed that prices, wages and the exchange rate were to be frozen over the next three months. Inspectors began monitoring price movements and the public was urged not only to fall into line but also to report any infringements. Thanks to the public's cooperation (an unusual feat in Israel) inflation was finally reined in. In the following two years it fell to 24 percent and then to 16 percent. Nevertheless, the sudden arrest of inflation put strains on the economy. Enterprises ran at reduced profit levels and many went bankrupt, causing a rise in unemployment.[69]

A government coalition based on a partnership between two opposing parties is usually fraught with friction, and the Shamir–Peres alliance proved to be no exception. After Shamir assumed the premiership on October 20, 1986, Peres pursued objectives over which they were in disagreement. The main bone of contention centred on Israel's policy with respect to the convening of an international conference to resolve outstanding issues between Israel and its neighbours, including the Palestinians. Shamir, who was against such a gathering, made it clear that his government would have no part of it. Peres, ignoring Shamir's ruling and his insistence that all diplomatic efforts to further an international conference be put on hold, carried on regardless. Shamir then circumvented the Foreign Ministry and its ambassador in the USA by dispatching Arens to Washington to explain to Secretary of State Shultz that it was pointless for the Americans to consider such an enterprise, since Shamir's participation would not be forthcoming.[70] Meanwhile, in the international arena, Peres spoke derisively about Shamir by suggesting that he was thwarting the peace process. In the end, the climate of opinion in Israel shifted somewhat towards Shamir's policy of depriving the PLO of involvement in any prospective Palestinian delegation and of resisting pressures brought upon Israel into making concessions that might adversely affect its security. Consequently, Shamir's political stock rose slightly in comparison with that of Peres.[71]

With the term of the government of rotational prime ministers drawing to a close, a general election was set for November 1, 1988. As can be seen in the Appendix, while Likud lost a seat, bringing its total to forty, the Maarah slipped from forty-four to thirty-nine mandates. Aggregating all the religious parties, all of which are usually inclined to support Likud, it is notable that, by increasing their representation of Knesset members from twelve to eighteen, they had become a far more formidable bloc. On this occasion Shamir, who could have assembled a government without the Maarah, chose to form a national unity coalition with it in which he was to be the exclusive prime minister. His reasoning was that, if he acceded to the outlandish demands of the religious and more right-wing minor parties, he would alienate many of his own supporters. Shamir's new government, inaugurated on December 22, 1988, contained five parties – Likud, Maarah, Shas, Mafdal and Agudat Yisrael. The Foreign Ministry went to Arens and Rabin remained minster of defence, while Peres had to make do with being minister of finance. Crucial decisions were to be determined by an inner cabinet of six Likud and six Maarah ministers.

A few weeks later Rabin suggested pacifying the Palestinians caught up in their intifada (see below) by offering them an election to set up a representative body to negotiate some form of autonomy with the government. Shamir gave Rabin his blessing provided the intifada was brought to a close. But, despite the fact that Rabin had released from captivity Faisal Husseini, a prominent West Bank Palestinian, and eased restrictions affecting the Palestinian populace, the Palestinians were adamant that they would not agree to the holding of any election while remaining under Israeli occupation.[72] Although Shamir seemed to have endorsed Rabin's approach, some crucial differences surfaced relating to the voting rights of Palestinians living in Jerusalem and as to whether the elections were meant to be municipal or general ones. Papering over such differences, a proposition known as the Shamir–Rabin proposal was submitted to cabinet for its approval. Twenty ministers were for it and six against. Among the naysayers were Sharon, Levy and Yitzhak Moda'i, who formed a cabal to neutralize what they saw as an inappropriate peace initiative.[73] In turn they submitted four demands of their own: the end of the intifada as a sine qua non for negotiating Palestinian elections, the continued expansion of settlements, an Israeli declaration that it would not accept any foreign (i.e. non-Israeli) sovereignty over the West Bank, and that there should be neither a Palestinian State nor any negotiations with the PLO. Bearing down on Shamir from another source was the United States, which sought three assurances of its own, namely the international supervision of any Palestinian election, the extension of the franchise to Jerusalem residents and the absence of restrictions on electoral propaganda. US Secretary of State James Baker also added that he expected a halt in settlement construction and the reopening of Palestinian schools. In response to such conflicting pressures, Shamir, in association with Arens, met with Palestinians known to be PLO supporters in an attempt to impress the USA, but instead merely incurred the wrath of the settlers.

By August 1989 the Egyptian president, Hosni Mubarak, came up with the idea of a trilateral conference in Cairo involving the Egyptians, Israelis and Palestinians to resolve all outstanding issues relating to the Palestinian elections. Among the preconditions for such an event was an understanding that both Palestinians living in Jerusalem and those who had been deported could be included in the Palestinian delegation. As far as Shamir was concerned, that was totally out of the question. Challenging Shamir, Peres in October pressed for a cabinet vote to accept Mubarak's stipulations, but he did not obtain the necessary numbers. It was at that point that Baker became more proactive, formulating a five-point plan of his own. Not wishing to offend the Americans, Shamir cautiously indicated a willingness to give serious consideration to Baker's proposals. That in turn provoked a fierce backlash from both Likud Knesset members and the extreme right-wing parliamentary groups, making Shamir sense that his hold over his party was being undermined. Accordingly, he reverted to his previously held negative position concerning the procedural arrangements for convening the conference. In early March 1990, the Likud government ministers announced that they would attend the conference in Cairo only if Baker stated that, in relation to both the Palestinian delegation and the ultimate elections, Palestinians living in Jerusalem would not participate. Baker tersely responded by demanding that, without further ado, the Israeli government should indicate once and for all whether or not it was going to attend.

Baker's dictate set off a whirl of events within Israel. Maarah Knesset members toyed with the idea of toppling the government. Shamir in turn announced that he was dismissing Peres, thus precipitating the Maarah's withdrawal from the government. Then, on March 15, the

Maarah proposed a Knesset resolution expressing no confidence in the government that was carried by a vote of sixty in favour as opposed to fifty-five against. With the government's downfall Peres was given the brief to head an alternative administration. He thought that he could count on the support of Shas members, who had absented themselves from the confidence vote, but once Rabbi Elazar Shach, the sage of Degel Hatorah (a Haredi party), decreed that it would be sacrilege to enter into an alliance with the Maarah, whose kibbutz members he termed "rabbit eaters," Rabbi Ovadia Yosef, Shas's patron and ultimate authority, felt constrained not to affront his esteemed cleric.[74] In short, Peres had finally to concede that he was incapable of forming a government with a commanding Knesset majority. The ball was then passed back to Shamir, who, with much coaxing, managed to bring under his wing Knesset members such as Moda'i, who had been on the verge of striking a deal with Peres, plus those from Tzomet, Moledet, Degel Hatorah and Tehiya whom he did not previously wish to include. Shamir's new government came to light on June 11, 1990. Arens became minister of defence, David Levy (who could not speak English) became foreign minister and Sharon took over the portfolio of housing and construction, which he used as a vehicle for settlement expansion.

During the 1980s there was a vast increase in the number of Israelis living in newly formed settlements in the occupied territories. Excluding those in East Jerusalem and its environs, the number of settlers rose from 2,500 in 1975 to 60,000 in 1985.[75] Among the new settlers were many who were motivated less by religious or national ideologies and more by economic considerations. Thanks to large government subventions, they could acquire far more commodious homes at prices that fell below those of smaller units within Israel proper.

Israel's Radical Right

The radical right as a distinct political movement never attained mass membership. In its heyday in the late 1980s its disparate groups secured only seven Knesset seats. But like, say, the radical Marxist left in the UK, its influence was far greater than its proportional representation. That was so since many within the ranks of the Likud, such as Sharon, and within the ranks of the National Religious Party (Mafdal), while not always in agreement with their methods, were sympathetic to their objectives and subscribed to the essence of their ideology. By 1988, for example, the political platform of Mafdal read like a Gush Emunim pamphlet.[76] Contrary to the way it has been perceived by the Israeli left, the mainstream radical right was not inclined towards fascism. But, while it has had no national socialist colouration, its compliance with the rulings of democratically elected governments had not been unconditional. It has been antipathetic to the Palestinians and Israel's Arab minority and has placed Jewish rights above those of all others. Perhaps it could best be described as having the characteristics of an ultra-nationalistic movement, with a large contingent of its members guided by religious dogma pertaining to Jewish claims to all of Palestine. Many of its religious members held that the settlement of Jews in the West Bank and Gaza was preordained as a means of ushering in the messianic age and of fulfilling God's promise to restore the Jewish nation in the Land of Israel. With that in mind, they submitted that elected politicians must not be allowed to frustrate God's will. However, by no means all members of the radical right were religious. Most of the leaders of radical-right Knesset parties such as Tehiya, Moledet and Tzomet were secular Jews convinced that it was in Israel's vital strategic interest to retain the conquered areas.[77] Failing that, they believed Israel's defensive posture would be weakened as intransigent Palestinians would be emboldened to step up measures to undermine the Jewish State, as indeed happened after Israel later vacated Gaza.

The appearance of a radical right would probably have been unthinkable had Israel not assumed possession of the West Bank, Gaza and the Golan Heights as a result of the Six-Day War. Essentially, its whole *raison d'être* is based on its perceived need for Israel to retain such territories for either religious or security reasons. While the movement was underpinned by students of the Jerusalem Yeshiva Merkaz Harav, who founded Gush Emunim, the arrival in 1971 from the USA of the charismatic Rabbi Meir Kahane added a darker side to it. Believing that the presence of Arabs both in Israel and in the occupied territories posed an existential threat to Israel, Kahane, through his newly formed party, Kach, advocated their forceful expulsion. He reasoned that Arab-Israeli citizens do not see themselves as Israelis. They feel no loyalty to the Jewish State and its institutions, they are hateful of the Jewish majority, and over time their intellectuals will become ever more uncompromising Palestinian nationalists.[78] The sad part about it all is that Kahane's prognosis has partially been realized. Unfortunately his abrasive political style and behaviour tended to aggravate matters. Until his arrival in Israel, the Gush Emunim and their followers aspired to maintain cordial relations with their West Bank Arab neighbours. But instead, as Ehud Sprinzak wrote, Kahane injected "Jewish violence and vigilantism into the complex of relations between Jews and Arabs in the West Bank."[79] The process was abetted by the government officially relying on settlers to assist in stamping out rebellious behaviour, such as rock throwing, which put people's lives at risk. By appealing to the settlers to defend themselves, the state implicitly conceded that it alone could not ensure law and order and that, in essence, the settlers were licensed to take the law into their own hands, which of course is just what many of them did. Not only did some of them indulge in killing and wounding Palestinians as well as damaging their property, but according to the 1982 Karp Report commissioned by Itzhak Zamir, the state's attorney general, of a sample of seventy cases involving such transgressions, fifty-three did not lead to prosecutions.[80]

Serious settler violence got off the ground in 1980. The catalyst for it was the shooting at close range of Yeshiva students as they wended their way to Beit Haddasah in the heart of Hebron. Six of the students were killed and another twenty were wounded. Before that, the settlers were subjected to a growing wave of Arab assaults. A hitherto unknown group, the Jewish Underground, led by Menachem Livni, Yehuda Etzion and Ben Shoshan, all members of Gush Emunim, was commissioned by angry settlers to avenge the killing of the Yeshiva students. A plan was concocted that entailed the maiming of five Palestinian West Bank mayors by placing and then setting off explosives in their cars. In only in two cases were they successful. The mayor of Nablus lost both legs and the mayor of Ramallah lost one. The explosive charge meant for the mayor of El Bira was detected, and an Israeli sapper was blinded as he tried to dismantle it.[81] However, the group's actions were widely applauded in settler circles and, taking comfort from such support, it set its sights on a far more daring and in fact far more damaging undertaking involving nothing less than the complete demolition of the Muslim Dome of the Rock situated on the Temple Mount. For that undertaking, large quantities of explosives were accumulated and more than twenty operatives were equipped with Uzi machine guns and gas canisters. But at the final hour, for want of the blessing of an approved rabbi, the project was aborted.

The Jewish Underground undertook two more operations, both of which were in response to deadly Arab attacks on Jews, and in both cases their actions were pre-sanctioned by rabbis. The first operation, on July 26, 1983, was directed against the Muslim College at Hebron. Two members of the Jewish Underground entered the building, firing bullets and hurling hand grenades, killing three Arab students and wounding thirty-three others. As in the intended Dome of the Rock enterprise, the second action, planned for April 1984, did not eventuate – not for lack of rabbinical backing, but because it was foiled by the Israeli authorities, who managed in the nick of time to round up all the conspirators. Had they not done so, five Arab buses crowded with passengers would have been blown up in revenge for similar attacks on Israeli buses.[82] Three of those implicated in the Islamic College attack received life sentences, but within less than seven years they were released through a presidential pardon, to be hailed as heroes by their supporters. It bears mentioning that many Gush Emunim members were appalled by the whole saga of the Jewish Underground and dissociated themselves from it.

The First Intifada

Since falling under Israeli rule in June 1967, the Palestinians had enjoyed significant improvements in their economic conditions and living standards. Between 1968 and 1991, per capita income rose from $165 to $1,713, while infant mortality kept falling, from sixty per thousand in 1968 to fifteen per thousand in 2000. By 1986, 92.8 percent of the population had access to electricity as opposed to 20.5 in 1967, and, similarly, 85 percent of homes had access to running water in 1987 as opposed to 16 percent ten years previously.[83] Illiteracy rates fell to far lower levels than those attained in other Arab countries and, while in 1967 there were no universities in the West Bank or Gaza, seven were eventually founded. On the other hand, during the 1980s a fall in oil prices led to a decrease in Palestinians working in oil-producing states, with the concomitant result that remittances to the West Bank and Gaza declined.

To a large extent the population was left to run their lives as they saw fit. There was no press censorship other than to matters relating to security issues. School curricula were untouched, the universities became hothouses for Palestinian extremism and non-violent anti-Israel manifestations were tolerated. Israel even turned a blind eye to a flow of PLO-controlled funds. Previous Israeli efforts to foster a local Palestinian leadership that would supersede the PLO faltered. Among such schemes was a move to establish, in the late 1970s, Village Leagues, to be run by respected elders vested with authority to dispense licences or favours to individual villagers. The elders, who were permitted to carry firearms, extorted fees for services that ought to have been gratis. Appalled by their greed and arbitrary abuse of power, Palestinians spurned them. The Israelis too were disappointed by their performance. By the mid-1980s, the leagues were wound down and some of their leaders were arraigned on corruption charges. Not unexpectedly, the PLO was able to solidify its influence and support.

Deprived of any reasonable measure to win the hearts and minds of the Palestinians, Israel, much to its later regret, supported the budding Islamic movement by even assisting it in setting up an Islamic Centre in Gaza and the al Najah University in Nablus. Once it became clear that Hamas was not simply a conservative social movement as originally perceived but also a militant terrorist one, Israel began circumscribing it and arresting its leaders.

The first intifada or mass revolt did not simply occur out of the blue. Rather there was an upward trend in Palestinian violence perpetrated against Israelis. On October 7, 1981, a day after Sadat was assassinated – that is, on the anniversary of the Yom Kippur War – rioting flared up in the West Bank and Gaza. Palestinians stoned Israeli vehicles and hurled Molotov cocktails at them. The number of recorded violent incidents grew year by year. By 1987 (excluding the month of December) such incidents exceeded those that occurred a year earlier by a margin of 150 percent in Gaza and 100 percent in the West Bank.[84]

If anything, the upward trend in violence ought to have alerted the Israelis to the fact that both a qualitative and a substantial change in the Palestinian will to challenge Israel's ability to govern the occupied territories was occurring. But since the upsurge in violence was instigated by individuals acting on their own devices, Israeli security agencies failed to discern that a popular and sustained uprising was in the making, an oversight also falling on the PLO leadership in Tunisia.

While there were of course some clear-cut cases of PLO-inspired operations, in general they were not out of the ordinary. A notable exception was the hijacking on April 12, 1984, by four Palestinian terrorists of an Egged bus containing forty-one passengers. The hijackers, who had threatened to blow up the bus, were demanding the release of 500 detainees in Israeli prisons and a free passage to Egypt. The bus was eventually intercepted as it sped into Gaza, and after a standoff an elite Israeli squad shot dead two of the hijackers and captured the remaining two, who were removed from the scene and then summarily killed by Ehud Yatom on the orders of Avraham Shalom, the director of the domestic intelligence service (Shin Beth). That extrajudicial execution caused a scandal in Israel. Despite official inquiries and a trial, none of those implicated served prison terms.[85]

On November 25, 1987, two Palestinians on hang gliders with small propellers powered by lawn mower-sized engines headed towards Israel from Southern Lebanon. One inadvertently landed in the IDF's border security zone and was shot and killed. The other reached a point in northern Israel not far from the Gibor IDF Nachal (Pioneering Fighting Youth) camp near Kiryat Shmona. After detaching himself from his hang glider, the infiltrator fired at two Israeli soldiers in a passing army vehicle, killing one of them and wounding the other. He then made his way to the army camp, where the sentry had absconded, entered it and began firing and hurling grenades at the surrounding tents. Before he was eventually gunned down, he succeeded in killing another five soldiers and wounding seven more.[86] The remarkable daring of the raid won the admiration of the Palestinians, who taunted the Israelis with the slogan "six to one" – that is, six IDF fatalities to the one assailant.

The IDF had begun to be seen by the Palestinians as a paper tiger. A cumulative series of events convinced them that the Israelis were losing their grip on power in the wake of an apparent decline in their resolve to uphold the full force of the law. This was manifested as early as April 1986, when the IDF opted not to deploy any of its troops while

Jafr al-Masri, the late mayor of Nablus, was being buried. During the funeral procession 10,000 mourners, some of whom were masked, filled the streets of Nablus openly brandishing PLO flags.[87] Elsewhere, over a period of months in 1986–7, rebellious residents in the Balata refugee camp on the West Bank began stoning Israeli vehicles approaching the camp. The Israeli authorities responded by suspending attempts to enter Balata, effectively conceding its self-rule. In August 1987 an Israeli soldier was shot and killed at midday on the main street of Gaza. None of the Palestinian passers-by offered him any succour or bothered to summon an ambulance. Consequently, Israelis shunned the main Gaza road, and by so doing they reinforced a growing Palestinian perception that they were losing their nerve.[88] By mid-November 1987 an intifada rehearsal took place in the Jabalya refugee camp in Gaza following the arrest of an Islamic Jihad firebrand. The residents rose up en masse, raining down stones on every IDF patrol day in and day out.[89] As Schiff and Ya'ari noted, "most of the [Palestinian] actions that were to characterize the uprising . . . had actually been current during the months before its outbreak."[90]

The intifada, which essentially means "shaking off," manifested the natural impulse of an occupied people to bring the occupation to a close. In the twenty years since Israel had taken possession of the West Bank and Gaza, a new generation of Palestinians had reached maturity having lived entirely under Israeli rule,without appreciating why that rule came about in the first place. What they did of course know is that their fate was not entirely in their own hands. They were regulated by Israeli authorities, and round about them they observed burgeoning Jewish settlements encroaching on their space and resources. In Gaza, for instance, the settlers, who represented 0.4 percent of the population, had been awarded some 28 percent of the state lands.[91] On the West Bank, Jewish settlers obtained twelve times more water per head than the Palestinians.[92] Unemployment was rising as the mushrooming Palestinian population outpaced the local demand for labour, and the education system turned out high school and college graduates who were over qualified for the posts available. Even under normal circumstances a country with an explosive population growth rate and massive youth unemployment would find itself with a volatile social situation.

Many of those who secured menial jobs in Israel were subject to both real and imaginary indignities that emanated from the arduous and lengthy process of commuting to work and from the insufferably haughty bearing of some of their employers. Labourers living in Gaza had to rise at the crack of dawn to pass through a tardy security control station manned by inexperienced IDF recruits overwhelmed by the volume of the people they had to vet. Those with regular employment continued on a journey lasting an hour or more to their workplaces, while less fortunate ones had to stand around waiting to be arbitrarily selected by Israelis in search of casual labour. At the end of the day, tired workers were not infrequently held up for a couple of hours or more at the Gaza Erez checkpoint. On eventually returning home, unfavourable comparisons between their living conditions and that of the Israelis could not help being drawn. For virtually all of them, as two prominent Israeli journalists concluded, "the contrast between the quality of life on the two sides of the Green Line [the 1967 border] was downright painful."[93] Over half the Gaza workforce and a third of the workers in the West Bank were employed in Israel.[94] Even though Palestinians working in Israel earned more than those in the occupied territories, they were rankled by the stark discrepancy between their wages and working conditions and those of Israelis performing similar tasks.

For generations past, the Palestinians have resented the mere existence of the state of Israel, a resentment fuelled by anti-Semitic aspects of Islamic theology, an artificial perpetuation of the Palestinian refugee problem and the notion, assiduously propagated by the PLO, of being the innocent victims of Jewish aggression.

The spark that ignited the flames was a traffic accident. An Israeli driver lost control of his truck at the entrance to Gaza, killing four Palestinians. Within no time at all a rumour circulated that the killing was quite deliberate, engineered as an act of revenge by a relative of an Israeli stabbed to death in Gaza two days beforehand.[95] Thousands of mourners at the next day's funeral for the victims began stoning an Israeli outpost alongside the Jabalya refugee camp. A day after that, in both Gaza and the West Bank, Palestinians gathered in mass protests, culminating in more upheaval. That was followed by a series of spontaneous strikes, including the closure of schools, which had the effect of augmenting the available pool of protesters. Constant clashes between the Palestinians and the IDF grew more violent and gave rise to mounting deaths and injuries. Even then the Israelis did not appreciate that they were dealing with a widespread uprising that was to last for years on end. Pointing to the predominance of young Palestinians confronting the Israelis, Shamir comforted himself with the false assumption that they did not represent the bulk of their people and that therefore the IDF was dealing with only a marginal sector of the Palestinian population.[96] Certainly the IDF had not been primed to cope with anything as extensive as the intifada proved to be. It took two weeks of constant rioting to convince the IDF substantially to reinforce its presence in Gaza and the West Bank. In the interim, the absence of an effective IDF response simply fuelled the Palestinian populace's appetite for more riotous behaviour. As a routine of civil insurrection unfolded, a vast array of TV reporters descended on the troubled sites. Viewing scenes, devoid of any context, of IDF baton charges against seemingly innocent civilians, world TV audiences began to perceive the Palestinians as Davids challenging Israeli Goliaths. Appreciating the propaganda value of such images, whenever overseas media reporters appeared, the Palestinians tended to raise the level of confrontation, goading the Israelis to be rough in subduing them.

The Israeli government made a determined yet unsuccessful attempt to suppress the intifada through the general use of limited and controlled force. In addition to the imposition of curfews and the forced opening of striking shops, it resorted to the use of tear gas, riot batons, rubber and plastic bullets, mass arrests and detentions, the demolition of houses of those with Israeli blood on their hands and, ultimately, banishment. The IDF was handicapped by having a limited number of soldiers on hand to suppress disturbances occurring simultaneously over an extensive front. It had not provided training in what amounted to standard policing measures involving riot control and other forms of civil disobedience, such as stone throwing, in which children participated in 60 percent of all incidents. To some extent, the lack of adequate riot control training plus the meagre concentration of troops at flash points caused soldiers fearing for their lives to open fire with live ammunition. As a result, the number of Palestinian fatalities soared. Rabin, at his wits' end, is reputed to have called upon the IDF to break the bones of those causing mayhem. Whether he actually issued that injunction is contentious. Menachem Brinker, in an article in *Haaretz*, claimed: "One cannot find a single person in Israel who heard Rabin utter such a thing. Rabin himself has flatly denied using such language."[97] Similarly, in his book *Justice under Fire*, the former chief army attorney Amnon Straschnov recorded: "As to the matter of whether Rabin said 'break their bones or break their arms or legs' there is no written material extant substantiating that."[98] By contrast, the pro-Palestinian Israeli journalist Amira Hass, by reporting Rabin's alleged remarks as if they were self-evident truths, had contributed to a widespread belief in their authenticity. In a well-cited article, she affirmed that, "When Palestinians are asked about Yitzhak Rabin, they remember a man who ordered Israeli soldiers to break their arms and legs."[99] Whatever Rabin actually said, it is generally agreed that he wanted the IDF to adopt stern policing measures. But although there were indeed a few disgraceful incidents, the worst being an unsuccessful attempt by one IDF squad to bury a party of Palestinians alive,[100] the plain truth of the matter is that the IDF ruled out raising the level of its operational violence to the point where it could have put an end to the confrontation. That led Shalom and Hendel, two distinguished academics from Ben-Gurion University, later to ask whether, in light of the heavy casualties that were sustained by both Israelis and Palestinians throughout the long duration of the intifada, which officially ended in 1993 with the onset of the Oslo Agreement (see next chapter), had the IDF indeed acted sharply and swiftly in the spirit of breaking demonstrators' bones, would far more people on both sides of the barricades have been spared?[101]

Within Palestinian communities in the occupied territories, local committees began to be formed to manage and coordinate the clashes. That caused the PLO leadership in Tunis, which had not fomented the riots, to fear being supplanted by fighters on the ground. To guard against such a contingency, a ship was commissioned to carry 131 exiled PLO members to the Israeli port of Haifa. They were to be accompanied by 200 journalists and a few pro-PLO Jewish Israelis. The ship, a ferry by the name of *Sol Phryne*, was renamed *al-Awda* (The Return) and was clearly meant to represent a Palestinian version of the famous Zionist ship *Exodus*. On February 15, 1988, hours before it was due to sail from Limassol, Cyprus, a limpet bomb attached to its hull by Mossad agents and frogmen of Flotilla 13, the Israeli equivalent of US

Navy SEALs, exploded. Water surged into the damaged area and the ship listed. There were no casualties, but the voyage had to be called off. In the end the PLO's concerns at finding itself out of the intifada loop were short-lived. A self-described United Command, which soon began to oversee the local intifada committees, reported directly to the PLO leadership by phone and fax, while the PLO funnelled vast sums of money into the occupied territories to help sustain the insurrection.

Attacking Israeli vehicles became a main tactic of choice. On July 16, 1989, a Palestinian grabbed the steering wheel of an Egged bus en route from Tel Aviv to Jerusalem, turning it so that the vehicle careened off the highway into an abyss. Sixteen passengers were killed.[102] During the first nine months of the uprising, 1,650 Israeli buses were stoned and thirty-nine torched.[103] Buses were not the only object to be scorched. By May 1988 Palestinians turned to arson as a weapon to destroy Israeli forests, orchards and field crops, mostly in Israel proper. At the year's end, some 1,300 forest and brush fires had ravaged 144,000 dunams[104] of Jewish land.[105]

Taking advantage of the general turmoil, Palestinians settled scores with rivals or with criminals and those affronting Muslim behavioural norms by accusing them of being Israeli collaborators and then killing them. Meanwhile, getting in on the act, a few Israelis took it upon themselves to kill Palestinians thought to be responsible for acts of terrorism. Some were arrested and given lengthy jail sentences, but those who were settlers were rarely apprehended; when they were, they were treated with kid gloves.[106] Settlers travelling in the West Bank and Gaza were particularly prone to be attacked. Since the IDF could not realistically protect each and every one of them, settler vigilantes took to beating their Arab neighbours and vandalizing their homes, vehicles and orchards.[107] Needless to say, their actions were not conducive to restoring calm. Complaining that the IDF was being derelict in its duty to protect them, settlers also turned their wrath against ordinary IDF recruits and high-ranking officers.

The intifada cost the Israelis lives, resources and adverse media reports. Further, by causing its army to be engrossed in what was essentially a law and order enforcement procedure, time spent in basic military training and field exercises was limited, constituting a threat to the IDF's war-waging capabilities. Israeli foot-soldiers in the West

Plate 4 *Intifada protestors in Ramallah, March 1988*

Bank and Gaza mobilized to contain the uprising found the task both daunting and demoralizing. The patience and restraint of young Israeli conscripts unremittingly up against furious and screaming civilians pelting rocks and Molotov cocktails at them was severely tested. On occasion even the moderate among them lost their self-control, joining their more unrestrained comrades by belting into any unfortunate rioter that came their way. Some Palestinians were so badly brutalized that they had to be hospitalized. Aggravating matters, not every Palestinian victim was necessarily implicated in the disturbances.

Precise information relating to the number of intifada victims on both the Israeli and Palestinian side, as well as the actual number of violent clashes, is not readily available. As has always been the case, casualty estimates of the IDF and the Palestinians are irreconcilable. The IDF for one does not include casualties inflicted by Jewish civilians or by Palestinians on one another.[108] It has been estimated that, by the end of June 1989, ninety Palestinians had been killed by their own people – some to settle personal scores, some for "moral" reasons and others for suspected collaboration with Israel.[109] For the three year period 1988–90, the IDF calculated that twenty-one Israelis were killed compared with

645 Palestinians. The respective figures for those injured are 4,170 and 13,648.[110] The lower ratio of Israeli deaths to casualties could partly be explained by the fact that the Palestinians were deploying less lethal means and by Israel having a more effective health delivery system.

The intifada had been enthusiastically supported by Palestinians at all levels – rich and poor, young and old, men, women and children. Once the PLO had firmly secured the baton of orchestrating the uprising, its standing among Arabs rose to unprecedented heights. Seeing which way the wind had been blowing, on July 31, 1988, King Hussein of Jordan reluctantly announced Jordan's formal disengagement from the West Bank, involving "the undoing of the legal and administrative bond between the two banks" … in response "to the will of the PLO."[111] Hussein's decision constituted a severe blow to the Israelis, who had entertained hopes of resolving the Palestinian predicament in the context of a deal with Jordan. With local Palestinian leaders being unwilling or too afraid of PLO reprisals to negotiate with Israel, members of the Israeli Peace Movement began to look longingly for signs of a moderating tendency within the PLO.

By November 15, 1988, such signs seemed to be in the offing. It was then that the Palestine National Council, meeting in Algiers, declared the establishment of a Palestinian State on the basis of the 1947 UN Resolution 181, which called for the creation of both a Jewish and an Arab state in Mandated Palestine. From that, those within the Israeli Peace Movement rashly concluded that the PLO had finally come to terms with Israel's existence. But that was not so. The National Council had also called for "the settlement of the issue of the Palestinian refugees in accordance with the pertinent United Nations resolutions," which is PLO parlance for the unlimited return of Palestinian refugees to Israel proper. Lest any PLO rank and filer be similarly misled, they were soon put right by the late Abu Iyad, the PLO's intelligence chief, who assured them that "the borders of our state noted [by the Palestine National Council Algiers declaration] represent only a part of our national aspirations. We will strive to expand them so as to realize our ambition for the entire territory of Palestine."[112] In the closed-door deliberations for obtaining the Palestinian National Council's approval of the declaration, Arafat's deputy, Salah Khalaf, explained that at first the state would be small but then, God willing, it would expand. Posing the question of how one might acquire all of Palestine, Khalaf answered "step by step."[113]

The following month, Arafat addressed the UN General Assembly. Normally it meets in New York but, since the United States refused to grant Arafat an entry visa, the Assembly obligingly held a special session in Geneva. At a press conference in the wake of his talk, Arafat announced: "We totally and categorically reject all forms of terrorism, including group and state terrorism."[114] He then went on to claim that the Palestinian National Council had accepted UN Security Council resolutions 242 and 238 and, as a result, the USA agreed to open a dialogue with PLO representatives. As Shalev observed, the US change of position was a significant political PLO achievement courtesy of the intifada.[115]

6

THE FATEFUL 1990s

In April 1989, the government grudgingly decided to fulfil its obligations to further Palestinian autonomy, as stipulated in the Israel–Egypt peace treaty. To that end, it indicated a new willingness to negotiate with Egypt and Jordan and to accept elected Palestinian members in the Arab state delegations. After it had conveyed its change of heart to the United States, the Americans requested that Israel halt the expansion of all its West Bank and Gaza settlements.

Meanwhile Shamir's government had to contend with a serious crisis emanating, on August 2, 1990, from Iraq's invasion of Kuwait and its subsequent annexation of that country. Iraq's action, riding roughshod over a peaceful neighbouring state and poised to do likewise to other regional oil producers, was regarded by the United States as totally unacceptable, and it promptly organized, under its leadership, a coalition of thirty-four countries, including Britain, Egypt, Saudi Arabia and Syria, in preparation for a military operation to liberate Kuwait. With war looming in the Middle East, Israel, pointedly excluded from the US-led coalition, was liable to be subjected to Iraqi missiles carrying chemical weapons. President Bush insisted that on no account was Israel to join in the fighting even if attacked. Should it do so, argued the Americans, the coalition would unravel, as Arab countries would be unwilling to be seen as being in any alliance with Israel. Dutifully,

Shamir personally informed Bush that he could rely on Israel exercising the utmost restraint.

As if to exacerbate further Israel's relations with its neighbours, on October 8, 1990, nearly two dozen members of a fanatical religious Jewish group, the Temple Mount Faithful, gathered at the Temple Mount supposedly to conduct prayers. After no more than ten minutes they were escorted off the site by police, but the damage had already been done. Their presence had aroused an Arab mob of between 2,000 and 3,000 that took to stoning Israeli police and Jewish worshippers at the Western Wall. The police withdrew and the Jewish worshippers were evacuated. The mob then stormed a nearby police station, where two officers had remained; they managed to escape, but that was not known. Thinking that the officers' lives were imperilled, a large rescue force arrived on the scene to be met by a hail of flying objects. The police first fired teargas canisters and rubber bullets and then, when that proved to be of no avail, live ammunition. At the end of it all, eighteen Palestinians were killed. Twenty-eight Jews and 150 Arabs were injured. The UN Security Council condemned Israel and called for a UN-sponsored investigation. When Israel rejected the Council's resolution, a further one was passed condemning Israel's refusal to cooperate with the UN inquiry. Despite the USA giving Israel to understand that it did not endorse the resolutions, there was indeed, as a French diplomat admitted, a clear-cut connection between their adoption and the attempts being made to consolidate a consensus in the Arab World against Saddam Hussein, the Iraqi dictator.[1]

On January 16, 1991, after Hussein failed to meet international deadlines to withdraw from Kuwait, the US-led armed forces coalition arrayed against him opened its military offensive with an air attack on Iraq. Two days later Iraq began launching Scud missiles on the Israeli cities of Tel Aviv and Haifa. All told, forty-two Scuds landed in Israel. Thanks to imprecisions in the missiles' guidance mechanism, only one person was killed directly, but fifteen others died from heart attacks, by suffocating while incorrectly fitting gas masks, or from reactions to a chemical-weapon antidote taken in panic.[2] For the Israelis cooped up in specially sealed rooms as a precaution against chemical weapons, and with their defence forces remaining idle for political reasons, it was a gruelling experience. The USA did, however, install four largely ineffectual Patriot anti-missile batteries in Israel manned by US personnel, complementing two other US batteries already in place and manned by Israelis. Apart from the cost to life and limb, the barrage of Scuds damaged over 3,000 apartments, displaced around 2,000 people and, by keeping many others away from work, adversely affected the economy. Fortunately Israelis were not constantly tied to their "safe" rooms. Infra-red sensors on US spy satellites detected heat ejected from Iraqi missiles being launched. The information was instantly relayed to a US ground station in Australia that telephoned it to a control centre in Washington, which then passed it on to Israel, giving the Israelis a two- to three-minute warning – time enough for them to "secure" themselves.[3]

As soon as the war ended, Bush, in an address to the US Congress, announced that, as a reward to the Arab states for participating in the US-led alliance that manifestly furthered their own interests, the United States was determined to establish a new order in the Middle East. For Israel that meant, at a time when it was in urgent need of a $10 billion loan from the Americans to assist it in absorbing what had become a mass immigration of Russian Jews, that the USA began tightening the conditions for its issuance. It required of Israel that it respond positively to US peace initiatives, that no Russian migrants be diverted to Jewish settlements in the West Bank and Gaza, and that no further such settlements be constructed.[4] Yet, far from yielding on the settlements, Israel stepped up the pace of their construction. It has been estimated that, in both 1991 and 1992, approximately 10,000 new settlement housing units were built.[5] Bush retaliated by suspending the issuing of promised assistance, and US Secretary of State James Baker added an extra measure of asperity to the American position by disdainfully providing Shamir with the White House telephone number, telling him to call once he had met the American settlement demands. To add insult to injury, Bush tactlessly and falsely claimed that Israel had benefited from US soldiers risking their lives in Iraq "to defend Israelis in the face of Iraqi Scud missiles."[6] US–Israeli relations had reached one of their lowest points in Israel's short history.

Having gained the cooperation of Russian President Mikhail Gorbachev, Baker, in August 1991, proclaimed that, under both his and Gorbachev's auspices, he was arranging for a conference to be held on October 30 in Madrid, to be attended by Israel, Syria, Jordan and Lebanon. Palestinians not nominally PLO members would be included among the Jordanian representatives. All the parties in question accepted Baker's invitation, with Shamir opting to head the Israeli delegation personally. The conference, which lasted three days, opened with statements delivered by each participant outlining their views and approaches in resolving the issues at stake. Agreement was reached for the setting up of ongoing bilateral and multilateral negotiations to obtain peace treaties between Israel and its neighbours. As for the Palestinians, a two-stage process was approved, involving an interim agreement to be followed by a final one, with deliberations to take place in Washington. None of the Madrid Conference-sponsored dialogues bore any fruit but, as outlined below, by means of other channels, agreements were reached with the Palestinians and with Jordan.

   In the wake of the Madrid Conference and its offshoots, Shamir's cabinet showed signs of faltering. By January 1992 the right-wing Tehiya and Moledet parties withdrew from the government in protest against what they regarded as an excessively generous offer of Palestinian autonomy. Realizing that his days as prime minister were numbered, Shamir persuaded the Maarah to agree to the scheduling of a general election on June 23, 1992. Gearing themselves up for the event, the Maarah, now known as the Labour Party (on account of Mapam's earlier withdrawal), chose Rabin to lead it, whereas the Likud re-endorsed Shamir. From Shamir's point of view, the timing of the elections was inauspicious. The economy was in the doldrums, with unemployment rising and with difficulties being experienced in settling the Russian Jewish immigrants. Hezbollah rockets were falling in northern Israel and Palestinian terrorist attacks within Israeli cities were on the rise. Increasing criticism was being levelled at the Likud's settlement policy, which was being seen not only as provocative but as wasteful of precious resources better employed elsewhere. During the campaign the contenders referred to their rivals in extraordinarily unflattering terms, making that election, in the words of one writer, "the dirtiest one in the history of Israel, a country which already had its share of dirty elections."[7] (For the results in detail, see the Appendix.) The clear winner was Labour, which gained five extra seats to reach a total of forty-four. Likud's loss was a heavy one, falling by eight seats to thirty-two, and could be accounted for by defections to Tzomet, Moledet and Mafdal, which collectively achieved an eight-seat gain. Within, by Israel's standards, a moderately short period of time, Rabin's government assumed office, on July 13, 1992. It consisted of Labour, Meretz, a new party combining Ratz, Shinui and Mapam, and the Shas Party (no longer reluctant to strike a deal with the non-kosher rabbit eaters), giving it a total of sixty-two seats. For the most part Rabin's new government could also count on the support of the five Arab Knesset members from Hadash and the Arab Democratic Party. Rabin held both the premiership and the defence portfolio, while Peres became the foreign minister. According to Professor Israeli, Rabin had stipulated that Peres was to confine his attention to the multilateral talks with the Arabs in Washington and not to concern himself with bilateral contacts with Palestinians.[8]

Indications of a change of government policy could be discerned in an explicit acceptance of the principle of yielding territory in the context of a peace agreement and of an expressed intention to slacken the pace of settlement construction. Rabin's new housing minister, Benjamin Ben-Eliezer, announced a total freeze of all new settlement construction in the West Bank and Gaza. In August 1992, the US government, now convinced that its demands had largely been met, finally authorized the $10 billion loan sought by Israel. As a mark of goodwill towards the new Israeli government, Baker agreed to the completion of the construction of about 10,000 settlement housing units for which work was already in progress. Consequently, the number of Israelis residing in settlements in the West Bank and Gaza rose by 32 percent, from 110,000 in 1992 to 145,000 in 1996.[9]

Regarding the general security situation, one of a series of acute crises began on December 13, 1992, when an Israeli border policeman by the name of Nissim Toledana was abducted in Lod by Hamas terrorists, who demanded the release of Sheikh Ahmed Yassin, a Hamas founding father held by Israel. The government refused to negotiate with the kidnappers until it received firm evidence that Toledana was still alive.[10] Two days later Toledana's body was found off the Jerusalem–Jericho highway. Israel's initial response was to round up around 1,000 Hamas members. But that was not enough to assuage the seething anger of the Israeli public, shocked by the brazenness of the action and the manner in which the policeman was killed. As a further means of punishing Hamas, 415 of its top-ranking personnel were deported to Lebanon. There the Lebanese army prevented them from progressing beyond a desolate buffer strip between Lebanese and Israeli forces, where the deportees set up camp. Before long, they were adopted as a cause célèbre by the international media, which highlighted their grim circumstances. Bowing to US pressure, Israel agreed to allow them to return, but not before a year had expired.

Meanwhile, there was still a need to counter a growing spate of Palestinian orchestrated violence in which even Tel Aviv streets were not spared. Believing that he had no option other than to adopt drastic measures, Rabin imposed, for an unlimited period, a total prohibition on Palestinians entering Israel from Gaza and the West Bank. While such a move had the desired security effect, it impacted adversely on Palestinians who had been employed in Israel and on those who relied on their services.

With specific sectors of the economy at a serious loss for staff, temporary work visas were issued to workers in Poland, Romania and Portugal, as well as Thailand and the Philippines. The unintended consequences of such a policy were soon apparent. Within a matter of a few years estimates put the number of foreign workers present in Israel at around 250,000.[11] In addition to siring offspring born in Israel, in some cases the foreign workers were able to send for their wives and children at home. Demands for the education of foreign workers' children were such that in one Tel Aviv primary school they were in the majority.[12]

The Oslo Accords and Associated Matters

In the early summer of 1992, Terje Roed Larson, the executive director of the Norwegian Institute for Applied Social Science, which monitored living conditions in the West Bank and Gaza, contacted Yossi Beilin, then head of the Israeli Economic Cooperation Foundation. The point of Larson's approach was to inform Beilin that he had strong reason to believe that the Palestinians had reached the conclusion that the continuation of the intifada was counterproductive and that it was in their best interest to seek a mutually acceptable agreement with Israel. Nothing of significance occurred until July, when Peres became Israel's foreign minister and Beilin his deputy, for it was then that Johan Holst, Norway's foreign minister, authorized Larson to notify Beilin that the Norwegian government was willing to offer its good services in facilitating a direct Israeli–Palestinian dialogue. Since it was technically illegal for Israelis to meet face to face with PLO members (a law that was promulgated in 1986 when Peres was prime minister), Beilin proposed to Larson that Yair Hirschfeld of Haifa University and Ron Pundik, an ex-student of his, informally probe the Palestinians to determine whether or not something positive could result from their alleged change of heart. At first the PLO did not deem it worth their while engaging with Beilin's nominees, but once they met with Hanan Ashrawi, a leading PLO figure living in the West Bank, she put them in touch with Abu Ala, the PLO's finance minister. On December 4, 1992, Hirschfeld and Pundik duly met with him in London, where it was agreed that their incipient dialogue be continued in Oslo. By late May 1993, Rabin, who had been briefed about the talks only in the previous February (two months after the Oslo talks had been in progress), suggested that Uri Savir, the director general of the Foreign Ministry, and Yoel Singer, a prominent lawyer with expertise in international law, be charged with coordinating them. The talks seemed to be reaching promising developments and Rabin wanted them placed in the hands of Israeli professionals. What probably made the normally cautious Rabin go along with the Oslo process was a general acceptance by the negotiating parties of "graduality [sic] in the transference of powers and authority from Israeli rule to the Palestinians."[13] With that in mind, Rabin felt reassured that Israel was not about to make a reckless one-off decision that could spell disaster. Nevertheless, Rabin's acceptance of the Oslo process was never wholehearted. In June, after reading a report not to his liking, he abruptly ordered a suspension of the Oslo talks, but Peres persuaded him that the unofficial Oslo channel was in fact a boon to the official one in Washington.[14] As the Israelis saw things, they were negotiating behind the scenes with the PLO to obtain their agreement on a set of proposals to be signed at the Washington Palestinian autonomy talks by Palestinian delegates not associated with the PLO.[15] That way they felt that they could have their cake and eat it, for, as Yigal Carmon explained, they hoped to "secure PLO sponsorship without having to accept the PLO's presence or its participation in implementing the agreement."[16]

By August Rabin was faced with a crisis. The Shas Party withdrew from the coalition over an issue relating to a High Court's ruling that one of its ministers, Aryeh Deri, be forced to step down since he was facing trial for corruption. That left Rabin with the official support of only fifty-six Jewish Knesset members. He could still of course count on the backing of five Arab members, but that placed him in an invidious position. Peres, realizing that there was little time left to wrap up unresolved Oslo negotiation issues, notified Holst that it was "now or never."[17] Holst in turn immediately contacted the PLO leadership, and on August 20 an agreement, known as the Declaration of Principles (DOP) or Oslo Accords, was finalized and initialled by Israeli and PLO negotiators in the presence of Holst and of Peres, officially in Oslo on another matter. Immediately thereafter, Peres and Holst flew to Washington to break the news to US Secretary of State Warren Christopher and Dennis Ross, President Clinton's special coordinator for Middle East Talks. On examining the Oslo document, Ross warned Peres that it was resuscitating a moribund PLO at a time when a local Palestinian leadership was coalescing in the occupied territories. Not taking kindly to Ross's remarks, Peres insisted that Israel was the best judge of its own interests.[18]

Meanwhile, Rabin invited two prominent US Jewish leaders, Lester Pollack and Malcolm Hoenlein, to travel to Jerusalem to meet with him and Peres. He was anxious to secure the support and understanding of the US Jewish establishment. At the meeting, after the Americans questioned the wisdom of rehabilitating Arafat, Rabin admitted that, while he shared some of their concerns, he was consoled by his belief that, "if the PLO proves to be unable or unwilling to combat terrorism, then the whole Oslo process would come to a halt."[19] Later, when the chief of staff, Ehud Barak, was apprised of the details of the Oslo Accords, he found little in them to reassure Rabin. As far as Barak was concerned, the Oslo process was flawed by not taking into account Israel's complex security needs.[20]

When the Oslo Agreement was forwarded to Haider Abdel Shafi, the head of the non-PLO Palestinian delegation in Washington, to be endorsed, he refused on the grounds that a high-ranking PLO leader ought to undertake that task. This presented Rabin with a predicament. If he abandoned the project he would be left exposed as having broken his long-standing promise not to bargain with the PLO without having anything to show for it. As a means of extricating himself and allowing the accords to be consummated, he insisted that the PLO abide by three key demands. It was to recognize Israel's right to exist, to cease all acts of terror and to expunge all clauses in its charter calling for Israel's destruction. One would normally have expected such demands to have preceded the opening of negotiations, not once they had been concluded, but in this case the Israelis had not originally intended officially to acknowledge the PLO as their negotiating partner. After a ten-day period of hectic quibbling, the PLO appeared to accept Israel's demands. Israel and the PLO would recognize each other, terrorism would be renounced and condemned, and the PLO Charter would be suitably amended. The recognitions agreed upon were not, strictly speaking, mutual. By Israel recognizing the PLO, there was an implicit acceptance of the legitimacy of the Palestinians seeking an independent state of their own. By contrast, the PLO's acceptance of Israel implied that the Palestinians accepted it as a state but not necessarily as a Jewish one. Commenting on the matter, Israeli wrote: "Any novice would have required reciprocity. But the Israeli team thought that the desire for peace in their self-styled 'peace camp' was so fervent that, as the PLO recognized Israel, that was an adequate equivalent."[21] To this day, the Palestinians remain adamant in regarding Zionism as a perfidious movement and in their refusal to recognize Israel as a Jewish State. As to the other PLO concessions, there were already indications of future equivocations and of various sleights of hand so as not to concede anything of substance. With their charter remaining untouched, the Palestinians held that they would simply declare that the contentious clauses were no longer valid. As to the matter of terrorism, the PLO argued that, like any national liberation movement, it had a legitimate right to have recourse to an armed struggle, and therefore it rejected Israel's call for an immediate end to the ongoing intifada.[22] However, in a letter to Rabin, Arafat did promise that he would punish anyone disobeying orders to suspend terrorist activity, and in a separate letter to Holst he indicated that he would make a general appeal to his people not to engage in terrorism. With all the loose ends tided up, a Declaration of Principles was agreed upon that envisaged the formation of an Interim Palestinian Self-Government Authority (PA), an elected

Plate 5 *Left to right: Rabin, Clinton and Arafat at the Oslo Accords signing ceremony at the White House*

Palestinian Council or Parliament and, within the very near future, the handing over to the PA of control of most of Gaza and of Jericho. Israel and the PLO were to negotiate the extent and means of widening the PA's control over further areas in the West Bank and, finally, the parties were to arrive at a Permanent Status accord based on UN resolutions 242 and 338[23] by no later than five years after ratifying the agreement.

Once the Declaration of Principles (DOP) had been endorsed by the PLO executive committee, it was to be signed on September 13, 1993, in Washington by Peres for Israel and by Mahmoud Abbas for the PLO. The PLO requested that the signing be witnessed by Clinton along with Rabin, Arafat, Christopher and the Russian foreign minister, Andrei Kozyrev. For President Clinton, plagued by problems with his health-care legislation, entering the international limelight as a sponsor of Middle East peace was a welcome relief. As he exclaimed to an aide: "Miracles do happen."[24] Rabin, by contrast, was none too keen to abide by the PLO request but succumbed to US entreaties provided that Arafat would neither carry a weapon nor wear a uniform. In the end, Arafat presented himself on the White House lawn in his trademark military attire, which, to make the most of a bad situation, the Israelis likened to an olive-green suit.[25] In his letter to Holst, in which he had promised that he would call upon Palestinians to desist from wanton acts of violence, Arafat indicated that he would do so once the parties officially signed the DOP. It was generally believed that he would fulfil that promise in his speech at the signing ceremony. Ehud Ya'ari, an Israeli military commentator, so confident that that would happen, kept reassuring his Israeli TV audience at every pause in Arafat's speech that "now" they would witness that historic moment. Finally, when Arafat reached his peroration, a crestfallen Ya'ar uttered, "He is not saying it!"[26]

The very day that Arafat was performing the role of peace-maker and basking in the adoration of politicians and the world media, a pre-recorded television address of his was broadcast in Jordan, informing his Arab audience that he had just accomplished the first step in the PLO's 1974 plan of dismantling Israel by stages.[27] During that month alone, he referred to that plan in the Arab media no fewer than a dozen times. In accordance with the plan the PLO would acquire whatever territory it could by means of negotiations and then use that land as a base for furthering its long-term objective of destroying Israel. Arafat's vision was shared by all his senior colleagues. To cite just one among countless examples, in November 1999, Orthman Abu Gharbia, the Palestine Authority's director of political indoctrination, held that an "independent Palestinian state, with Jerusalem as its capital, is not the end of the process but rather a stage on the road to a democratic state in the whole of Palestine."[28] Interestingly, the Israeli historian Benny Morris drew attention to the fact that, during the 1970s and early 1980s there were indeed some genuine PLO moderates, as opposed to the sham ones, who conducted a dialogue with individual Israelis in search of a true two-state solution. But from 1978 to 1983 the best known among them, Said Hamani, Izz al-Din Kalak and Issam Sartawi, were all gunned down by Palestinian extremists.

Arafat's failure to denounce violence at the Oslo signing ceremony could not be attributed to any oversight due to the excitement of the occasion. Rather it was a deliberate calculated omission. When at the beginning of the following month thirty Israelis were injured in a Hamas attack and Arafat was asked to condemn that incident, he replied that, just as the Israelis respected their hard-line internal opponents, so he too could not be expected to do otherwise with regard to his fractious rivals.[29] A further taste of things to come was provided in November. After two separate killings of Israelis committed by Fatah, Arafat's own organization, it took the application of relentless pressure by President Clinton and Rabin to elicit from Arafat a half-hearted rebuke.[30]

In arriving at the Olso Accords, Rabin finally accepted that the PLO, even with its dismal track record, was the only representative of the Palestinians. Furthermore, because it was at its lowest ebb, Rabin concluded that that time was a propitious one in which to engage it.[31] Should the PLO not honour its commitments, so he thought, Israel would be entitled to reassume control of territories that it had already ceded and, if need be, deport its leaders.[32] However, it was assumed that the likelihood of the PLO not living up to its newly declared role of peace-maker was small. With the PLO attaining significant Israeli concessions, it seemed axiomatic that it made no sense for it to provide cause to be deprived of further such benefits. Therefore a vested Palestinian interest in favour of ending the Israel–Palestine conflict was expected to emerge. As to general security matters, the government was confident that it had found a reliable partner, one that had a common interest in suppressing the more extreme Palestinian Islamists vying for leadership of the Palestinian national movement. Addressing the Knesset, Rabin glorified the Oslo Accords as an opening of a gateway to peace and of an end to acts of terror. But Knesset members were not all so sanguine. While sixty-one voted to approve the Oslo Accords, fifty voted against, eight abstained and one was absent.[33] Earlier on, at the signing ceremony of the Declaration of Principles, Rabin declared that "Today, here in Washington, at the White House, we will begin a new reckoning in relations between peoples, between parents tired of war, between children who will not know war."[34] Unfortunately such a statement was not underpinned by any solid evidence that the PLO had indeed changed.

One of the shortcomings of the Oslo Accords was that they failed to provide Israel with an enhanced sense of security. Palestinians claim that a massacre by a Jew of their brethren on February 25, 1994, sparked most of the subsequent suicide attacks. The massacre in question was perpetrated by an individual Israeli extremist, Dr Baruch Goldstein, who on his own initiative gunned down Arab worshippers in cold blood at the Cave of the Patriarchs in Hebron. Twenty-nine people were killed and 125 wounded. Goldstein, who was in turn overpowered and slain by surviving Palestinians, had been a member of the Jewish terrorist group Kach, founded by Rabbi Meir Kahane. The group was banned in the immediate aftermath of the massacre. For many years prior to Goldstein's outrage, Israeli citizens were subject to numerous terrorist attacks that led to massacres. If the Palestinians were aroused by Goldstein to seek vengeance, thirteen well-organized "reprisals" that followed would by any standards be regarded as excessive. Nevertheless, there is no denying that the terrible slaughter wrought by Goldstein certainly inflamed Palestinian passions and almost certainly induced Palestinian individuals to volunteer for suicide bombing missions.[35] In an attempt to curtail the provocative stance of Israeli extremists, the government determined to evacuate a hard core of them living in Tel Rumeida in central Hebron. The settlers in question, consisting of only seven families, quickly gathered support from four prominent rabbis, who ruled that their eviction would violate Jewish law, a ruling that was endorsed by the majority of Israel's Orthodox rabbis.[36] On conferring

with his security advisors, who warned of impending violent confronta-
tions with the settlers, Rabin reluctantly backed down.[37]

Although disturbed by manifestations of Arafat's duplicity, the
Israelis were inclined to gloss over them as fading remnants of a passing
phase in his conflict with them. They fooled themselves into believing
that what really counted was the putting in place of a recognized and
mutually accepted mechanism that would regulate Israeli–Palestinian
relations in a manner conducive to the promotion of peace and goodwill. The first step taken in that direction was the conclusion on May
4, 1994, of the Gaza–Jericho Agreement, which made allowances for an
Israeli handover of control to the Palestinian Authority (PA) of most of
Gaza and a small area encompassing Jericho. At the signing ceremony
in Cairo, Arafat at first and for no apparent reason refused to append his
signature to the maps attached to the document. In front of the world's
television cameras, pandemonium broke out on the stage as people tried
to reason with him. Only after the Egyptian president, Hosni Mubarak,
cornered Arafat and demanded of him not to disgrace the occasion or
embarrass Egypt as its host did he sign. As a witness to Arafat's bizarre
behaviour, Uri Savir later wrote: "The outrageous scene on the stage
left a bitter taste in our mouths. Here was a man who had gained for
his people an absolutely unprecedented achievement behaving in a way
that flouted the norms of relations between national leaders."[38]

The Gaza–Jericho Agreement detailed the responsibilities of the
PA and the procedures for carrying them out. Among other things,
allowance was made for the formation of a Palestinian Police Force
consisting of no more than 9,000 recruits.[39] In this regard what the
Israelis conceded was extraordinarily magnanimous, for, as the writer
Gal Luft emphasized: "Rarely in modern history has a nation, strug-
gling for its independence, been granted permission by its own military
occupier to establish a quasi-military armed force and to handle its own
security matters independently."[40] The Palestinian Police Force was
to be the exclusive Palestinian organization bearing arms. In terms of
article IX, section 3, of the agreement, no other organization or individual could manufacture, sell, acquire, possess or import weapons and
explosives – an article that was contravened right from the start. More
to the point, article XII, section 1, of the agreement read: "Israel and
the Palestinian Authority shall seek to foster mutual understanding

and tolerance and shall accordingly abstain from incitement, including hostile propaganda, against each other and, without derogating from the principle of freedom of expression, shall take legal measures to prevent such incitement by any organizations, groups or individuals within their jurisdiction."[41]

It took no more than six days for Arafat, on May 10, 1994, to make an incendiary speech before a congregation of a Johannesburg mosque. Unaware that he was being recorded, he justified his signing of the Oslo Accords with reference to the ten-year treaty that Muhammad concluded with the Quraish tribe to obtain access to Mecca. Within two years, after gaining sufficient strength, Muhammad abrogated his pact with the Quraish by vanquishing them. With the implication of such a comparison being patently clear, Arafat concluded his speech by calling upon all Muslims to join in a Jihad to liberate Jerusalem, the eternal capital of Palestine.[42] Rabin was aghast, demanding of Arafat a reaffirmation of his commitment to the Oslo Accords. Even Yossi Sarid, a dyed-in-the-wool left-wing peace advocate, then minister of the environment, called upon Arafat to retract his Johannesburg statement and to show that he was unflinchingly willing to put an end to Palestinian terror.[43] Ignoring all Israeli qualms, Arafat continued to cite how Muhammad deceived the Quraish tribe.[44]

A month later, Arafat triumphantly entered the Gaza Strip in a large motorcade. The seat on which he was sitting was raised in order to facilitate the illegal entry of four terrorists. Among them was Jihad Amarin, who masterminded the fatal 1974 attack on a school in Maalot that led to the deaths of twenty-five Israeli civilians, including twenty-two children. Only after Rabin issued Arafat with an ultimatum did the proscribed men leave for Egypt.[45] If anything, that incident should have served the Israeli leaders with a clear indication of the nature of their prospective "peace partners." But they continued to treat Arafat as a responsible person, and to their dismay Amarin later reappeared, as a colonel in the Palestinian Police in Gaza, to play a lethal role in the al-Aqsa Intidafa (described in the next chapter).

All the while, the PA proceeded to consolidate itself and to strengthen its grip on Palestinians in Gaza and the West Bank. It lost next to no time in building up an armed force far in excess of the limit of 9,000 men specified in the Gaza–Jericho Agreement and when, on September

28, 1995, that limit was extended to 30,000 in terms of the Israeli–Palestinian Interim Agreement, Oslo II, (see below),[46] it had already surpassed that figure. The 1998 budget of the Palestinian Legislative Council included outlays for the salaries of 40,000 security personnel,[47] but there were grounds for believing that the actual number could well have been 50,000,[48] or at least certainly more than 45,000.[49] Infringements of the Oslo Agreements were not confined to armed force manpower quotas but also applied to the quantity and quality of weapons. The limit of firearms to be held by the PA police was set at 15,240, but by 2001 probably four times as many weapons were in use.[50] Ignoring the restriction that they were to bear only light weapons, the PA police also acquired rocket-propelled grenades, mortars, mines and anti-aircraft guns.[51]

In addition to enhancing his armed forces, Arafat embarked on a series of steps to ensure that the PLO assumed full control of all PA institutions. As envisaged by the Declaration of Principles, elections for the Palestine Council were to be held in July 1994, but Arafat, needing more time to undermine any opposition, secured Israel's consent to hold them in January 1996. With Hamas boycotting the election, Fatah gained fifty-five seats in the eighty-eight-member council. The council, which remained largely inactive, simply became a rubber stamp of the executive authority. That meant that Arafat, unhampered by any checks and balances, ruled by decree.[52] Top priority was accorded to the dismantling of the Palestinian independent press existing under Israeli rule to replace it with PA-controlled newspapers and broadcasting media. Dissident journalists were subject to threats and violence, and many were arrested.[53] As for the general population, key elements were wooed through bribery and through the provision of employment in the PA armed forces and other bodies. The social fabric of people in Gaza worsened in the early years following the Oslo Agreement. As Sara Roy, a reporter sympathetic to the PLO, regretted, there was much "anger in the street over what is seen as protection of corrupt individuals by Arafat and certain ranks of Fatah."[54]

So endemic is PA corruption that it has become a defining feature of the PA's administration. According to the BBC, the IMF estimated that, between the years 2000 and 2004, the PA had been receiving international aid to the tune of more than $1 billion per annum and that, in

2003, *Forbes* magazine estimated Arafat's net wealth to be $300 mil-lion.[55] Arafat's economic advisor, Mohammad Rashid, shrewdly played the system. For investors, contractors and other businessmen to be able to operate in PA-held areas, they needed to get Rashid on board by pro-viding him with a lucrative share of their profits. Consequently Rashid became the owner in part or in full of numerous companies, ranging from advertising, to gasoline, to communications, to cement, to electric-ity.[56] Monopoly rights were issued to specific companies empowering them alone to import products, such as gasoline, cement, cigarettes, steel, paint, milk powder and other items, from various Israeli sources and to sell them at inflated prices without fear of being undercut by any rivals. As a result, Palestinian consumers were needlessly out of pocket by hundreds of millions of dollars.[57] Not only did the new tycoons harm the pecuniary interests of their customers but, in at least one instance, the health interests of the latter were given short shrift. Towards the end of 1996, Husam Hadar, a member of the PA parliament, noticed something strange. In the middle of one night, in a warehouse adja-cent to his house, Israeli trucks were loading up spoilt flour recently imported from Romania. Hadar followed the trucks to discover that the flour was delivered to an Israeli packing company to be repackaged as if fine and wholesome. When Hadar tried to expose the scam he was warned that his parliamentary immunity would be removed and that he would be prosecuted. Summing up the sorry episode, Hikmat Zaid, chairman of the Palestinian parliament's Economic Committee, described the affair as a "serious crime against the Palestinian nation aided and abetted by senior PA officials."[58]

Arafat and Rashid had been the only signatories to a large and secret account held at Bank Leumi, Tel Aviv, funded by money that would otherwise have been subject to the control of the Palestinian Treasury Office.[59] The amounts involved were colossal, rising from $71 million in 1994 to $2.3 billion in 1998.[60] That meant that, in the course of time, 80 percent of the PA's financial resources were personally controlled by Arafat and Rashid.[61] In 1998, the EU discovered that a disbursement of $20 million for the provision of low-cost housing was used to construct luxury apartments for PA officials.[62] Below the big shots, smaller fry such as officers of the security forces shook down private individuals for cash and even helped themselves to privately owned land.[63]

Perhaps the one good thing that the Oslo Accords facilitated was the achievement of an Israeli–Jordanian peace treaty. Many years before peace was formalized between Israel and Jordan the two countries communicated with each other in irregular clandestine encounters. Relations were generally cordial and mutually helpful. For example, as already mentioned in earlier chapters, Israel in September 1970 readied its forces to confront a Syrian invasion of Jordan, and on September 25, 1973, King Hussein returned the favour by furtively flying to Israel to warn Meir in person that Syria and Egypt were on the threshold of attacking the Jewish State. Yet, even when Israel and Egypt arrived at a peace settlement on March 25, 1979, Hussein did not follow suit. He would have liked to have done so but his hands were tied. Lacking a solid and vibrant economic base, he was in no position to alienate wealthy Arab oil states, nor did he wish to antagonize his more powerful Syrian and Iraqi neighbours. Internally, the Palestinians, who constituted a majority of the population, would not have taken kindly to his officially coming to terms with Israel. But when, by virtue of the Oslo Accords, the PLO solemnly recognized Israel and forswore the use of violence, Hussein felt that the time had finally arrived to sue for peace. After brief negotiations, Israel and Jordan reached agreement for the conclusion of a peace treaty. It was formally consummated on October 26, 1994, at a ceremony attended by US President Clinton at the Arava Crossing, where Rabin signed on behalf of Israel and the Jordanian prime minister, Abdul-Salam al-Majali, on behalf of his country. More than 4,500 other guests, including twelve foreign ministers, were present. Arab and non-Arab Muslim states that were represented were Tunisia, Morocco, Oman, Qatar, Malaysia and Mauritania. President Mubarak of Egypt, who had strained relations with King Hussein, and Arafat, who objected to a clause in the treaty specifying that Jordan had an historic role as guardian of Jerusalem's holy Muslim shrines, were both absent. The treaty provided for a fully comprehensive peace entailing diplomatic relations and cooperation concerning tourism, water, energy, transportation, environmental protection, agriculture and economic development.

On September 28, 1995, a further interim agreement, Oslo II, was reached. With great flourish its signing took place in Washington in the presence of Rabin, Peres, Clinton, Mubarak, Hussein and other foreign ministers. In essence, Oslo II entailed graduated Israeli withdrawals from parts of the West Bank in exchange for a recommitment on the part of the PA to improve security and to continue to strive for better Israeli–Palestinian relations. The agreement delineated three areas in the West Bank. In what was called Area A, the PA would enjoy full jurisdiction. In Area B, the PA's jurisdiction would be confined to civil matters, with Israel retaining responsibility for security. Finally, in Area C, Israel for the time being would retain full jurisdiction. Allowance was made for a fully functioning Palestinian legislative council and an independent judiciary as well as for joint IDF and PA police patrols. The PA was also duty bound by clause 2 of article XVI of the agreement, which read: "Palestinians who have maintained contact with the Israeli authorities will not be subjected to acts of harassment, violence, retribution or prosecution."

All major Palestinian cities save for Hebron fell into Area A, while 450 other Palestinian towns were included in Area B. The transfer of most of Hebron to Area A was to be effected on March 28, 1996. Areas A and B together contained 96 percent of the West Bank population – that is, the civic affairs of just about all Palestinians in the West Bank were to be placed under PA control.[64] While being happy to assume whatever concession Israel was prepared to make, the PA, as was its practice on each and every other occasion, had no intention of fulfilling its side of the bargain. Far from standing by its signed commitment to enhance general security, it arrived at an arrangement with Hamas which allowed the latter to continue to conduct acts of terrorism as long as they were outside the bounds of Area A. Putting it bluntly, Salim Zanoun, the PA official who negotiated with Hamas, declared: "Everyone must understand that we are not the defenders of the Zionist entity."[65]

Conceding that the PA's performance record in living up to its obligations as laid down in the DOP was anything but satisfactory, Rabin, on October 5, 1995, nonetheless implored the Knesset to ratify Oslo II. After a stormy debate, it did so with a razor-thin majority of sixty-one in favour to fifty-nine against. Had the anti-Zionist Arab-dominated Communist Party and the Arab Democratic Party not supported the motion, it would certainly have been defeated. By now Rabin was well and truly locked into a policy about which he had originally expressed grave misgivings. Years earlier he wrote: "It is not surprising that a decisive majority of Israelis are strongly opposed to such an 'option' [of awarding the Palestinians a mini-state]. Even though positions change over time, I am very doubtful that we would ever be able to relate with understanding and moderation to a program liable to bring about our ruin."[66]

On November 4, 1995, a mass rally was held at the Kings of Israel Square in Tel Aviv (later renamed Rabin Square) in favour of the Oslo Accords. A festive crowd sprinkled with families carrying toddlers holding balloons listened cheerfully to speeches by Rabin and Peres. The rally climaxed with the two men joining the vocalist Mira Aloni and all those present in singing the rousing and moving "Song for Peace." Rabin stood there beaming, relaxed and feeling at one with the supportive crowd. After continually having been denigrated in demonstrations organized by the Likud, the settler movement and religious extremists, in which posters were bandied about depicting him as a Nazi and a traitor, the large turnout in that Tel Aviv square yielded him immense comfort.

At the conclusion of the rally Rabin made his way to an awaiting car parked behind the town hall. At the point when the prime minister was about to enter the vehicle, Yigal Amir, a law student at Bar Ilan University, who had escaped the attention of security officials, fired three shots at him from a Beretta semi-automatic pistol. As Rabin was being rushed to Ichilov Hospital, where he subsequently died on the operating table, his supporters were stricken with grief. They mourned not only the loss of a beloved leader but also the loss of a man who embodied their dreams and who gave them cause to hope that such dreams would be realized. Throughout his life, Rabin devoted himself to defending and providing security to his people. Having joined the Palmah (a Jewish strike force) at the age of nineteen, he fought in Israel's War of Independence and, after rising through the IDF ranks, became chief of staff in 1964. With his intelligence and devotion to detail, Rabin meticulously prepared the IDF to emerge victoriously from the Six-Day War. Following his term as chief of staff, he turned his hand to diplomacy. It seemed at the time that Rabin was an improbable statesman, for he did not strike one as being a man of the world. He was ill at ease in engaging in small talk, he had to learn late in life to knot a tie, and he lacked certain social skills such as an ability to glide across a dance floor. Nevertheless, by his modesty, unpretentiousness and straightforwardness, he captivated the echelons of the US administration, winning their hearts and minds. While at no time did Rabin ever hate the Arabs, he was extremely wary of them and their motives. He was a reluctant recruit to the Oslo Accords but, fearful of missing a rare opportunity for attaining peace, he suppressed his misgivings and strove towards ensuring that the accords would yield Israel the serenity for which it so much yearned.

The assassination of Rabin induced many Israelis to take stock of the consequences of employing reprehensible smear tactics in attacking their political opponents. Before the event, Binyamin Kahane, the son of the late Meir Kahane, the founder of Kach, had stated that "there are people who think that the solution to Israel's problems lies in the liquidation of Rabin and Peres."[67] The assassin personally had drawn inspiration from obscurantist rabbinical sources that furnished him with a questionable religious pretext to commit murder. While no rabbi had actually authorized Amir to kill Rabin, some rabbis had begun openly to air ancient edicts suggesting that it was incumbent upon a Jew to slaughter another Jew who endangered his community and the lives of its members. Amir, in referring to such a ruling, known as "din rodef," informed his investigators that, without believing in God, he would have been incapable of carrying out his nefarious deed.[68]

The void left by Rabin was filled by Peres, who, in stepping up to assume his mantle, comfortably secured a vote of confidence in his new government. Like Rabin before him, Peres managed the Ministry of Defence, while the foreign affairs portfolio went to Barak.

Seven days after Rabin's death, Arafat once again showed his disdain for the Oslo Accords by declaring in a PA broadcast that "the struggle will continue until all of Palestine is liberated."[69] Then on January 30, 1996, at a secret gathering of Arab diplomats in Stockholm's Grand Hotel, Arafat avowed that the final-stage agreements between the Palestinians and Israel would ultimately bring about Israel's collapse. Warming to his theme, he predicted that the PLO would establish a purely Palestinian State, for, by making life "unbearable" for them "by psychological warfare and by means of [an Arab] population explosion," Jews would not wish to live there.[70] Although the Scandinavian press reported Arafat's speech and the Israeli government had evidence of its authenticity, Ehud Ya'ari wrote that it "chose not to challenge Arafat on his vision of the New Middle East."[71]

The official Israeli response to Arafat's breach of faith and to his and other PLO leaders' explicit intentions of exploiting the Oslo Accords as a means of destroying Israel is redolent of the failure of Israeli intelligence on the eve of the Yom Kippur War. Although IDF intelligence had accumulated ample material evidence that Egypt and Syria were in the process of preparing for a major assault on Israel and that their D-Day was fast approaching, intelligence chief preconceptions to the contrary held sway. Similarly, as more evidence was gathered by Israeli intelligence relating to the PLO's true intentions, the government and its peace movement backers gave it scant regard. Dazzled by the promise of a new peaceful era that the Oslo Agreements seemed to offer, they were determined not to be distracted by any unpleasant details. Gone was the post-Yom Kippur War resolve never again to allow highfalutin abstractions to hinder the IDF and the government in arriving at a true assessment of reality. Moshe Ya'alon, who in July 1995 was appointed as head of the IDF's intelligence branch, observed such a process at first hand. He summed up his experience as follows: "In the course of years, the Oslo conceptualization was compelling. It was impossible to challenge it. Whoever openly came out against the Oslo consensus was labelled in the public arena as an 'extremist,' and therefore marginalized. All information that ran counter to it was brushed aside and every critical voice was stifled."[72]

Within a mere nine-day period between February 25 and March 5, 1996, fifty-nine Israelis were killed and hundreds were wounded as a result of suicide bombing attacks. Most of the bombs involved were prepared by Yahya Ayyash, who had a degree in electrical engineering. On January 5 he was killed as Israelis detonated, by remote control, a rigged cell phone he was using at the time. Arafat, in commemorating his death at a memorial assembly, likened him to a "shahid" (martyr).[73]

In March 1996, Nabil Shaath, the PA's planning minister and leading negotiator, speaking at a Nablus symposium televised by PA television, expounded the PA's attitude to the adoption of violence. He enunciated that, as long as Israel goes forward [with the peace process] there are no problems, which is why we observe the agreements . . . But if and when Israel will say, "that's it, we won't talk about Jerusalem, we won't return refugees, we won't dismantle settlements and we won't retreat from borders," then all acts of violence will return. Except that this time we'll have 30,000 Palestinian soldiers who will operate in areas in which we have unprecedented elements of freedom.[74]

Coming from a so-called moderate, Shaath's statement amounted to a declaration that the PA would continue the farce of pretending to cooperate with Israel only as long as it continued to succumb to PA demands.

No matter how one looks at it, the Oslo Agreements were an unexpected boon to the PLO. Since the 1982 Israeli invasion of Lebanon, its fortunes had steadily declined. It had to abandon its headquarters in and evacuate its forces from Lebanon to replant them in Tunisia, far from its theatre of war. By 1991, with the fall of the Soviet Union and of other communist regimes, the PLO lost its world power sponsor, which had furnished it with arms and training and furthered its cause in the UN and other international bodies. Then, in the 1991 Gulf War, it misplayed its hand by throwing in its lot with Saddam Hussein, depriving itself of almost $1 billion in revenue from Saudi Arabia and the Arab Gulf States, as well as further antagonizing the United States.[75] Given that loss, IDF intelligence, not anticipating the Oslo Accords, concluded that the PLO in Tunisia was heading towards oblivion.[76] For, in essence, as Efraim Karsh remarked, "by the early 1990s, the PLO had become a regional pariah, with Arafat on the brink of political extinction."[77]

Miraculously, through the Oslo Agreement, the Israelis brought the PLO in from the cold by recognizing it, enabling its leaders and militia to resettle on Israel's doorstep and assisting it in re-equipping its forces. The PLO became accepted as a responsible peace-seeking body by Western powers, who provided it with generous amounts of foreign aid. Since then it has never looked back. Mahmoud Abbas, who unjustifiably acquired the reputation of being a moderate Palestinian leader, is on record as having stated before a body of Fatah leaders: "Israel committed the mistake of its life when it signed the Oslo agreement . . .

in accordance with the Oslo agreement we have assumed land without giving anything in return leaving the final stage open. The fact that final issues remain unresolved does not mean that we have given up on them."[78] Chief among the ultimate PLO objectives, as continually stressed by Abbas, is the return to Israel proper of all Palestinian refugees and their offspring.

In the 1992 election campaign, Rabin had promised that he would attain an Israeli–Palestinian agreement within nine months, and the Oslo negotiations presented him with a rare opportunity for realizing his promise. Rabin endorsed the Oslo process with little forethought. Consequently, as retired General Ephraim Sneh wrote: "The Palestinians faced an Israeli government that was less suspicious of them, less cautious, more eager for an agreement and more amenable to concessions."[79] Support for Sneh's analysis is provided in an interview conducted by Ari Shavit with Yossi Beilin for the March 7, 2007, edition of *Haaretz*. After being appraised by Beilin that he could not recall any serious discussion either in the Rabin government or in the Israeli negotiating team as to the expected nature of a final settlement arising from the Oslo talks, Shavit responded: "I don't understand. In 1992 a government was elected, in 1993 you created the Oslo process. At no stage did you ask yourselves where all that might lead?" To Shavit's question, Beilin answered in one word: "No."[80] To make matters worse, in arriving at the Oslo Accords, there was, not counting Rabin, absolutely no input from any Israeli intelligence or security expert. Peres harboured a jaundiced view of intelligence agents, believing that they were incapable of grasping reality and the sea changes occurring in the PLO. Their absence in the negotiations was touted by him as a plus, for, as he proudly maintained, there would have been no agreement had members of the intelligence community been a party to the talks.[81]

As the PA continued to violate the Oslo Agreements, the Israeli government still held that both it and Arafat were joint allies in combating terrorism. From time to time, Israeli government ministers, such as Sarid, argued that, since the terrorists were patently seeking to sabotage it, Israel needed to expedite the peace process.[82] In practice that meant caving in more readily to Arafat's demands, irrespective of whether or not the PLO was reciprocating in good faith. Even when

the Israeli government forcefully called in vain upon the PLO to dismantle the terrorist infrastructures of Hamas and the Islamic Jihad, it
never seriously contemplated suspending the implementation of the
Oslo Agreements in the face of PLO non-compliance. By that time,
be it noted, the PLO was far more powerful than its Islamic rivals and,
when it suited it, it had shown no hesitation in challenging them. For
example, on November 18, 1994, PA forces in Gaza fired on a crowd
outside the Palestine Mosque who were protesting against the arrest of
Hamas members. As a result thirteen people were killed and over 150
wounded.[83]

Instead of taking the PLO to task for not clamping down on Hamas
for engaging in anti-Israel terror activities, the government and most of
the Israeli media complained that critics of the Oslo Accords were, like
Hamas and the Islamic Jihad, destroying the country's newfound peace
prospects. Complicating the issue, Oslo Accord opponents included
groups, such as the Gush Emunim, that would have rejected any deal
with the Palestinians, no matter how reasonable, if it meant relinquishing even minuscule sections of the West Bank. Therefore, there was an
element of truth in the charge that those who railed against the government were unwilling to do what it took to resolve the Israel–Palestine
conflict. The upshot of it all was that some of the country's jeremiahs
were so tainted in many people's eyes that they simply could not bring
themselves to examine their tidings with any air of detachment.

Putting aside the role of anti-peace extremists, the Rabin–Peres government and the Israeli intelligentsia's general readiness to condemn
those holding genuine reservations about the wisdom of yielding to
PLO demands when in turn nothing of substance was attained, plus
a government-felt need to increase the rate of yielding concessions
as terrorist actions escalated, has been presciently analyzed by the
psychiatrist Kenneth Levin.[84] Essentially, Levin argues that a large
proportion of Israelis, as with the Jewish people throughout much of
their history, suffer from battered child syndrome. Take the case of
an innocent assaulted and abused child who is constantly told by his
callous and abusive parents that he merits punishment because his
behaviour displeases them. Unable to comprehend that it is not his but
the parents' behaviour that is questionable, the child internalizes the
parents' admonitions by concluding that he is entirely at fault and that

the remedy lies in his altering his behavioural pattern to suit them. This causes him to feel that he himself has some control in alleviating his situation, and if at first he does not obtain a satisfactory outcome that must surely mean that he has not quite reached an acceptable level of goodness. Similarly, many Israelis delude themselves into thinking that they have some freedom of action in improving relations with their neighbours. That would generally hold true if their neighbours were responsive to reasonable overtures, but this does not apply to the PLO and Hamas, which can be placated only by Israel's downfall. Not willing to come to terms with such a scenario, Israelis continue to favour conciliatory gestures and, when that does not resolve matters, erroneously conclude that they are not being conciliatory enough.

By way of illustration, Levin refers to Mordechai Bar-On, an historian and onetime Knesset member for Shalom Ahshav (Peace Now), who wrote that it is "a moral obligation for Israel to resolve the hundred-year conflict with its Arab neighbours."[85] Bar-On's views, in Levin's opinion, imply "that Israel is capable by its own actions of bringing about peace and that if the conflict remains unresolved it is because Israel has failed to meet its moral obligation."[86] Had Bar-On written "try to resolve" instead of just "to resolve," it would have been a different matter but, as Levin continues, Bar-On's failure not to do so reflected his belief that Israel had "the capacity to bring about the wished-for resolution through a self-reform that answers the other sides' indictments."[87] The Israeli journalist Ari Shavit captured the spirit of the Israeli peace movement of the time in writing that he and his fellow pro-Oslo supporters

> were infected with a messianic craze ... All of a sudden, we believed that the great global changes underway at the end of the millennium were signalling to us that the end of the old Middle East was near. [We kept] harbouring the notion that everything was really much more simple, that if we only pulled back, if we only recognized Palestinian statehood ... we would be able to breathe in that exhilarating, heady aroma of the end of history, the end of wars, the end of the conflict.[88]

Interestingly, a founding leader of Hamas, Sheikh Hassan Yoesef, is reported to have revealed that "the members of the Israeli peace camp who have been speaking about the need to terminate the occupation have reinforced our decision to press ahead with suicide attacks."[89]

Not only have the Israelis been misled but so have virtually all Western leaders who accepted Arafat's positive statements at face value. Delighted that the long-standing Middle East conflict seemed about to end, they were not prepared to countenance any doubts. As far as they were concerned, the PLO had acted graciously in jettisoning its refusal to recognize Israel, and it would have been churlish of the Israelis to nit-pick about some of Arafat's minor infractions. Apart from sheer wishful thinking, there were at least two other factors that swayed them. Since the Oslo Accords provided the PLO with a clear pathway for achieving a Palestinian State, they deduced that the PLO had a vital interest in cooperating with Israel to ensure the smooth realization of its national aspirations. However, that sophistry was conjured up by fallaciously assuming that the Palestinians would behave like Westerners, a fault that lent itself to the overlooking of facts that proved the contrary. Finally, with saturated media reports graphically covering Israel's attempts to suppress the intifada through the eyes of journalists who saw the Palestinians as a downtrodden people deprived of their rights, it seemed beyond belief that the PLO would ever be a party to any act that would extend Palestinian statelessness.

In the 1996 Israeli general elections, held on May 29, for the first time in Israel's history, voters cast two ballots, one for their choice of prime minister and one for their choice of party. In terms of a newly passed law, the prime ministerial candidate receiving more than 50 percent of the votes cast was entitled to form a government, irrespective of the number of Knesset seats held by his party. With Peres pitted against Netanyahu, the elections took on an American flavour. Not only did Arafat appear to be barracking for Peres, but so too was US President Clinton, who persuaded his public relation's expert, Douglas Schoen, to visit Israel with a view to providing Labour with electoral guidance.[90] Peres had been counting on gaining votes from Israel's Arab community. However, on April 16, an Israeli error of judgment in artillery shelling during Operation Grapes of Wrath, designed to curb Hezbollah's shelling of northern Israel, led to the death of 106 civilians in the Lebanese town of Qana. Voicing the Israeli Arabs' disenchantment with Peres, Arab Knesset member Abdul Wahab Darawsheh pronounced that

Peres was a "murderer of women and children," and that "Israeli Arabs are going to punish Peres for his brutality" by not voting for him.[91] By so doing they contributed towards a slender victory for Netanyahu, who won 50.5 percent of the popular vote against 49.5 percent for Peres (for the results in detail, see the Appendix). One might also cite a growing sense of public insecurity resulting from terrorist atrocities that worked against Peres, along with a public relations blunder that occurred in April 1996. At the conclusion of a specially convened session of the Palestine National Council (PNC), Arafat issued a statement that the PLO Charter had been revised in accordance with his previous promises. Without examining the relevant resolution, Peres blithely proclaimed: "This is the most significant ideological development in more than one hundred years of conflict between Israel and the Palestinians."[92] A few days later Peres had egg on his face when the acting chairman of the PNC, Salim Zanoun, explained that "there were no specific sections of the Covenant that were deleted."[93]

Netanyahu's new government, formed in June 1996, contained a large number of parties. Apart from the Likud–Gesher–Tzomet bloc, it included Mafdal, Yisrael Be'Aliyah (a party of Russian migrants), Shas and the Third Way (a party against ceding the Golan Heights). Later it was also joined by United Torah (a Haredi party). David Levy became the government's foreign minister and Yitzhak Mordechai the minister of defence. Netanyahu was reluctant to have Sharon in his cabinet, but Levy forced his hand by making that a condition for his participation. Not wishing to award Sharon a ministerial position at the expense of any other, Netanyahu appointed him minister of the specially created portfolio of national infrastructure.

On assuming power, Netanyahu wished to moderate the pace of unilateral concession-making until the Palestinians satisfactorily fulfilled their obligations. In this respect, he lifted the settlement freeze policy of the previous government that had limited construction to Jerusalem and within large well-established settlement blocks. But he was subject to a never ending stream of strident criticism emanating from the Israeli media, the Labour–Meretz opposition parties, the Israeli peace movement, Israeli writers and a large segment of the Israeli academic community. The media in Europe and the United States as well as the US administration shrilly echoed Netanyahu's internal detractors. To no small extent, the Israeli encroachment on East Jerusalem gave rise to legitimate concerns. Some Arab houses were demolished on the grounds that they lacked prior building approvals, which were not easy to obtain, and in one instance a facility for handicapped youth was razed.[94] Nonetheless, Netanyahu's reasonable demands that the PA abide by both the spirit and the letter of the Oslo agreements were interpreted as a devious ploy to stymie the peace process.[95] On August 14, 1996, having made no progress on the Palestinian compliance issue, Netanyahu, bearing the weight of irresistible pressure brought to bear on him, reluctantly decided to resume negotiations with Arafat, a decision made easier by a temporary reduction of Palestinian violence from early March to early September 1996.

With the resumption of high-level Israeli–Palestinian talks, Arafat fell back on the use of force as a means of extracting additional benefits. In the process he emulated his hero Haj Amin al-Husseini, the pro-Nazi mufti of Jerusalem, who instigated the Arab Palestinian riots of 1929 by suggesting that the Jews had breached the status quo in the vicinity of the al-Aqsa Mosque, a device to which Arafat resorted not only then but again in late September 2000, when he initiated a second, more lethal intifada. In the first instance, in September 1996, a modification of an excavated tunnel provided the pretext.

Soon after the 1967 Six-Day War, an archaeological project was undertaken in the interest of providing historic insights on the Western Wall and its surroundings. Over time a shaft extending up to almost 500 metres in length was excavated, exposing the rest of the Western Wall and remains of ancient streets, masonry and other features. After 1987, the tunnel, which is more than 200 metres away from the al-Aqsa Mosque, was opened to tourists, but they had to backtrack to the sole entrance. On September 24, 1996, to alleviate tourist congestion, a doorway was added that enables visitors to exit the tunnel onto the Via Dolorosa. Beforehand, in January 1996, an agreement was reached between the Israeli authorities (then under Peres's premiership) and the Islamic Waqf entrusted with the control and management of the al-Aqsa Mosque. In return for permission granted to the Muslims to clear the debris and clutter and to pray in what is known as Solomon's stables, an underground area beneath the Temple Mount, the Waqf agreed to accept Israel's tunnel modifications. But on the day the new doorway opened, the Voice of Palestine, broadcasting from Jericho, appealed to the Palestinian masses to rise against what it described as Israel's "criminal scheme."[96] Confronted by Walter Rodgers of CNN, who was baffled by Arab opposition to what seemed to be "essentially a tourist attraction," a senior PA official, Saeb Erekat, confected an explanation whereby for years the Israelis had planned to open the tunnel in order to supplant the al-Aqsa Mosque with a new Jewish temple.[97] The next day Arafat, in a speech in Gaza broadcast on the PA media, upped the ante by reminding his listeners that, "to the believers who fight for Allah, kill and are killed, heaven is promised."[98] As if on cue, students from Bir Zeit University, arriving in busloads, converged on an IDF checkpoint outside Ramallah. As they pelted Israeli soldiers with Molotov cocktails and rocks, Palestinian police supporting them began firing at the Israelis.[99] In the ensuing four days of general and widespread mayhem, fifteen Israeli soldiers and approximately sixty Palestinians were killed.[100]

For Arafat, the course of events was very rewarding. Israel was universally denounced by the international media for its "provocative actions," and Western governments strongly censured Netanyahu for sabotaging the peace process. The Palestinians in turn were seen as unfortunate victims of an obdurate occupying force, and Arafat soon found himself hosted in Washington by a concerned US president, who failed to veto a UN Security Council resolution condemning Israel. Without any grounds, Clinton demanded positive gestures from Israel, including the closure of the tunnel.[101] Had world governments and members of the media adopted even a reasonable measure of objectivity, they would not have fallen for Arafat's subterfuge. Weeks beforehand, Arafat appealed to the Palestinians to attend en masse the Friday services at the al-Aqsa and other mosques as a means of expressing their displeasure at the slowed pace of the implementation of the Oslo Accords. But there was no discernible response. Then, much to his relief, the opening of the new tunnel doorway provided a welcome opportunity to inflame passions over what was skilfully presented as a provocative and threatening Israeli act. The Palestinian recourse to violence was pre-planned. On September 2, 1996, Mohammad Dahlan, head of Palestinian Preventive Security in the Gaza Strip, remarked on Israel Radio (Kol Yisrael) that, "If Israel continues with its policies, the [Palestinian] Authority does not rule out using its men and the arms it holds." Finally, on the day that the violence erupted, Muhammad Nashashibi, a PA cabinet minister, admitted that Arafat and his entire cabinet had "given a green light for escalation by all means in the West Bank, Gaza and Jerusalem."[102]

The tunnel doorway riots turned out to be a PA dress rehearsal for the initiation of the al-Aqsa Intifada, which commenced in September 2000. Those still holding that the Palestinians genuinely believed that the doorway opening amounted to a violation of the sanctity of the al-Aqsa Mosque ought well to consider the fact that, after the rioting had been subdued, Palestinians resumed normal living as if nothing had happened. At no time in all their subsequent negotiations with the Israelis did the PA ever demand that the controversial doorway be sealed.

Despite all his reservations, Netanyahu, edged on by the United States, proceeded to honour Israel's contracted Oslo obligations. Though he expected the Palestinians to reciprocate, which they clearly did not, he unwillingly found himself in the process of adhering to Oslo II's requirements to disengage from most of Hebron. By the end of November 1996, when all details were cut and dried, Arafat unexpectedly hesitated in giving his go-ahead lest that would lessen the international pressures to which Netanyahu was subject.[103] However, on January 15, 1997, the Hebron Accord was duly signed by both parties and approved the day after by the Knesset. Dennis Ross, on behalf of the USA, provided the Israelis and the Palestinians with what he termed a "Note for the Record," which summarized Israel's commitments to undertake the first of three general deployments specified in Oslo 11 by March 1997, to release certain Palestinian prisoners and to resume final-status negotiations. For their part, the Palestinians were still to amend their National Charter and combat terrorism.

There was an interesting internal side issue relating to the Knesset endorsement for the Hebron Accord. Rabbi Aryeh Deri, one of the founders of Shas, was due to be tried for accepting bribes while serving as the minister of internal affairs. To avoid being defined by the court as a person of immoral turpitude, and thus be deprived of the right to sit in the Knesset, he is alleged to have approached Netanyahu with a proposition. If Netanyahu would appoint Roni Bar-On (a Likud stalwart) as the government's attorney general, who would then agree to a plea bargain in exchange for ensuring that the court would not officially stigmatize Deri and thereby disqualify him from the Knesset, Deri would guarantee that Shas would vote in favour of the Hebron Accord. Sure enough, Bar-On was duly appointed on January 10, though he resigned two days later in the face of a public outcry that he was ill-suited to the post. Apart from anything else, he had no distinguished legal credentials. As for Deri, he was found guilty and sentenced to a three-year prison term.

On January 16, immediately after the Israelis had withdrawn from the ceded parts of Hebron, the remaining Jewish enclave was bombarded with stones, Molotov cocktails and even gunfire. With that pattern of behaviour continuing into the months that followed, the Israeli Foreign Ministry compiled a special report detailing the PA's non-compliance with its contracted obligations. Points listed included failures to amend the PLO Charter, to suppress terror and violence, to curb incitement to violence, to dismantle terrorist structures, to detain terrorists, to hand over wanted suspects to Israel, to confiscate privately held weapons and to adhere to the maximum permitted Palestinian Police Force size.[104]

Given that the USA, in its "Note for the Record," had succinctly clarified its understanding that both parties to the conflict had to meet their obligations, Israel did not take kindly to US demands that it ought to improve on its territorial offer due in a forthcoming round of concessions when PA responsibilities still remained essentially unfulfilled. What particularly irked Netanyahu was the fact that, in order to persuade both his government colleagues and then the Knesset to endorse the Hebron Agreement, he had promised that henceforth "the fulfilment of the undertakings of one side would be dependent upon fulfilments by the other side."[105] Furthermore, he was adamant that Israel, at its sole discretion, would determine the extent of any further land transfers.[106] Netanyahu's confidence that such promises were sustainable was fortified by a letter he received from Warren Christopher, the US secretary of state, reassuring him that "there would be no new agreements until the PA complied with the old ones."[107]

With the PA failing to curb violent attacks upon Israelis, Netanyahu, against his better judgment, agreed to attend a summit with Arafat and President Clinton to be held on October 15, 1998, at the Wye River Conference Center, in Maryland, USA. At that gathering, Clinton so insistently tabled his proposals that Netanyahu felt that, had he rejected them, his relations with the US administration might well have been seriously impaired. Accordingly, Netanyahu accepted them. The decisions arrived at were incorporated into the Wye River Memorandum, signed on October 23. They called for an Israeli transfer of land amounting to 13 percent (not the 7 percent that Israel originally wanted) of the West Bank from Area C to areas A and B. In the process, 14.2 percent of land in Area B was to be shifted to Area A. Replicating previous agreements, the Wye River Memorandum listed measures to be taken by the PA in relation to changing its charter and curbing Palestinian violence.

On November 11, 1998, the Israeli government formally agreed to endorse the Wye Agreement on the understanding that the PA would expunge from its charter clauses calling for Israel's destruction, that a third deployment of Oslo II would not entail more than 1 percent of West Bank land, that thirty terrorists released from PA custody would be redetained, and that Israel would be entitled to disassociate itself from the agreement should the PA not honour its commitments.[108] Then on November 17 the government forwarded the agreement to the Knesset for its ratification, which it duly provided.

Visiting Gaza on December 14, 1998, Clinton, in addressing members of the Palestine National Council, made a heartfelt plea for them to amend their charter. As Martin Indyk, the US ambassador to Israel, described the scene: "Tears were running down the faces of the Palestinian delegates as they rose to vote overwhelmingly to annul the clauses in their covenant that called for the destruction of Israel."[109] Though that choreographed performance may have been enough to convince Clinton and Indyk that the PLO had finally come to terms with Israel's existence, high-ranking Palestinians were not of that view. According to a *World Tribune* report, the Palestine National Council vote called for the formation of a committee to amend or redraft the covenant, but as yet it had not done so.[110] Writing in 2003, Zeev Begin, quoted Salim Zanoun, the chairman of the Palestinian National Council, as having publicly admitted that the Palestinian Covenant had not been annulled.[111] Zanoun's statement was confirmed by Farouk Kaddoumi, the PA's foreign minister, in an interview given on April 22, 2004, to the Jordanian newspaper *al-Arab*. In the words of Kaddoumi: "The Palestinian national charter has not been amended until now. It was said that some articles are no longer effective but they were not changed."[112] Even had the charter been altered, the issue is in fact a red herring. What really counts is whether or not the Palestinians have truly come to terms with making an historic compromise with Israel. On that score, the historical record is not reassuring.

Towards the end of his term of office, there was a widespread feeling that Netanyahu had not lived up to the hope he engendered that he would break with Peres's practice of yielding to the PA while gaining nothing in return. Instead he followed a similar pattern, except that in his case it was accompanied by a tough rhetorical façade. Nor did he perform any better on the northern front. Peace was no closer with Syria, while in Lebanon Hezbollah continued to exact a high toll of Israeli lives. In the entire period over which his government presided, seventy-eight Israelis died in Lebanon and many more were wounded.[113]

Ehud Barak, who had newly acquired the leadership of the Labour Party, took advantage of Netanyahu's declining popularity by presenting himself as a well-decorated warrior who, as an alternative prime minister, could be relied upon not to jeopardize Israel's security. Promising to withdraw from Lebanon in the context of a peace treaty with Syria within a year of his attaining power, Barak tempted voters by offering them a timely exit from that blood-soaked quagmire. Barak's candidacy also derived a boost from an unexpected quarter – Arafat, who appealed to Israeli Arabs to vote for him.[114]

On May 17, 1999, when the next general election was held, Barak routed Netanyahu, acquiring 56.08 percent of the popular vote as opposed to 43.02 percent for Netanyahu. In that election the Labour Party stood on a common ticket called One Israel that also included Gesher and Meimad, a moderate pro-peace religious party. One Israel secured twenty-six Knesset seats, while Likud's representation slumped to nineteen. Because electors voted separately for both a prime minister and a party, they were able to indicate their preferences for a prime minister without necessarily supporting his or her party. This resulted in the parties associated with the contestants for the premiership incurring heavy losses in favour of minor ones (see Appendix). After some prolonged negotiations, Barak on July 6 formed a government made up of One Israel, the Center Party, Meretz, Shas, Yisrael Be'Aliyah and

Mafdal. In addition to being prime minister, Barak held the defence portfolio. David Levy was at first foreign minister and Peres minister of regional cooperation.

An innovative aspect of Barak's approach was a desire to dispense with the notion of further successive land handovers to the PA and instead to make a direct move to a final-status agreement. Such an approach met with PA resistance, for it conflicted with Arafat's strategy of maximizing the amount of land transferred to the Palestinians without them having to agree to a final settlement. But, following in the footsteps of his predecessors, it was Barak who yielded. By September 1999 he found himself at Sharm el Sheikh negotiating a new timetable for fulfilling Israel's Wye Agreement land-transfer commitments. In the end they were completed in March 2000.

Nor did Barak achieve his coveted deal with Syria. To that end he was prepared to offer the maximum concessions possible, as he demonstrated in December 1999 in his talks in Washington with the Syrian foreign minister, Farouk Shara. The talks soon reached a sticking point for, if news leaks are to be believed, Barak offered an Israeli withdrawal from the Golan Heights to the original 1923 international frontier. That, however, was deemed insufficient by the Syrians, who insisted on Israel yielding a strip of land along Lake Galilee that Syria had seized in the Israeli War of Independence. The Syrians certainly did not lack for chutzpah. Although, like their fellow Arab leaders, they constantly chanted the mantra that all territory taken by force had to be relinquished, they insisted on being exempt. Throwing all prudence to the wind, Barak responded by expressing a willingness to improve on what was meant to be his final offer. He would accept the 1967 border provided that it was situated 100 metres away from Lake Galilee, which was to remain under full Israeli sovereignty. But it was all to no avail. Syria severed all contacts with Israel, and by February 2000, when Clinton met Hafez Assad, the Syrian president, in Geneva, he was told in no uncertain words that, no matter how generous Barak might be, Syria would never sign a full peace treaty with the Jewish State.[115] In any case, according to Assad, the *entire* lake would have had to have been handed over to Syria.[116] Barak's futile overtures to Assad did not meet with Israeli appreciation, especially since, in early February, the Syrian newspaper *Tishreen*, the regime's official mouthpiece, declared the Holocaust to be a myth and labelled Israel as "the plague of the third millennium." Yossi Klein Halevi, an eminent and well-respected Israeli journalist, summed up the feeling of many Israelis in writing that "The notion of Israel surrendering its most strategic territory, along with one-third of its water sources, to an old, sick dictator whose regime may not outlast him was merely an insane gamble with the country's future." But now, in light of the Syrian anti-Semitic outbursts, "it is also a national disgrace."[117]

An inability to attain peace with Syria did not deter Barak from withdrawing all Israeli forces from its security zone in Southern Lebanon. This he did in May 2000, when the IDF, with little advanced notice, unilaterally pulled out, leaving its ally, the Christian-manned Southern Lebanese Army, in the lurch. As a result, the Southern Lebanese Army disintegrated. Before the event, for Israelis who expressed qualms about the forthcoming arrangements, Amos Oz, a leading Israeli writer and peace advocate, offered solace by claiming: "The minute we leave south Lebanon we will have to erase the word Hizbullah [sic] from our vocabulary, because the whole idea of the State of Israel versus Hizbullah was sheer folly from the outset. It most certainly will no longer be relevant when Israel returns to her internationally recognized border."[118] Unfortunately, things did not quite work out that way. Despite Israel receiving informal assurances that the Lebanese Army would take possession of the land forfeited by Israel and that the UN forces would monitor the area in question to ensure that it would not be used as a guerrilla staging post, Hezbollah moved in in force, along with advanced missiles and other forms of weaponry supplied by its Iranian sponsor.

With Israel's pursuit of peace with Syria having reached a dead end, and with the country having finally withdrawn from Lebanon, the slate was seemingly clear for Barak to devote his full attention to outstanding issues with the Palestinians. In lieu of continuing with a piecemeal approach, as already mentioned, Barak thought it expedient to move directly to final-status talks so as to resolve the Israel–Palestine conflict once and for all. However, all omens radiating from the Palestinian side were far from encouraging. Intelligence reports suggested that the PA was intent in stoking up anti-Israel feelings both in the areas under its control and among Arabs in Israel proper. The target populations were subject to a never ending stream of traditional PLO propaganda, with a mix of crude anti-Semitism and a long-standing assertion that the Palestinian claim to all the land from the River Jordan to the Mediterranean can never be compromised. In communicating in Arabic with his own people and with those of the wider Arab World, Arafat made it clear that he had no intention of arriving at a final accord. What he did have in mind was a unilateral declaration of independence backed by general world opinion that did not necessitate Israeli approval. From such a nascent state, he hoped to whittle Israel away in stages.[119]

Barak hit upon the idea of appealing to Clinton to cajole Arafat into coming to the bargaining table by deploying the full weight of his office – an idea to which Clinton was well disposed. At first, Arafat resisted Clinton's overtures, claiming, among other things, that final-stage negotiations were somewhat premature, since the Palestinians had still to complete their preparations for such an encounter. Such reasoning was at odds with threats, which the PA began to issue repetitively, that, unless all issues were soon resolved, it would unilaterally declare an independent Palestinian State. Eventually having run out of excuses, Arafat agreed to attend a trilateral United States–Israel–Palestine summit to commence on July 11 at Camp David.

As the parties assembled at their US meeting place, support for Barak's government was beginning to falter. An inkling of the type and scope of the concessions that Barak was prepared to make began to filter into the public domain, and many of his coalition partners began to be filled with serious misgivings. Shas, Mafdal and Yisrael Be'teinu withdrew from the government on July 10 and 11. That meant that Barak could count on the overt support of only thirty-two Jewish Knesset members and the tacit backing of ten anti-Zionist Arab members.[120] Refusing to let domestic political considerations sidetrack him, Barak, for the full seventeen days that the talks lasted, showed a remarkable willingness to do whatever it would take to bridge the gap between the Israeli and Palestinian positions. When at first his initial submissions were deemed to fall short of Palestinian demands, Barak eventually improved upon them by seemingly reaching the limit, from an Israeli point of view, of what he could possibly concede. His closing bid amounted to a willingness to hand over Gaza and approximately 91 percent of the West Bank, as well as sections of Jerusalem. The Palestine state was to be demilitarized, and for a limited period Israel was to hold a thin strip of the southern Jordan Valley. Palestinian refugees would be able to settle in the new Palestinian State but not in Israel.[121]

Never before had an Israeli prime minister considered such an extensive withdrawal. Previously, Israeli leaders of all political persuasions had automatically ruled out dividing Jerusalem. As an article of religious and national faith, an undivided Jerusalem was to remain under Israel's sovereignty in perpetuity. Of all nations currently extant, only the Jews have had the city as their historic capital. In no phase of their relatively brief existence has Jerusalem ever been the capital of the Palestinians. Apart from anything else, if one includes both its eastern and western sections, Jerusalem since 1874 has constantly had a Jewish majority.

No less startling was Barak's readiness to vacate almost the entire Jordan River Valley. As mentioned in chapter 1, soon after the 1967 war, Yigal Allon, the commander of the Palmah, devised a plan for an eventual partitioning of the West Bank that became known as the Allon Plan. This allowed for Israel to forfeit a significant proportion of the West Bank while maintaining a Greater Jerusalem area, the Judean Desert and the Jordan Valley. Areas to be allotted to the Palestinians comprised a region north of Jerusalem embracing the cities of Nablus, Jenin, Tulkarm, Ramallah and Jericho, as well as a smaller stretch of land south of Jerusalem that included Hebron and Bethlehem. To a large extent, Allon's plan was favoured by the Labour Party, but it was also in part acceptable to right-wing politicians, given that it included the retention of the Jordan Valley as Israel's defensive border in the east. On that score there was no dissension. Yet Barak offered to throw in most of the Jordan Valley. One might have expected that his efforts to meet the Palestinians more than half way would have met with some expressions of appreciation. But senior members of the PA regarded his gestures with derision and Barak himself as a "lemon" to be squeezed over and over again, to derive one concession after another.[122] Consonant with that approach was Mahmoud Abbas's statement: "Personally I cannot move one step forward. The other party [Israel] has to come our way on *all* the issues on which it procrastinates."[123]

To the chagrin of both Clinton and Barak, Arafat insisted that no agreement would be reached unless Israel acceded to his demand to accept the right of all Palestinian refugees and their descendants to return to their former homes in Israel as it existed before the Six-Day War. For good measure, Arafat also rejected any formula for shared sovereignty of the Temple Mount. As far as he was concerned, the Jews never built a temple there in the first place and, for good measure, he preposterously claimed that Jesus was not only a Palestinian but also the first Palestinian shahid.[124]

What was particularly telling was Arafat informing Clinton that a decision on his part to accept shared sovereignty over the Temple Mount would amount to his signing his own death warrant.[125] At the heart of the matter lies a dysfunctional Palestinian society incapable of reaching a genuine peace settlement with Israel. Apart from Arafat's own personal feelings, which in practice were in tune with his constituency, his mullahs had given him food for thought that he could ill afford to ignore. On July 21, the imam of al-Aqsa, speaking from his pulpit, pontificated on the nature of the Israeli–Palestinian conflict. In his judgment, all Palestinian land held by Jews, including "the land that was occupied in 1948," is inalienable Islamic land. Consequently, any agreement that allows for Israel's continued existence is treasonable. Three days later, while the Camp David summit was still in progress, the mufti of al-Quds, Ikrama Sabri (who was chosen by Arafat), issued a fatwa forbidding Palestinian refugees from accepting financial compensation in exchange for not being repatriated.[126] Reflecting on the Palestinian rejection of Barak's offer, Mahmoud Abbas declared that anyone subject to the illusion that the Palestinians would ever forego their "right" of return to Israel would simply be misleading himself. He and his colleagues felt no compunction at having missed an historic opportunity, since no such opportunity ever existed.[127]

7

THE AL-AQSA INTIFADA

After rejecting Barak and Clinton's joint efforts to arrive at a final settlement, Arafat returned home to a hero's welcome and was lauded for
not forsaking his people in their principled struggle for "justice." On
the eve of the talks, Arafat's approval rating had slumped to 40 percent
of the population, but afterwards it exceeded 70 percent.[1] His account
of his stance at the Camp David talks was well appreciated. At a mass
rally, Arafat proclaimed: "We told the Israelis that we demand not only
the Haram Ash-Sharif [the Temple Mount], the Church of the Holy
Sepulchre and Armenian Quarter but Jerusalem in its entirety, all of
Jerusalem, all of Jerusalem. If that does not please them they can jolly
well drink water from the Dead Sea."[2] Arafat once more pronounced
that the return of the Arab refugees to their homeland was an inviolable
sacred tenet. To obviate any misunderstanding, Abbas specified that,
"When we talk about the Right of Return, we talk about the return of
refugees to Israel, because Israel was the one who deported them and
it is in Israel that their property is found."[3] According to an official
Palestinian account of the talks, the Palestinians also demanded a *full*
Israeli withdrawal to the pre-1967 war boundaries. Once that had been
attained, they would be willing to negotiate minor adjustments, involving no more than 1.5 percent of the area of the West Bank in return for
twice as much land from Israel.[4]

Buoyed by his newfound popularity, Arafat planned his next move, which amounted to assuming a violent offensive. As in the case of the tunnel riots, an ideal pretext came to hand, this time in the form of Sharon paying a visit to the Temple Mount. Sharon, who had recently succeeded Netanyahu as leader of the Likud, believed that a short walking tour of the Temple Mount would bolster his credentials as an ardent nationalist. The visit was coordinated with the Muslim Waqf, and Jibril Rajoub, the PA security chief, had assured Israel's minister of internal security, Shlomo Ben-Ami, that he foresaw no problems provided that Sharon did not enter either of the two mosques.[5] After all, as Shalom and Hendel wrote, "Sharon, a member of the Knesset, had merely requested permission to visit an area under Israel's sovereignty."[6] Nonetheless, the PA began making extensive preparations to make political capital out of the situation. Feigning concern that it might lose control over events, it designated Saeb Erekat to approach Dennis Ross, President Clinton's Middle East envoy, at his hotel in Washington to plead with him to use his influence over Barak to have the visit cancelled. As Ross wryly noted, the meeting seemed more like a perfunctory attempt on Erekat's part to have been seen as having issued a warning of dangers ahead, for the meeting took place at 11 p.m. Israel time on the night before the event.[7]

On Thursday September 28, 2000, surrounded by his bodyguards and many other security officials, Sharon spent no more than forty-five minutes at the Temple Mount. During that time he dutifully refrained from entering the Dome of the Rock and the al-Aqsa Mosque and made no statement.[8] The occasion passed without any serious incident other than a few sporadic Arab clashes with the police involving relatively minor injuries, but nonetheless the Palestinians soon worked themselves into a lather. When, by contrast, a far graver affront had been administered to the Israelis, they remained calm. In December 1999, the Waqf, without the legally required authorization of the Antiquities Authority, commissioned bulldozers to excavate tons of material on the Temple Mount where the ancient Jewish Temples were sited. Dismissing Israeli protests, the Waqf's spokesman, Adnan Husseini, argued that there was no "need to have contact with anyone. Every piece of stone on the Temple Mount is Islamic property."[9]

The day after Sharon's Temple Mount visit, Muslims attending the

Friday service at the al-Aqsa Mosque were subject to a rousing call to rise to the defence of Islam. In a fit of fury they made a beeline for the top of the Western Wall, whence they hurled previously piled rocks and even Molotov cocktails at the Jewish worshippers below. Israeli snipers fired both live ammunition and rubber bullets at the rioters, killing seven of them.[10] Thus was the al-Aqsa Intifada inaugurated, at a time when the PA had full or partial control over 98 percent of the Palestinian population.[11] In practice, one could say that it began earlier that morning when, at 6.45 a.m., an IDF soldier on a joint patrol with a member of the PA preventive security force was killed by his Palestinian counterpart, who shouted "Allahu Akbar" (God is the greatest) as he shot him.[12]

Almost universally, the media attributed the cause of the senseless bloodshed, which continued without interruption until February 2005, to Sharon's disregard for Muslim sensibilities. But the Palestinians knew better. In March 2001, speaking at a Palestinian refugee camp in Lebanon, Imad al-Faluji, the PA communications minister, told a crowd of listeners: "Whoever thinks that the Intifada broke out because of the despised Sharon's visit is wrong. The Intifada was planned in advance." Al-Faluji then added:

> Just as the national and Islamic Resistance in South Lebanon taught [Israel] a lesson and made it withdraw humiliated and battered, so shall [Israel] learn a lesson from the Palestinian Resistance in Palestine. The Palestinian Resistance will strike in Tel Aviv, in Ashkelon, in Jerusalem, and in every inch of the land of natural Palestine. Israel will not have a single quiet night. There will be no security in the heart of Israel.[13]

Then on May 28, 2002, at a rally in Gaza, Brigadier Mazen Izz al-Din, chief of political indoctrination of the PA security forces, pronounced: "We have to be truthful and honest and spell it out. One day history will expose the fact that the whole Intifada and its instructions came from Brother Commander Yasser Arafat."[14] Even Arafat's widow, Suha Arafat, in an interview on Dubai TV, wanted it known that her late husband had told her in July 2000 that he was going to start an intifada.[15]

Before the onset of the al-Aqsa Intifada, a number of warnings of an impending collision were made known in Palestinian publications.

In an interview with the official PA newspaper, *al-Hayat al-Jadida*, published on August 24, 2000, Freih Abu Middein, the PA minister of justice, let it be known that "violence is near and the Palestinian people are willing to sacrifice even 5,000 casualties."[16] Similarly, on August 30, 2000, the PA morning paper *al-Sabah* assured its readers: "We will advance and declare a general Intifada for Jerusalem. The time for the Intifada has arrived; the time for Jihad has arrived."[17] Harbingers of an impending explosion were evident well beforehand. Three years earlier, on August 5, 1997, Arafat *openly* exhorted Fatah leaders to prepare for a violent showdown with Israel. He declared: "Ahead of us is a conflict far greater than we encountered in the past. We are all living shahids ready to renew our commitment to a path of armed struggle that we took upon ourselves many years ago."[18] Arafat's colleagues hardly needed any encouragement. In March 1997, Marwan Barghouti, a leading light among Fatah's Tanzim fighters, in addressing the Palestinian Legislative Council, extended his deep condolences to the family of the Hamas terrorist who blew himself up at the Apropo Café in Tel Aviv, killing three young women (one of whom was pregnant) and wounding twenty-eight others. Barghouti's sentiments were thunderously applauded by all in the chamber.[19] Finally, even the Israelis had some foreknowledge of the looming conflict. On July 23, 2000, the IDF chief of staff, Shaul Mofaz, told a Knesset committee that the PA had been smuggling in weapons in preparation for an armed struggle.[20] He could just as well have added that the PA had begun hoarding food and other provisions, including medicine on a massive scale.[21] One of the things that troubled Mofaz was the agenda of the PA youth camps, attended by 25,000 Palestinian teenagers. John Burns, reporting for the *New York Times*, visited one such camp in the summer of 2000. There he witnessed "a mock kidnapping of an Israeli leader by masked Palestinian commandos, ending with the Israeli's bodyguards sprawled dead on the ground. Next there is a mock attack on an Israeli military post ending with a sentry being grabbed by the neck and fatally stabbed. Finally there is the opportunity to excel in stripping and reassembling a real Kalashnikov rifle." One of the camp guides proudly quoted Arafat as saying "This is the generation that will plant the Palestinian flag on the walls of Jerusalem."[22]

An important factor that encouraged the PA to undertake a popular uprising against the Israelis was the IDF's unilateral withdrawal from

Southern Lebanon in the previous month of May. Far from being seen as an orderly departure, the withdrawal was perceived as a rout. Just two days after the last Israeli soldier left Lebanon, Hezbollah's leader, Hassan Nasrallah, made a grandiloquent victory speech that left a deep impression on the Palestinians. Among other things Nasrallah stated: "My dear brothers, I say this to you. With all its weapons Israel is weaker than cobwebs."[23] That assessment was shared by leading figures in both Fatah and Hamas, who reasoned that, if the IDF left Lebanon after sustaining an average of only twenty-five fatal casualties per year, surely it would be unwilling to continue retaining the occupied territories in the event of Palestinian terror exacting a far higher price.[24]

Having turned down a generous Israeli final settlement offer and offering in return a well-planned outbreak of sustained violence and bloodshed, the Palestinian leadership went to great pains to portray the intifada as a struggle to rid Palestine of Jews. In an official PA TV broadcast on October 2, 2000, an announcer proclaimed: "The existence of Israel has numbered only fifty-two years, whereas the Palestinians have been here for thousands of years. We are the indigenous population and in the end we shall expel the invaders, irrespective of how long it takes."[25] Sahir Habash, a member of the Fatah Central Committee, explicitly stated in January 2001 that it is "impossible to maintain any co-existence between Zionism and the Palestinian National Movement."[26] On July 2, 2001, after being asked by US journalist Jeffrey Goldberg as to what would be expected of Israel to bring the uprising to a close, Barghouti replied: "We need one hundred percent of Gaza, one hundred percent of the West Bank, one hundred percent of East Jerusalem, and the right of return for refugees." When Goldberg sought to establish whether or not the conflict would be resolved in the unlikely event of all such PA demands being met, Barghouti smiled, emitted an expletive and said: "Then we could talk about bigger things . . . I've always thought that a good idea would be one state for all the peoples . . . a secular democratic Palestine?"[27] In other words, the struggle was a zero-sum game in which there was no point in coming to any negotiated terms with Israel other than its acceptance of its own demise. That brings us back to the basic question actually posed by Barak – namely, why did Arafat resort to widespread violence just when he was being offered the prospect of becoming the first president of an independent Palestinian State? The answer to such a question can only be because Arafat was under no circumstances willing to agree to a partitioned Palestine in which an independent Jewish state would coexist side by side with an Arab one.

During the first few days of the intifada, clashes occurred between Israeli soldiers and Palestinian protesters at various checkpoints in the occupied territories. Far from being spontaneous, they were incited by members of Fatah with Arafat's connivance.[28] During the first month of the uprising, 141 Palestinians and eleven Israelis were killed.[29]

Of the many encounters taking place in the occupied areas, one in particular had a significant impact on the course of events to follow and, considering its importance, is being dealt with here at some length. It was reported by France 2, a French public-owned national television channel, that on September 30, 2000, a twelve-year-old Palestinian boy, Muhammad al-Dura, and his father, Jamal, were caught in crossfire at the Netzarim Junction in Gaza between IDF forces and PA police. Huddled behind a concrete barrel alongside a wall, Jamal, shielding his frightened son, tried to alert the Israelis to the fact they were innocent civilians who had inadvertently stumbled there. Ignoring his frantic appeals, Israeli soldiers fatally shot Muhammad and wounded Jamal. All this was supposedly filmed live by a France 2 photographer, Talal Abu Rahmeh, who later testified under oath that the Israelis had intentionally murdered the boy in cold blood.[30] The footage, generously released to all interested parties, was universally broadcast. According to Charles Enderlin, a France 2 journalist who was the film's commentator (though at the time of the reported events he was attending an interview with Marwan Barghouti), the terrible moments of the child's death throes were edited out because they were "too unbearable."[31] In PA-controlled areas, images of the dead boy lying at the feet of his distraught father were extensively replicated and distributed. They became a ubiquitous symbol of Israeli infamy, and, as they became seared into Palestinian minds, there was no shortage of volunteers seeking to avenge Muhammad, "the first al-Aqsa child martyr." Moreover, the pictures, well enlarged, were prominently displayed in just about every anti-Israel rally throughout Europe and even within parts of America.

At first, the Israelis accepted a measure of responsibility for the tragedy and promised to investigate it. In the course of their inquiries they determined that it would have been impossible for the IDF to target the unfortunate pair, as they were not in the line of fire from the IDF's sole nearby outpost, where all its troops were concentrated. Furthermore, as Nidra Poller wrote, IDF soldiers "had reported nothing resembling what Enderlin described, for the simple reason that they had seen nothing."[32] Other inconsistencies began to emerge. The France 2 photographer retracted his testimony of the boy's death being a willful Israeli murder. When French journalists Luc Rosenzweig and Denis Jeambar asked France 2 to show them the scene of Muhammad's final moments, they were informed that, contrary to Enderlin's assertions, no such footage existed.[33] Even more damning, Rosenzweig and Jeambar had obtained a photograph of a dead child, identified as Muhammad al-Dura, who had been admitted to a Gaza hospital hours before the alleged incident. The dead child's face did not resemble that of the boy filmed by France 2. Finally, Philippe Karsenty, the founder of the French online watchdog Media Ratings, accused France 2 of staging the al-Dura "killing." As a result, Karsenty was sentenced by a French lower court for libeling France 2 and Enderlin. But on May 21, 2008, the Court of Appeal vindicated him. Influencing the court's decision was the testimony of the historian Professor Richard Landes, who, after viewing previously unavailable footage, found that the violence had been staged.[34] In a post-trial statement Karsenty declared: "A child cannot move, lift his head, arm and leg, stare at the camera and still be considered 'dead.' One need only look at France 2's own footage to realize that the 'death' scene was faked."[35] However, for Karsenty the matter did not rest there. On February 28, 2012, the French High Court rendered the Court of Appeal's verdict redundant on the grounds that it overstepped its bounds in ordering France 2 to send Karsenty the rushes (unedited footage) of its contentious TV report.[36] For France 2 to get off the hook because the Court of Appeal had exceeded its authority does not automatically mean that Karsenty's strictures were unfounded.

By coincidence, nearly two weeks earlier, on February 15, 2012, the same French High Court acquitted Dr Yehuda David, of Israel's Tel Hashomer Hospital, of slandering Jamal al-Dura, the dead boy's father. Jamal had shown the media scars on his body that he claimed were the result of his having been wounded by the IDF. David revealed that, in reality, the scars resulted from surgery performed on Jamal some years before the al-Dura affair. Jamal had been admitted to Tel Hashomer Hospital after having been assaulted by members of Hamas who suspected him of collaborating with Israel. Jamal sued David for libel and at first won his case on a technicality. A Paris court ruled against David on the grounds that he had unethically released Jamal's medical records, but the French High Court overturned that decision. Speaking to journalists after being vindicated, David exclaimed: "It means that I spoke the truth, and the father just lied. We managed to deconstruct their false statements. All the scientific evidence that we collected for the past 12 years proves that the incident was staged and fake. They made up the father's injury, and the IDF troops never shot the boy."[37]

A few days after the al-Dura incident, on October 1 to be exact, Israeli Arabs joined in the mayhem, and in the ensuing ten days thirteen of them were killed by the IDF and law-enforcement agents. The focal point of the disturbances was in the Galilee, but they also spread as far afield as Jaffa and to Bedouin settlements in the Negev. The Arabs' anger was vented by stoning cars and by burning banks and government buildings. Fortunately for Israel, a forceful military and police response soon succeeded in putting a stop to such occurrences[38]

The al-Aqsa Intifada was far more violent than the first intifada. From its inception, it involved the Palestinian use of firearms, and as it progressed Israelis were subjected to planned operations intended to kill as many of them as possible. Within a short time span, it ceased to be a popular uprising as was the case with the previous one. The practice of Palestinian gunmen firing from among and behind civilian crowds caused civilians to shy away. In the process, they conceded the struggle to armed organizations. The latter in turn were not only not unified and centrally controlled but vied with one another for the esteem of the Palestinian populace. Prominent among them were Hamas, the Tanzim (an organization associated with Fatah), the al-Aqsa Martyrs Brigade (with close ties to Arafat) and, finally, the Islamic Jihad, which rivaled Hamas. The progress of the intifada was neither consciously orchestrated nor coordinated by any Palestinian high command, and Arafat's influence on the course of events was more in the nature of his passively acquiescing to initiatives proposed by those who assumed command of fighter units rather than his issuing of explicit instructions. While he retained a measure of control over the activities of the Fatah-related bodies by virtue of his being the major source of their funding, not once did he try to stem the ongoing bloodshed.[39] Meanwhile, Hamas renewed dispatching suicide bombers to Israel proper, a step avoided by Fatah until over a year later, for initially it sought to confine itself to the waylaying of IDF troops and the attacking of West Bank Jewish settlers, including women and children.

In the very early stages of the Intifada, Gilo, an Israeli suburb of Jerusalem established in 1973, was subject to regular rifle fire from the nearby Palestinian town of Beit Jala. The IDF returned fire but refrained from entering Beit Jala, since it was in an Area A Palestinian zone. Feeling the brunt of the IDF retaliations, some of the Beit Jala inhabitants turned to Arafat in the hope that he would put a stop to the actions of the local gunmen. The latter in turn took it out on Beit Jala civilians by extracting "Intifada taxes," sexually molesting and even raping two of their women, and killing those suspected of cooperating with Israel.[40]

On the Israeli side there was also a pronounced tendency to resort to gunfire, except that the IDF was both responding to and anticipating perceived threats. It did not hesitate to make use of tanks, helicopters and, on occasion, fighter planes. In Gaza it demolished a fair number of Palestinian homes and cleared a large number of trees alongside roads on which Jewish settlers travelled[41] – a move described by the Israeli journalists Amos Harel and Avi Issacharoff as "pure vandalism."[42] To deter would-be infiltrators from approaching the wired fence that marked Gaza's northern boundaries, a no-man's land was designated and the army was instructed to shoot at anyone encroaching upon it.

In the midst of all this carnage, on October 4, a theatre of the absurd transpired in the US embassy in Paris as Barak and Arafat met in a forlorn attempt to carve out a ceasefire agreement. Arafat, playing the victim, demanded both the establishment of an international commission of inquiry to investigate the IDF's conduct and the stationing of foreign observers in the area. That claim was given short shrift by Barak, who in turn asked Arafat to rein in Barghouti and the Tanzim under his control. At that point Arafat put on a vaudeville act, pretending never to have heard of such a person. His behaviour was so absurd that even his aides could not control their laughter.[43] That was the second time that Arafat had ridiculously professed not to know of a prominent Palestinian terrorist. (In 1996 when requested by Moshe Ya'alon, then head of IDF intelligence, that he arrest Mohammad Deif, the mastermind of Hamas's suicide bombing offensive, Arafat, after bellowing "Mohammad who?," turned to Mohammad Dahlan, sitting beside him, to ask "Have you ever heard of such a bloke?" Dahlan, who went to school with Deif and who had been in an Israeli prison with him, played along with Arafat by also denying all knowledge of Deif's existence.)[44] Soon afterwards Arafat suddenly declared the Paris meeting over and that he was leaving, prompting US Secretary of State Madeleine Albright to run after his car in the embassy grounds while shouting to the guards to close the gates.[45] Arafat then returned with Albright and finally agreed to a ceasefire. But after dining with French President Chirac he backtracked by refusing to sign the ceasefire document.[46]

When at times the IDF overreacted, thus causing needless deaths, its level of deliberate personal brutality fell short of that shown by the Palestinians. Take for example the case of what became known as the lynching in Ramallah. On October 12, 2000, two IDF reservists, one a father of three and the other newly married, mistakenly drove into Ramallah. There they were detained by PA police, who would normally have handed them over to the Israeli authorities, but on that occasion they took them to the local police station. On hearing that Israeli soldiers were in the building, a vast crowd of Palestinians gathered and surrounded it. Soon some of them burst into the station, where they laid into the two unfortunate men by stabbing them, gouging out their eyes and disemboweling them. So disfigured were they that they could subsequently be identified only by means of dental records. Hearing on Israeli radio that two IDF soldiers were in the custody of the PA police, the anxious wife of one of them tried contacting her spouse on his cell phone. The call was taken by someone with a strange voice, blithely informing her that he had just murdered her husband. Shortly thereafter, the crowd, baying for Jewish blood, received satisfaction when one of the victims was tossed out of a first-floor window, where Aziz Salha, a Palestinian policeman, jubilantly appeared and raised his blood-soaked hands. Among the crowd was Mark Seager, a British photographer, who afterwards wrote:

My God, I thought, they've killed this guy. He was dead, he must have been dead, but they were still beating him, madly, kicking his head. They were like animals . . . it was the most horrible thing that I have ever seen and I have reported from Congo and Kosovo . . . there was such hatred, such unbelievable hatred and anger distorting their faces . . . I'll never forget this. It was murder of the most barbaric kind. When I think about it, I see that man's head, all smashed. I know that I'll have nightmares for the rest of my life.[47]

A large component of the international media tried to extenuate the atrocity by referring to Palestinian losses since the commencement of the intifada and/or other long-standing Palestinian grievances, such as the expansion of Israeli settlements. For example, writing in the *Washington Post* nearly a year later, Lee Hockstader asserted that "People's emotions were boiling over because of Palestinian teens shot by Israeli soldiers . . . Israel's settlements and occupation were on Salha's mind . . . he was a calm, good-natured and athletic kid."[48] The shallowness and lack of concern of the international "quality" media for the real causes of such savage behaviour is legendary. Staring in the face of every reporter was a never ending stream of vile anti-Semitic harangues, propagated by the PA and by others under its auspices, inciting Palestinians to undertake such gruesome deeds. The day after the Ramallah lynching, no less a person than Dr Ahmad Abu Halabiya, a member of the PA-appointed "Fatwa Council" and former acting rector of the Islamic University in Gaza, gave a sermon at a mosque in Gaza *which was broadcast live by the official PA television*. Among other things, this is what he had to say: "The Jews are Jews, whether Labor or Likud . . . they are all liars . . . They are the terrorists. They are the ones who must be butchered and killed . . . Allah will torture them at your hands . . . Have no mercy where they are, in any country . . . Wherever you meet them, kill them."[49] By any criterion, Halabiya's adjuration was heady stuff, though not pungent enough for the likes of William Orme, who, writing in the *New York Times*, could only bring himself to report: "'Whether Likud or Labor, Jews are Jews,' proclaimed Sheik Ahmad Abu Halabaya [*sic*] in a live broadcast from a Gaza City mosque."[50] Orme's dispatch conveyed not the slightest hint that Halabiya's message was, by any civilized standards, beyond the pale.

Plate 6   *Aziz Salha jubilantly raising his blood-soaked hands after taking part in the killing of Israeli reservists*

If an award were to be given for the most egregious and craven journalistic performance with regard to the Israeli–Palestinian conflict, Ricardo Cristiano would be a commendable candidate among a field of many serious contenders. On October 18, 2000, so alarmed was he that he might be mistaken by the PA for having been involved in filming the Ramallah lynching, he placed a notice in the PA's official newspaper, *al-Hayat al-Jadida*, that read:

My dear friends in Palestine. We congratulate you and think that it is our duty to put you in the picture of what happened on October 12 in Ramallah. One of the private Italian television stations which competes with us filmed the events [*sic*] . . . the public impression was created as if we [Radiotelevisione Italiana] took these pictures. We emphasize to all of you that the events did not happen this way because we always

respect the journalistic procedures of the Palestinian Authority . . . You
can be sure that this is not our way of acting. We will not do such a
thing.[51]

In responding to the outbreak of the intifada, the Israeli government
exhibited elements of schizophrenia. On the one hand, the IDF did not
hesitate in returning fire arising from Palestinian gunmen, and Barak
even made noises about sterner countermeasures to follow. On the
other hand, Barak, still thinking that a deal with Arafat was worth pursuing, was loath to adopt measures that might further alienate him. On
November 1, Peres met with Arafat at Dahaniya International Airport
in Gaza, where it was agreed that, at 12 p.m. the following day, Barak
and Arafat would simultaneously announce that they had ordered a total
ceasefire. But when the time came Arafat was immersed in a PA leaders'
meeting and supposedly for that reason could not fulfil his side of the
bargain.[52] If that was not clear enough, three hours later the detonation
of a car bomb in Jerusalem, killing two Israeli civilians, blew away, for
the time being, Israeli illusions that any return to normality was on the
immediate horizon. Barak and his remaining cabinet members failed
to grasp the fact that Arafat was delighted to be seen both by his own
people and by the rest of the Arab World as a newfound Saladin. The
intifada had energized him, and in its early months he was euphorically
riding on cloud nine.[53]

By early December, Barak, realizing that he had lost the necessary
Knesset support to remain in office, resigned and set February 6, 2001,
as the date for an election to determine Israel's next prime minister. In
the transition period until the swearing in of a new government, he and
his ministers retained their posts. Unfazed by his anomalous position,
Barak persisted in seeking to resolve all outstanding issues with the
PA. One of his decisions involved agreeing to Clinton's own proposals for an Israel–Palestine peace submitted on December 23. Clinton's
"parameters" amounted to Israel handing over Gaza and between 94
and 96 percent of the West Bank, which would all be demilitarized.
Jerusalem was to be divided and shared along Jewish–Arab ethnic lines;
the Palestinians were to have sovereignty over the Temple Mount, the
Israelis over the Western Wall, and both would share sovereignty over
the area beneath the Temple Mount. The Palestinian refugees would

be given unrestricted rights to return to the new Palestinian State, but Israel would have full discretion in deciding whether or not to accept any within its frontiers. On December 28, the Israeli cabinet voted to accept Clinton's parameters. But on January 2, 2001, Arafat effectively rejected them. Among the items he found to be unacceptable were the sharing of sovereignty under the Temple Mount and the exclusion of the rights of Palestinian refugees to return to Israel proper.[54] Arafat's rejection was roundly criticized by Prince Bandar of Saudi Arabia and Nabil Fahmy, the Egyptian ambassador to the USA. Bandar considered Arafat's obduracy as a crime against the Palestinians, while a little later Crown Prince Abdullah told Clinton that it was widely known that Arafat's word could not be taken at face value.[55]

Then over the week January 21 to 27, 2001, Barak's ministers attended a conference at Taba in the Sinai, where they negotiated with their PA counterparts. The talks were pointless. Neither Barak nor Arafat participated, Clinton was no longer president, and Bush, his successor, had withdrawn his support for the parameters. Even so, the Israelis upped their offer to hand over to the Palestinians 97 percent of the West Bank while not explicitly rejecting the right of return of displaced Palestinians. It was a better deal than that submitted by Barak at Camp David and the contents of Clinton's parameters. But the PA delegates, Abu Ala and Mohammad Dahlan, admitted to Gilad Sher and Yisrael Hasson that Arafat was not interested in a settlement.[56]

Given that public support for Barak's leadership and policies had plummeted, his conduct as a caretaker prime minister can only charitably be described as irregular. The Israeli electorate was not impressed. Standing against Sharon for re-election, Barak was trounced. He obtained only thirty-eight percent of the total votes cast, as opposed to the 62 percent share that went to Sharon.

The irony of it all is that the Palestinians, who despised and feared Sharon more than any other Israeli politician, and who used the latter's visit to the Temple Mount as an excuse to launch an unprecedented wave of anti-Israel violence, found that their very actions set the stage for his rise to power. Despite his colleagues' misgivings, Arafat indicated that he was not in the least perturbed. "On the contrary," he boasted, "we'll defeat him just as we did in Lebanon." Listening in astonishment, Erekat asked: "How exactly did we win if he expelled us from there and forced us to move to Tunisia for over ten years?" Arafat answered with some classic Arab curses.[57]

Since the election was only to decide the next prime minister, Sharon, in forming his new government, had to take into account the fact that each party's share of Knesset seats remained unaltered. He opted for a broad-based national unity government made up of Likud, One Israel, Shas, United Torah (an Ashkenazi Haredi God-fearing party), Yisrael Be'Aliyah, Ichud Leumi–Yisrael Beiteinu (a right-wing pro-settler party headed first by Rehavam Ze'evi and then by Avigdor Lieberman) and Gesher. Peres became foreign minister and Binyamin Ben-Eliezer minister of defence. Sharon's government was sworn in on March 7, 2001. As for Barak, he resigned from the Knesset and for the next few years did not play an active role in politics.

In the same month that Sharon became prime minister, the Palestinians launched their first fatal suicide bombing since the commencement of the al-Aqsa Intifada. Adapting to his newfound responsibilities, Sharon moved rather cautiously. His government's responses to Palestinian violence were similar in kind to all previous ones, with two notable exceptions. First, he ruled out negotiating with the PA while Israelis were being subject to Palestinian assaults and, second, he intended to suspend cash transfers to the PA arising from the income taxes of Palestinians working in Israel. With regard to the first point, it turned out that Sharon, like all his predecessors, failed to abide by his own pronouncements. Very soon into his term of office, low-level negotiations were resumed with the PA with the intention of preparing the way for a face-to-face meeting between Sharon and Arafat. While the groundwork was being prepared for such an encounter, it was Arafat who balked and, as a result, all such efforts came to naught. As for the second point, the USA, not taking kindly to the view that it was reasonable to deny one's adversary funds that financed its militia, insisted that the remittances be continued. Then, hopping aboard the bandwagon of the clamorous international critics of Israel's defence measures, the US secretary of state, Colin Powell, censured Sharon for employing excessive and disproportionate force.[58] Powell's hypocrisy was widely noted in light of his own defence doctrine, which stated that, when at war, the United States should not stint on using all manner of force at its disposal. On May 22, 2001, Sharon declared a unilateral ceasefire. The

IDF would no longer initiate any actions and its soldiers would open fire only in situations where their lives were clearly at risk. Israel asked the Americans to use their influence to persuade Arafat to do likewise, but Arafat, deriving encouragement from growing international support, would have none of it.[59]

Meanwhile, the Tanzim led by Marwan Barghouti, in addition to confronting IDF forces, chose to fire on settlers in the West Bank as they travelled in cars lacking bullet-proof armour. The settlers were picked off early in the mornings en route to work or at sunset as they returned home. Of the ninety Israelis killed in the first half of the year, eighteen were West Bank settlers.[60] In turn, some settlers took the law into their own hands, killing eight Palestinians and setting off, in a Palestinian school, an explosive device packed with nails and screws that wounded five pupils.[61] Before long a number of unauthorized new settler outposts emerged, but that did not perturb Sharon, who regarded them as a blessing. In 1998, while serving in Netanyahu's government, Sharon told the settlers that each of them ought to "seize another hill and widen the area. Everything that is taken will be in our hands. What is not taken by us will be in their hands."[62]

On June 1, 2001, after attempting to uphold his unilateral ceasefire declaration, Sharon was presented with a serious dilemma. That day, at the Dolphin Disco in Tel Aviv, a Palestinian suicide bomber blew himself up, killing twenty-one Israelis, mostly teenagers, and wounding 120 others.[63] Deferring to international pressure, Arafat issued a cursory condemnation of the massacre. Then he promptly wrote a letter to the parents of Said al-Hotari, the murderer, commending their son's deeds. After describing the killer as a heroic martyr, Arafat went on to suggest that he was the very "model of manhood and sacrifice for the sake of Allah and the homeland."[64] Al-Hotari himself would have concurred, for in a testament he had left behind he claimed: "There is nothing greater than being martyred for the sake of Allah, on the land of Palestine. Cry in joy my mother, hand out candy, my father and brothers, for your son awaits a wedding with the 72 black eyed virgins in heaven."[65] At an emergency cabinet meeting, Sharon demanded that Arafat be finally designated as an enemy and that the government should once and for all come to terms with the real situation on the ground rather than the prevailing imaginary one. But, ever beholden to his delusions and ready to serve as Arafat's advocate, Peres swayed a gullible cabinet to accept that he remained Israel's stalwart peace process partner. As the cabinet meeting dragged on, Peres learned from Joschka Fischer, the German foreign minister visiting Israel at the time, that Arafat was willing to declare, *in Arabic and on Palestinian television*, his acceptance of a ceasefire. With that in mind, it was resolved that Israel would reaffirm its commitment to do likewise.[66] Needless to say, Arafat once again was not true to his word. At the time that his announcement was expected, Arafat stood at the side of Miguel Moratinos, the European Union Special Representative for the Middle East Peace Process, while Moratinos announced in English that a ceasefire had been agreed upon. Arafat himself said nothing. The most he could do was to nod his head feebly.[67]

Arafat was not of course the only senior Palestinian leader to speak with a forked tongue. Faisal Husseini, poised to succeed him and constantly exuding an impression of being a benign moderate playing a "pivotal role in pursuing accommodation with Israel," did much the same.[68] Upon the latter's sudden death of a heart attack in June 2001, Meron Benvenisti, a former deputy mayor of Jerusalem, described him as "a man that you could find a shared language with."[69] What Benvenisti did not appreciate was the scope of Husseini's discourse. In an interview given to the Egyptian journal *al-Arab* weeks before he died and published posthumously on June 14, 2001, Husseini likened the PLO to a Trojan horse that, given a foothold on territory controlled by Israel, would eventually overrun the entire Jewish State. For the time being he differentiated between PLO strategic goals and what he termed "phased goals," leaving no doubt that, since "Palestine in its entirety is an Arab Land," the long-term goal is "the liberation of historical Palestine from the [Jordan] River to the [Mediterranean] Sea."[70]

The next devastating Palestinian terrorist event occurred on August 9, 2001, when 22-year-old Izz al-Din Shuheil al-Masri, from an affluent land-owning West Bank family that ran a prosperous restaurant in Jenin, entered the Sbarro pizzeria in downtown Jerusalem carrying a bomb in a guitar case. He had been escorted to the entrance of the store by Ahlam Tamimi, a twenty-year-old female university student posing as a Jewish tourist. The two had casually strolled through Jerusalem's city streets, audibly speaking English. Al-Masri's bomb, detonated in

Plate 7   *Israeli police and rescue workers gathering bodies in the wake of a
Palestinian suicide bombing*

the midst of a school holiday, took the lives of fifteen people, including
seven children. Close to 130 sustained mild to severe injuries. As a correspondent of *The Guardian* reported the scene, "Bodies hurled through
the windows lay sprawled on a road strewn with pizza slices, cardboard
boxes, shattered glass, and blood. There were people and babies thrown
through the window and covered with blood. The whole street was
covered with blood and bodies: the dead and the dying."[71] Students of
al Najah University in the West Bank town of Nablus were so proud
of that atrocity that they opened an exhibition on campus containing a full-sized replica of the obliterated Israeli restaurant containing
mock-up body parts, clothes depicted as being bloodstained, and strewn
pieces of pizza. Al-Masri's female escort, Tamimi, was arrested and, for
what it was worth, sentenced to a long term of imprisonment. Freed in
October 2011 in partial exchange for the release of the kidnapped IDF
soldier Gilad Shalit, she was asked whether she regretted what she had
done. She replied: "Absolutely not. This is the path. I dedicated myself
to Jihad for the sake of Allah, and Allah granted me success. You know
how many casualties there were? This was made possible by Allah. Do

you want me to denounce what I did? That's out of the question. I would do it again today, and in the same manner."[72]

Sharon's patient wait for Arafat finally to lose all his credibility with the US administration finally seemed to bear fruit. On January 3, 2002, the Israeli navy and air force intercepted and captured the ship *Karine A* in the Red Sea and brought it to Eilat. There its cargo, generously supplied by Iran, containing 50 tons of advanced weaponry including Katyusha rockets, rifles, mortar shells, mines and a variety of anti-tank missiles, was unloaded and laid out on the pier. Israel accused Arafat of being responsible for attempting to smuggle the weapons in question, but he strenuously denied the charge. His denial was contradicted by the ship's captain, Omar Akawi, who in a jail interview with Jennifer Griffin of Fox News confirmed that the weapons were intended for the Palestinians.[73] The Americans, sharing Israel's assessment that Arafat was behind the whole affair, insisted that he accept the fact that he had a major hand in it. Contributing to Bush's general disenchantment with the Palestinians was their unbridled and public display of elation on hearing the news of 9/11. Arafat, ever so compromised, suppressed all media images of his people celebrating the occasion and made a splash of donating blood for the Twin Tower victims.

In March 2002 there was a dramatic upsurge in Palestinian violence: 117 Israelis were killed as opposed to thirty in the month before. For the first time since the outbreak of the al-Aqsa Intifada, Arafat's Fatah organization consigned more terrorists to Israel proper than Hamas and the Islamic Jihad combined.[74] The most lethal incident occurred on March 27, when a Hamas suicide bomber detonated his device in the restaurant of the Park Hotel in Netanya amid a congregation of Jews celebrating Passover. Thirty people, mainly senior citizens, were killed and 140 were wounded. Paramedics arriving on that macabre scene, where corpses and the injured were sprawled all over the place, had to triage the victims as best and as rapidly as they could.

For Sharon, that was unquestionably the last straw. In an impassioned televised speech, after noting that his country was at war – a war for its existence – Sharon went on to remind his audience: "We have done all we could to achieve a ceasefire and in return we have received nothing but terror, terror and more terror." Arafat, in Sharon's eyes, was "an enemy of Israel," of the entire free world, and a danger to the whole Middle East region.[75] Accordingly, the IDF was authorized to undertake a massive sweep into PA-controlled areas in order to "root out the terrorist infrastructure in the Palestinian territories."[76] Under the rubric of Operation Defensive Shield, a wide-ranging operation went into effect. At the cabinet meeting that approved the project, there were differences of opinion as to what was to become of Arafat. Sharon and his Likud colleagues wanted to deport him, but that was opposed by the Labour Party ministers. Peres in particular, anxious to avoid the adoption of drastic measures, turned to Sharon and, as if the Oslo Accords were still a going proposition, exclaimed: "You are destroying my life's work."[76] Eventually, after hours of soul-searching arguments, a compromise was reached. The cabinet, while designating Arafat as an enemy, decided that, "at this stage," he would merely be isolated. Peres, it might be added, seemed to remain quite impervious to disclosed information based on seized PA papers that Arafat had been actively pursuing a course of violence against Israel. On being asked by Ronen Bergman how he felt when he read such documents, he replied:

> According to the way I see things, Arafat was drawn in by the course of the events and was not an active initiator of them. It is difficult for me to assume that he ignited the PA fuse. Based on my wide experience, I would also suggest that one should relate to written documents as with conversation texts, with a certain degree of skepticism.[78]

Operation Defensive Shield, which commenced a few hours before midnight on March 28, involved the regaining of complete control of all towns and cities of the West Bank except for Hebron and Jericho. Gaza was left untouched, as a strengthening of the fence surrounding it plus an IDF warning that anyone approaching a kilometre strip adjacent to it (on the Gaza side) would be shot, proved to be effective in preventing terrorist acts from being launched there. Over 30,000 soldiers were deployed, more than would be the case four years later in Israel's Second Lebanese War. Sharon, in addressing the Knesset a few days later, urged the IDF "to strike at anyone bearing arms and to silence those that attempt to oppose and endanger Israel's armed forces without harming the civilian population."[79]

The IDF penetrated deeply into Ramallah where, after four days of intermittent fighting, the Muqata, Arafat's headquarters compound, was surrounded and sealed off. The 400 or so Palestinians trapped with Arafat were in desperate straits. They had barely any food and little water and their sanitary conditions were dreadful. However, the IDF soon restored water and electricity and permitted the delivery of fresh food and medicine to Arafat and his associates. Rummaging through parts of the compound, the Israelis discovered small arms stockpiles, sabotage equipment, heavy weapons proscribed by the Oslo agreement, and documents detailing Arafat's involvement in the intifada.[80] That particular arms cache was just one among many found during the IDF's onslaught. Throughout the West Bank a massive quantity of weapons were seized, including thousands of assault rifles and handguns, tens of machine guns, hundreds of kilograms of dynamite, and forty suicide bomber belts ready for immediate use.[81]

In the course of the Muqata siege, a group of Western pro-Palestinians, masquerading as "peace activists," circumvented IDF roadblocks and burst into the Muqata to offer Arafat support. There they agreed to attempt to smuggle out some twenty Palestinians posing as members of their group and to alert the Tanzim and al-Aqsa Martyrs Brigade as to the nature of the IDF's dispositions. As they sauntered forth, the IDF forestalled most of them but a few managed to escape. Hours later, with Israel's enemies emboldened by their recent acquisition of crucial intelligence, a fierce six-hour battle ensued, culminating in the deaths of ten Palestinians and many more wounded. No casualties were inflicted on any Israelis. The affair put paid to Arafat's hope of breaking through the Israeli siege to emerge as the hero of the day.[82]

On learning that the six assassins of Rehavam Ze'evi were ensconced in the Muqata, Israel demanded custody of them as a precondition for ending the siege. Ze'evi, a government minister of tourism, had been gunned down in the Jerusalem Hyatt Hotel at around 7 a.m. on October 17, 2001, in revenge for the targeted killing on August 27 of Abu Ali Mustafa, the leader of the Popular Front for the Liberation of Palestine. On April 14, 2002, the US secretary of state, Colin Powell, accompanied by Anthony Zinni, the US envoy to Israel and the PA, met with Arafat in an attempt to iron out obstacles to the lifting of the Muqata siege. Powell demanded of Arafat that he hand over Ze'evi's killers, accept the US George Tenet Plan, and acknowledge culpability for the arms smuggling attempt of the vessel *Karine A*. On June 10, 2001, Tenet, acting on behalf of President Bush, had drafted a peace plan that included the acceptance of a mutual comprehensive ceasefire facilitated by the security forces of both sides working together to resolve contentious matters. In the end Arafat wrote to Bush confirming the PA's implication in the *Karine A* affair, but he failed to yield on Powell's first two points.[83] Not satisfied, Powell publicly condemned Arafat for misleading both the USA and the world.

The issue of Arafat providing a safe haven for the assassins was ultimately resolved after a series of Egyptian, Jordanian and European delegations hammered out a deal acceptable to both sides. In essence, the killers of Ze'evi were to be transferred from the Muqata to a jail in Jericho, where they were to be guarded by British warders. On May 1, 2002, after the transfer was effected, Israel lifted the Muqata siege. Nearly four years later, when Hamas won the Palestinian legislative elections in January 2006, it was presumed that the assassins would be released, which induced the IDF to raid the Jericho prison to bring them to justice in Israel. In mid-2010, Erekat, the PA's chief negotiator, drafted a letter to Ahmed Saadat, convicted of orchestrating Ze'evi's murder, conveying to him his "strongest emotions of solidarity and brotherhood." Erekat concluded by congratulating Saadat for exhibiting "steadfast resistance that has become the stuff of legend, during which many martyrs fell."[84]

During the IDF offensive in Bethlehem, more than 100 armed members of Fatah, Hamas, Islamic Jihad and the PA security forces barricaded themselves inside the Church of the Nativity, where scores of priests, nuns and other church officials were also present. The Vatican complained that the occupation of the holy places by armed men was "a violation of a long tradition of law that dates back to the Ottoman era."[85] The IDF refrained from storming the church. As the thirty-nine-day standoff continued, conditions there deteriorated. The gunmen, who defecated throughout the church, tore up sacred texts for toilet paper, stole church jewelry and damaged holy statues, survived by helping themselves to the food stored for the clergy. After protracted negotiations, they were allowed to leave without their weapons provided that thirteen of them were exiled to Europe and twenty-six others were moved to Gaza.[85]

Further to the north, Nablus (or Shehem in Hebrew) was retaken by the IDF at a cost of one fatality as opposed to some seventy Palestinian ones. However, in Jenin, Israeli troops paid dearly for their efforts. Some of their losses could be attributed to the fact that, in the main, few of the soldiers in question had any prior urban combat experience or preparation for fighting in densely populated areas. In addition, they were inappropriately issued with relatively long-barreled M-16 rifles that hindered their manoeuvrability in confined spaces.[87]

Their major objective was to penetrate the refugee camp, overwhelm it and neutralize the terrorist threat that emanated from it. Given that so many Palestinian suicide bombers were nurtured, briefed and dispatched from that specific camp, Jenin acquired the sobriquet "the city of martyrs."[88] Before proceeding further, a word or two about the term "refugee camp," as it applies in the West Bank and Gaza, is apposite. For most people, the term "refugee camp" conjures up an image of people living under canvas or in temporary makeshift abodes. While that was so when such camps were formed in the wake of Israel's War of Independence, it is no longer the case. The "refugees" – that is, largely second- or third-generation Palestinians descended from the original camp inhabitants, who are in point of fact living in what they regard as Palestinian territory – currently occupy solidly built structures connected to a power grid. Although by no means lavish, they compare well with homes in which Arab masses generally dwell in, say, rural Egypt.

The Jenin refugee camp was defended by a few hundred gunmen from the Palestinian Authority and from various terrorist organizations, who in the course of time had moved in from Gaza and even from Jordan. Anticipating an IDF incursion, the area was protected by a widespread placement of lethal devices among houses and alleys. Some of the booby traps were in fact effectively large bombs containing 250 pounds of explosives, more than ten times the amount of the 25-pound payload of the standard suicide bomber.[89]

Incorrectly believing that most of the camp's residents were still present, there were differences among IDF commanders as to how to proceed. Most thought it prudent for the infantry to advance tentatively in order to minimize civilian casualties, and in some places they covered only 50 metres per day. While that provided less risk to the lives of non-combatant Palestinians, it exposed the Israelis to avoidable dangers, which in turn caused far more to be killed in Jenin than in any other West Bank city. Dissenting from his fellow officers, Lieutenant Colonel Ofek Buchris pursued a more aggressive approach that involved concentrations of anti-tank missiles and the use of heavily armoured Caterpillar D-9 bulldozers to widen alleys that were merely 3 feet across. One bulldozer alone triggered 124 separate booby traps on a single day,[90] which indicates just how hazardous it was for the Israeli infantry. The dangers that the IDF encountered were later outlined to a UK journalist Jonathan Cook, as he interviewed a "revered" bomb-maker named Omar for an Egyptian journal. In their discussion, Omar disclosed that he and his comrades had planned

> to trap the invading soldiers and blow them up . . . We had more than 50 houses booby-trapped around the camp. We chose old and empty buildings and the houses of men who were wanted by Israel because we knew the soldiers would search for them . . . We cut off lengths of mains water pipes and packed them with explosives and nails. Then we placed them about four metres apart throughout the houses in cupboards, under sinks, in sofas.

In his article Cook went on to remark that "the fighters hoped to disable the Israeli army's tanks with powerful bombs placed inside rubbish bins on the street." Such bombs, connected by wires, were to be remotely triggered.[91] Nevertheless, as the Israelis advanced, the terrorists fell back to the more heavily protected camp's centre. There they were pounded by Cobra helicopters and finally, on April 11, after nine days of fighting, they surrendered.

In the immediate aftermath of the battle, Israel met with a cacophony of nefarious international slander orchestrated by the Palestinians and their supporters. Without a shred of evidence, Jenin, described by Arafat as the "Palestinian Stalingrad," was reputed to have become the scene of a massive Israeli-perpetrated massacre. Not batting an eyelid, leading PA spokesmen such as Nabil Shaath and Saeb Erekat pronounced that no fewer than 500 Palestinians had been slaughtered.[92] Most of the world media accepted the PA's version of events as if it reflected self-evident truths. On April 18, 2002, the BBC quoted a British forensic expert who, after visiting Jenin, declared that "the evidence before us at the moment doesn't lead us to believe that the allegations are anything other than truthful."[93] The UK newspaper *The Independent* claimed on April 19 that "Israeli officials were desperately scrambling to explain the war crimes committed at Jenin refugee camp as the international furore over the devastation rose to new heights yesterday,"[94] and the next day falsely asserted that "enough is already known about what went on in Jenin to say Israel has committed an appalling atrocity."[95] Leading British and other European politicians spoke of Israel as if it were a rogue state. In addressing the European Parliament, Christopher Patten, the European Union External Relations Commissioner, stated that the "Israelis can't trample over the rule of law, over the Geneva conventions, over what are generally regarded as acceptable norms of behaviour."[96] Joining in the refrain, Mary Robinson, the UN High Commissioner for Human Rights, added that the international community cannot permit the "the wanton killings of Palestinian civilians and the destruction of the civilian infrastructure to support life. It cannot be right to wage war on civilian populations." UN officials were particularly scathing. The Secretary General, Kofi Annan, decreed that "the situation is so dangerous and the humanitarian and human rights situation so appalling" that it merited the dispatch of a force there. Peter Hansen, the Commissioner-General of UNRWA, claimed that he had "hoped the horror stories coming out were exaggerations as you often hear in this part of the world, but they were all true." Adding his piece, Terje Roed-Larsen, the UN's Special Coordinator for the Middle East Process, informed reporters: "We have expert people here who have been in war zones and earthquakes and they say they have never seen anything like it . . . Israel has lost all moral ground in this conflict."[97]

In the end it transpired that the actual death toll amounted to fifty-three Palestinians, of whom only five were civilians. Israel, by contrast, lost twenty-three soldiers and incurred the wounding of fifty-two others.[98] That of course did not deter the Secretary General of the UN, Kofi Annan, from appointing a three-person UN investigative committee, consisting of Martti Ahtisaari, Sadako Ogata and Cornelio Sommaruga, to ascertain exactly what had occurred in Jenin. Martti Ahtisaari, its chairperson, had subsequently condemned as "completely inexcusable" the deadly Israeli attack on a flotilla carrying aid for Gaza.[99] (With regard to that incident, the UN later exonerated Israel.)

Sadako Ogata, a former UN High Commissioner for Refugees, had been known to be partial towards the Palestinians and, finally, Cornelio Sommaruga, former head of the International Red Cross, had previously castigated the IDF for "the sufferings of the Palestinian people and the destructions of property." What is more, he exhibited profound animus to Israelis and Jews generally by refusing Israel Red Cross membership on the grounds that the country's corresponding organization bore as its emblem the Star of David, which he claimed would be akin to accepting an organization whose emblem was a swastika.[100] However, he had no problem with the Muslim Red Crescent.[101]

Peres, as Israel's foreign minister, signalled his acceptance of Annan's inquiry commission. But Giora Eiland, head of the IDF's Planning Directorate, who had a more realistic appreciation of the likes of its appointees, alerted Chief of Staff Mofaz to the high probability of the UN commission falsely accusing Israel of committing war crimes, thus paving the way for an international force to be stationed in the region. As a result, the matter was brought before the cabinet. There it was decided that under no circumstances would Israel have anything to do with the commission. That being the case, Annan on July 2 dismantled it, making do with a report that ironically confirmed that there had indeed been no massacre in Jenin.[102]

Despite resistance to the IDF's initiatives turning out to be generally unexpectedly weak, the Palestinians continued to pursue acts of terror, albeit on a reduced scale. From the commencement of the IDF's offensive on March 28 up to April 30, forty Israelis were killed in Israel proper, not counting the thirty-four killed in combat. On the Palestinian side, and extending the period to May 10 when the siege of the Bethlehem Church of the Nativity ended, 261 Palestinians had been killed, thousands were wounded and thousands detained.[103] The PA lost its full autonomy in Zone A, and, with Israel determined to preempt, as much as was humanly possible, further outbreaks of violence, the Palestinians were forced to cope with burdensome roadblocks and checkpoints throughout the West Bank. Furthermore, the PA had alienated the Bush administration. After it became clear that Arafat would not comply with US demands that he agree to an unconditional ceasefire and all that it entailed, Bush on June 24, 2002, in a televised address, finally declared: "I call on the Palestinian people to elect new leaders, leaders not compromised by terror. I call upon them to build a practicing democracy, based on tolerance and liberty."[104]

Apart from its military actions, by far the most major step taken by Israel to protect its citizens was the construction of a security barrier that ran close to the pre-Six-Day War border. The go-ahead for it was authorized by the cabinet on June 23, 2002. During the thirty-five years since June 1967 when Israel first occupied the West Bank there was no such barrier. During that period, Palestinians were generally afforded relatively easy access into Israel in search of employment and, in certain cases, health care. Israel did not at first aspire hermetically to compartmentalize the two populations, and all references to the security barrier as an "Apartheid wall" are grounded in arrant baleful intent. There is one, and only one, factor that led to its establishment, and that is the orgy of violence unleashed by Palestinians soon after the signing of the Oslo Accords. The construction of the security barrier was first mooted as early as 1995 after a suicide bomber killed twenty-one Israelis. Rabin very much favoured it, but opposition to it by Peres and Shlomo Ben-Ami, among others, as well as financial constraints and bureaucratic inertia, stood in the way. Ben-Ami's reasons were rather quaint. He thought that any intention to construct the barrier would adversely reflect Israel's "lack of faith in the maturity of the Palestinians and the seriousness that guides their efforts to build their promised state."[105]

Later Barak tried to reinvigorate moves to commence the barrier's construction, but time was not on his side. A unity government formed in 2001 did not take kindly to the idea. Sharon feared that a barrier close to the pre-1967 frontier would demarcate the western border of a future Palestinian State, while Peres, as Harel and Issacharoff noted, "still held that it was possible to arrive at a settlement with Arafat that would make the barrier superfluous."[106] Only by mid-2002, when faced with a large groundswell of public opinion calling for such a barrier, did Sharon relent. Once he had done so, he propelled the project forward with the same drive and enthusiasm that he had shown for settlement construction in the 1970s.[107] In the process, some Palestinians living around the barrier's pathway were subject to various deprivations such as loss of land and or ready access to it. To some extent, in a landmark decision, such impositions were remedied by the Israeli Supreme Court, which on June 30, 2004, ordered the repositioning of 30 kilometres of the barrier northwest of Jerusalem. The court's president, Aaron Barak, while accepting the legitimacy of the creation of the security barrier, ruled that the IDF had to maintain a balance between Israel's defensive needs and the rights of the Palestinians affected.[108]

Meanwhile, in Israel in October 2002, the Labour Party withdrew from the government. The move was essentially the outcome of an internal party issue. Up until then Ben-Eliezer had served as Labour leader after having succeeded Barak, but a new leadership ballot was set for November 19. With an eye on party primary voters, Ben-Eliezer engineered an exit from the government on the grounds of opposing state funding for settlements. However, he lost to Amram Mitzna, the left-wing mayor of Haifa, who favoured pursuing further negotiations with Arafat and, if that fell through, for Israel to withdraw unilaterally from Gaza and most of the West Bank under the protection of a security fence. In the general elections to the Knesset held on January 28, 2003, Likud secured thirty-eight seats while Labour–Meimad gained only nineteen, as opposed to the twenty-six secured by it and its electoral allies in the 1999 elections (see the Appendix). Once again, Sharon wished to include Labour in his government, but for the time being the party rejected his offer. Instead, he formed a coalition of Likud, Shinui (an anti-clerical free-market liberal party), Mafdal, Haichud Haleumi (a right-wing national party) and Yisrael Be'Aliyah. All told the coalition commanded sixty-eight seats. Silvan Shalom became foreign minister, Shaul Mofaz minister of defence and Netanyahu minister of finance.

On the international front attention was focused in the latter half of 2002 and into 2003 on a so-called Road Map for peace in the Middle East. It evolved from a European Union interest in securing a definitive end to the Israel–Palestine conflict and from Bush's perceived need to be seen to be furthering the establishment of a Palestinian State as a means of gaining Arab support for his war against terror and for his involvement in Iraq. As a precondition for the US releasing the details of its Road Map, the PA was to establish an office of prime minister with full executive authority that would have reduced the scope and power of the president. In March 2003 Arafat finally gave ground by appointing his loyal lieutenant Mahmoud Abbas in that new role.

The subsequent release of America's Road Map in April 2003 contained the usual list of PA obligations to dismantle terrorist organizations and to confiscate illegally held weapons, and so on. For its part, Israel was expected to withdraw to positions it held before the outbreak of the intifada, remove outpost settlements erected since March 2001, and place a total construction freeze on all its other settlements. All this was to be achieved in what was designated as the first phase. In the second phase, to be completed by the end of 2003, there was to be an establishment of an interim Palestinian State leading to a full peace agreement in 2005. A quartet of Europe, the USA, Russia and the UN were to oversee the Road Map's application. On June 4, 2003, at a summit in Aqaba (Jordan), Bush, Sharon and Abbas met to reaffirm their determination to realize the Road Map's essential objectives. But, in the end, nothing changed. The PA continued with European, Russian and UN connivance to flout all its commitments, while Israel was no longer inclined to make unrequited concessions. Once Bush endorsed Sharon's plan to vacate Gaza in 2005 (see chapter 8), he effectively conceded that the Road Map was a dead letter.

The al-Aqsa Intifada continued to take its toll. Then some light appeared at the end of the tunnel: on November 11, 2004, Arafat died in a Paris hospital of unspecified causes, leaving a legacy of needless bloodshed and suffering. For a man who, as Jeff Jacoby of the *Boston Globe* aptly encapsulated, encouraged the killing of innocent Israelis, who lied, cheated and stole, and "who inculcated the vilest culture of Jew-hatred since the Third Reich," he was remarkably extolled by fawning Western journalists.[109] This had been the case despite the thousands of incriminating documents found by the IDF with Arafat's signature authorizing the payments of sums of money to various groups organizing suicide bombing missions and to the families of the so-called Palestinian martyrs killed in the process. The authenticity of such documents had been verified by Jibril Rajoub and Mohammad Dahlan, both senior Palestinian security officials.[110] Brushing aside all the evidence to the contrary, Derek Brown in *The Guardian* described Arafat as exhibiting extraordinary courage as a peace negotiator, while the BBC's Barbara Plett admitted to crying when she saw the ailing Arafat being airlifted from Ramallah to Paris. As Jacoby derisively remarked, the likes of Plett "do not seem to have any trouble reporting, dry-eyed, on the plight of Arafat's victims ... That is, when they mention them."[111] Arafat was succeeded by Abbas, who in January 2005 assumed the presidency of the PA after an election in which he gained 63 percent of the vote.

At a summit meeting held on February 8, 2005, at Sharm el Sheikh attended by Sharon, Abbas, President Mubarak of Egypt and King Abdullah II of Jordan, the al-Aqsa Intifada was deemed to have ended. From its beginning in September 2001 up to July 2004, Israel had encountered 133 separate suicide attacks.[112] But, as Operation Defensive Shield progressed, the incidence of suicide bomb attacks declined sharply. In 2003 there were twenty-six such occurrences, in 2004 twelve, in 2005 eight, in 2006 six, and in each of the years 2007 and 2008 just one.[113] All told the intifada claimed the lives of some 3,212 Palestinians and 1,009 Israelis.[114] Of the Palestinian fatalities, 1,542 were combatants killed by the IDF while 406 were killed by fellow Palestinians. In other words, 45 percent of all Palestinians killed by Israelis were civilians. On the Israeli side, with only 215 combatants killed, civilian deaths amounted to 78 percent of the total.[115] In addition to the dead, the seriously wounded – that is, those that were severely burnt, blinded or lost limbs – continued to suffer for years on end.

Thanks to a combination of the security barrier, a depletion in terrorist ranks as a result of the IDF's Operation Defensive Shield, and the resumption by the IDF of an effective presence on the West Bank that facilitated a marked improvement in its intelligence-gathering ability, the policy of giving the IDF more or less free rein to quell the uprising was highly successful. In the process it dispelled the myth that force alone could not put an end to the intifada. That myth was unthinkingly derived from the experiences of colonial countries striving to secure their independence. Conveniently forgotten is the fact that the Israeli–Arab conflict is essentially a war for the survival of the Jewish State.

While the international media dutifully reported Palestinian atrocities, it never really conveyed a clear understanding of what the Israelis were experiencing. Since no single place was immune from Palestinian attacks at any time, whether in the centre of the country or in peripheral areas, in streets, buses, shopping complexes, markets, restaurants, hotels, clubs, universities, and so on, no one felt secure in the conduct of their daily lives. The practice among the suicide bombers of disguising themselves variously as Hasidim, women (as was the case in the Park Hotel), Jewish settlers or tourists[116] made people even more neurotic.

David Grossman brilliantly captured that phenomenon in his novel *To the End of the Land,* where the central character, while sitting in a bus in Jerusalem, scrutinizes each incoming passenger for tell-tale signs of their being a Palestinian terrorist. So concerned were Israelis that many of them minimized the amount and extent of their entry into public spaces, avoiding, wherever possible, public transport and entertainment venues. For similar reasons, the tourist industry slumped. Taking stock over what led to such a situation, Efraim Karsh contrasted the experiences of Ireland and Israel. In Ireland, the dismantling of the arms of the IRA was a precondition for a peaceful outcome. In the occupied territories, Israel saw the arming of the PLO, despite its abysmal previous track record, as a key to peace and security. "Where did such blind faith come from?" he asked.[117]

8

BEYOND THE AL-AQSA INTIFADA

Israel's Disengagement from Gaza

On November 18, 2003, at a conference in Herzliya sponsored by the Institute for Policy and Strategy, Sharon proposed unilaterally disengaging from Gaza, an idea that evolved during a series of consultations held over weekends at his farm. The participants included Sharon's two sons, Omri and Gilad, his current and previous senior advisors, Dov Weissglass and Uri Shani, and the advertising executives Reuven Adler and Eyal Arad, none of whom had any special expertise in security matters.

At stake was the total withdrawal of 7,500 Israelis from twenty-one settlements.[1] The proposal ran counter to everything for which Sharon had hitherto stood. A year beforehand, in the run up to the January 2003 general election, Sharon had inveighed against the Labour Party for including a Gaza withdrawal plan in its electoral platform. As far as he was concerned, the settlements in Gaza equalled Tel Aviv in importance.[2] More specifically, in 2000 Sharon wondered, "What will we do once we withdraw from Gaza and find, as we inevitably will, that Arafat or his successors have stepped in and the squads of terrorists are operating again from there into Israel, murdering and destroying? What will we do when the Katyusha fire starts hitting Sderot . . . and Ashkelon . . . and Kiryat Gat?"[3]

Just why Sharon had a change of heart remains unclear. In his Herzliya speech he explained that the "purpose of the 'Disengagement Plan' was to reduce terror as much as possible, and grant Israeli citizens the maximum level of security. The process of disengagement would lead to an improvement in the quality of life, and will help strengthen the Israeli economy." Furthermore, the intention was to "relieve the pressure on the IDF and security forces in fulfilling the difficult tasks they are faced with."[4] According to *Newsweek*, it had been taking 3,000 soldiers and tens of millions of dollars per year to guard the Gaza settlers.[5]

Various commentators attributed other motives to Sharon's volte-face. Among speculations were his hopes that the Palestinians would respond by making peaceful gestures of their own, that the United States would acquiesce in an Israeli annexation of part of the West Bank, that an Israeli initiative would forestall unwelcome US pressures on Israel to make unwanted concessions and, finally, that attention would be deflected from impending corruption charges that Sharon was facing and which were seriously damaging his personal ratings. Added to all that, Weissglass offered what may well have been his own preferred objective. In an interview with Ari Shavit of *Haaretz*, he predicted that the disengagement plan would freeze the peace process, "and when you freeze that process, you prevent the establishment of a Palestinian state, and you prevent a discussion on the refugees, the borders and Jerusalem."[6]

Members of Sharon's own party, Likud, were up in arms against his proposal. In a referendum conducted on May 2, 2004, to determine whether or not it should become official party policy, naysayers accounted for 60 percent of the total votes cast.[7] Their opposition to the pull-out was shared by adherents of the settler movement, religious parties and right-wing nationalists. (In July 2005 a group of rabbis invoked God to send angels of destruction to kill Sharon.)[8] Some high-ranking IDF officers, including General Moshe Ya'alon, expressed their concern that a unilateral Israeli withdrawal from Gaza would jeopardize the country's security. Prominent among leading Likud opponents was Netanyahu, who was reported as presciently declaring: "I am not willing to be a party to a move that ignores reality and blindly advances toward the establishment of an Islamic terrorist base that threatens the state."[9] However, Sharon, with the support of a majority of the population, was undeterred. In January 2005, to circumvent the erosion of his parliamentary support, he formed a national unity government to include the Labour Party. As a result, he was able, on February 16, 2005, to secure Knesset approval for his plans, with fifty-nine members voting in favour as opposed to forty against.[10]

The evacuation of the settlers began on August 15, 2005.[11] To facilitate the process, some 55,000 Israeli soldiers and police were deployed. Most settlers left of their own accord but others, who were in emotional turmoil, had to be forcefully removed. The extreme distress displayed by resisters who had for many years lived and raised their families in Gaza affected many soldiers, who were moved to tears. By September 11 it was all over: 2,530 homes were razed, as were all but two synagogues. The forty-eight bodies in Gush Katif's cemetery were exhumed and reburied in Israel. Greenhouses purchased for $14 million by US Jewish donors for the benefit of the PA were left intact.[12]

Israel's gesture, involving so much traumatic dissension, of voluntarily and unilaterally vacating Gaza enabled Palestinians living there to structure their lives independently. Almost immediately after the final IDF soldier departed, Palestinians, firing guns into the air and waving Hamas and Fatah flags, surged into the deserted settlements, where the remaining synagogues were demolished, items of value found among the ruins looted and the greenhouses destroyed. PA police standing by proved to be incapable of intervening.[13]

Organizations such as the UN and motley anti-Israel NGOs maintain that, because it continues to control access to Gaza, Israel has not really terminated its occupation there. One wonders whether, during World War II, if the Allies had surrounded, say, Italy and sealed its borders, they would have been deemed responsible for the welfare of the Italians on the grounds that they were an occupying force. According to article 42 of the Hague Regulations Respecting the Laws and Customs of War on Land, "Territory is considered occupied when it is actually placed under the authority of the hostile army."[14] Weighing the issue, Pnina Sharvit-Baruch, head of the international law division at the IDF Military Advocate General's Office, concluded that, because Israel has no effective control over Gaza and the Hamas government is quite capable of exercising effective powers of government therein, "there is no valid legal basis to regard Israel as the occupying power of the Gaza Strip."[15]

More to the point, Israelis had been concerned as to whether or not its unilateral withdrawal had been worthwhile. On that score a subsequent consensus turned out to be negative. In the first four months alone following the Israeli exit, some 283 rockets were launched from Gaza into Israel,[16] and, as is well known, Israeli security in areas within reach of Gaza worsened. In a poll conducted in 2009, 68 percent of Israeli respondents who had previously been in favour of the withdrawal from Gaza regretted having supported it.[17] Even Peres, who in 2005 had labelled withdrawal protestors as shlemazels (habitual failures or chronically inept),[18] later confessed that, "had the disengagement been a success, we would have repeated it in the West Bank."[19]

Sharon's Exit from the Political Scene

On September 24–5, not long after the Gaza pull-out, Hamas fired a number of rockets into Israel, to which the IDF responded by bombing suspected launching sites. Such events tended to strengthen Netanyahu's hand in his drive to displace Sharon as the Likud leader. In a ballot held on September 27 to determine the party leadership, Sharon beat Netanyahu by a rather narrow margin – 52 to 48 per cent.[20] Sharon of course could have continued to function as usual, but he didn't. Conscious of his tenuous position and the growing embitterment against him in party ranks (on the previous Sunday at a Likud convention his microphone had twice been disconnected), plus the fact that opinion polls indicated that he would do far better forming a new party of his own, he decided to do just that. His decision was precipitated by the Labour Party under its newly appointed leader, Amir Peretz, resolving on November 20 to withdraw from the coalition, thus bringing the government down. On November 21, while still retaining the premiership, Sharon resigned from the Likud to establish a new party called Kadima (Forward). He was joined by a number of prominent Likud members as well as some deserters from the Labour Party. For example, Peres, smarting from losing the Labour Party leadership ballot to Peretz (whom he thought he could manipulate to prevent a Barak comeback),[21] and tempted by an offer of securing a cabinet portfolio in any future

Sharon government, bolted from Labour to support Kadima. The move was widely seen as a blatantly opportunistic one. One Labour Knesset member, Ophir Pines-Paz, forecast that Peres "will be remembered as someone who abandoned his home, which he led for dozens of years, in favour of an 'instant career' party that no one knows where it came from or where it's going."[22] Meanwhile, Netanyahu, on December 20, finally assumed control of the remnants of Likud.

Sharon was unable to enjoy the fruits of his newfound enterprise. On December 18, 2005, he suffered from a moderate stroke that seemed to be manageable, but on January 4, 2006, a second and far more severe one required extensive brain surgery, from which Sharon never regained consciousness, finally expiring on January 11, 2014. Ehud Olmert, acting as deputy prime minister, managed the affairs of state and steered Kadima through the general election held on March 28, 2006. Kadima won handsomely, attaining twenty-nine seats as opposed to twelve for Likud (see Appendix). After the usual post-election coalition bargaining, Olmert emerged on May 4 to head a government made up of Kadima, Labour, Shas and Gil (the pensioners' party), commanding sixty-seven of the 120 Knesset seats. Peretz became minister of defence and Tzipi Livni foreign minister. As will shortly be seen, the appointment of Peretz to the Defence Ministry was ill-advised. He had in the past shown little interest in security matters, and he himself was aware of his lack of qualifications for such a crucial post.[23] It has been argued that Olmert chose Peretz out of partisan political considerations, knowing full well that he was not up to the job.[24] If that was indeed the case, it indicates a reckless disregard for Israel's security. In addition, Shimon Peres was appointed as a co-vice premier with Haim Ramon, who also held the Ministry of Justice portfolio and, as with Peres, was a former Labour member who deserted the party in 2002 following an unsuccessful leadership challenge against Amram Mitzna. In Israel it would seem that the age of politicians living up to their avowed principles had long since ceased. On January 31, 2007, Ramon was convicted for indecent assault and sentenced to community service.[25] He was not the first Israeli minister to be so indicted. In March 2001 Yitzhak Mordechai, who was both the minister of transport and, like Ramon, vice premier in Rabin's government, was convicted of sexually assaulting two women and given an eighteen-month suspended sentence.[26]

Palestinians at Loggerheads: An Internecine Dispute

On January 25, 2006, elections held for members of the Palestinian Legislative Assembly resulted in a sea change in the Palestinian political landscape. Hamas emerged victorious, winning seventy-four of the 132 seats in parliament, while the previous ruling group, Fatah, gained only forty-five seats. As a result, the Palestinian prime minister, Ahmed Qureia, was superseded by the Hamas leader, Ismail Haniyeh.[27] In March 2007 a Palestinian unity government headed by Haniyeh was formed, with most of its members being associated with Hamas. Relations between Hamas and Fatah had become increasingly strained, with sporadic acts of mutual violence becoming the norm. Matters reached a climax in June in Gaza, where tensions between the two groups were most acute. Bitter fighting transpired, with the combatants attacking one another's key posts. Hamas, with a much larger following and with more dedicated cadres, prevailed. Thoroughly overpowering Fatah, it laid claim to absolute control of the whole of Gaza. More than 100 people were killed in the fighting and approximately 100 Fatah members sought refuge in Israel.[28] What is startling about the conflict was the degree of gratuitous cruelty that both sides visited upon each other. On one occasion Hamas members captured Mohammed Sweiki, a Fatah security officer, and threw him off the roof of a fifteen-storey apartment building. In return a Hamas operative was thrown from the twelfth floor of a building.[29] Others were attacked in hospitals[30] or pursued and shot in public areas.[31] From Israel's perspective, the Hamas takeover presaged heightened security risks.

The Second War in Lebanon

Israel's foes in its second war in Lebanon were neither the Lebanese army nor the general Lebanese people. Rather, Israeli forces were pitted against those of Hezbollah, the "Party of God," created in 1982 by Iran, which has since provided it with a munificent annual stipend, amounting in 2005 to $100 million.[32] Hezbollah's aims are spelt out in an open letter, "The Hezbollah Program." After outlining its plans for Lebanon, the letter continues: "Our primary assumption in our fight against Israel states that the Zionist entity is aggressive from its inception, and built on lands wrested from their owners, at the expense of the rights of the Muslim people. Therefore our struggle will end only when this entity is obliterated."[33] Hezbollah's grievance with Israel has less to do with its actions and far more to do with its existence. Led by Sheikh Hassan Nasrallah, the movement has extended financial, training and material support to Hamas and the Islamic Jihad in Palestine as well as to the Fatah-aligned Tanzim and al-Aqsa Martyrs Brigade.

Hezbollah does not confine itself to direct attacks on Israel. On March 17, 1992, it detonated a bomb in the Israeli embassy in Buenos Aires, killing twenty-nine people and wounding over 250 others. Among the victims were Israeli diplomats, children, Christian clergy from a church located across the street, and other passers-by. Then on July 18, 1994, Hezbollah struck again, bombing the Jewish Community Centre in Buenos Aires, bringing about a death toll of eighty-seven and over 100 injuries. The slaughtering of innocent diaspora Jews was in accordance with a 1992 Hezbollah statement affirming its anti-Semitic credo, which in part read: "It is an open war until the elimination of Israel and until the death of the last Jew on earth." This was followed up in 2002 by their leader Sheikh Nasrallah advising Jews to migrate to Israel to "save us the trouble of going after them worldwide."[34] No matter how outrageously Hezbollah behaves, like Hamas or the PLO, it can always count on the automatic support of leading Western radical intellectuals. Even the European Union refuses to define it as a terrorist organization. In May 2006, just before the onset of the Second Lebanese War, Naom Chomsky spent eight days as Hezbollah's honoured guest in Lebanon, where he duly and publicly endorsed its "right" to bear arms.[35] He can be seen on YouTube deferentially removing his cap on being introduced to a local Hezbollah leader and was quoted by New TV (Lebanon) as having said: "A victory achieved by the resistance [the term by which Hezbollah often refers to itself] is a victory for all people that fight injustice and oppression."[36]

What could well be described as a dress rehearsal for the war in 2006 took place ten years earlier. After its northern sector had been subject to an unusually large and sustained Hezbollah rocket bombardment, culminating in a salvo that exacted thirty-eight casualties, Israel on April 11, 1996, activated Operation Grapes of Wrath. Meant to be a campaign of retribution, Operation Grapes of Wrath involved the combined action of Israel's army, air force and navy. With Southern Lebanon being extensively pommelled, Arab civilians began fleeing northwards en masse. Meanwhile Hezbollah rockets continued to rain down on Israeli towns and villages, prompting a similar, albeit comparatively smaller, civilian displacement. As already mentioned in chapter 6, a UN post in the village of Qana was inadvertently shelled, causing the deaths of over 100 Lebanese civilians seeking shelter there. The international uproar that followed served to bring the Israeli campaign to an abrupt end, and by April 17 the IDF had withdrawn and terminated all its military engagements, with little to show for its efforts.[37]

The spark that caused the 2006 war was the Hezbollah abduction on May 12 of two IDF soldiers, Ehud (Udi) Goldwasser and Eldad Regev, while on border patrol. That was not the first time that IDF soldiers had been kidnapped. On October 7, 2000, Adi Avitan, Benyamin Avraham and Omar Swaid were captured by the Hezbollah after sustaining injuries from a roadside bomb on the Israeli side of the Mount Dov border. In relation to this particular incident there was a sequel that brought little credit to the UN. The Hezbollah attackers had originally entered Israeli territory dressed as UN personnel and driving vehicles with UN-like markings. After the IDF troops were seized the vehicles used by the Hezbollah were abandoned. The entire operation was witnessed by UNIFIL personnel from an observation post on a hill just over 350 metres away. Somehow or other, the Israelis acquired knowledge of the fact that an Indian UNIFIL soldier had videotaped the kidnapping and therefore wished to view it as a means of identifying the Hezbollah attackers. At first, top UN officials, including Secretary General Kofi Annan and Terje Roed-Larsen,[38] the special Coordinator for the Middle East Peace Process, denied all knowledge of it, but on July 6, 2001, they admitted to its being in their possession. When Ben-Eliezer, Israel's defence minister, demanded a copy, he was turned down on the spurious grounds that UNIFIL was not prepared to provide intelligence material to any party in the conflict. But, as Dore Gold, who was previously Israel's ambassador to the UN, so pointedly wrote, the strict impartiality that UNIFIL "was supposed to observe applied to Lebanon and Israel, not to a terrorist organization. And Hizballah [sic] was not, to use UNIFIL's bureaucratically sterile language, just a 'party' in this dispute, it was the aggressor."[39] The most the UN was prepared to do was to let the Israelis see an edited version that hid the identity of the kidnappers. What it did not hide was the glee and laughter of UNIFIL troops as they watched the kidnapping, with one of them yelling "They're screwing the Jews."[40] By November the IDF finally determined that all three of its abducted soldiers were dead.[41] Their families accepted such findings and mourned for them,[42] By Israel agreeing to the release on January 29, 2004, of 430 Palestinians, some Arab prisoners and a German, as well as the bodies of sixty others, in exchange for the remains of the three IDF soldiers and an Israeli businessman taken under murky circumstances, Hezbollah was emboldened to attempt even more kidnappings. Considering the scale of the Israeli handover, as well as the IDF's restraint in the wake of the abduction (Israel did not retaliate), Hezbollah's strategy seemed to work like a charm.

The kidnapping of Goldwasser and Regev was meticulously planned and executed. Observation cameras near the chosen site were disabled by sniper fire and, as a decoy, heavy shelling erupted along the entire frontier. The lead vehicle of two Humvees in which Goldwasser and Regev rode was hit by two upgraded Russian-made RPGs and immobilized. The two Israelis, already wounded, were yanked out of the Humvee and taken across the border in a jeep that headed northwards. An IDF retaliatory attack was hastily improvised, but the sole tank involved encountered a massive bomb that killed all four of its crew. To retrieve their bodies, a small infantry detachment was dispatched to the area. It soon came under heavy mortar fire that led to the death of one of them. Barring the two that were abducted and including three Israelis killed when the Humvees were attacked, the IDF's total losses for the day amounted to eight.[43]

To understand why Israel went to war following the Goldwasser–Regev capture, one has to take into account the kidnapping of Gilad Shalit less than a month earlier and its subsequent impact. On June 25, a Hamas unit in conjunction with members of two allied organizations suddenly emerged from a hitherto concealed tunnel just north of Kibbutz Kerem Shalom along the Israel–Gaza border. Taken by surprise, members of an Israeli tank crew were shot. Two were killed and, of the remaining two who were wounded, Shalit was whisked off to be incarcerated over the next five years somewhere in Gaza. By the time other units of the IDF arrived at the scene of the attack, it was already too late to give chase to the abductors. All requests by the International Red Cross to visit Shalit were flatly rejected.

Considering that, during the interval between Israel's total evacuation of Gaza in September 2005 to June 2006, Israel had been subjected to thousands of rockets and mortars being fired at it from Gaza, the abduction of Shalit solicited a forceful response. In what was dubbed Operation Summer Rain, the IDF on June 28 entered Gaza at various points. Bridges were destroyed, Gaza's sole power station was partially crippled, and the Gaza International Airport was occupied. A widespread bombardment and ground skirmishes caused extensive damage and the loss of the lives of 450 Palestinians. By contrast, only one Israeli was killed, and that was due to friendly fire. But, despite all efforts, Shalit's whereabouts remained unknown. From that experience, Olmert resolved to change the rules of the game. Henceforth, he warned: "Israel's response would prove to the terror organizations that the abduction of Israeli soldiers is of no benefit to them."[44] In an attempt to fulfil his promise, Olmert, in cooperation with Dan Halutz, the chief of staff, and Amir Peretz, the minister of defence, and without any serious pre-planning or consideration, rushed in to wage war against Hezbollah.

Hostilities, commencing the very day of the abduction, took the form of IAF planes bombing sixty-nine bridges and other objectives in Southern Lebanon in an effort to seal off Hezbollah escape routes. The scale of the attacks surprised Nasrallah, who thought that, because of Israel's previous mild record in responding to Hezbollah's hostage-taking, there was little chance that it would embark on so bold an adventure. As he reasoned: "It never happened that a state launches a war against another for a few apprehended soldiers and a few others killed."[45] On July 13, the IAF, in a 34-minute strike involving laser-guided ordnance, destroyed almost all of Hezbollah's Fajr-2 missiles, with a 45-kilometre range. A few days later, most of Hezbollah's Fajr-5 missiles, with a 75-kilometre range, were similarly eliminated. However, the IAF could not neutralize the enemy's large stock of other rockets concealed in private houses and other obscure places throughout Southern Lebanon. Some such rockets eventually reached as far south as Haifa. Hezbollah missile sites were not the only objectives targeted. Roads, bridges, power stations and Beirut International Airport were also bombed. On July 14 attention was focused on pounding Dahlia, a section of Beirut in which Hezbollah headquarters, as well as offices and apartments housing Hezbollah members and its supporters, were located. As a result, Dahlia residents fled from their homes in their thousands. That night Nasrallah appeared live on al-Manar television advising viewers to avert their gaze westwards towards the Mediterranean. There they would witness, he assured them, the destruction of an Israeli vessel that was a party to the IAF's bombing of Beirut. Sure enough, an Iranian C-802 shore-to-ship missile struck the Israeli missile boat *Hanit*, setting it aflame and killing four sailors.[46] For some reason the *Hanit* had not activated its electronic countermeasures. During July 15 and 16 villagers in the south of Lebanon were inundated with flyers dropped from overhead IAF planes advising them to leave their homes and to seek shelter further north. Before long a mass exodus of people numbering close to three-quarters of a million headed towards Beirut, imposing intolerable strains on the country's capacity to care for them. A crowning achievement for the IAF was its successful mission, accomplished on July 17, in which eighteen out of a possible twenty-one Zalzal-2 missile launchers were demolished. The missiles in question, carrying a 400- to 600-kilogram warhead, had the capability of hitting Tel Aviv. Not unpredictably, Hezbollah did not take it all lying down. It constantly launched batteries of rockets, disrupting civilian life in Israel's far north. Most rockets fell in open areas, but from time to time they inflicted damage to life and property.

On July 17 Olmert addressed the Knesset. His presentation was considered enthralling both on account of its rhetorical qualities, described by the media as Churchillian, and because of its firm stance. Olmert listed Israel's preconditions for ending the fighting: securing the release of Goldwasser and Regev, the cessation of Hezbollah rocket attacks, the displacement of Hezbollah from Southern Lebanon and the entry there of the Lebanese army. While Olmert's speech did much to raise public morale, it did little towards unravelling the conflict. Once Hezbollah realized that it was up against the sustained might of the IDF, which it could not defeat in a broad head-on collision, it settled for a more realistic outcome. It concluded that, if, at the end of the day, it simply emerged intact after offering sustained resistance and after having fired its rockets without let-up, it could lay claim to victory merely on the grounds that the IDF had failed to vanquish it. With such thoughts uppermost in mind, Hezbollah resolved to carry on fighting come what may. Given that Israel for one reason or another was ill-prepared to deal Hezbollah a mortal blow, Olmert's parliamentary address was meaningless. On subsequently being asked why he raised false public expectations, especially in relation to the release of the two abductees, Olmert replied he was duty bound to instil a ray of hope for the soldiers' return.[47]

After a week of fighting, when the IAF was beginning to run out of bombing targets, a stalemate was in the offing. It seemed that, for Israel, there were only two courses of action. Either it could seek an acceptable ceasefire agreement or it could widen its offensive. The first option was barely considered, since Israel felt that its hammering of Hezbollah was just commencing and that it could ultimately bring that organization to its knees. The country was enjoying a rare bout of international support. Not only was the United States firmly behind it, but so too were Canada, Australia, the UK, France and other European countries. While they voiced reservations about the IAF's bombardment of civilian centres, they nonetheless encouraged Israel to take an even more combative stance. More strikingly, even many Arab regimes, highly censorious of Hezbollah, were hoping that Israel would subdue it. Among such countries were Saudi Arabia, Egypt and Jordan, not to mention the Lebanese prime minister, Fouad Siniora, whose associates, as Harel and Issacharoff wrote, "asked the United States to see to it that Israel did not end the war after only a few days."[48]

From Israel's point of view, it had impulsively entered the war without a clear-cut conception of what it could realistically achieve and without mobilizing its reserves. To a large extent, the fault lay with Dan Halutz, who had risen through the ranks of the air force to become chief of staff. He was the first and most probably the last IDF officer to do so. Looking at the general picture through the eyes of an airman, Halutz had utter faith in the ability of the air force alone to decide the war's outcome. So self-assured was he that when, on the evening of the opening day of the war, the foreign minister, Tzipi Livni, asked how long it was expected to last, Halutz replied: "It'll be over tonight. A few hours. Maybe tomorrow morning."[49] As the war proceeded and Hezbollah rockets rained down on northern Israel, Halutz continued to reject Peretz's suggestions that large contingents of ground forces be dispatched to Southern Lebanon. Two reasons can be adduced to account for Halutz's stand. First, he still believed that, with sufficient pressures brought to bear by the IAF, Hezbollah would either see the error of its ways and agree to withdraw from Southern Lebanon or it would be compelled to do so by the Lebanese government and its allies. Second, Halutz, who had participated in the 1982 Israeli invasion of Lebanon, was keenly aware of the fact that a large section of the population was opposed to that war and the manner in which it had been prosecuted. The last thing he wanted was to be seen as reinvading Lebanon, with all the bloodshed that would entail. He was reputed to have said at a GHQ meeting that "a ground offensive is the place where we stand a chance of leaving IDF soldiers dead in southern Lebanon."[50]

There were also other factors militating against the use of large numbers of ground troops. In the recent past, the IDF's overall battle readiness had depreciated. After the fall of Saddam Hussein, the risk to Israel of a full-scale war receded. As a consequence the size of Israel's tank corps was somewhat reduced by dissolving, in 2003, the Kfir tank brigade. (A few years earlier, the 211th tank brigade had been disbanded.) IDF budget cuts imposed by the Treasury took their toll both in the tank corps and in infantry units. When tank reserves eventually went into Lebanon they found to their dismay that their vehicles lacked smoke shields.[51] In the war, thirty tank crew members were killed and over 100 wounded, and 108 tanks were hit.[52] Apart from economies in general maintenance, weapons and ammunition supplies (just over a week into the war, the IDF had to turn to the USA for replenishments), there was a general decline in training standards. Battalion commanders went into action without ever organizing a battalion field exercise, and divisional commanders were not trained for their jobs since the division commander course had been abolished.[53] For the most part the IDF's readiness for battle was impaired by its preoccupation with the al-Aqsa Intifada, where it honed its skills in suppressing small-scale, poorly coordinated and inexperienced fighting units. Dealing with the well-structured, highly motivated and disciplined Hezbollah organization was an entirely different matter. Mistakenly, many officers thought that the lessons learnt in Gaza and the West Bank were also applicable in Lebanon.

By way of a compromise between not authorizing any use of ground forces and giving in to a growing clamour for their extensive involvement, Halutz, with Olmert's support, agreed to accord them a minor role. They were to conduct limited raids on objectives stationed close to the frontier involving what amounted to hit-and-run operations. It was not intended that positions taken would be retained for more than a brief interlude. The attacking units were meant to be small-scale ones and their missions were not always determined on the basis of strategic necessity. For example, the town of Bint Jbeil, with a population of 40,000 and situated 4 kilometres from the border, was singled out as a target primarily for its symbolic value. It was there that Nasrallah gave his victory speech in the wake of the IDF's withdrawal in 2000 from Lebanon, and it was thought that its capture, even if fleetingly, would undermine Nasrallah's standing.[54] The battle for the town, commencing on July 24, resulted in ten IDF fatalities, with very little to show for it. Contrary to expectations, Bint Jbeil was never captured.

Realizing that all was not well, the cabinet on July 27 finally authorized the mobilization of 2,000 to 3,000 reservists to be on stand-by should the general staff finally decide to use them. Then, on July 30, the IDF encountered a serious setback after the IAF had bombed the town of Qana, causing a building to collapse. Buried below the rubble were twenty-eight civilians, of whom about half were children.[55] In light of a previous IDF engagement with Qana in April 1996, in which more than 100 Lebanese civilians met their death from an artillery barrage, the latest incident led to an international condemnation of Israel. The next day, Israel suspended its air offensive for a 48-hour period to enable the matter to be investigated.[56] Once Hezbollah had responded to the Qana disaster by firing 156 rockets on a single day, the second highest figure since the start of the war, Halutz finally came round to the view that there was indeed no alternative other than for extensive ground forces to comb through Southern Lebanon in order significantly to diminish Hezbollah's rocket-launching capability. On being asked why it had taken him so long to arrive at such a decision, Halutz spuriously replied that "the Israel public was not yet ready to accept a penetration into Lebanon on July 12."[57] In the meantime, Israelis had been fleeing from the northern towns and villages in search of safety from the hazards of Hezbollah's Katyusha rockets. On August 6, a Katyusha rocket slammed into an IDF vehicle transporting soldiers stationed at Kfar Giladi. Twelve were killed. It seems that unlike the civilians, who were usually in shelters, the soldiers were rather cavalier about safety procedures and were wearing neither protective vests nor helmets.[58]

By August 7 preparations were completed for a ground offensive scheduled to commence during the night of August 9. But, as the IDF was about to learn, needless procrastinating was not without cost. Had Israel acted earlier it would have found itself unhindered by other countries and regimes, then eagerly awaiting Hezbollah being routed by the IDF. But circumstances had now changed. The Lebanese government had indicated an unexpected willingness to place its own forces in Southern Lebanon, and the UN Security Council had begun deliberating on a ceasefire. With the UN clock ticking, Olmert estimated that the IDF probably had less than four days' grace to accomplish its new assignment, barely enough time even to complete its first phase – namely, the reaching of the Litani River.[59] Yet such an assessment did not deter Halutz, who, in his new guise as an ardent advocate of the use of ground forces, held that the mission should proceed regardless.[60] Peretz was of similar mind. On August 8, he had consulted with a group of retired generals. Asking them whether or not he should give his blessing to a large ground offensive, they replied that, if there was time enough, by all means, but not otherwise. Subsequently Peretz would defend his actions by asserting that he had the generals' endorsement, neglecting to mention their caveat regarding any time constraint.[61]

On August 9, Halutz, at a cabinet meeting, outlined the IDF's plan of attack. It involved three divisions that, after racing to the Litani River, would then proceed to erode Hezbollah's military structure and presence in Southern Lebanon. According to Halutz, the whole process was expected to last three to four weeks. Such an assumption, given a UN resolve to bring the war to a close as soon as possible, was highly fanciful. The day before, fearing that Halutz's scheme might go awry, Olmert outlined the plan to Shaul Mofaz, the minister of transport, who had previously served as the IDF's chief of staff and then minister of defence. Mofaz proposed an alternative that, in his view, would have been easier to implement given the time factor and that would have devastated Hezbollah. It involved the seizure, by two airborne IDF divisions, of the high ground overlooking the Litani River, thus presenting the enemy with a formidable force to their rear. After that, two brigades in the south could mop up any residual resistance.[62] Olmert, much taken by Mofaz's suggestion, believed that the IDF now had an optimal strategy. But when the cabinet met the next day he deferred to Halutz, on the grounds that a cabinet rejection of Halutz's plan in favour of that of Mofaz would constitute "a blow to the security establishment."[63]

The IDF rapidly went into its pre-invasion mode, stationing all troops at their start-off positions. Just as they were about to advance, Olmert ordered the operation to be postponed for 24 hours to take stock of international opinion. The next day, much to the consternation of Peretz and Halutz, Olmert decided to extend the military freeze by yet another 24 hours. Meanwhile, on August 11 (it was already August 12 in Israel), the UN Security Council unanimously adopted a resolution calling for a ceasefire. In response, the Israeli Ministry of Foreign Affairs issued a declaration that read in part: "While the resolution does not contain everything that we strove to achieve at the outset . . . it constitutes a good starting point for changing the regional reality in the direction that Israel and Lebanon want to go."[64] On August 12, both Israel and the Lebanese government accepted the UN resolution and set the ceasefire date for August 14. Olmert was in a quandary. The time left to conduct a new campaign was no more than 35 hours, yet he did not want to continue to turn down Peretz's persistent calls for the IDF to be given free rein. Finally, Olmert gave the IDF the all clear. Reflecting on the operation, Ya'alon, the previous serving chief of staff, concluded that the decisions taken had to do more with internal political considerations than with state-security matters.[65]

At 9 p.m. on August 12, 9,800 IDF troops entered Southern Lebanon for the final day and a half of the war. It was far too late for the IDF to achieve significant breakthroughs but not late enough for it to incur additional casualties – in this case, thirty-three deaths. When Mofaz was informed of the commencement of the ground offensive, he warned Olmert, "You're not going to gain anything except get a lot of good men killed."[66] Nor was Mofaz alone in that assessment. Once the ceasefire went into effect and Israel was committed to withdraw from the small amount of Lebanese territory that it had gained, irate journalists confronted Brigadier-General Guy Tzur of the northern command, asking, "What the hell did the soldiers die for?" Tzur evasively replied by suggesting that such a question should rather be directed to his superiors.[67]

In the war as a whole, 119 IDF personnel and forty-four Israeli civilians were killed.[68] Israel's losses specifically from Hezbollah rocket attacks amounted to fifty-three fatalities (including both soldiers and civilians), 250 severely wounded and 2,000 lightly wounded. Hundreds of private dwellings, several public utilities and dozens of industrial plants were damaged. Some 250,000 civilians abandoned the northern part of Israel in search of safer areas further south, while in overall terms around 1 million huddled in bomb shelters.[69] On the Lebanese side over 1,000 people perished, nearly half of whom were believed to be civilians. Right until the final moment of battle, the IDF was unable to staunch the flow of rockets into Israel, amounting to close to 4,000 in number.[70] To review Israel's general conduct and management of the war, a government-appointed committee of inquiry chaired by the retired judge Eliyahu Winograd was commissioned. His co-investigators were Professor Ruth Gavizon, an expert on constitutional law, Professor Yehezkel Dror, an expert on policy-making, and the retired major-generals Menahem Einan and Dr Haim Nadel. The commission issued an interim report on April 30, 2007, and a final one on January 30, 2008.

In its final report it concluded: "We regard the second Lebanon war as a serious missed opportunity. Israel initiated a long war, which ended without its clear military victory. A semi-military organization of a few thousand men resisted, for a few weeks, the strongest army in the Middle East, which enjoyed full air superiority and size and technology advantages." The report went on to stress that both the military and the political leadership shared the blame for the IDF's less than optimal achievements, citing the fact that the IDF commenced "its ground operation only after the political and diplomatic timetable prevented its effective completion."[71] Olmert, Peretz and Halutz were all seriously reprimanded. The interim report blamed Olmert for acting with undue haste without any detailed knowledge of the IDF's capacity to wage war and without seeking such knowledge. Peretz was held to account for making decisions without due consultation with appropriate experts, thereby lessening the IDF's ability to perform optimally, whereas Halutz failed to alert the government of IDF shortcomings in relation to a ground offensive and misled ministers to believe that "the IDF was ready and prepared and had operational plans fitting the situation."[72] Olmert, who accepted "the full responsibilities for the failures of the war," refused to resign.[73] (Both Peretz and Halutz had already done so before the publication of the interim report.) Harel and Issacharoff neatly summed up Israel's lacklustre military performance as being due to "a rare combination of inexperience, lack of understanding, self-destructive internal rivalry and overweening pride."[74]

Nevertheless, given that the IAF had undertaken numerous effective bombing missions and that more than 170,000 artillery shells had been fired into Lebanon, there is little doubt that Hezbollah suffered a grievous blow. On August 10, in an interview with Lebanon's New TV station, Nasrallah said: "You ask me, if I had known on July 11 ... that the [kidnapping] operation would lead to such a war, would I do it? I say no, absolutely not."[75]

The UN Security Council resolution (UNSCR 1559) adopted on August 11 was quite specific about the need for the implementation of measures to ensure "the disarmament of all armed groups in Lebanon, so that ... there will be no weapons or authority in Lebanon other than that of the Lebanese State." All that prompted Livni, as Israel's foreign minister, to expect the UN Interim Force in Lebanon (UNIFIL) "to control the passages on the Lebanese Syrian border, to aid the Lebanese army in deploying properly and to fully implement UNSCR 1559, particularly in disarming Hezbollah."[76] But Major-General Alain Pellegrini of UNIFIL was emphatic that "the disarmament of Hezbollah is not the business of UNIFIL."[77] Rather, it was a "strictly Lebanese affair" to be resolved by the Lebanese themselves, which meant that the UN resolution's call for the prevention of hostilities, "including the establishment between the Blue Line and the Litani river of an area free of any armed personnel, assets and weapons other than those of the Government of Lebanon and of UNIFIL," was nugatory.

On Wednesday July 16, 2008, just over two years after the start of the war, a prisoner exchange between Hezbollah and Israel was scheduled to take place at the Rosh Hanikra border crossing. In return for the release of four terrorists and 197 bodies of Hezbollah and other Arab fighters, Israel was to receive Goldwasser and Regev. Hezbollah had not divulged any information whatsoever relating to the well-being of the kidnapped Israelis. The general consensus within the IDF top echelon was that they had most probably died of wounds resulting from their capture. Their families were advised accordingly, but since the information was not definitive they continued to nurture hopes of eventually seeing them alive. Even the IDF had some reservations, for a helicopter was put on standby to fly them to hospital should the need arise.[78] Sky News reported that, early on the morning of the day in question, "Miki Goldwasser went shopping. She said she wants enough food in the house for when her son, Ehud, returns . . . she was quoted as simply saying she can't wait to hug him."[79] Like the rest of the Israeli public, the families of both abductees watched the handover procedure live on television. When the final moment came, a Hezbollah spokesman nonchalantly announced that "the soldiers [sic] Goldwasser and Regev will now be released." That was just the sort of announcement that the families in question were hoping to hear, but almost instantly their hopes were cruelly dashed as two black coffins were brought forward, causing a wail of unmitigated grief to resound throughout the Goldwasser and Regev households.

Towering among the four terrorists that Israel freed was one Samir Kuntar, who, on April 22, 1979, after killing an Israeli policeman, entered an apartment in Nahariya, an Israeli coastal town, and made off with a young man and his four-year-old daughter. As Kuntar and his party were about to board a dinghy to return to Lebanon, Kuntar shot the father, Danny Haran, at close range and bludgeoned his daughter Einat to death by bashing her skull against a rock with a rifle butt. The anguished mother, Smadar, while hiding from Kuntar in the apartment's crawl space, inadvertently caused the suffocation of her two-year-old daughter Yael in her attempts to keep her quiet.[80] It was Kuntar's freedom to which Nasrallah was most committed. He had promised the Kuntar family that he would secure their son's release, and the kidnapping of Goldwasser and Regev was executed precisely with that in mind. On his return to Lebanon, Kuntar was hailed as a national hero. A public holiday was proclaimed to commemorate the occasion and he was publicly welcomed by Nasrallah and then later by Iran's president, Mahmoud Ahmadinejad. In November 2008, on a visit to Syria, Kuntar was awarded the Syrian Order of Merit, the country's highest accolade. Photographs of him on his release reveal a healthy, well-nourished middle-aged man, who, while imprisoned in Israel, was allowed to marry a local Arab, to have conjugal rights and to graduate from the Open University of Israel in social and political science.[81] By contrast, on the very day that the two unfortunate Israelis were kidnapped, a request by the International Red Cross for one of their doctors to examine them was brusquely dismissed.[82]

Operation Cast Lead

Between 2005 and 2008, a total of 5,447 rockets and 4,108 mortars were fired at southern Israel from Gaza. Although over that period only fifteen Israelis were killed,[83] the never ending discharge of rockets demoralized and terrorized Israeli civilians, making their daily lives all but intolerable.[84] As Yonatan Yagodovsky, of the Magen David Adom (Israel's Red Cross organization), described the situation: "The problem for most people was not being hit but the fear, uncertainty and stress." In essence, this affected over 800,000 people living within rocket range.[85]

To a large degree Israel had reacted by targeting individuals, organizations or sites associated with the dispatch of Palestinian missiles. But such measures were evidently insufficient, for shortly after each reprisal the rocketeers resumed business as usual. A distinct step towards a full-blown crisis occurred on November 4, 2008, when a small unit of the IDF entered Gaza to destroy a suspected tunnel being built for the purpose of kidnapping Israeli troops. In the firefight that followed, six Hamas gunmen were killed. The raid so incensed Hamas that, despite a supposed truce, which in any event it regularly violated, it stepped up the pace of its rocket launching to such a degree that, in the month of November alone, some 190 missiles were fired.[86]

Matters reached a head when a six-month truce between Israel and Hamas brokered by Egypt expired on December 19, 2008. The following day some sixty rockets and mortars were fired at Israel.[87] With warnings by Olmert of dire consequences lest Hamas failed to desist being ignored, the IDF on December 27 inaugurated Operation Cast Lead. The operation opened with some sixty IAF aircraft and helicopters bombing Hamas structures and personnel, killing among others the Gaza police chief, the police commander for central Gaza, and the head of the Hamas bodyguard unit. In search of a safe refuge, some Hamas leaders found shelter in the Israeli-built basement of Shifa Hospital, knowing full well that the IAF would leave the hospital untouched.[88] Hamas replied to the Israeli attacks by intensifying its rocket shelling. Meanwhile Israel began mobilizing 6,500 of its reservists,[89] who went into action on January 3, 2009. Their entry into the Gaza arena was preceded by a massive artillery barrage spanning the Gaza frontier. Three infantry brigades, drawn from the paratroopers, Golani and Givati, entered Gaza from different vantage points, while the 401st Armoured Brigade blocked accesses to Gaza City. Fierce fighting arose on the outskirts of that city, and eventually the IDF began to penetrate it. The IDF made steady progress and, by January 13, was approaching the headquarters of Hamas's preventive security building. While all this was going on, the UN Security Council on January 8 passed a resolution calling for a complete and immediate ceasefire, which was ignored by both sides.

An unavoidable aspect of fighting in densely populated urban areas is that innocent civilians are invariably killed. The worst of such incidences was supposed to have taken place on January 6 at the al-Fakhura school in the Jabalya refugee camp, where it was claimed an Israeli shell had fallen. The UN and numerous NGOs wasted no time in alleging that, as a consequence, forty-two people lost their lives. However, by January 27, the UN's Office for Humanitarian Affairs (OCHA) clarified its previous report by stating that "All of the fatalities took place outside rather than inside the school."[90] That is, the school was not shelled after all. Moreover, the IDF disputed the death toll, claiming that only twelve people were killed, of whom nine were members of Hamas engaged at the time in firing mortars.[91] Partly because of the international hue and cry resulting from the "al-Fakhura school massacre," on January 7 Israel made a humanitarian gesture by opening up a relief shipment corridor into Gaza and by agreeing to suspend fighting for three hours per day. Finally, on January 17, Israel announced a unilateral ceasefire and began drawing its campaign to a close.

The fighting in Gaza claimed the lives of ten IDF soldiers (four due to friendly fire) and three Israeli civilians.[92] According to IDF estimates,

1,166 Palestinians were killed, 709 of whom were identified as fighters and 457 as civilians.[93] The IDF figures chime with an admission made in November 2010 by a senior Hamas official that, in the war, up to 750 Palestinian fighters were martyred.[94] By contrast, NGOs produced figures suggesting that the overall Palestinian death toll was higher and the number of fighters lower. For example B'tselem, an Israeli NGO renowned for its regular criticism of the IDF, claimed that, out of a total of 1,385 supposedly killed, 762 were civilians.[95] B'tselem claimed that it "cross-checked the information with investigations carried out by Palestinian and international human rights organizations and with information on various websites and blogs, including those of the military wings of armed Palestinian groups."[96] It is hardly surprising that B'tselem's estimates, as noted by a correspondent of *The Guardian*, were "broadly in line with research from Palestine human rights groups."[97]

Israelis had mixed feelings as to whether or not Operation Cast Lead ought to have been regarded as a success. David Makovsky, a former executive editor of the *Jerusalem Post*, believed that there were good grounds for assuming that concrete achievements were attained, since the ability of Hamas to fire rockets into Israel had been degraded at very little cost to the IDF in terms of loss of life.[98] That such an achievement resulted from Hamas not offering serious resistance to Israeli ground troops must surely, in Makovsky's view, be attributed to the IDF's fine mettle. Other Israeli defence analysts begged to differ. As far as Stuart Cohen of the Begin Sadat Center for Strategic Studies was concerned, by declaring a unilateral ceasefire, Israel's "political and military leadership (after engaging the enemy without a coherent strategy other than to negatively impact on it) had run out of ideas of what more could be done."[99] They brought their campaign to a close without extracting any formal concession from Hamas, which survived the day undefeated to continue firing rockets into Israel, albeit on a reduced scale. Weapons continued to flow into Gaza, and Gilad Shalit remained in captivity until October 18, 2011. Israel made much of a claim that, when all is said and done, the operation restored the IDF's deterrence. But, as Cohen posited, "The side intent on attaining deterrence is never in a position to determine whether or not that aim has been achieved." The problem, as Cohen saw it, was that no concrete or tangible aims were formulated, such as "the conquest of a particular slice of territory, control over a strategically important resource, the surrender of a hostile government, or in the present context, the repatriation of a soldier held captive."[100] Martin Sherman, a research fellow in security studies at Tel Aviv University, basically concurred with Cohen's analysis. After noting that the IDF had in no way imposed its will on Hamas, he concluded that that failure emanated from a relatively recent Israeli phenomenon, namely "a loss of faith in victory, both as a valid cognitive concept and as an attainable military objective." In his view, "credible 'pictures of victory' require a credibly decisive victory. And a credibly decisive victory can only be attained if it is believed possible."[101]

Whether or not Operation Cast Lead was a well-executed military venture is a moot point. What is incontestable is that it gave rise to a sweeping and effective international anti-Israel campaign whereby the country was stigmatized as an aggressor bent on terrorizing Palestinians by an iron-fisted IDF engaged in war crimes and crimes against humanity. Governments, the media at large and global NGOs were scathing in their criticism of the IDF's putative recklessness and disregard for human life. Amnesty International accused it of causing wanton destruction as a result of not distinguishing between military and civilian targets. For good measure, it claimed that, while Hamas or other Palestinian fighters did not use civilians as human shields, Israel, in certain cases, did.[102]

As damning as such reports were, none was as detrimental to Israel's reputation as the Goldstone Report, submitted to the UN Human Rights Council on September 29, 2009. It was commissioned by the UN Human Rights Council at a ninth special session held on January 9 and 12, 2009, in the form of Resolution S-91, which read, in part: the Council "resolves to dispatch an urgent, independent international fact-finding mission, to be appointed by the President of the Council, to investigate all violations of international human rights law and international humanitarian law by the occupying Power, Israel, against the Palestinian people ... particularly in the occupied Gaza Strip, due to the current aggression." No mention was made of any human rights violations by the Palestinians, and since, as the resolution makes clear, Israel had already been prejudged as a wanton aggressor, one might reasonably wonder why there was any need for such a fact-finding mission in the first place. Mary Robinson, formerly UN High Commissioner for Human Rights, was first approached to head the investigation, but declined, saying: "Unfortunately, the Human Rights Council passed a resolution seeking a fact-finding mission to only look at what Israel had done, and I don't think that's a human rights approach."[103] When the post was subsequently offered to Justice Richard Goldstone, a South African human rights lawyer, he accepted, but with minor qualms. Like Robinson, he was aware of the irregularity of singling out Israel and asked the Council president to extend his brief to include Hamas. The president concurred but did not have the authority to alter a resolution, and the Council never formally amended it.[104]

Mirroring the Council's prejudices were the preconceptions of Goldstone's three co-investigators, Professor Christine Chinkin of the London School of Economics, Hina Jilani, a Pakistani jurist, and Desmond Travers, a retired colonel of the Irish Defence Forces. Chinkin had appended her signature to a joint letter to the *Sunday Times* that appeared on January 11, 2009. The letter read in part: "Israel's bombardment of Gaza is not self-defence, it's a war crime ... The rocket attacks on Israel by Hamas, deplorable as they are, do not, in terms of scale and effect amount to an armed attack entitling Israel to rely on self-defence ... Israel's actions amount to aggression, not self-defence ... its invasion and bombardment of Gaza ... [is] contrary to international humanitarian and human rights law."[105] On October 11, 2005, Jilani told journalists that "Israel is depriving Palestinians of their basic human rights using security as an excuse."[106] Inadvertently revealing her distinctive investigative style and legal philosophy, she maintained that "it would be very cruel not to give credence to the voices of the victims."[107] Of the three, Travers seemed to have been obsessed with a fantasy that the Israelis had deliberately targeted Irish peacekeepers in Southern Lebanon. This dissonance with reality was highlighted by his ludicrous claim that, in the month preceding Operation Cast Lead, the number of rockets fired into Israel by Hamas "was something like two."[108] With pronounced hyperbole, Travers insisted that "Gaza has now come into the history books in the same way as Guernica, Dresden, Stalingrad. Gaza is a gulag, the only gulag in the Western hemisphere."[109] Although there is no record of Goldstone having previously disparaged Israel, the stance he would take was foreshadowed by his signing an open letter (along with Jilani and Travers, among others) addressed to UN Secretary General Ban Ki-Moon, calling for a prompt, independent and impartial investigation that "would provide a public record of gross violations of international humanitarian law *committed*."[110] While elsewhere in the letter the word "alleged" appeared, it seems beyond belief that Goldstone and the other distinguished jurists involved would have been unaware of the fact that they were in effect attesting that "violations of international humanitarian law" had indeed been committed. After all, their letter concluded with the declaration that "the events in Gaza have shocked us to the core."

Goldstone and members of his panel did all that was expected of them. They dutifully compiled a report that was exceedingly harsh in its criticism of Israel. Although Hamas was also called to account, the overwhelming thrust of their report was directed against the IDF. Bearing the UN imprimatur, the Goldstone Report has been widely brandished by anti-Zionists, anti-Semites and radical Islamists as an effective device in tarnishing Israel's international standing.

In essence, the Goldstone Report concluded that "there was strong evidence to establish that numerous serious violations of international law, both humanitarian law and human rights law, were committed by Israel."[111] More specifically, Israel was accused of applying disproportionate force, wilfully killing and wilfully causing suffering to civilians, using them as human shields and deliberately targeting industrial sites and water installations in order to deprive Gazans of the means of their subsistence. The report concluded that the IDF had committed war crimes "and, in some respects, crimes against humanity."[112] Finally, Goldstone and his associates stipulated that their report be tabled by the UN Human Rights Council to the UN Security Council, even though the UN Human Rights Council can report only to the UN General Assembly.

According to a ruling of the International Criminal Court, as summarized by Peter Berkowitz, "States not only have the right but also the primary responsibility to prevent, control and prosecute atrocities."[113] Therefore Israel, when it refused to cooperate with Goldstone's kangaroo court, was acting within its legal rights. In the absence of Israel's involvement, a good deal of the Goldstone mission's evidence was derived from sources in Gaza under the watchful eye and help of Hamas functionaries and from members of NGOs all renowned for their deep antipathy to Israel and its defence forces. Consequently, the picture that emerged was at variance with the historical record.

In practice, Israel had taken a number of measures to forewarn civilians of impending attacks and to advise them to vacate specific areas. This was done by IAF planes dropping hundreds of thousands of leaflets and by notifying thousands of Gazans by cell phone. According to *Haaretz*, an Israeli newspaper widely regarded by the international media fraternity as a reliable information source,

> The IDF has also used what they are calling "roof knocking" operations, in which they inform the residents of suspected buildings that they have 10 minutes to leave the premises. In some cases, residents of suspected houses have been able to prevent bombing by climbing up to the roof to show that they will not leave, *prompting IDF commanders to call off the strike*.[114]

What impressed Anthony Cordesman, who currently holds a chair at the Washington Center for Strategic and International Studies and who previously was the director of intelligence assessment in the Office of the US Secretary of Defense, was the care Israel had taken to avoid civilian losses. In a post-war study of Operation Cast Lead, Cordesman wrote:

> The IAF did make a systematic effort to limit collateral damage. It developed detailed targeting plans to identify sensitive areas and targets. It prepared for fighting in an urban environment by developing highly detailed maps that tracked Hamas movements, facilities, shelters and tunnels and the location of sensitive facilities like schools, hospitals, and religious institutions. It planned and executed strikes using the smallest possible weapon, and coordinated both air strikes and the use of artillery weapons using GPS to try to [decouple] military targeting from damage to civilian facilities.[115]

Similarly, Colonel Richard Kemp, one-time commander of British forces in Afghanistan, had on October 2009, a month after the Goldstone Report was released, explicitly informed the United Nations Human Rights Council that, in Gaza, the IDF "did more to safeguard the right of civilians in a combat zone than any other army in the history of warfare."[116] Referring to statistics derived from a UN study, Kemp noted that the worldwide average civilian to combatant death ratio was three to one, as it was in Afghanistan. In Iraq and Kosovo it was believed to be four to one and in Chechnya and Serbia higher still. By contrast, in Gaza it was less than one to one.[117] Given that many Hamas fighters had donned civilian clothes,[118] some of the dead Palestinians identified as civilians might well have been combatants, thus lowering the civilian to combatant ratio in Gaza even further.

The charge of the Goldstone Report that Israel sought to deprive the people of Gaza of the means of subsistence is belied by the IDF having opened up corridors for the supply of basic provisions. (According to Cordesman, "States do not have an obligation to provide humanitarian relief to their enemies or to enemy populations in wartime.")[119] Rather than accusing Israel of systematically using civilians as human shields, it would have been far more pertinent for Goldstone and his team to focus on Hamas. The practice of using civilians as human shields has been openly and even proudly admitted by Hamas spokesmen. For example, Fathi Hammad, a Hamas MP, declared on al-Aqsa TV: "For the Palestinian people death has become an industry ... that is why they have formed human shields of the women, the children, the elderly and the mujahideen [fighters] in order to challenge the Zionist bombing machine."[120] Human Rights Watch noted that, consistent with their disregard for the well-being of their own civilians, Palestinian armed groups "placed fellow Palestinians at grave risk of Israeli counter-attacks by firing rockets from within or near populated areas ... residents felt endangered and angered by the militants' use of their area as a launching site."[121] Finally, because total Israeli losses in Operation Cast Lead were a minute proportion of the losses of the Palestinians, the Goldstone Report complained that the IDF employed disproportionate force, a claim fervently endorsed by many European states. Yet, during the war in Kosovo, Europeans, Americans and Turks participated in a NATO alliance that, between March and June 1999, in Operation Allied Force, conducted a bombing campaign that led to the deaths of at least 500 civilians and fewer than 170 Serbian soldiers.[122] No member of the NATO forces suffered casualties, and the issue of proportionate force never troubled them or anyone else.

On April 2, 2011, in an article in the *Washington Post*, Goldstone, to his partial credit, wrote:

> If I had known then what I know now, the Goldstone Report would have been a different document... [Palestinian] civilians were not intentionally targeted as a matter of policy ... The final report by the U.N. committee of independent experts – chaired by former New York judge Mary McGowan Davis – that followed up on the recommendations of the Goldstone Report has found that "Israel has dedicated significant resources to investigate over 400 allegations of operational misconduct in Gaza" while "the de facto authorities (i.e., Hamas) have not conducted any investigations into the launching of rocket and mortar attacks against Israel."

Goldstone's partial recantation (he still insisted that the mission conducted itself according to the highest standards of probity) went some way towards redressing the damage inflicted, but remnants, albeit attenuated, of the unjust legacy of his report still linger.

The *Mavi Marmara* Affair

On May 31, 2010, six ships, described by their sponsors as the "Gaza Freedom Flotilla," were intercepted in international waters of the Mediterranean by the Israeli navy. The vessels, which set out from ports in Ireland, Turkey and Greece and converged 30 miles south of Cyprus, were ostensibly on a mission to convey humanitarian aid to Gaza. However, that was by no means their sole or even major pursuit, for an offer by Israel to enable them to utilize land crossings from Israel into Gaza was turned down. Three of the six vessels carried no cargo whatsoever, and on the *Mavi Marmara* there were close to 600 passengers with *only* their personal effects.[123]

The flotilla had been jointly organized by the Free Gaza Movement and the Turkish Foundation for Human Rights and Freedoms and Humanitarian Relief, known as IHH. Both bodies ally or identify themselves with Hamas and share a common desire to hasten the demise of the Jewish State. With that in mind, their real objective in organizing the flotilla was to nullify Israel's sea blockade of Gaza to facilitate the flow of armaments to Hamas. Lest it needed spelling out, the leading financial backer of the flotilla, Yasser Qashlaq, a Palestinian-Lebanese businessman,[124] delineated what he ultimately had in mind. In an interview on May 17, 2010, on Hezbollah's al-Manar TV, Qashlaq informed his interlocutor that eventually "these ships will carry these [Israeli] dregs of European garbage back to their own countries [in Europe]." Then, addressing the Israelis directly, he declared: "Don't be misled . . . You will never be able to make peace with us . . . There is no reason for coexistence."[125]

In the early hours of May 31, the Israel navy broadcast the following message to the oncoming boats:

> You are approaching an area of hostilities, which is under a naval blockade. Gaza coastal area and Gaza Harbor are closed to maritime traffic. The Israeli government supports delivery of humanitarian supplies to the civilian population in Gaza Strip and invites you to enter Ashdod port. Delivery of supplies will be in accordance with the authorities' regulations and through the formal land crossing to Gaza and under your observation, after which you can return to your home ports.[126]

In reply, someone from one of the ships' radios was heard to snarl, "Shut up. Go back to Auschwitz."[127]

Five of the six vessels offered no physical resistance to the Israeli navy's efforts to tow them to the port of Ashdod, but not so the *Mavi Marmara*. Included among them were forty hard-core members of IHH, who had embarked in Turkey well ahead of the other passengers and who were not subject to security checks. Among items in their possession were gas masks, bulletproof vests and walkie-talkies.[128] They commandeered the ship's upper deck and readied themselves to do battle against any Israeli naval personnel daring enough to challenge them. There is no question that they anticipated a violent encounter. In preparation for the forthcoming showdown they amassed a large quantity of knives, daggers, slingshots, chains and metal bars.[129] Meanwhile they fortified their spirits by singing "Khaybar, Khaybar. Oh Jews, the army of Muhammad will return," in reference to the 628 Jews massacred in Arabia at Muhammad's behest.[130]

At around 4.30 a.m., after the *Mavi Marmara* categorically refused to comply with an Israeli navy request that it stop and allow its men to take possession of the ship, the Israelis attempted to board from two approaching speedboats. But on meeting with a torrent of miscellaneous objects hurled at them, and after their ladders were rendered inoperable, they turned back. The IDF then sent in a helicopter, from which soldiers rappelled onto the top deck of the vessel. As they touched down they were mauled by a frenzied mob of IHH members striking them with metal rods and attempting to throw them off the ship.[131] According to the Meir Amit Intelligence Center: "During the first stages of the fighting three IDF soldiers were taken hostage, wounded and moved below decks ... they were brutally beaten with wooden clubs, stabbed and choked."[132] It took two more helicopters bringing in extra reinforcements to subdue all opposition and to assume full control of the vessel. Considering that IDF fighters in the first landing party found themselves with their lives at risk – nine had been injured, two had been shot and one stabbed in the stomach – permission was finally given for the landing party to respond with live ammunition. Up to then, no shots were fired by any IDF soldier. Outnumbered and fighting at very close range against Islamic fanatics wielding pikes, poles, knives and daggers, as well as at least three handguns that had been snatched from the Israelis, it is no wonder that nine of those attacking the Israelis were killed and fifty-three were wounded.[133] Eight of the nine killed belonged to the IHH or affiliated groups and all except one of the wounded were Turks. Furthermore, seven of those killed had previously expressed their intention to die as shahids (martyrs).[134]

Mindful of the need to mobilize the media in their anti-Israel vendetta, a lounge of the *Mavi Marmara* was fitted to provide foreign journalists with individual panel desks and access to the internet. The moment the IDF attempted to board the vessel, the ship-bound journalists assiduously set to work, beaming out their anti-Israel dispatches. Their versions of events fell on fertile grounds. There was an immediate eruption of hateful anti-Israel sentiment that reverberated throughout the world. Almost all "quality" newspapers and TV stations ran stories that the Israelis had shown themselves to be pirates of the sea, murdering innocent passengers whose only interest was in relieving the poor starving people of Gaza.

On June 7, 2010, the UK *Financial Times* editorialized that, "by behaving as though it were above the law, Israel is steadily alienating international public opinion and *eroding its legitimacy*."[135] *The Economist* on June 5, 2010, opined that "Israel resorts to violence too readily . . . it tends to shoot opponents first and ask questions later." The BBC pontificated that the matter was "not just about this single incident at sea, serious and deadly though it was . . . It is about a pattern of violent and disproportionate behaviour, with Israel playing to its own rules rather than international law."[136] On the diplomatic front, the UN Security Council "condemned those acts which had killed hundreds of civilians and wounded many more," while the UN Human Rights Council censured "in the strongest terms the outrageous attack by the Israeli forces against the humanitarian flotilla of ships which resulted in the killing and injuring of many innocent civilians."[137] Patrick Goodenough of CNS News captured the tone of the UN Human Rights Council's deliberations by reporting: "Piracy, act of aggression, brutal massacre, atrocious act, war crime, unprovoked, unwarranted, murderous attacks, act of terrorism, crime against humanity and violation of international law were some of the terms used by HRC envoys to describe Monday's pre-dawn interception at sea. The pro-Palestinian activists onboard the ships were characterized as peaceful, innocent, noble, unarmed and defenseless."[138] In an article fittingly titled "An Irrational Obscene Hatred," William Shawcross pointed out that "the Israeli ambassador to the EU was harangued and abused in the European Parliament Foreign Affairs Committee. No one was interested in his explanation, and when he showed images of IDF soldiers being beaten with iron bars on the *Mavi Marmara*, MEPs [members of the European Parliament] asserted the film was faked propaganda."[139]

As to be expected, it was in the Middle East where the denunciation of Israel was most strident and where the Palestine Authority president, Mahmoud Abbas, called for three days of mourning for the victims of Israel's "massacre."[140] But the epicentre of it all was Turkey, where the country's prime minister, Recep Tayyip Erdogan, had already realigned his foreign policy to win the hearts and minds of Arabs in order to become the region's pre-eminent power. With that in mind, Erdogan had made a conscious decision to forego commercial and military ties with Israel. Before the *Mavi Marmara* had departed from Turkey, Israel pleaded in vain with the Turkish government not to allow it to set sail.

Writing in the English-language edition of *Hurriyet*, Barcin Yinanc complained that officials in Erdogan's ruling Justice and Development Party "were not convincing at all when they said they could not stop the ship [*Mavi Marmara*] carrying humanitarian aid to Gaza from leaving Turkey. They could have stopped it if they wanted to, [but] did they want to? Not at all."[141] In the same edition, Semih Idiz affirmed that "there can be no mistake that the Erdogan government is morally and politically behind this group, the IHH, that has now gained international fame according to some, and notoriety, according to others."[142] Courting close and fraternal ties with Hamas, Erdogan stated: "I do not think that Hamas is a terrorist organization . . . They are Palestinians in resistance, fighting for their own land."[143] Erdogan's strictures on Israel were withering in the extreme. In a discourse summarized by Joshua Teitelbaum as amounting to "calls for a Jihad against Israel," Erdogan demanded a formal apology from Israel and compensation for Turkish losses. Much to his satisfaction he became the darling of the Arab World.[144] Since then, Turkey has not only continued to excoriate Israel in the ugliest of terms but has thrown its weight beyond the movement to delegitimize the Jewish State, accusing it of it being in constant breach of international law.

A rare document examining the flotilla incident with a degree of objectivity was the UN Palmer Report, commissioned in August 2010. It was chaired by Geoffrey Palmer, former prime minister of New Zealand, and its other members were Alvaro Uribe, former Colombian president, Joseph Ciechanover Itzhar, former director general of the Israeli Ministry of Foreign Affairs, and Süleyman Özdem Sanberk, a veteran senior Turkish diplomat. The report was submitted to the UN Secretary General in September, 2011. Below are some of its main findings:

> The naval blockade was imposed as a legitimate security measure in order to prevent weapons from entering Gaza by sea and its implementation complied with the requirements of international law. (p. 45)

> If the flotilla had been a purely humanitarian mission it is hard to see why so many passengers were embarked and with what purpose. Furthermore, the quality and value of many of the humanitarian goods on board the vessels is questionable. (p. 47)

The flotilla acted recklessly in attempting to breach the naval blockade. The majority of the flotilla participants had no violent intentions, but there exist serious questions about the conduct, true nature and objectives of the flotilla organizers, particularly IHH. The actions of the flotilla needlessly carried the potential for escalation. (p. 48)

Soldiers landing from the first helicopter faced significant, organized and violent resistance from a group of passengers when they descended onto the *Mavi Marmara*. . . . In the face of such a response, the IDF personnel involved in the operation needed to take action for *their own protection and that of the other soldiers*. (pp. 56–7; emphasis added)

Israel's decision to board the vessels with such substantial force at a great distance from the blockade zone and with no final warning immediately prior to the boarding was excessive and unreasonable:
    a. Non-violent options should have been used in the first instance. In particular, clear prior warning that the vessels were to be boarded and a demonstration of dissuading force should have been given to avoid the type of confrontation that occurred;
    b. The operation should have reassessed its options when the resistance to the initial boarding attempt became apparent so as to minimize casualties. (p. 54)

In the main, Israel accepted the gist of the report's findings and, while it had reservations about the criticism of the conduct of its forces, agreed, in conformity with the report's recommendation, to express regret and offer compensation. Turkey, by contrast, totally rejected the report's conclusions and demanded a full apology.[145]

The Ongoing Quest for Peace

In early 2007, the United States decided to become more proactive in resolving the Israeli–Palestinian conflict, partly on account of a new commitment given to moderate Arab regimes in order to secure their support in its efforts to contain Iran.[146] Accordingly, on November 27 a large international conference was convened at the US Naval Academy in Annapolis. Forty-nine countries and international organizations were invited. At the conference Olmert and Abbas agreed to undertake weekly bilateral negotiations in an effort to reach an agreement, based on the acceptance of a two-state solution, before the end of 2008. As a result, numerous encounters took place, either between the two of them alone or in the presence of their senior colleagues and advisors.[147] During that time the construction or expansion of settlements in the West Bank continued without interruption. By September 16, 2008, Olmert presented Abbas with his final offer. It amounted to Israel annexing roughly 6.4 percent of the West Bank, where there was a large concentration of Jewish settlers. In return, Israel would forego parts of its own territory, amounting to an area equivalent to 5.8 percent of the West Bank. A not insignificant portion of such land would consist of prime agricultural soil adjacent to Gaza currently cultivated by Israeli farming communities such as Be'eri, Kissufim and Nir Oz.[148] More to the point, as Aluf Benn noted, "The implementation of the Olmert plan would require the evacuation of tens of thousands of settlers and the removal of hallmarks of the West Bank settlement enterprise such as Ofra, Beit El, Elon Moreh and Kiryat Arba, as well as the Jewish community in Hebron itself."[149] While it is unlikely that a government led by, say, Netanyahu would make such a sweeping offer, it does go to show, especially when one factors in the twenty-one settlements that Sharon had dismantled in Gaza, that the existence of Jewish settlements across the previous 1967 armistice lines does not necessarily constitute a primary obstacle in reaching an Israeli–Palestinian peace agreement. Furthermore, to afford a territorial link between the West Bank and Gaza, Olmert was willing to provide the Palestinians with a tunnel under their own control. It would be subject to Israeli sovereignty but without any Israeli presence. With regard to Jerusalem, Olmert (who was once mayor of that city) told Greg Sheridan, an Australian journalist: "While I firmly believed that historically and emotionally, Jerusalem was always the capital of the Jewish people, I was ready that the city should be shared. Jewish neighbourhoods would be under Jewish sovereignty. Arab neighbourhoods would be under Palestinian sovereignty, so that it could be the capital of a Palestinian state."[150] In addition, Olmert envisaged that the holy basin of Jerusalem containing sites sacred to Jews, Muslims and Christians would not fall under the sovereignty of any state but would instead be jointly administered by Saudi Arabia, Jordan, the Palestinian State, Israel and the United States.

Olmert's offer was the most far-reaching one that the Israelis were ever likely to make. Where he did adhere to the mainstream consensus was in his refusal to accept the Palestinian demand for an unrestricted "right of return" for Arab refugees who were either displaced or fled from the Jewish State. As a gesture he was prepared to accept 1,000 per year for up to five years on the understanding "that would be the end of the conflict and the end of claims."[151] In their final meeting, Olmert showed Abbas a map that embodied his ideas. Abbas would have liked to have taken the map with him, but Olmert would agree only on condition that they both signed it, indicating that they both endorsed the essence of what the map projected. Not being prepared to commit himself, Abbas promised to return the following day accompanied by his experts. But, as Olmert sadly recalled, "The next day Saeb Erekat rang my advisor and said we forgot we are going to Amman today, let's make it next week. I never saw him again."[152]

Leaving aside the issue of the refugees' "rights of return," rights regarded by the Palestinians as inalienable and non-negotiable, Erekat provided yet another explanation as to why Abbas walked away from Olmert's offer. On March 27, 2009, on al-Jazeera TV, Erekat recalled a conversation between President Clinton and Arafat at the fateful Camp David talks. According to Erekat, Clinton had assured Arafat that he was on the threshold of becoming the first president of a Palestinian State with East Jerusalem as its capital, if only he would acknowledge that the Temple of Solomon is located underneath the Haram Al-Sharif (the Temple Mount). Arafat indignantly replied: "Jerusalem will be nothing but the capital of the Palestinian state and there is nothing underneath or above the Haram Al-Sharif except for Allah." Erekat then concocted a conversation between Olmert and Abbas in which, after Olmert outlined his suggestion for dealing with the Jerusalem's holy basin, Abbas, following in Arafat's footsteps, exclaimed: "I am not in a marketplace or a bazaar. I came to demarcate the borders of Palestine, the June 4, 1967 borders, without detracting a single inch, and without detracting a single stone from Jerusalem, or from the holy Christian and Muslim places." That, in Erekat's words, was "why the Palestinian negotiators did not sign."[153]

Within a few months after his final meeting with Abbas, Olmert was no longer in power. His popularity had flagged owing to the IDF's lacklustre performance in the Second Lebanon War and his being subsequently censored by the Winograd Commission, but above all he was under a cloud of suspicion for corruption and was heading towards his day in court. By not contesting his party's September 2008 leadership primaries, he had left the field clear for Livni to emerge as his successor. After a failed attempt on Livni's part to form a new government, an election was called for February 2009, and in the meanwhile Olmert stayed on as caretaker prime minister. The election produced a technical victory for Kadima in that it attained one seat more than its Likud rival, but Netanyahu stole the show by being able to assemble a coalition, a feat beyond Livni's reach. The other electoral casualty was Labour, whose Knesset representation fell from nineteen to thirteen seats, putting it in fourth place after Likud, Kadima and Yisrael Beiteinu (see Appendix). After years of being either in government or being a credible alternative, Labour had sunk to a new low. Its decline was due to its being identified with the failure of the Oslo Accords, its dilution of core values such as its militant Zionist stance of bygone years, the permeation into its ranks of materialistic careerists, and the relative increase of Mizrahi and Russian Jews, who were by no means natural Labour supporters.[154] On March 31, 2009, Netanyahu formed a broad government consisting of Likud, Labour, Yisrael Beiteinu, Shas, Habayit Hayehudi (a new orthodox religious party) and United Torah. Barak (who had returned to the political arena in 2007) was minister of defence and Avigdor Lieberman foreign minister. The government, with its distinct right-wing colouration, and with some constituent elements not likely to accept any reasonable compromise, was not as keen to reach out to the Palestinians as Kadima had been. Although on September 2, 2010, it did enter into negotiations with the PA in Washington, the talks did not amount to much. During the next few years the atmosphere surrounding Israeli–PA contacts was one of mutual suspicion and distrust. The Palestinians, running with a call from President Obama for an Israeli freeze on settlement construction, insisted that talks be suspended until Israel complied. On Israel's part, the adamant refusal of the PA to recognize Israel as a Jewish State, its continued engendering of anti-Israel hatred through its educational institutes and media, and its slavish public adoration of convicted suicide bombers and others with Jewish blood on their hands left a nasty taste in Israeli mouths. Through the PA's attempts to bypass Israel by appealing to the UN and other international organs to adopt resolutions on issues that it had been committed to resolve with Israel in direct talks, the Israeli government lost interest in trying to meet it half way. Accordingly, throughout the government's four-year term, an Israeli–Palestinian rapprochement was put on hold.

9

SOCIAL AND ECONOMIC DEVELOPMENTS

This chapter provides an overview of a few chosen aspects of Israel's domestic social and economic environment. It commences with the immigration of Russian and Ethiopian Jews, continues with an account of the Israeli Arabs and ultra-orthodox Jews, and concludes with a brief description of Israel's economic performance and related matters. The topics in question do not embrace every single social phenomenon. Rather they serve simply to present the reader with a reasonable *glimpse* of some prominent features of Israel's complex society.

Russian Jews

In the years between 1948 and 1971, in keeping with the Soviet Union's obdurate refusal to grant exit visas to all but a minuscule number of its citizens, very few Soviet Jews succeeded in migrating to Israel. But, by the early 1970s, in the framework of a détente between the Soviet Union and the United States, the Soviet Union partially relented. With the Soviet economy becoming increasingly hard pressed, in part as a result of the Cold War arms race, the Soviets sought to augment their trade with the West. That provided them with a strong interest in securing Most Favoured Nation Status from the USA, allowing for the reduction of import tariffs on their goods. In 1974, taking advantage of the Soviets' newly disclosed vulnerability, the US Congress, by means of the Jackson–Vanik Amendment to the US–Russian trade agreement, linked the level of trade liberalization to the level of permitted Soviet Jewish emigration. To a certain extent, the Soviets responded positively by, among other things, waiving the emigration tax (levied according to specific occupations) on would-be Jewish émigrés.[1]

The Jackson–Vanik Amendment would probably not have eventuated had it not been for the daring of a small group of Soviet refuseniks (those denied exit visas) who had planned to commandeer a compact Antonov airliner to escape to Sweden. Posing as guests en route to a locally based wedding, they reserved all of the plane's twelve passenger seats in order to assume full operational control of the aircraft (one of their members had formerly been a fighter pilot). On June 15, 1970, as they assembled at Smolnoye Airport near Petrograd, they were all promptly arrested. At their subsequent trial, they were charged with high treason. Two of their leaders, Mark Dymshits and Eduard Kuznetsov, were sentenced to death, while the rest were condemned to long terms of imprisonment. The courage and desperation of the would-be hijackers generated a worldwide response of sympathy to the plight of Russian Jewry. Their cause was taken up by Jews throughout the diaspora and Israel as well as by various governments, trade unions and statesmen.[2] Not being totally deaf to outside criticism, the Soviet regime commuted the death sentences on Dymshits and Kuznetsov to fifteen-year prison terms.

Nevertheless, throughout the 1970s a series of restrictive bureaucratic practices prevailed. Aspiring emigrants could obtain exit visas only if they were able to verify that they wished to leave the Soviet Union to be reunited with relatives living abroad. Once that was done, supporting employer references had to be submitted. Such a requirement placed potential emigrants in a bind, for, by disclosing to their employers their migration intentions, they frequently jeopardized their immediate employment and hence their prospects of emigrating. Finally, coveted exit visas were issued in restricted numbers, with the quotas varying among the various Soviet regions. (Given that these regions included areas where the populations were not ethnic Russians, it is strictly speaking invalid to label all the émigrés as Russians, but for the sake of convenience, and in accordance with general usage, that practice is upheld here.) The main criterion determining visa quota ceilings was the extent to which Jews were contributing to critical economic and defence sectors. As a consequence, less highly educated Jews living in Tajikistan, Uzbekistan, Azerbaijan and Georgia fared better than Jews living in Russia and the Ukraine.[3] Such Jews maintained a far stronger affiliation to Judaism than their Russian and Ukrainian counterparts.

Between 1971 and 1973, a fervid desire to live in a Jewish State constituted the main motive for seeking exit visas, and therefore those that arrived in Israel in that period were in the main avowed Zionists. After 1974, when Soviet Jewry was confronted with a resurgence of anti-Semitism that included restricting the right of entry of Jews into institutes of higher learning, the Jewish exodus from the Soviet Union consisted predominantly of those with little interest in settling in Israel. Their choice was also influenced by the 1973 Yom Kippur War, which highlighted Israel's vulnerability. Although Jewish émigrés were issued with exit visas for Israel, on their journey, broken at Vienna, many chose to divert to the West, especially to the USA and Canada. That was facilitated by the United States recognizing them as refugees (who did not need to be processed as standard immigrants) and by the US Hebrew Immigrant Aid Society (HIAS), which offered economic support and other forms of assistance.

After the Soviet invasion of Afghanistan in December 1979, US–Soviet relations once again soured and, as a consequence, the number of Jews permitted to leave the Soviet Union substantially declined. Many of those who showed an interest in leaving were prosecuted, with some, such as Anatoly (subsequently Natan) Sharansky, who had been arrested in 1977, being subject to lengthy prison sentences involving hard labour.

With the advent in the late 1980s of the policy of Glasnost, introduced by the new Soviet leader Mikhail Gorbachev, which entailed extended free speech and openness in government, Jewish emigration flourished. Not only did the Soviet Union liberalize Jewish emigration, but economic woes and a more blatant manifestation of anti-Semitism emanating from the new direction that Russia had embarked upon lent a strong impetus for Soviet Jews to seek a better life abroad. The deteriorating Russian economy worked both ways. It not only provided an

incentive for Jews to emigrate but also induced policy changes facilitating that emigration, so as to eliminate residual Western objections to
trading with and investing in the Soviet Union.[4]

Most of the new Jewish émigrés would gladly have proceeded to
the USA, but a change in October 1989 in US policy ensured that an
overwhelmingly large proportion of them went to Israel. The change
emanted in no small part from Prime Minister Yitzhak Shamir importuning George Shultz, the US secretary of state, to curb the American
intake of Soviet Jews and from a ballooning out of US expenditures
incurred in accepting Soviet Jews as refugees. In accordance with the
US Refugee Act of 1980, each individual was to be issued with housing,
medical care, employment and, if necessary, retraining.[5] Now that the
Soviet Union had begun dismantling its politically oppressive system,
the United States felt justified in acceding to Shamir's request not to
confer refugee status on the Soviet migrants. The upshot of it all is that,
whereas in 1989 only 12,000 Jews settled in Israel, a year later 185,000
did so, and by June 1992, 400,000 had arrived.[6] All told, between 1970
and 2009, 1,049,230 Jews immigrated to Israel from what had previously been the Soviet Union.[7] By that terminal year they accounted for
15 percent of Israel's total population and 17 percent of its Jewish one.[8]

Unexpectedly, the mass entry of Soviet Jews was not at first seen as
a boon by all Israelis. *Some* within the Mizrahi community resented
their arrival, fearing that it would rebound to their disadvantage. In
January 1990, at a meeting between Yossi Beilin, then deputy minister
of finance, and a group of young disaffected Mizrahi Jews living in a
poor area of Jerusalem, one of the latter remarked: "We remain the
cannon fodder of the state while everyone pays heed to the [Russian]
Ashkenazi migrants."[9] The Haredim considered the Russians a threat to
their share of Knesset seats, as did Israeli Arabs. But what really caused
a furore was the inane statement made in October 1994 by Ora Namir,
the minister of labour and welfare, in an interview with the newspaper
Haaretz. In essence Namir declared: "I feel very uneasy about the Soviet
Jewish migration that has occurred in the last two and a half years. One
third of the immigrants are elderly, one third are seriously crippled and
almost a third are single parent mothers."[10] Namir's statement, which
reflected more on her unsuitability for high office than anything else,
was taken as an insult by Soviet Jews, who justifiably felt that their

welcome mat was wearing thin. They were already as a group being stigmatized for the few bad apples among them who were involved in prostitution, crime and alcohol abuse and for the unsavoury behaviour of a handful of prominent Russian Jewish oligarchs. Such slurs were totally unwarranted for, in the most part, the Russian Jews turned out to be exemplary citizens, bringing much credit to Israel.

The arrival of so many Soviet Jews within such a short time span did of course initially impose a tremendous strain on the Israeli economy. The unemployment rate rose appreciably, reaching a level of 10.6 percent in 1990 as opposed to 4.8 percent a decade earlier. Many of the newcomers encountered tremendous difficulties in securing jobs, since either their professional qualifications were not recognized or the general demand for their skills was rather low or, in some cases, negligible. This was particularly the case with regard to the medical profession, as, in 1990 alone, around 6,000 doctors arrived in a country that already sustained one of the world's highest doctor to patient ratios. Similarly, by 1991 there were proportionally thirteen times as many engineers among the Russian immigrants as among Israelis.[11] The situation was perhaps even more daunting for the multitude of musicians and university researchers and teachers that sought placements in institutions and bodies which already had their full staff complements. The arrival of so many musicians prompted the quip that, if a Russian immigrant disembarking from a plane was not carrying a violin, he or she must surely have been a pianist.

To gain employment many individuals had to retrain or enter into an alternative field, with both options entailing high adjustment costs. Some, such as Soviet doctors, were required to pass a qualifying examination. In 1990, of those who undertook that examination, 70 percent failed.[12] A survey undertaken in 2000 disclosed that, of the Russians who had been in Israel for five years or more, only 27 percent were engaged within their original professional or academic field.[13] Being forced to accept posts that fell far short of the social status and relative income level that they had enjoyed in the Soviet Union, many felt demeaned but, to their credit, did not hesitate in working wherever an opportunity arose. As evidence for that, practically every supermarket was manned by credentialed Russian professionals. What was startling about the Russians was their positive attitude, for many regarded their dismal situation as ephemeral, and their bold expectations of better things to come tended to be self-fulfilling.[14]

Heightening the migrants' initial tribulations was a scarcity of housing. The state had made great strides in trying to redress the housing issue but, given the nature of building construction, it took time for shortages to be reduced. Up until July 1990, each immigrant received a grant to assist them to settle in. Unlike the situation confronting the immigrants arriving during the early 1950s, temporary housing or absorption centres were generally not accessible to the Soviet Jews, who, by and large, had to find their own accommodation in the open market. As they attempted to do so, sudden increases in demand for housing caused rents to rise sharply. To alleviate the housing crisis, immigrants were put up in hotels and hostels, where a single room was allocated per family. When that proved to be of little avail, Sharon, as minister of housing, began to import mobile homes, which, like the first two options, still did not resolve the problem. Exacerbating the issue, with fewer Palestinian labourers available (on account of the intifada), and with the Russians unable or unwilling to replace them, the pace of the construction of new apartment complexes slackened. The Shamir government hoped, with offers of cash subsidies, low interest mortgages and income tax breaks, to induce Russian Jews to take up residence in the West Bank and Gaza.[15] But with the Russians expressing a distinct preference for living in and around Tel Aviv and other established cities, where employment and other social amenities were more readily available, no more than 1 to 2 percent of them responded to such inducements. One way by which many Russians coped with their hardships was to live in common either with another Russian family or with elderly veteran relatives. That enabled them to minimize their expenses and to accrue public benefits denied them as single family units.[16]

The Russian migrants experienced two aspects of culture shock. In the first instance, the actual country of Israel did not meet their expectations. As they saw things, "They had arrived in a tiny Levantine country with mosques, camels, heat and an abysmal theatre ... they expected heroism and found hedonism."[17] Second, many of the mostly secular Russian Jews experienced rather unpleasant brushes with Israel's religious establishment. Yitzhak Peretz, of the Haredi party Shas, who became minister of absorption in 1988, was concerned more with attending to migrants' spiritual "needs" than their material ones. This was manifested by his attempts to funnel them into religious ulpans (Hebrew language institutes) rather than secular ones, his attempts to discourage them from taking up residence in kibbutzim, his concern to ensure that all Russian Jews were duly circumcised, and his allotting them Hebrew names. Peretz's approach aroused widespread resentment among Russian migrants,[18] many of whom (possibly in excess of 350,000) were not strictly Jewish.[19] They were eligible for immigration to Israel by virtue of having a Jewish spouse or a Jewish grandparent,[20] or by having being categorized as a Jew by the Soviet authorities. For them to marry Jews, conversion to Judaism became a necessity, since in Israel one cannot obtain a civil marriage. Unfortunately, the Jewish clergy authorized to oversee conversions imposed highly stringent conditions, by insisting that prospective Jews become more pious than is the norm for the non-Haredi (God-fearing) community.

With Russian immigrants representing close to a fifth of Israel's Jewish population, a thriving Russian communal subculture developed; there arose numerous Russian newspapers and journals, Russian TV, nightclubs, restaurants, clubs, theatres and bookshops, as well as two political parties, Yisrael Be'Aliyah and Yisrael Beiteinu. All these not only alleviated the migrants' sense of alienation but, by providing them with mutual support in finding jobs and housing, as well as information in navigating Israeli bureaucracy, also made daily life far easier for them. For the elderly finding difficulties in acquiring a working knowledge of Hebrew, the Russian communal subculture enabled them to live contentedly in Israel within their Russian cocoons. It is not clear to what extent that subculture will endure, but for the time being the Russians have imparted an enhanced aspect of pluralism and ethnic diversity to Israeli society. Ardently pursuing enlightened education[21] and excellence in personal and public life, and having a healthy respect for knowledge and work, the Russians have been a boon to Israel.[22] Not only have they enhanced Israel's population, but they have greatly increased the country's endowment of scientists, engineers, doctors, teachers and technicians and have paved the way for Israel's impressive advancements in high technology-based industries and in stimulating the country's general economic growth.[23] They have left their mark in the field of commerce and industry as well as in the arts and sport. In the realm of music, thanks to the Russian Jews, more ensembles and performing groups have come into being, yielding listening pleasure to Israelis living away from major cities; as for sport, Soviet Jewish athletes have excelled in the international arena, conveying a sense of pride to the country as a whole. The mass arrival of Soviet Jews has added significantly to the state's military strength, for Israel's Russian Jewish community provides a quarter of recruits serving in the IDF.[24] Of no less relevance, it has also gone some way towards safeguarding Israel's character as a Jewish State with a distinctly Jewish majority.

With some justification, Russian Jews like to think of themselves as migrants who have been absorbed into mainstream Israeli society through their own efforts and who have saved Israel from itself and its enemies.[25] They certainly rejuvenated classical Zionism in their near universal rejection of post-Zionism, harbouring instead a strong commitment to Israel as a Jewish State that need not apologize for its existence. The flow of benefits has not been unidirectional, for the Russians too have gained. A survey of Russian Jews who had lived in Israel for over a decade revealed that some 79.5 percent were satisfied with their final absorption and that moving to Israel was for them a good move,[26] even though most of those surveyed would *originally* have preferred to have gone to the USA.[27]

Ethiopian Jews

According to the Israel Central Bureau of Statistics, by the end of 2011 there were 125,400 Jews of Ethiopian origin living in Israel. Of those, 81,900 were natives of Ethiopia and 43,500 were born in Israel to Ethiopian fathers.[28] Although they began entering Israel in discernible numbers from the late 1970s, there were two periods during which Ethiopian immigration spiked. The first relates to the years 1983 to 1985 and the second to 1990 to 1992.

The Ethiopian Jews had for ages lived in total isolation from all other Jewish communities. Calling themselves the Beta Israel (the House of Israel), they liked to think of themselves as being descendants of the Israelites, but most scholars agree that they are indigenous Ethiopians who adopted Judaism, probably sometime during the Middle Ages.[29] To all intents and purposes they were akin to their Christian neighbours in language, dress, diet and family life.[30] But, by not accepting Christianity, they were deprived of their land and thus had to survive as tenant farmers and as craftsmen. By so doing the men became smiths, weavers, carpenters and masons and the women potters.[31] Smithing was generally regarded with repugnance and, both on that account and because of their landless status, their non-Jewish neighbours named them "Falashas," meaning "landless" or "strangers."

Cut off from their inception from the entire Jewish World, they based their faith exclusively on the Old Testament, being unaware of the Talmud (a rabbinical compendium of Jewish oral law) and its commentaries. They had no knowledge of the Jewish festivals of Hanukkah and Purim, the custom of bar mitzvahs, the wearing of skullcaps and prayer shawls, and the lighting of Friday night candles. But in many other respects they had all the hallmarks of orthodox Jewry. Ritually cleansing themselves beforehand, they scrupulously honoured the Sabbath, refraining from all manner of work including the kindling of fires. They fasted on Yom Kippur, they did not eat forbidden food, and their womenfolk separated themselves during their menstrual periods. As for Jews throughout the world, their prayers, offered while facing in the direction of Jerusalem, were interwoven with invocations to return to the land of Israel.[32]

Only in the late nineteenth century was any meaningful contact established between Beta Israel and outside Jewish bodies, when in 1867 the Alliance Israélite Universelle sent Joseph Halévy as its emissary to Ethiopia (then Abyssinia). There Halévy concluded that the Beta Israel were indeed bona fide Jews. In 1904, Halévy's pupil Jacques Faitlovitch visited the country for an extended period, during which time he introduced the Beta Israel to mainstream Jewish practices by establishing a school for their children and by arranging for promising youngsters to travel abroad to acquaint themselves with the ways of the wider Jewish world, so that on their return they could assume leadership roles within their own community.

By the 1950s, the Beta Israel had incorporated post-biblical holidays into their calendar and were becoming more recognizably Jewish. Still the Israeli government showed little interest in them. In the early 1970s when the subject of their immigration to Israel was mooted, Prime Minister Golda Meir was reputed to have exclaimed, "Don't we have enough problems?"[33] Such a remark may have inspired Natan

Peled, then minister of immigrant absorption, to have a report prepared expressing doubt about the Beta Israel's Jewish credentials. But in February 1973, before it was released, Ovadia Yosef, the Sephardi Chief Rabbi, in response to a plea by Ethiopians already in Israel, deemed that the Beta Israel were descendants of the lost tribe of Dan and were therefore Jewish. In that case, Ovadia Yosef concluded, it was incumbent upon the state to rescue them by hastening their immigration to Israel.[34] In 1974, Shlomo Goren, the Ashkenazi Chief Rabbi, after having at first rejected Rabbi Yosef's ruling, reluctantly accepted it, thus paving the way for the Rabin government in 1975 to acknowledge officially that the Beta Israel were entitled, under the law of return, to immigrate to Israel.

When Begin assumed power in 1977, he seized upon the idea of orchestrating Israel's intake of Ethiopian Jews, partly to show to his Mizrahi supporters that he was no Ashkenazi bigot and partly as a demonstrable retort to the UN General Assembly's branding of Israel as racist.[35] With that in mind, he negotiated an arrangement with Mengistu, Ethiopia's Marxist dictator, to provide him with arms in exchange for his granting the Beta Israel exit visas. Unfortunately, when Dayan in an interview in Zurich publicly disclosed the transaction, Mengistu, under Arab pressure, called off the deal. Determined to find a way to reach the Holy Land, many Ethiopian Jews began furtively slipping into Sudan, from where they hoped the Israelis would rescue them. Their epic journey, which lasted several weeks or more, was both arduous and fraught with danger. Many died en route as well as from diseases contracted in overcrowded unsanitary Sudanese compounds. Eventually, the Israelis rose to the occasion by organizing an airlift, named Operation Moses, which took place between November 1984 to January 1985 and which culminated in around 8,000 Ethiopian Jews being flown to Israel.[36] Reporting on that operation, William Safire wrote: "For the first time in history, thousands of black people are being brought into a country not in chains but in dignity, not as slaves but as citizens."[37] Not all the Ethiopian Jews languishing in Sudanese camps were included in Operation Moses on account of its being prematurely terminated because of widespread press coverage that complicated Sudan's relations with other Arab states. But, luckily, more were ferried to Israel a few weeks later by the US air force.

In November 1989 after a hiatus of sixteen years, Ethiopia and Israel resumed diplomatic relations.[38] The restoration of official ties between the two countries resulted from American efforts to achieve some mutual understanding between the USA and Ethiopia. For that purpose, Herman Cohen, the assistant secretary of state for Africa, paid a call to Mengistu in August of that year. Among other things, Cohen had indicated that a liberalization of emigration – which Mengistu correctly assumed referred to Ethiopian Jews – would be taken as a friendly gesture towards the United States. Accordingly, Mengistu allowed for a modest monthly departure of 500 people. However, Susan Pollack, who was present in Ethiopia at that time on behalf of the American Association for Ethiopian Jews (AAEJ), became convinced that the Beta Israel of Gondar province, where the main concentration of Ethiopian Jews lived, were in grave danger. Ethiopia was in the throes of a general uprising, and elders from Gondar panicked and appealed to Pollack for assistance. Pollack's response was to arrange for as many Jews as possible to seek safe haven in the country's capital, Addis Ababa, a course of action that was not warranted from the point of view of the well-being of the Beta Israel, for they were not in any immediate peril. Fighting was not raging in their villages, neither was there a famine or an infectious epidemic. Moreover the Jews' Christian neighbours were not harassing them.[39]

Nevertheless, under Pollack's leadership, the AAEJ began trucking Jews from Gondar to Addis Ababa, while others came pouring in under their own steam. By early June 1990 there were 8,500 Jews in the capital and thousands more to come. Cared for by the American Jewish Joint Distribution Committee (JDC) they were placed in camps and, wherever possible, in rented houses, some of which were little more than animal pens. Exposed to malnourishment and disease, and for the first time in their lives to HIV, the Beta Israel were in urgent need of being airlifted to Israel. But by July Mengistu had brought emigration to a standstill. What followed was a tortuous and lengthy process of Israeli and Jewish Agency officials negotiating with Mengistu to permit their exit. During the following months, Ethiopia erratically allowed for a modest outflow, but it was far too limited in scope and did little to redress the distress of the hordes of Jews trapped in the capital. On May 20, 1991, with the rebels closing in on Addas Ababa, Mengistu fled the country to seek sanctuary in Zimbabwe. When the regime was about to topple, a deal was finally struck. In exchange for $35 million, the government would allow, within a 36-hour period, for Israeli planes (without their markings) to land at the capital's airport and to scoop up all the Jews awaiting them.

The airlift, which took the name Operation Solomon, began on May 24, 1991. In preparation, fifty-nine absorption centres and 250 buses, each with an Amharic speaker, were secured, as were doctors, nurses and social workers. Seats and bathrooms were removed from most of the forty-one El Al and military planes involved in order to accommodate more passengers, with time being of the essence.[40] In place of the removed seats, the passengers sat on rubber foam covered by thick black plastic. The mission was completed in just over 34 hours, by which time 14,310 Ethiopians, including eight that were born in mid-flight, had landed in Israel.[41] Meeting them at Ben-Gurion Airport were leading government dignitaries and social workers ready to attend to their immediate needs. The festive mood of the official and professional welcoming party was palpable.[42] It was a great moment for Israel, which, while buckling under the weight of a massive Russian immigration, still found the resources and initiative to rescue brethren in desperate straits who would of necessity continue to require state assistance upon their arrival.

The Jewish Agency and the Israeli government expended a Herculean effort to facilitate the absorption and integration of the Beta Israel into Israeli society. Considering the cultural background of the Ethiopian immigrants, both bodies had their work cut out for them. Emanating from a subsistence village economy in which most people were illiterate, the newcomers were confounded by services and commodities that the average Israeli took for granted and thus had to be inducted into their usage. Although they were provided with Hebrew lessons, generally speaking, only relatively younger Ethiopians acquired a measure of fluency in that language. In terms of housing, at first many of them were provided with mobile homes on the outskirts of urban areas away from sources of employment. But in the course of time, thanks to generous government loans, they were able to acquire somewhat more congenial living quarters. Understandably, given a starting base that entailed low educational standards, a lack of any skilled training and an

Plate 8   *Ethiopian Jews on flight to Israel*

unsatisfactory knowledge of Hebrew, they were relegated to the bottom
rung of Israel's economic ladder. As a result, on entering the workforce
the Ethiopian immigrants earned less than 30 or 40 percent of what
Arabs were earning for comparable work. However, as they continued
to accumulate work experience their salaries rose.[43]

While striving to surmount the innumerable natural obstacles with
which they had to contend, the Beta Israel had also to cope with religious bigotry and racial prejudice stemming from minority groups. At
first the rabbinate insisted that many of the Ethiopian Jews undergo
a conversion process, to which the Beta Israel vehemently objected.
Eventually, the rabbinate partially modified its stand by limiting its
directive to a small number of seemingly warranted cases among
the Falasha Mura, whose forebears had been forcibly converted to
Christianity but who had secretly upheld their Jewishness. In their case,
many were required to be remarried. As one such immigrant, Kasta
Kamuchi, who had been married for fifty years, recounted: "They told
us that we had to go to Jerusalem. They took 30 to 40 of us in a bus to
the rabbinate building. After they drew the blood [from their penises

as a symbolic circumcision] and we dipped in the mikvah [a ritual bath] they gathered us, all the men and women, in the hallway. Once inside the room, they spread over us a tallit [prayer shawl] that acted as a canopy and then I had to break the glass." On being asking how he felt, Kamuchi replied:

> I was only saddened, angry, frustrated. I already have grandchildren. They told us that it's a big day for us because today we were becoming Jewish, but it's hard to be happy on a day like that. In our opinion, we are Jews. We kept all religious laws in Ethiopia, we lived a modest but good life with our wives; but here they treat us like we're gentiles.[44]

Considering that Russian immigrants of doubtful Jewish affinity were never subject to such indignities, one cannot help concluding that, with regard to the Ethiopians, an element of racism was at play. But, to its credit, the government was not prepared to sit by idly when in August 2009 three semi-private Haredi (God-fearing) schools in Petah Tikvah denied entry to Ethiopian Jewish children. Prime Minister Netanyahu, by threatening to withhold funding from such schools, ensured that the children in question were duly admitted.[45] Nonetheless, cases of clear prejudice against the Beta Israel continue to surface from time to time, and fears are sometimes expressed that a large concentration of them within a given place could lead to a depreciation of property values and an increase in crime. In many respects such attitudes are similar to those that were articulated by veteran Israelis in relation to the influx of Mizrahi Jews at the beginning of the 1950s. At that time, the mayors of Tel Aviv and Ramat Gan, who felt that the proximity of reception centres for the newcomers would affect their lifestyles unfavourably, compelled the government to place them in less salubrious localities.[46] The public's view of the migrants from Arab countries was expressed in a leading Israeli newspaper (*Haaretz*) as follows: "You will find among them [the immigrants] dirt, card games for money, drunkenness and fornication. Many of them suffer from serious eye, skin and venereal diseases, not to mention immorality and stealing."[47] As for the prime minister of the day, David Ben-Gurion, he thought of the Mizrahi migrants as "riffraff and human dust, without any language, education or roots and without imbibing the tradition and vision of the nation."[48]

With regard to the Ethiopian Jews, nothing vaguely like that had been expressed by any high-ranking Israeli politician, official or newspaper. Just as, at first, there was little commingling between Ashkenazi and Mizrahi Jews, so too will the passage of time be kinder to the Ethiopians.

Some progress has indeed been made. Two Ethiopian Jews served in the Knesset that was dissolved in January 2013, and two served immediately in the successive one. Of the latter, one is a woman, Penina Tamnu-Shata, who migrated at the age of three and who subsequently became an attorney. The other is Shimon Solomon, who had been a director of an immigrant absorption centre in Beersheba. Both are members of Yesh Atid, Yair Lapid's party. Within the army, Issachar Makonnen and Tzion Shenker serve as lieutenant-colonels and, within the diplomatic corps, Belanesh Zevadia was in 2012 appointed as the Israeli ambassador to Ethiopia. Having arrived in Israel at the age of seventeen, she graduated from the Hebrew University and went on to obtain an MA degree. Ethiopian Jews have been entering into such diverse fields as medicine, rabbinical studies, education, sport, music and entertainment.

As impressive as such achievements are, the Ethiopian Jewish community still has a long way to go. Largely mired in poverty, its progress is hindered by a number of problematic issues. School drop-out rates are inordinately high and, concomitant with that, delinquency is rife. The same applies in the army, where many go AWOL. Desertions occur partly as a result of Ethiopian conscripts being plagued by pangs of conscience for not being available to assist their parents and siblings.[49] Traditionally, the Ethiopians lived within a framework of an extended family but, on coming to Israel, their extended families began to fragment, to be replaced by nuclear ones with high divorce or separation rates. Consequently, more than half of Ethiopian Jewish children live in single-parent households.[50] As has been well established, a high incidence of single-parent households is in itself a significant cause of poverty. To help redress such problems, free academic summer camps have been set up to assist Ethiopians preparing for their final-year school examinations. For those that succeed in gaining entry into a higher education institute, tuition and residential fees are fully state funded. Despite all the problems associated with some Ethiopian conscripts, the army assists them by extending their skill base and by incorporating them into the wider Israeli society. For many, their spell in the IDF has afforded them with a leg-up. But, all good efforts aside, it takes more than a generation or two for an *entire* community that was recently anchored in a pre-industrial subsistence economy to adjust successfully to life in a modern society.

Israeli Arabs

Until the Six-Day War most Arabs in Israel accepted the appellation "Israeli Arabs." Their acquiescence reflected a defeatist attitude born of the trauma they encountered in being swiftly transformed from a constituent part of the mainstream population of an undivided Palestine to a small minority in a newly formed Jewish State. Subject until 1966 to military rule that restricted their freedom of movement, and being regarded as a potential fifth column, they were generally anxious not to rock the boat. After the Six-Day War, when they were able to re-establish direct contact with their kinsmen in the West Bank and Gaza, and with the advent of an increasingly assertive Palestinian national movement, many of them began to refer to themselves as Palestinians. However, since the majority of Israeli Arabs have, through various opinion polls, expressed an unwillingness to contemplate leaving Israel to settle in an independent Palestinian State, they are in this respect (and in this respect only) similar to some in the USA that refer to themselves as, say, Italian Americans. That being the case, the term "Israeli Arabs" is retained here as a term that is consistent with the fact that, in certain key respects, the Arabs of Israel have undergone a measure of Israeli acculturation that distinguishes them from other Palestinians.

Needless to say, the Israeli Arabs remain distinctly different to Jewish Israelis. They are more traditional, they speak Arabic as opposed to Hebrew, they subscribe to a different religion – with the proportion of active adherents being twice as high as with the Jews – the social behaviour of their women is far more regulated, they are more obliged and respectful to their extended families, and they live in separate areas even within mixed towns and cities. While they are less inclined to conduct impersonal relations, they tend to be polite and are generally less self-assertive than Jewish Israelis.[51] Social interaction between Arabs and Jews is very limited and intermarriages are rare, if only because Arabs

and Jews are, in the words of an Israeli writer, "ideologically and con-
sensually non-assimilating groups."[52]

Most Israeli Arabs live in the Galilee, in the Little Triangle adjacent
to the 1967 border with Jordan, in the Northern Negev and in various mixed towns such as Haifa, Jaffa, Acre, Lod and Ramle. They are
not a homogeneous community, since they include Muslims,(mainly
Sunnis), Christians (of various denominations), Druze and Bedouins.
The Muslims (including the Bedouins) represent approximately 82
percent of the total, while the share of both the Christians and Druze is
9 percent respectively.[53]

At first the Israeli Arabs represented no more than 12.5 percent of
the population. But, by 2012, even after the massive immigrations of
Jews from Arab countries, Europe, Russia and Ethiopia, 20.6 percent
of Israelis were Arabs. That resulted from the Arab fertility rate constantly exceeding the Jewish one. The Arab population had for some
time sustained an annual natural population growth rate of 4.5 percent, which was one of the world's highest rates and in excess of the
population growth rates in Arab counties.[54] The margin between the
Arab and Jewish population growth rates has been steadily declining,
but presently it is still significant, standing at 2.4 for Arabs compared
with 1.8 for Jews. A number of factors account for the decline in Arab
fertility rates. They include improvements in Arab education generally
and for women in particular, the decline of the Arab rural economy, the
increased costs of raising children in a growing advanced economy, and
a more extensive use of contraceptives.[55] Despite a deceleration in the
Arab population growth rate, Israeli Arabs are likely to become even
more relatively numerous. Some scholars speculate that, by 2030, no
less than 30 percent of Israelis would be Arabs.[56]

Although, in law, they have acquired the same rights as all other
citizens, Arabs are relatively disadvantaged, experiencing higher than
average poverty and unemployment rates. They have access to fewer
educational resources, and in the past their municipal councils had
been grossly underfunded.[57] A large proportion of their land holdings
had been sequestrated, and the demolition of homes deemed to be illegally constructed occurs from time to time.[58] This has been particularly
galling for the more than 80,000 Negev Bedouin, who live in illegal
settlements lacking access roads, running water, electricity, schools and

clinics.[59] Such deprivations are rarely experienced by unauthorized Jewish settlements in the West Bank. The matter of Arab-Israeli land loss has been a big bone of contention. Over the years, between 50 to 60 percent of land originally held by Arabs had been expropriated.[60] The Or Commission determined that the state had indeed been remiss in not allocating land to the Arab sector "according to the same egalitarian principles it uses with other sectors."[61] Partly as a consequence, population densities in Arab municipal areas have risen sharply. Furthermore, about a fifth of the Arab population living in Israel during its War of Independence became "internal refugees" following the razing of their villages and the government's refusal to allow them to reoccupy them.[62]

Arab advancement has been hindered by hiring prejudices against them, both in the public and the private sector. Well-educated Arabs experience far higher unemployment rates than well-educated Jews and, generally speaking, Arab workers obtain wages 11 percent lower than Jews with comparable qualifications.[63] The Arabs enjoy few high-ranking connections within the establishment, less access to state land and fewer state handouts by virtue of their political parties not being represented in Israel's coalition governments.

Not all Arab deprivations are necessarily the outcome of discrimination. Even though the Arabs have little political influence, that in itself is not necessarily a significant factor. After all, the Haredi community remains poverty stricken years after exacting large amounts of public funding on account of its highly placed political leverage. Arab relative poverty rates stem in no small part from inferior educational attainments, large family sizes and low female employment participation rates.

On the eve of the formation of Israel, the proportion of Arab Muslim children attending primary school was 30 percent compared with 90 to 100 percent for Jews. Arab parents limited the number of years their boys spent in school so that they could help in cultivating their land. As for girls, only 10 percent received any basic education, and fewer than 1,000 Arab students attended one of the two available Arab high schools.[64] By the early twenty-first century, entry rates into primary schools had become more or less the same for both Arabs and Jews. However, school drop-out rates are still higher in the Arab sector, and far more Arab teachers lack adequate tertiary education and training.

In most Arab homes there is only a single male earner. In 2006 only 19.1 percent of Arab women had outside employment compared with 56.2 percent for Jewish ones.[65] This discrepancy has arisen from Arab families choosing to have far more children than Jews and from a religious-cultural constraint that discourages Arab women from entering the general workforce. A profusion of children tends to militate against high educational accomplishments, thereby lowering each child's prospective income.

Further burdening Arab households is an exceptionally high incidence of children born with congenital disorders and deformities, resulting from the widespread practice of first-cousin marriages.[66] The offspring in question impose extra monetary costs on their parents and face specific difficulties as potential earners in later life. All these issues are endogenously induced and cannot be ascribed to discrimination. They are almost exclusively confined to the Arab Muslim population and not to Arab Christians, whose family sizes, workforce participation rates and marriage customs are in keeping with the Jewish population, *as are their average incomes and educational attainments.* In this regard, the relative situation of Muslim communities in Europe is instructive. For example, in the UK in 2007, Bangladeshi and Pakistani Muslims earned on average £180 per week in comparison with the weekly national average earnings of £332. Lest one think that discrimination is at play here, Hindus from India obtained the same average earnings as the whites. Interestingly, the 2007 wage gap in Israel between Arabs earning an average monthly income of 5,230 shekels and of Jews earning 7,178 shekels was far lower than the gaps between Muslims and non-Muslims in the UK.[67] From such data, Oz Almog, one of Israel's leading sociologists, concluded "that by any measure the Arabs in Israel are far better off than their brethren in Europe."[68]

Although in the past local Arab councils were considerably financially deprived, that is no longer the case. Since 2010 they have been receiving more government funds on a per capita basis than Jewish-run councils. That is, they now enjoy a measure of positive discrimination. The public infrastructure of many Arab townships still leaves much to be desired, but some of the inadequate services that they provide, particularly poor sewage disposal, emanate in no small part from an unwillingness on the part of Arab councils to impose appropriate usage charges.[69]

Despite all the obstacles that Israeli Arabs have faced, their lot has improved immensely, allowing them to enjoy a far higher standard of living than is the norm within neighbouring Arab countries. Within Arab villages (other than in the Negev) only a sparse number of old-style antiquated houses remain. By 1981, after a steady rate of village reconstruction, "90–95 percent of village buildings were completely new."[70] In some cases, grand multi-storey villas with spacious courtyards have arisen.[71] Currently, 92.6 percent of Arabs are owner-occupiers as opposed to 70 percent of Jews.[72]

Life expectancy for Arab women rose from 71.9 years in 1970–4 to 77.4 in 1994–8, while, for men, it rose from 68.5 to 74.2 years.[73] Such figures reflect better medical delivery systems, diets, education and general incomes. In the field of education, great strides have been made. By comparison with the situation in 1948, when 70 percent of the Israeli Arabs were illiterate, in 1988 this figure was only only 15 percent,[74] and these were mainly remnants from that earlier era. (In 2010, the illiteracy rate was 28 percent in Egypt and 17 percent in Syria.)[75] Similarly, the proportion of the Arab community attending university rose from 0.6 percent in 1956–7 to 7.1 percent in 1998–9.[76] To ensure their access to higher education, a special effort has been made to provide Arab students with university dormitory accommodation.[77]

Arab homes are fitted with modern appliances in a measure that is beginning to be compatible with general living standards in advanced countries: 55 percent of Arab households own a car, 85 percent have telephone lines, 72 percent computers, 97 percent television sets, 70 percent microwaves, 65 percent air-conditioners, and 30 percent clothes dryers and dishwashers, while 45 percent travelled abroad between 2002 and 2007.[78] Clearly what is at issue is relative and not absolute poverty.

Israeli Arabs are not entirely absent in prestigious posts in key areas of Israeli society. Salim Joubran was one of a panel of three judges on Israel's Supreme Court which, in November 2011, upheld the conviction of a former Israeli president, Moshe Katzav, on rape charges. (Israel is constantly maligned as being an Apartheid state. Yet it is unimaginable that, during the era of Apartheid in South Africa, a black man could not only have become a Supreme Court judge but also have been party to the deliberations of the criminality of a former high-ranking state official.) Israeli Arabs can be found as professors in Israeli universities, as doctors in leading hospitals and as holding senior positions in the diplomatic corps. For example, in mid-2012, Naim Araidi, an Israeli Druze, was appointed ambassador to Norway. George Deek, a Christian Arab, who had been the deputy Israeli ambassador to Nigeria, was made Araidi's deputy.[79] Professor Majid al-Haj is Haifa University's vice-president.[80] In 2007, the Western Galilee Hospital on the outskirts of Nahariya (a predominantly Jewish town) appointed an Arab Israeli, Dr Massad Barhoum, as its director,[81] and in 2009, Dr Suheir Assady became the first Arab-Israeli woman doctor to head a hospital department – in this case, the Department of Nephrology at Haifa's Rambam Hospital.[82] Rambam Hospital was also the first to appoint an Arab woman doctor, Dr Rania El Hativ, as a plastic surgeon.

As already indicated, there have been some significant indications of the regime's willingness to extend benefits to its Arab citizens. Child allowances, which were originally intended for the families of IDF veterans, were extended in 1993 to the Arab sector, and the inauguration in 1995 of the National Health Law bestowed medical benefits to Israeli Arabs that they did not previously enjoy. More specifically, there has been a significant increase in university scholarships allocated to Arab students.[83] Finally, in terms of general benefits, in 2006 Arabs received a higher percentage of their gross income in the form of government transfers while paying a lower percentage in taxes and other imposts than Jews.[84]

Some writers and commentators have recommended allowing the Israeli Arabs the distinction of being a national minority with *collective rights*, including full control of their educational institutions and official recognition of their representative bodies.[85] In arriving at such a standpoint, they tend to refer to the resolution of ethno-national conflicts in other countries. Yet the situation in Israel is quite unique and cannot be addressed by borrowing procedures successfully employed elsewhere.

Take, for instance, two significant minority communities in the United States that had previously been subject to widespread discrimination – the Jews and the black Americans.[86] In neither case were these communities linked to surrounding Jewish or African states whose populations far exceeded those of the USA and who were bent on destroying America. Both Jews and black Americans, far from being inimical to America as a state and to its central values as embodied in its constitution, desperately wished to be accepted into the American fold as loyal citizens enjoying equal rights and sharing equal responsibilities, as exhibited by Jewish and African Americans becoming GIs during World War II. By contrast, the Arabs in Israel regard themselves as being affiliated to the greater Arab nation in the Middle East and North Africa numbering in excess of 300 million. In essence, the Israeli Arabs are, as Moshe Ma'Oz suggests, a "minority with psychological convictions of a majority."[87] Muhammad Dahlah, one of the founders of Adalah (the Legal Centre for Arab Minority Rights), claimed that "The notion of being a minority is foreign to Islam. It is appropriate for Jewry but not for Islam. A moment's glance would suggest that we are not really a minority. In Israel there is a majority that is really a minority and a minority that is really a majority."[88]

While currently a large proportion of Israeli Arabs would rest content if their living conditions and opportunities were on a par with those of Jewish Israelis, there is a growing strain among them that have adopted the call of either Fatah or Hamas to challenge the very legitimacy of the Jewish State. To that extent they are becoming real as opposed to potential fifth columnists. In stark contrast to the mindset of other alienated minorities that have yearned to be fully accepted and incorporated into the social and political framework of the countries in which they live, the Arab-Israeli radicals would rather strive for the "de-Israelification of Israel's Jews"[89] and the replacement of Israel by an Arab Palestinian State that would almost inevitably be a Muslim one.

The process of Israeli Arabs becoming more radicalized began to be heralded in the 1970s by the appearance of bodies such as the National Committee of Arab Councils and Mayors and the National Committee for the Defence of Arab Land. In 1982 the Supreme Monitoring Committee on the Affairs of Arab Citizens was established to become the unofficially recognized representative of Israeli Arabs. On the party political front, a number of Arab parties emerged, all of which are hostile to Israel as a Jewish State.

Arab-Israeli radicals have fuelled Arab resentment by regularly commemorating two events that attract a mass following. The first relates to what is now known as "Land Day." It originated on March 30, 1976, when a series of demonstrations were organized by Rakah (an

Arab-dominated communist party) to protest against the government's intention to expropriate approximately 21,000 dunams of land in the Galilee as part of a program to boost the presence of Jews there. Only 31 percent of the land in question was Arab owned, some of which was to be allocated to the Arab village of Majar for its expansion and to other Arab towns for the construction of public buildings.[90] The Arabs and their followers complained that the police acted wantonly against citizens peacefully voicing their opposition to land seizures. As a result, six Arabs were killed and many more were wounded. By contrast, a *Jerusalem Post* editorial contended that the police "were attacked with stones and firebombs," and that "Land Day was in fact born in violence, the product of a political party that proudly waved the dubious banner of Marxism–Leninism."[91]

The other seminal day in the Arab-Israeli almanac is the annual memorial on May 15 of the Palestinian Naqba (Catastrophe) that occurred in 1948 when Israel was established and attacked by its neighbours, thus giving rise to the Palestinian refugees. Israeli Arabs attending such gatherings, where keynote speeches bewail the rise of Israel as an act of colonial piracy and plunder, assert their desire to purge Israel of all elements of Jewish statehood.

The official views of the new breed of Arab radicals can be discerned in four key documents that were released in 2006–7: *The Future Vision of the Palestinian Arabs in Israel*, *An Equal Constitution for All*, *The Democratic Constitution* and the *Haifa Declaration*. Known collectively as the "Vision Documents," they constitute the main substance of Arab-Israeli radical demands. Typically, the Haifa Declaration (published by Mada al Carmel and financed by the European Union) opens by declaring: "We reaffirm our attachment to our Palestinian homeland,"[92] which implies that the land over which Israel has sovereignty belongs inherently to the Palestinians and not to the Jews. This is confirmed in pages that follow, where it is stated: "Towards the end of the 19th century, the Zionist movement initiated its colonial-settler project in Palestine. Subsequently, in concert with world imperialism and with the collusion of the Arab reactionary powers, it succeeded in carrying out its project, which aimed at *occupying our homeland* and transforming it into a state for the Jews." To redeem itself, the state of Israel is required to recognize the historical injustice that it committed against the Palestinian people through its establishment, to accept responsibility for the Naqba, which befell on all parts of the Palestinian people, and also for the war crimes and crimes of occupation that it has committed in the Occupied Territories. Reconciliation also requires recognizing the Right of Return, ending the Occupation and removing the settlements from all Arab territory occupied since 1967.[93]

Up until the early 1990s, any articulation of support or endorsement of the PLO would have been regarded by almost all Jewish Israelis as being beyond the pale. Therefore, Israeli Arabs were generally loath to disclose openly the fact that many of them were at one with the aims and objectives of Israel's arch enemy. But the onset of the Oslo Accords in September 1993 changed all that. Once the Israeli government officially recognized the PLO and referred to Arafat as their "peace partner," with whom they were prepared to negotiate a settlement involving a substantial transfer of land to the Palestinians as a prelude to securing a permanent settlement, it became acceptable to associate with and promote PLO interests.

In October 2000, radical Israeli Arabs threw in their lot with the PA-inspired insurgents of the al-Aqsa Intifada by instigating riots within Israel proper. In the process, ten Arabs were shot dead by the police and many others were injured. Considering the seemingly heavy-handed police response, the government commissioned an official inquiry headed by Justice Theodor Or. It was to investigate, among other things, both the immediate and long-term underlying causes of the riots. In its report, released on September 1, 2003, this is how it described the rioters' behaviour:

Against Israeli citizens and members of the defence force various means of assault were brought to bear. These included the throwing of Molotov cocktails, the hurling by slingshots of metal ball bearings at high velocities, stone throwing, rolling burning tyres and, in a few isolated cases, resorting to live fire. Jews were attacked on the roads because they were Jews and their property was destroyed. In one case, a Jewish passer-by was killed. Some attempts were made to prevail upon local Jewish settlements and to threaten them. Major traffic axes were blocked for a time and access to Jewish townships was seriously impaired.[94]

Assiduously and openly propounding the notion that Israel is essentially a racist fascist state lacking legitimacy, radical Arabs have shown no qualms in overtly siding with and egging on Israel's deadly foes even while Israel had been locked in combat with them. In 2006, during the Second War in Lebanon, radical Israeli Arabs barracked wholeheartedly for the Shiite Arabs of Hezbollah. The Union of Arab Community Based Associations, known as Ittijah, accused Israel of the murder of Arabs in Haifa by means of Hezbollah-dispatched rockets! In similar vein, Azmi Bishara, the former Arab Knesset member of the Balad Party, addressing a protest meeting in Nazareth as the war raged, called for "solidarity with the free Lebanese, heroes up against the Zionist war machine."[95] More egregiously, Bishara was accused in 2007 of conveying strategic information to Hezbollah that assisted it in locating appropriate rocket targets. Rather than stand trial and defend the charges against him, Bishara fled the country.[96] Before that, in June 2000, at a "Hezbollah Victory Festival" held in Umm el-Fahm in northern Israel on the occasion of Israel's unilateral withdrawal from Lebanon, Bishara told the assembly that "Hezbollah has won. For the first time since 1967, *we* have tasted victory. Hezbollah has every right to be proud of its achievement and to humiliate Israel."[97]

Let us return to the reforms advocated by well-meaning social scientists that incorporate awarding the Israeli Arabs the distinction of being a national minority with collective rights, including full control of their educational institutions, official recognition of their representative bodies and the provision of positive affirmative action programs.[98] Such policy prescriptions reflect a Western desire to foster ethnic and religious pluralism. Should Israel recognize its Arab citizens as a national minority with *collective* rights, a Pandora's box would be opened paving the way for Israel initially to become a bi-national as opposed to a Jewish State. Relentless Arab pressure would then be unleashed to obtain official acceptance of, say, Naqba Day, which celebrates Zionist perfidy. The Arabs would demand equal treatment with regard to the immigration of both Jews and Arabs, a claim which the Supreme Court of Israel might well uphold, since it would be consistent with any recognition of Arab *national* rights. That would result in the repatriation of millions of Palestinian refugees, which would subsequently lead to the replacement of Israel by a Palestinian State.

There are of course aspects of the Jewish State with which Israeli Arabs may understandably feel ill at ease. These include the national anthem, the state's flag and symbols, and the preferential treatment given to Jewish immigrants. It is not infrequently argued that Israel is alone among democratic states in according an elevated status to the religion, language and ethnic identity of its majority, but that is not the case.[99] In the UK, only a practising member of the Church of England can become head of state. Greece, in which there is a Muslim minority, has a constitution that designates the Greek Orthodox Church as the country's "prevailing religion." Unlike the Muslim clergy, the Greek Orthodox ones receive state salaries. Moreover, descendants of Greeks living abroad are eligible for the immediate bestowal of citizenship the moment they take up Greek residence. Similarly, the German Federal Republic extends automatic citizenship to all Volksdeutsche from Eastern Europe and the former Soviet Union, even though many of them have been away from Germany for hundreds of years. In India, Hindi and English are the county's two official languages, yet Hindi is spoken by only a third of the population. Within Canada, the state of Quebec, where 20 percent of its residents speak English, French has become the sole official language and English signage in public places is prohibited. As for flags, in Norway, Finland, Denmark, Sweden, Switzerland, Britain and Greece, where in some case there are large Muslim minorities, the national flags contain Christian crosses.[100]

Haredi Jews

Haredi Jews are characterized by their extreme piety, their black garments devised in a bygone age in Eastern Europe, their adoration and slavish worship of their rabbis, their use of Yiddish as a spoken language, their concentration in their own neighbourhoods, their own school system, and their avoidance of most things modern, such as modern literature, sport, music, film and television.[101] While to the non-informed they appear to be a homogenous group, they are in practice divided into various sects, with loyalties to specific rabbis within a dynastic chain.

For the most part, with the exception of Shas and Chabad, the Haredim (plural of Haredi) are anti-Zionists, believing that is sinful to pre-empt God's work by creating a Jewish State in advance of the coming of the Messiah. One sect in particular, the Neturei Karta, is so opposed to Israel's existence that it openly makes common cause with the PLO. Its emissaries have even appeared at a Holocaust Denial conference in Teheran.

The Haredim are financially worse off than the Arabs, with half their families in 2001 being officially deemed relatively poor as opposed to 40 percent of Israel's non-Jewish population.[102] In terms of absolute poverty entailing a designated breadline, the Haredim are twice as impoverished as Israel's non-Jews. As with the Arabs, large families, a low female workforce participation rate and far less education and fewer suitable job skills are factors accounting for their inferior economic status. But, more significantly, Haredi men are not inclined to hold down regular jobs, for 60 percent of those between the ages of twenty-five and fifty-four simply do not work.[103] Rather, they prefer to wile away their days in yeshivot (Jewish seminaries), for which they receive from the state 900 shekels per month, while IDF conscripts obtain between 360 and 700 shekels.[104] Only in Israel do Haredi men baulk at full-time employment, for their counterparts living abroad rarely remain in full-time yeshiva study beyond age twenty-five.[105] As a case in point, in the Montreal Hasidic community, only 6 percent of men aged twenty-five and above are full-time yeshiva students.[106]

Haredi primary and high schools generally do not teach scientific subjects, not to mention secular history and modern languages. Even so, in July 2008, the Knesset passed a law granting them state funding without subjecting them to any effective checks to establish whether or not they provide their students with even a minimum of general non-religious knowledge.[107] Many Haredi schools receive top-ups in state funding on the basis of fraudulent reports issued by their own inspectors.[108] As a community, the Haredim have also been recipients of various state welfare handouts, including child allowances, disability allowances, reduced health insurance premiums and subsidized public transport. Furthermore, they are almost completely exempt from income and municipal taxes.[109] In fact the Haredim are welfare spongers par excellence. Only 18 percent of their income is derived from

Plate 9 *A Haredi father with two of his children*

working, while 39 percent comes from government transfer payments (most of which are meant to cover expenses from studying in yeshivot), 32 percent from child allowances, and the remaining 11 percent from other largely nebulous government sources.[110] Among the few Haredim that do work, tax evasion is rife.[111]

While, in 2010, the Haredim made up 13 percent of the state's Jewish population, because of their birth rates far exceeding those of the non-Haredi Jews, their proportion is projected to rise by 2030 to 20 percent.[112] Before the establishment of Israel in 1948, Haredi families were similar in size to those of other orthodox Jews living in British Mandated Palestine. But they rose rapidly from the late 1970s, when the Likud government began increasing welfare payments to them.[113] Being exempt from military service, the Haredim marry and have children at a younger age. The government child support system has been structured in such a way that payouts for each additional child rise exponentially, providing an incentive for an enlarged family. High fertility rates are also encouraged by leading elements of the Haredi community. Heads of yeshivot benefit from greater total fees, their rabbis enjoy the kudos of a growing flock, and their political leaders gain extra parliamentary representation.

Given the high population growth rates of both the Haredi and Arab communities, there is a strong possibility that, within the span of a few generations, non-Haredi Jews might well constitute a distinct minority not only of the entire population but also of all Jews. Professor Arnon Soffer fears that the rapid population growth of anti- and non-Zionist communities will, if they continue, be reflected in an adverse change in the composition of the Knesset, causing it to be dysfunctional and inducing ever increasing numbers of non-Haredi Jews to emigrate.[114]

One of the biggest bugbears relating to the Haredim is that, with a few exceptions, unlike most of the rest of the Jewish population, they do not serve in the army. This arose as a result of Ben-Gurion, Israel's founding prime minister, agreeing to exempt a group of Haredi Talmudic scholars from military service. Ben-Gurion's concession (made in 1947) was based on a desire to draw the Haredi community into the general fold to secure its support in the Zionist bid for statehood. Also Ben-Gurion had empathized with the devastating loss of Haredi scholars emanating from the Holocaust. At the time, the number of exempt scholars amounted to no more than 400. Today, the number of full-time yeshiva scholars exempt from the IDF is equivalent to 13.8 percent of all Israeli males subject to the draft.[115] In absolute terms, in 2010, 61,000 Haredi men under the age of forty were able to avoid military service.[116] The cosy exemption that the Haredim have enjoyed was officially enabled by the passing of the Tal Law in August 2002. In accordance with that law, a student who attends a yeshiva for 45 hours per week and who does not engage in any other occupation is eligible for military exemption. The Tal Law not only deprived the IDF of recruits, it also made sure that none of the draft avoiders entered the labour force. This meant that the dwindling relative non-Haredi Jewish community was left to bear the full brunt of sustaining the economy and defending the country. Such a situation is of course untenable. On February 21, 2012, the Supreme Court determined that the Tal Law violated the right of the majority of Israelis to equal treatment under the law and that the Knesset could therefore not extend its application beyond August 1, 2012.[117] At the time of writing (July 2013) theoretically all Jews, without exception, have become eligible for conscription.

Apart from Haredi non-participation in the country's defence and civil economy, there have been other instances in which the conduct of Haredim has invoked the displeasure of non-Haredi Jews. In Jerusalem there is a public bus in which men sit at the front and women at the rear! On one occasion a Jewish woman from Canada entered the bus and sat down among the men. After refusing to budge she was set upon, pushed to the floor and assaulted.[118] On another occasion, a woman who converted to Judaism under the auspices of the Orthodox Chief Rabbinate was married by a recognized orthodox rabbi. However, Haredi Rabbi Yehuda Wolpe, the Chief Rabbi of Rishon Letzion, not only refused to issue the newly married couple with a marriage certificate but also rescinded the bride's conversion on the grounds that it did not meet his exacting standards.[119] Rabbi Wolpe's predecessor, the Haredi Rabbi Baruch Shimon Solomon, had refused to marry Jews from India unless they underwent a ritual immersion as a conversion ceremony. As one of them complained: "We are Israeli citizens, we did our army service, we are Jews. It has hurt my parents deeply that their Judaism has been called into question."[120]

The Haredim constantly oppose the freedom of action of

non-Haredi Jews. They have tried to prevent the opening of a public swimming pool in Jerusalem, as well as cafés and restaurants plying their trade and motorists taking to the roads on Saturdays. A study undertaken by Abraham Farver revealed that, during the 1980s, there had been a marked increase in Haredi intimidation of secular Jews in Jerusalem, especially against single women, marked by beatings, breaking into homes and even the firebombing of apartments.[121] In June 2012, in this case in Beit Shemesh, a woman retrieving her seven-month-old baby from a car was stoned by Haredim, who considered her to be immodestly dressed.[122] In addition, Haredim regularly deface posters in which women are depicted. On an El Al flight from Zurich to Ben-Gurion Airport, a group of Haredim who had not buckled up while the plane was taking off and who continued to busy themselves in their overhead lockers became enraged when a movie was soon being shown. After shouting in vain that it be switched off, they covered the screen with a blanket, to the understandable annoyance of the non-Haredi viewers. Attorney Ran Oren, who was on that flight, recalled that the movie was simply a family drama with no unsavoury aspects whatsoever.[123] El Al now provides a movie-free section on its flights to the USA.[124]

Haredim have participated in most Israeli coalition governments as ministers that affect the population at large. They not only use their political clout to extract scarce economic resources for the exclusive benefit of their own communities, but they make decisions that are totally out of keeping with the non-Haredi population. For instance, in 2010 the Haredi deputy minister of health, Yakov Litzman, initially refused to approve the construction of an extension of the emergency department of Barzilai Hospital in Ashkelon, on the grounds that the new building would encroach on an ancient burial site – in which it was not even certain that any Jewish remains were present. Bowing to his objections, described by Benny Vaknin, the mayor of Ashkelon, as enshrining "the dead at the expense of the living,"[125] the government arranged to place the extension some distance away from the existing hospital complex, at greater expense and at an enhanced threat to emergency proceedings by not linking it directly to existing surgical theatres and radiology departments.

There is within Israel a crying need to ensure that the Haredim be drafted into the army on the same basis as all other conscripts and to incorporate them more fully into the workforce. No mainstream secular political party is calling for measures that would seriously undermine the continued existence of the various Haredi communities. As the Lubavitch Chabad community has shown, one can live a pious life in a modern society while still being savvy in modern technology. A large-scale entry of the Haredim into the army and workforce would have the effect of diminishing, if not eradicating, the endemic hostility of non-Haredi Jews towards them. It would also redeem the Haredim from poverty and provide them with an improved standard of living. In this respect, there would be no zero-sum gain, for Israeli society as a whole would benefit.

Israel's Economic Performance

Meeting with unstable international economic conditions during the first decade of the twenty-first century, characterized by the burst of the IT bubble during 2000–1 and the global recession of 2007–9 in the wake of a sharp collapse of US property and share prices, the Israeli economy nevertheless fared relatively well. Only twice did it waver – in 2001, when real GDP growth remained stationary, and in 2002, when it fell by roughly half a percent.[126] In those two years, the violence of the al-Aqsa Intifada was largely to blame. Thereafter Israel attained a real GDP growth rate that exceeded that of most other OECD countries (it had become an OECD member in September 2010). As a result, the unemployment rate in 2011 fell to 5.6 percent.[127]

During the period under review, Israel surged ahead in the development of new technology, establishing its place among world leaders, as exemplified by its achieving "the highest density of start-ups in the world" and having more of its companies listed on the New York NASDAQ stock-exchange market "than all companies from the entire European continent."[128] Israel became the first non-US country in which state of the art corporations such as Intel, Microsoft and Apple have established research and development centres. The Intel branch has developed to such an extent that it has become one of the country's largest private employers.[129] Israeli technological breakthroughs have been both numerous and diverse. They include, but are not limited to, vastly improved Intel Pentium computer chips that have revolutionized the cell-phone and computer laptop industries; a stent that is inserted in blocked arteries; the PillCam video capsule, which travels through the small intestine, transmitting vital information; new methods in drip irrigation; a device for preventing cot deaths in babies; a mechanism for blocking electrical current surges; a product enabling the detection and counting of harmful microorganisms in a matter of minutes; an optical heart-beat monitor; firewall software; and inventions in clean air and solar power.

In analyzing the circumstances that gave rise to Israel's newfound technological prowess, Senor and Singer identified various factors that have collectively provided Israel with a keen competitive edge.[130] As to be expected, they relate largely to the nature of Israel's human capital. Israel is exceptionally blessed with a workforce richly endowed with scientists and engineers with expertise in a broad variety of disciplines. This has resulted from the Russian Jewish immigration, which initially created a market glut of technicians and professionals, and from Israel's own system of education, which contains universities and research institutes of world-class standard. While that may be a necessary condition for generating technical innovations, it is not a sufficient one. In Israel's case, some of the extra ingredients required are to be found in the country's unique social environment, bred in part by the IDF, which trains conscripts of almost all ranks to confront problems under stress, adopt personal initiatives, challenge prevailing dogmas and systems, and not to live in fear of or be shamed by failure. Moreover, some of the IDF's specialized technical units foster problem-solving within a team framework, which gives rise to strong social and collaborative ties transferable to civilian life. In addition, Israel's generally informal and egalitarian culture, where one is respected less for one's rank and position and more for one's performance, and where there is a willingness to criticize freely and to take on good advice, are also crucial factors. Finally, expansions and improvements in Israel's public infrastructure, particularly in road systems and the country's rail network, as well as radical economic reforms in the field of finance facilitating venture-capital investments, have also been of crucial importance.

In addition to new product creations, the Israeli economy benefited from its thriving tourist sector, which has emerged from the doldrums resulting from the eruption of the al-Aqsa Intifada. In 2012 it attracted

3.5 million foreign tourists, an all-time record number, prompting the minister of tourism to note that tourism is now one of the country's major engines of growth.[131] Israel also has a thriving diamond-polishing industry, is a prominent exporter of military equipment, and has well-developed chemical and pharmaceutical plants. In terms of energy resources, Israel's future looks secure, for in 2009 a significant natural gas field was located in the Mediterranean approximately 90 kilometres west of Haifa. A year later it was discovered that an even larger source of gas exists in a field near to the one found in 2009. According to an article in *Bloomberg Businessweek*, Israel's gas potential could well be worth $240 billion, more than enough to meet its local demand for 150 years based on current consumption rates.[132]

As well as the Israeli economy has performed, it is not free of problems. Aside from those beyond its control, such as the international economic climate, the government's budgetary deficit in early 2012 was running at 4.2 percent of GDP at a time when full employment prevailed.[133] This means that both expenditure cuts and tax rises are called for, which is easier said than done, for income inequality and the incidence of poverty are both relatively high.

In 2005, as measured by the Gini coefficient for disposable income[134] – that is, income after taxes and government transfers – only four of the then twenty-eight OECD countries had a more unequal distribution of income than Israel.[135] The countries in question were the USA, Portugal, Turkey and Mexico. The wage gap in Israel, as measured by the ratio of wages of those in the top income decile to those in the lowest, exceeds that of all OECD countries.[136] Although Israel has a minimum wage regime, it is not strictly enforced.[137] In practice the economy manifests aspects of dualism. Professionals and skilled workers fairly high on the income ladder draw salaries that are commensurate with those of most OECD countries. For example, dentists charge "Western fees" and managing directors of banks and large accounting firms earn in excess of $1 million per year. However, those at the lower end of the income ladder with no marketable skills are paid such paltry sums that they have in effect become the working poor. Instances are occasionally reported in the media of households with empty refrigerators being dependent on soup kitchens and general charity. For reasons given above, poverty is concentrated particularly in the Arab and Ultra-orthodox Jewish communities, where workforce participation rates are low, families are large and education is below national standards.

Foreign Workers in Israel

Within Israel there is a large pool of foreign migratory workers, who constitute 11 percent of all private-sector employees – a high percentage in international terms.[138] Soon after the Yom Kippur War in 1973, some 120,000 Palestinians from the West Bank and Gaza began streaming into Israel on a daily basis to undertake menial low paid work, particularly in the agricultural and building sectors.[139] When in late 1993 the Palestinians began launching suicide bombing missions against Israeli civilians, the flow of Palestinian workers into Israel was severely staunched. But, with Israeli employers having become dependent on cheap migratory labour, the government turned to other sources further afield, with the result that in 2012 there were some 250,000 foreigners on a temporary work visa. They include Chinese construction workers, Filipino home health-care aides and Thai farmhands, as well as other Asians, Africans and Eastern Europeans, who work as maids, cooks, nannies, home cleaners and restaurant dish washers, etc.[140] The migratory workers perform tasks that permanent residents are unwilling to undertake, thereby contributing to the well-being of the locals. Without them, many of Israel's old-age homes would not be economically viable and, by the same token, building costs would be much higher. Drawn to Israel in search of prospects for earning more than is available to them in their home countries, *some* have been exploited by rogue Israeli employers, who withhold their passports and cheat them out of their due wages.[141] On other occasions, migratory workers were not given their overtime allowances, a practice which is contrary to Israeli law.[142]

Critics suggest that the presence of foreign workers depresses wages for the unskilled and that labour-intensive production techniques are needlessly perpetuated in industries at a time when the country as a whole is becoming relatively more capital abundant.[143] As a result, some industries become reliant on a regular infusion of cheap foreign labour. However, not all Israeli economists are of that view.[144]

Unwelcome social problems may arise as a result of foreign workers staying for some time. Criminal activity and alcohol abuse, which the public *perceives* as being higher than average, may result partly from most migratory male workers being separated from their families. Israel now also has to confront the fact that it is not easy dispensing with foreign workers once their visas expire. Some in Israel who have overstayed have de facto spouses and families. At first the government served them notice that they had to leave. But in August 2011, deferring to a groundswell of public protest, it decided that, provided the migrant parents entered Israel legally, they and their children could obtain residency rights if each child had entered the country before the age of thirteen, had lived there for at least five years, was either in school or about to enter first grade, and spoke Hebrew fluently[145] Not all foreign workers have entered the country legally. From around 2007, refugees from Southern Sudan began crossing the Sinai Desert to infiltrate into the southern seaport of Eilat. By 2012, their numbers had reached an estimated 7,000 in a city of 55,000 inhabitants.[146] Of late, the government has erected secure fencing along the border near Eilat, making it next to impossible for more Sudanese to enter the country. Meanwhile, the regular denizens of Eilat are torn between those who would like to have the refugees expelled and those who would like to grant them some legal status, permitting them to seek employment, thus avoiding having a wayward population of young men loitering in the streets with no source of income.[147]

The Process of Change in the Kibbutz Movement

In October 1910, a group of ten men and two women set up a collective farm near the shores of Lake Kinneret (Sea of Galilee), which they named Degania. Based on full equality, with everyone receiving the same monthly wage, Degania is regarded as Israel's founding kibbutz. However, in its formative years, with its small and intimate membership, it exhibited more of the features of an extended family than those of the far larger kibbutzim that were to follow. The first settlement that incorporated most of the distinguishing characteristics of a fully fledged kibbutz was Ein Harod, established in 1922. From then on, as Jewish immigration into British Mandated Palestine gathered apace, kibbutzim began to be established in rapid succession. By 2013 there were 256 kibbutzim with a membership of 106,000 people.[148]

Over the years there have been various strands within the kibbutz movement. At the helm were three federations, each affiliated to a particular party within the labour movement, followed by two far smaller groupings, one religious based and the other with a liberal political disposition. Nevertheless, one can confidently assert that all kibbutzim were essentially cut from the same cloth in that they all aspired to create the kernel of a democratic, egalitarian and just society. Their structures and way of life were of the same kind. Above all, they were agricultural enterprises in which all members were on the same level in that, while no one was financially remunerated, they all shared equal entitlements to accommodation, food, clothing and other items and services that met their basic needs. The entitlements extended to use only and not to ownership. Thus a member's private quarters, furniture and other appurtenances were formally the property of the collective. Private income from external sources was for the most part disallowed. The few that earned outside incomes had to transfer them to the kibbutz. All partook of their meals in the communal dining hall. Children slept apart in a children's home supervised by other members. Individual work assignments were determined on the basis of the kibbutz's economic and social priorities, which meant that members had to accord preferences to communal imperatives over personal ones. They complied largely because critical decisions were taken collectively in general meetings in which all could and were expected to participate and vote. Settlement coordinators were chosen by ballot and had limited terms of office. *Theoretically*, there was nothing personal to be gained by serving in any managerial position.

Despite all the limitations that kibbutz life imposed, such as depriving individuals of the freedom to determine both their consumption patterns and their career paths (especially for women) and restricting their family integrity, the kibbutz was in its heyday a cynosure for Zionist idealists seeking to further the foundation and then strength of Israel. Placing national objectives above all, kibbutzim were established in remote and desolate areas, where they played a pivotal role in Israel's defence and in redeeming land for the Jewish people. For the most part, the land on which kibbutzim settled was barren and was either swampland, strewn with rocks or desert land. This meant that, in the early years, kibbutz members led Spartan lives, sleeping in tents while striving to cultivate their miserable allotments. In the realm of defence, kibbutz members, as supreme patriots, met with a death rate far higher than their proportion in Israel as a whole. For that they were widely admired and enjoyed a fair measure of general esteem.

As Israel passed through its turbulent infancy, the economy began to flourish, as did the kibbutzim. Agriculture became more mechanized and, to maintain full employment for all its members, the kibbutzim reluctantly turned to industry, setting up various factories to produce goods primarily for the export market. In the process, many kibbutzim were compelled to take on outside labour, a practice which was at odds with a cherished principle to remain exclusively dependent on their own manpower resources. The new industries, which by 1980 accounted for almost half of kibbutz income,[149] gave a welcome boost to rising living standards. Members acquired television sets for their own private use, tennis courts and swimming pools were built, café-like services in kibbutz club houses were improved, and members were better clothed. Gradually, pressures began to mount for family homes to be extended to accommodate children, and in many kibbutzim car pools were made available for weekend recreational travel.

By the late 1970s, kibbutz children could no longer be relied upon to stay on in their communities. After concluding their three-year national army service, like many other Israelis, they acquired a wanderlust that took them backpacking for an additional year to the far ends of the earth. In the process, their personal horizons widened, leading many to re-evaluate the desirability of kibbutz living. Israel's pioneering era had become a thing of the past. An ethos of dedication to national causes was replaced by an overriding materialistic culture, whereby the seeking of personal advancement and gratification became the norm. In that climate, the social significance of kibbutzim was increasingly seen as being irrelevant, with the IDF remaining the only Israeli institution deemed worthy of civic support and service.

Because the above mentioned developments progressed slowly and relatively evenly, they did not present the kibbutz movement with any specific challenge to its continuity. That changed in the 1980s. In 1983, the value of bonds issued by leading banks, which had been artificially inflated by the banks themselves, had collapsed. Kibbutzim and their organizations were prime victims, as they had invested heavily in such bonds in the hope of securing their assets against the soaring rate of inflation.[150] In addition, many kibbutzim had borrowed heavily and, with a sharp rise in interest rates, had accumulated a huge burden of debt, amounting by 1989 to $5 billion.[151] Some of the loans were meant to finance the operative capital required for kibbutz industries, but a large proportion of the money was used to invest in quality of life improvements. The upshot of it all was that many kibbutzim were in deep financial straits, made worse by a contemporaneous sharp drop in the price of cotton, the kibbutz movement's main agricultural cash crop.[152] Kibbutzim had also to grapple with an aging population. The proportion of those in the above sixty-five age group had risen from 6.8 percent in 1977 to 10.2 percent in 1990,[153] which resulted in increased monetary outlays for the care of elderly members. There is no state pension plan in Israel, and many kibbutzim had used up their pension funds to pay off debts or did not have any pension funds in the first place.[154] In 1988–9, wracked by a crisis of confidence in the kibbutz movement's future, for the first time ever, the total number of kibbutz members fell.[155]

Except for the few which were wealthy and solvent and could readily weather the storm, the kibbutzim had of necessity to undergo various degrees of structural reform. The sum total of measures adopted varied considerably, and what follows are merely examples of some of the more typical ones. One common denominator is that they allowed for individual choices, initiatives and responsibilities, characteristics that had up to then been alien to the kibbutz way of thinking. To rationalize and economize on consumption, members had to pay for items consumed either out of a budget allocated to them, from money privately earned, or from a combination of the two. When, for instance, people ate in the communal dining room, they were billed for dishes chosen. Alternatively, if anyone wished to prepare their own food, they were billed for items taken from the kibbutz general store. Similarly, the usage of electricity in members' homes was metred and charged. Private bank accounts were sanctioned as were monetary gifts from external sources. Finally, members received full ownership of their living quarters.

In terms of production, salaries were issued for work performed within the kibbutz, and each economic sector began to function along the lines of profit and not necessarily output maximization. Heading each branch was a manager who, like the new kibbutz general manager, was paid a differential salary, as were certain other members in keeping with their relative labour productivity. Members were encouraged to seek outside work if they could earn more than the kibbutz could afford to pay them, but some of their salary was requisitioned to finance remaining common kibbutz services and functions. By the same token, outsiders were taken on to fill various posts now vacant. As one kibbutz member observed, in the early morning hours as cars go out, others come in, bringing in service workers and other hired hands.[156]

The changes undergone in many kibbutzim have been quite comprehensive. In some cases, even the communal dining room is no longer used. Full equality has fallen by the wayside and many critical decisions are made by outside professionals. Yet the reforms have restored the kibbutz movement's confidence. No longer fulfilling a pioneering calling, kibbutzim are luring new members with offers of an attractive rural lifestyle within a communal setting. To that extent, they seem to have prospects for a bright future, as attested by the fact that many kibbutz children who had previously left are now returning.[157]

CONCLUSION

Since its inception in 1948, Israel has been plagued by unremitting attempts to eliminate it. In fact, the day after it declared its independence it was assailed by four regular Arab armies, which it heroically warded off at the cost of 6,000 lives. After that, Israel braced itself for a planned Arab "second round." That was played out first in 1956, when Israel routed the Egyptian army in Sinai, and then again in 1967, when Egypt, Jordan and Syria were jointly on the verge of attacking the Jewish State. Their attempts were foiled by the IDF's daring six-day pre-emptive strike. Having so utterly routed their enemies, the Israelis expected that they would forswear future attempts to vanquish them. But that was not to be. No sooner had the guns fallen silent then the PLO resorted to a torrent of terrorist attacks, killing 175 Israelis in the course of a single year. That was to be followed by a war of attrition on the Egyptian front, which concluded in August 1970 with Israel having suffered 727 fatalities, a figure not far short of the number sacrificed in the Six-Day War. For some unaccountable reason, the Israelis regarded themselves as having emerged from the war of attrition as victors. Abounding in unbridled optimism, their leaders hubristically predicted that, for the next decade at least, Israel would not be at war. Yet three years later, caught off guard, the country found itself at the point of being simultaneously overrun by both heavily armed and heavily manned Syrian and Egyptian forces. Recovering from its initial shock, the IDF was able to turn the tide, but at the cost of 2,656 of its soldiers. Finally, by 1979, a ray of light emerged following the conclusion of a peace treaty between Israel and Egypt. Although the treaty did not yield all expected of it, it has ensured that, since the 1973 Yom Kippur War, Israel has thus far been spared the ordeal of combating a nation-state army.

That did not of course mean that Israel was spared the anguish of continuous terrorist attacks and the necessity to suppress them. Initially, the main brunt of such attacks was conducted by Arafat's Fatah, the leading PLO faction. First they emanated from Jordan and, when the PLO was ejected from there, from Lebanon. In the process, the PLO began to acquire heavy weaponry to upgrade its military capability. To stymie the PLO's plans, the IDF in June 1982 launched a campaign to eradicate its presence in Southern Lebanon. While it succeeded in that task, even bringing about the PLO leadership's displacement to Tunisia, the combined cost of the operation and the IDF's first year of occupying Lebanese territory amounted to the loss of 516 men. The next serious encounter with the Palestinians arose in the context of the al-Aqsa Intifada, initiated by the PA in September 2000. In that episode, in which Israelis were subject to multiple suicide bombings and other forms of lethal terrorist activity, the death toll reached 1,009. After the al-Aqsa Intifada was wound down in February 2005, a year and a half later the Israelis in Southern Lebanon lost a further 163 citizens, including forty-four non-combatants, while engaging in a prolonged operation against Hezbollah. As if all that was not enough, the emergence in Gaza of Hamas as a dominant force, brimming with rockets, presented Israelis living in the southern region of their country with serious security threats and disruption to their daily lives.

Israel is unique among the nations of the world in that there has been no intergenerational let-up in girding for war. Young men attaining the age of eighteen are generally liable to be conscripted for three years' military service, with a high probability of seeing active combat. The weight of military obligations and their perils hangs so heavily in the air that the thought of grim tidings is constantly at the back of people's minds. Golda Meir revealed that she was frightened to telephone members of both her immediate and extended family to ask them how they were faring. In the same vein, she never inquired of friends as to whether they had heard from their sons.[1]

Addressing the problem of Israel's continuity, Dayan in August 1969 told a group of IDF officer graduates that Israelis had to steel themselves, both morally and physically, for a protracted struggle and that they ought not to be tempted "to draw up a timetable for the 'achievement of rest and peace.'"[2] To prevail, Israelis would have to have faith in the righteousness of their cause, "a faith that hardens them against spiritual depression, weakness, inaction and destruction." Apart from faith, they would need courage and fortitude to "endure the struggle throughout the generations and in changing circumstances."[3] While, for the most part, Israelis have lived up to Dayan's injunctions, they have never lost sight of the cost in human lives of preserving their state. Since Israel is a relatively small country, an unusually large proportion of the population has either direct or indirect knowledge of an individual cut down by the enemy, either on the battlefield or in the country's urban and rural areas. The collective memory of the fallen is perpetuated by the country's Memorial Day, when bereaved parents, spouses or children attend to the graves of their beloved ones and when, at the sound of sirens, all traffic comes to a halt and people stand in a moment of silence in tribute to those who have paid the ultimate price.

Israeli yearnings for peace are genuine. Despite all their bluster, the Israelis ceded the entire Sinai peninsula in return for peace with Egypt. Under Barak's term as prime minister, the offer to the Syrians was not only to vacate the Golan Heights but also to allow them to approach within immediate reach of the Sea of Galilee – an offer that was promptly rejected. As for the Palestinians, Barak in 2000 was prepared to yield all of Gaza, 97 percent of the West Bank and the Arab quarters of Jerusalem in exchange for peace. Then in 2008 Olmert was even more conciliatory. While wishing to retain 6.4 percent of the West Bank, he was prepared to compensate the Palestinians with an equal amount of Israeli acreage that would have also included a land link between Gaza and the West Bank. In Jerusalem, sovereignty of the Old City, in which the holy sites of all three monotheistic religions are situated, was to be vested in an international condominium consisting of Saudi Arabia, Jordan, the Palestinian State, Israel and the United States. On both occasions, the PA, without submitting any counter-offers, turned down the Israeli ones.

Plate 10 *Standing in silence in tribute to those fallen in defence of Israel*

The Palestinians assert that a fair share of the blame for the failure of the "peace process" can be attributed to Israel. Since the signing of the Oslo Accords, there has been over a threefold expansion of the number of settlers living in the West Bank, rising from 110,600 in 1993[4] to 300,150 in 2012.[5] The settlers like to believe that their presence does not cause any exacerbation in Israeli–Palestinian relations, but that is certainly not the case. From a Palestinian perspective there is nothing more humiliating and rankling than to confront Jewish settlements perched on surrounding hills, threatening to transform their social landscape. For with settlements come special settlement access roads, roadblocks, IDF patrols and, in many instances, unfriendly neighbours, some of whom are inclined to take the law into their own hands and, when aroused, to uproot and despoil Arab villages and their land. Discounting those settlers attracted to the West Bank purely for material reasons, such as cheap subsidized housing, and those with a genuine desire to forge friendly relations with the local Palestinians, the settler movement at heart serves to ensure that the West Bank would ultimately become an integral and inseparable part of Israel. That the settlements have flourished with the full support of both Labour and non-Labour governments could well cast doubt on Israel's willingness to resolve the ongoing Israeli–Palestinian conflict. However, the fact remains that the existence of settlements did not deter Barak or Olmert from expressing a willingness to forego most of them in exchange for peace.

Added to the litany of Palestinian complaints is that they have been patronized by the Israelis, who have granted them concessions for good behaviour while withholding the same whenever their demands were not met. However, what is conveniently overlooked is the constant and systematic violation and even abrogation of virtually all Palestinian obligations contracted under the Oslo Accords and subsequent agreements. The PA had solemnly accepted that it was to suppress terrorist violence and to maintain only *one* paramilitary police force, not exceeding 30,000 men and bearing light arms only. Its educational and other institutions were to promote Israeli–Palestinian peaceful coexistence. There was to be a democratically elected president and a democratically elected legislative body (Abbas still holds power four years after his term of office expired). Palestinians who had previously collaborated with Israel were to be unharmed, and all outstanding issues were to be settled by direct negotiations between the interested parties. Not one of these obligations did the PA fulfil. In fact, far from clamping down on terror, by initiating the al-Aqsa Intifada the PA actually orchestrated it.

Within Palestinian society there exists an abiding hatred of Israelis that has been consciously instilled by the Palestinian leadership, both in the past and in the present. The inculcation of the most extreme of anti-Jewish and anti-Israeli sentiments commences in kindergarten and school, where children are taught that the entire region from the River Jordan to the sea constitutes Palestinian territory and that Israel within its 1949 borders occupies land illegitimately wrested from them. Israel is white-washed out of all school maps and Israeli cities are listed in song and poetry as Palestinian ones to which the children are destined to return. Above all, suicide bombers are slavishly adored. Their pictures grace the walls of practically every classroom and the students are encouraged to emulate them. City squares, sports venues and teams, and other like associations, as well as public landmarks, are named after the most egregious Palestinian murderers, who are regarded as embodying the supreme virtues of the Palestinian people. Far from being ashamed or distancing themselves from the dastardly deeds perpetrated by their "freedom fighters," the PA is more than proud of them, *officially* according them respect and gratitude. Take, for instance, the insertion in July 2013 of photographs of five Palestinian terrorists and a summary of their feats on the official Facebook page of the Enlistment and Organization Commission of Fatah. Accompanying the photograph of Abdullah Barghouti, currently serving sixty-seven life sentences for organizing various acts of murder, is a list of his "accomplishments." It reads as follows: "The Sbarro restaurant operation in Jerusalem which killed 15 Zionists, the Moment Café operation which killed 11 Zionists, the Sheffield Night Club operation which killed 15 Zionists, the Hebrew University operation which killed 9 Zionists, the Ben Yehuda pedestrian mall operation which killed 11 Zionists."[6]

The adulation of terrorists emanates from the very pinnacle of the PA leadership. In July 2010, on the occasion of the death of Muhammad Daoud Oudeh, the organizer of the Munich Olympic Games massacre, Abbas sent a telegram of condolences to the deceased's family. In it he described Oudeh as a prominent Fatah leader and a wonderful brother and companion who, as a relentless fighter, devoted himself in defence of the Palestinian revolution.[7]

The wish list of the PA as repetitively articulated by its leadership and media outlets includes Israel's acceptance of the right of return of all Palestinian refugees and Palestinian control of the Old City of Jerusalem in its entirety, foreclosing Jewish access to the plaza facing the Western Wall, where the establishment of an Arab housing estate has been flagged.[8] Not only would the Old City be *Judenrein* (Jew free) but so too would the future Palestinian State. As Abbas declared: "In a final resolution, we would not see the presence of a single Israeli – civilian or soldier – on our lands."[9] Finally, far from being willing to recognize Israel as a Jewish State (which was the explicit intention of the November 1947 UN resolution favouring the partition of Palestine), the PA has called upon Israel to acknowledge its role in the creation of the Palestinian Naqba (tragedy), which, as Mustafa Barghouti, a member of the PLO Central Council, claims would be "a first step towards accountability and a just solution to this conflict."[10] The effrontery of it all is breathtaking. After having embarked upon a failed campaign to stifle Israel at birth, the Palestinians expect of Israel that it would contritely apologize for that failure.

Whichever way one looks at it, at this moment in time there is no indication that the PA is genuinely willing to come to terms with Israel's existence. It is of course not beyond the bounds of possibility that some sort of deal or agreement could be hammered out as a result of US arm twisting, but there is no way, given Hamas's control of Gaza and Abbas's tenuous hold on the West Bank, that any such deal would once and for all resolve the Israeli–Palestinian conflict. The sad fact of the matter is that it will continue to remain insoluble until such time as the Palestinians accept the right of Israel to exist as a Jewish State, just as they expect the Israelis to accept their prospective state as a Palestinian one.

A continuation of the status quo is not without cost. It leaves the Palestinians discontented and infused with a feeling of being victimized, whereas Israel of necessity needs to uphold a constant state of vigilance against potential outbreaks of Palestinian-initiated violence. For Israel, the only saving grace is that the Palestinians do not constitute an existential threat. But the same cannot be said of Iran, whose leaders have brazenly expressed their intention of wiping Israel off the face of the earth. In furtherance of that objective, the development of an Iranian atomic bomb has taken pride of place. The United States, despite all assertions to the contrary, is unlikely to deploy force to frustrate the Iranians and, as much as the Israelis may be tempted to go it alone, such an option is fraught with risk. An IDF operation to neutralize Iran's nuclear capability would be extremely complex, with a good chance of failure. Even if successful, the Iranians are likely to effect a formidable response and, if that were not enough, would be sure to resurrect their nuclear program in less accessible locations. As much as the author would like to be proved wrong, an Iranian acquisition of an atomic bomb seems inevitable. Without minimizing the gravity of the Iranian threat, Israel, with its ingenuity in devising defensive mechanisms against ballistic weapons, may, in good time, acquire adequate countermeasures, not to speak of the unmentionable means of deterrence already at its disposal. Unfortunately, there remains a legitimate concern that Iran's leaders might well determine that the loss of a million or so of their own people in a nuclear exchange with Israel would be but a small price to pay in furthering the will of Allah.

Despite Israel's manifold security concerns, the situation within the country is surprisingly rosy – one might even say upbeat. Like all European and North American countries, Israel has its share of intractable social problems, manifested by, among other things, pockets of poverty, rising alcohol and drug abuse, juvenile delinquency and violent crime. Nevertheless, the country can be credited with many outstanding achievements. In a world buffeted by economic turbulence, its economy has been exceptionally stable and buoyant. During the 2009–12 global economic crisis, the growth of Israel's GDP exceeded that of all other OECD countries.[11] Its 2013 unemployment rate, at 6.2 percent, was less than the European average, including that of the UK, France and Germany.[12] Assisted by an influx of private foreign investment in high-technology industries, Israel has made great strides in the export of sophisticated manufactured products. Over the previous two decades there has been a marked increase in average personal incomes, and in general terms the country is blessed with a modern road network, an efficient public transportation system, and good educational and health facilities. It has all the trimmings of an affluent Western society, with modern multi-storey shopping complexes, an array of fine widely patronized restaurants, and a variety of leisure facilities, including social clubs, art, music, theatre and cinema venues, as well as popular beaches and national parks. The social fabric and cohesion of the country has constantly been improving, with ethnic rifts narrowing and with the Russian Jews becoming fully integrated.

It is worth recalling that in 1948, at Israel's humble beginnings, it had merely 650,000 mostly Jewish citizens, an irregular militia with no heavy weapons or planes, and an economy with next to no foreign reserves. From such a parlous state, after fighting for its very survival, Israel went on to absorb Jews in distress from post-World War II displaced camps in Europe, Jews fleeing persecution in the Middle East and North Africa, and finally Jews from the ex-Soviet Union and Ethiopia. Today Israel stands tall, with a diverse population of just over 8 million, of whom 6 million are Jews. It is a viable open democratic state based on the rule of law with a high standard of living, enviable scientific and cultural achievements and a first-rate defence force. According to a poll conducted in 2012, 92.7 percent of the Jewish population are proud to be Israelis.[13] It would seem that their pride is based on good cause, for a 2011 Gallup poll ranked Israel seventh in the world in terms of happiness.[14]

Appendix:
General Election Results

November 1965

Hamaarah: alignment of Mapai and Ahdut Ha'avodah	45 seats
Gahal: Herut and Liberals	26 seats
Mafdal: Israel Religious Party	11 seats
Rafi: splinter group from Mapai	10 seats
Mapam: Zionist Marxists	8 seats
Agudat Yisrael: non-Zionist religious party	6 seats
Independent Liberals	5 seats
Pro-alignment Arab lists	4 seats
Rakah: anti-Zionist communists	3 seats
Maki: non-anti-Israel communists	1 seat
This World-New Force: led by a dissident journalist, Uri Avneri	1 seat

October 1969

Maarah: alignment of the Labour Party and Mapam	56 seats
Gahal	26 seats
Mafdal	12 seats
Agudat Yisrael	4 seats
Independent Liberals	4 seats
National List	4 seats
Rakah	3 seats
Pro-alignment Arab lists	4 seats
This World-New Force	2 seats
Free Centre: short-lived offshoot from Herut	2 seats
Po'alei Agudat Yisrael: workers' party of Agudat Yisrael	2 seats
Maki	1 seat

December 1973

Maarah	51 seats
Likud: Gahal plus Free Center and National List	39 seats
Mafdal	10 seats
United Torah: Agudat Yisrael and Po'alei Agudat Yisrael	5 seats
Independent Liberals	4 seats
Rakah	4 seats
Ratz: civil rights movement founded by Shulamit Aloni	3 seats
Kidmah Ufituah: minority list supporting Maarah	2 seats
Moked: communist-inclined party	1 seat
Arab list representing Bedouins	1 seat

May 1977

Likud	43 seats
Maarah	32 seats
Democratic Movement for Change: Liberals and others disenchanted with the mainstream parties, headed by Yigael Yadin	15 seats
Mafdal	12 seats
Hadash: a new name of Rakah	5 seats
Agudat Yisrael	4 seats
Flatto-Sharon (individual list)	1 seat
Shlomzion: list headed by Arik Sharon	2 seats
Mahaneh Sheli: list head by peace promoter Arie Lova Eliav	2 seats
United Arab List: supporting Maarah	1 seat
Po'alei Agudat Yisrael	1 seat
Ratz	1 seat
Independent Liberals	1 seat

June 1981

Likud	48 seats
Maarah	47 seats
Mafdal	6 seats
Agudat Yisrael	4 seats
Hadash	4 seats
Tehiya: a nationalist part supporting Gush Emunin	3 seats
Tami: Movement for Heritage of Israel, a traditional Sephardi party	3 seats
Telem: Movement for National Renewal, founded by Dayan	2 seats
Shinui: secular liberal party	2 seats
Ratz: Movement for Civil Rights	1 seat

July 1984

Maarah	44 seats
Likud	41 seats
Tehiya–Tzomet	5 seats
Mafdal	4 seats
Hadash	4 seats
Shas: a new party of Sephardi Haredim	4 seats
Shinui	3 seats
Ratz	2 seats
Yahad: founded by Weizman, who had left Likud	3 seats
Progressive List for Peace	2 seats
Agudat Yisrael	2 seats
Morasha Poalei Agudat Yisrael: a short-lived party formed by Haim Drukman from Mafdal and Avraham Verdiger from Agudat Yisrael	2 seats
Tami	1 seat
Kach: formed by Meir Kahane and barred from contesting future elections on account of its racist ideology	1 seat
Ometz: previously Telem	1 seat

November 1988

Likud	40 seats
Maarah	39 seats
Shas	6 seats
Agudat Yisrael	5 seats
Ratz	5 seats
Mafdal	5 seats
Hadash	4 seats
Tehiya	3 seats
Mapam	3 seats
Tzomet	2 seats
Moledet: founded by Rehavam Ze'evi to promote the voluntary exodus of Arabs from the West Bank	2 seats
Shinui	2 seats
Degel Hatorah: a splinter group from Agudat Yisrael of non-Hassidic Haredim	2 seats
Progressive List for Peace	1 seat
Arab Democratic Party: formed by Abdulwahab Darawshe, who had left the Maarah	1 seat

June 1992

Labor	44 seats
Likud	32 seats
Meretz: a new party consisting of Ratz, Mapam and Shinui	12 seats
Tzomet	8 seats
Mafdal	6 seats
Shas	6 seats
Yahadut Hatorah: an alliance of Degel Hatorah and Agudat Yisrael	4 seats
Hadash	3 seats
Moledet	3 seats
Arab Democratic Party	2 seats

May 1996

Labour	34 seats
Likud–Gesher–Tzomet (Gesher was formed by David Levy after defecting from Likud)	32 seats
Shas	10 seats
Mafdal	9 seats
Meretz	9 seats
Yisrael Be'Aliyah: party of Russian migrants headed by former refusenik Natan Sharansky	7 seats
Hadash	5 seats
Yahadut Hatorah	4 seats
The Third Way: formed by Labour defectors who were against Israel ceding the Golan Heights	4 seats
United Arab List: party in favour of a Palestinian State in the West Bank, Gaza and Jerusalem	4 seats
Moledet	2 seats

May 1999

One Israel: a bloc of Labour, Gesher and Meimad, a moderate religious party favouring peace and against imposing religious practice by legislation	26 seats
Likud	19 seats
Shas	17 seats
Meretz	10 seats
Yisrael Be'Aliyah	6 seats
Shinui: a breakaway party from Meretz in 1997, fiercely secular	6 seats
Center Party: formed by Yitzhak Mordechai as a halfway station between Likud and Labour	6 seats
Mafdal	5 seats
Yahadut Hatorah	5 seats
United Arab List	5 seats
Haichud Haleumi: right-wing party alliance	4 seats
Hadash	3 seats
Yisrael Beiteinu: formed by Avigdor Lieberman as a hard-line national party with a secular bent	4 seats
Balad: a party made up largely of Arabs, with a few Jews, against the notion of Israel being a Jewish State	2 seats
Am Ehad: a breakaway group from Labour fostering socialism	2 seats

January 2003

Likud	38 seats
Labour–Meimad	19 seats
Shinui	15 seats
Shas	11 seats
Haichud Haleumi: right-wing alliance	7 seats
Meretz	6 seats
Mafdal	6 seats
Yahadut Hatorah	5 seats
Hadash	3 seats
Am Ehad	3 seats
Balad	3 seats
Yisrael Be'Aliyah	2 seats
United Arab List	2 seats

March 2006

Kadima	29 seats
Labour–Meimad	19 seats
Shas	12 seats
Likud	12 seats
Yisrael Beiteinu	11 seats
Ichud Leumi–Mafdal	9 seats
Gil (New Pensioners' Party)	7 seats
Torah and Shabat Judaism: Haredi party	6 seats
Meretz	5 seats
United Arab List	4 seats
Hadash	3 seats
Balad	3 seats

February 2009

Kadima	28 seats
Likud	27 seats
Yisrael Beiteinu	15 seats
Labour	13 seats
Shas	11 seats
United Torah	5 seats
Ra'am Ta'al: an Arab party	4 seats
Ichud Leumi	4 seats
Hadash	4 seats
Meretz	3 seats
Habayit Hayehudi: an orthodox party	3 seats
Balad	3 seats

Glossary

Agudat Yisrael An ultra-orthodox political party

Ahdut Ha'avodah A social-democratic labour party with a tendency to promote a hard-line approach to the Israel–Arab question.

Aliyah The process of a Jew migrating to Israel

Ashkenazi A Jew of European origin

Barmitzvah A ceremony entailing a thirteen-year-old boy reading from the Torah (five books of Moses) in which he officially becomes recognized (for religious purposes) as a man

Center Party A short-lived party founded in February 1999 from among mainly disgruntled Likud and Labour members

Chabad A Hasidic movement in orthodox Judaism with headquarters in Crown Heights, New York

Degel Hatorah An Ashkenazi ultra-orthodox political party

Gahal A right-wing political bloc consisting of the former Herut and Liberal parties

Gesher A party founded in March 1966 by David Levy after he lost the Likud leadership ballot

Hadash A predominantly Arab party with a large communist component

Hanukkah Jewish festival of lights commemorating the rededication of the Holy Temple after a successful revolt against Greek rule

Haredi An ultra-orthodox Jew

Hasid (adjective Hasidic) A member of a branch of ultra-orthodox Jewry that promotes spirituality through mysticism

Herut A right-wing political party founded in 1948 by Menachem Begin advocating Jewish sovereignty over all of historic Palestine

IAF Israel Air Force

IDF Israel Defence Force

Kach Extreme anti-Arab party founded by Meir Kahane

Likud A centre-right party founded by Menachem Begin in 1973

Maarah An alignment of Labour parties

Mafdal Israel Religious Party

Mapai A social democratic party that prevailed in Israel's early years

Mapam A Marxist-Zionist party

Meimad A moderate religious Zionist party

Mizrahi In the modern sense, a Jew of Middle Eastern or North African origin

Moledet Right-wing party advocating Arab emigration

Morasha A short-lived religious party

Mossad Institute for intelligence and special operations

Ometz A small breakaway party from Likud

Palmach A strike force in Israel's War of Independence

Pesah Passover

Progressive List for Peace An alliance of Jewish and Arab left-wing socialists

Purim Jewish festival memorializing Jewish redemption through the medium of Queen Esther

Rafi A breakaway party from Mapai led by David Ben-Gurion

Ratz Civil rights party advocating the separation of religion and the state

Shas A Haredi party found by Mizrahi Jews

Shinui Movement for Social Change party

Tami A Mizrahi-dominated party

Tehiya An extreme right-wing party

Telem A small short-lived party founded by Moshe Dayan

Tzomet A secular right-wing nationalist party

Ulpan Institute for the study of Hebrew

United Torah Haredi party of Ashkenazi Jews

Yeshiva College for studying the Torah

Yishuv The Jewish population in the pre-Israel period

Yisrael Be'Aliyah A party founded by Russian Jews headed by Natan Sharansky

Yom Kippur The Day of Covenant

NOTES

Introduction

1 Benson 1997, p. 133.

2 Tal 2004, p. 156.

3 Morris 2008, p. 204.

4 Kimche and Kimche 1960, p. 161, and Morris 2008, p. 88.

5 Luttwak and Horowitz 1975, p. 30.

6 As quoted by Lorch 1961, p. 152.

7 Ben-Gurion 1971, p. 180, and Joseph 1960, p. 158.

8 Hurewitz 1950, p. 155.

9 Van Creveld 1998, p. 99.

10 As quoted by Ben-Gurion 1969, p. 489.

11 See Pappe 2006.

12 See Stein 2009, p. 70.

13 Gelber 2006, p. 103.

14 Kimche and Kimche 1960, p. 122.

15 See Morris 2008, p. 146.

16 Shapira 2004, p. 372.

17 As quoted by Morris 2008, p. 409.

18 As quoted by Karsh 2008, p. 26.

19 Oz 2004, p. 342.

20 Black and Morris 1991, p. 38.

21 Schechtman 1952, p. 5.

22 Al-Haj 2004, p. 110; emphasis added.

23 See Teveth 1990, p. 224.

24 See Morris 2001.

25 As quoted by Lorch 1961, pp. 82–3.

26 As quoted by Karsh 2008, p. 27.

27 As quoted by Morris 2008, p. 162.

28 As quoted by Gelber 2006, p. 115.

29 Flapan 1987, p. 97.

30 See Harkabi 1967, p. 6.

31 As quoted by Peters 1984, p. 22.

32 As quoted by Bodansky 2002, p. 323.

33 Ben-Gurion 1969, p. 370.

34 Lissak 1999, p. 18.

35 Ibid.

36 As quoted by Hacohen 2003, p. 69.

37 Ibid., p. 92.

38 Ibid., p. 143.

39 Halevi and Klinov-Malul 1968, p. 77.

40 Gross 1997, p. 140.

41 Ben-Gurion 1969, p. 385.

42 Gross 1997, p. 143, and Horowitz 1967, p. 37.

43 Bar-On 1994, pp. 133–4.

44 Cohen 1964, p. 484.

45 Sheffer 1996, p. 798.

46 Cohen 1964, pp. 450–1.

47 Shlaim 2000, p. 56.

48 Sheffer 1996, p. 844.

49 As quoted by Shalom 1996, p. 118.

50 Golani 1998, p. 22.

51 Sheffer 1996, p. 627.

52 Gabbay 1959, p. 445.

53 Sheffer 1996, p. 503.

54 Eytan 1958, p. 73.

55 As quoted by Tessler 1994, p. 329.

56 See Shalom 1995, pp. 154–5.

57 Dayan 1976 (Hebrew edn), p. 110.

58 Luttwak and Horowitz 1975, p. 101.
59 Dayan 1976 (Hebrew edn), p. 111.
60 Milstein 1989, p. 108.
61 Tal 2004, p. 77.
62 As quoted by Gabbay 1959, p. 504.
63 As quoted by Ben-Gurion 1969, p. 521.
64 As quoted by Lorch 1961, p. 461.
65 All the information in this paragraph is derived from Ye'or 2005, p. 42.
66 Black and Morris 1991, p. 101.
67 Sheffer 1996, p. 863.
68 As quoted by Bar-On 1994, p. 32. The statement was drafted by Evelyn Shuckburgh on behalf of the UK and Francis Russell on behalf of the USA. Both were senior foreign affairs bureaucrats.
69 See Bar-Zohar 1975, p. 1165.
70 As quoted by Gabbay 1959, pp. 424–5.
71 Morris 2001, p. 299.
72 As quoted by Ben-Gurion 1971, p. 527.
73 As quoted by Meinertzhagen 1959, p. 352.
74 As quoted by Ben-Gurion 1969, p. 535, who in turn sourced the material from *Foreign Affairs*, January 1957.
75 Kyle 1991, p. 102.
76 Shlaim 2000, pp. 183–4.
77 It might be contended that it is illegitimate to include Transjordan. However, consider the following hypothetical scenario: Suppose that in 1921, when Transjordan was formed, the British also allocated to it the West Bank and Gaza and declared the remaining land to be Palestine. By that logic, Israel by the end of 1948 would have possessed the totality of the Palestinians' homeland.
78 Gilboa 1968, p. 40.
79 Becker 1984, p. 256.
80 Ibid., p. 41.
81 Ibid., pp. 41–2.
82 Ibid., p. 44.
83 Segev 2005, p. 235.
84 Such was the opinion of Yisrael Lior. See Haber 1987, p. 152.
85 As quoted by Gluska 2004, p. 110.

86 As quoted by Oren 2002, p. 64.

87 Dayan 1976, p. 310.

88 As quoted by Shaham 1998, p. 254.

89 As quoted by Oren 2002, p. 84.

90 Kimche and Bawly 1968, p. 99.

91 Dayan 1976, p. 311.

92 Ibid., p. 305.

93 As quoted by Kimche and Bawly 1968, p. 131.

94 Gilboa 1968, p. 192.

95 As quoted by Dayan 1976, p. 314.

96 As quoted by Kimche and Bawly 1968, p. 100.

97 Ibid., p. 101. What is not appreciated by many Westerners even to this day is that, within the Arab World there is a culture of bloodlust and revenge. To some extent this emanates from strongly held beliefs in the sacredness of personal and national honour, and that any derogation of this necessitates a violent response. However, not all Arab heads of state are so inclined. Despite all conflicts with him, Israel held a high regard for the integrity of King Hussein, and upon his death Israeli flags flew at half-mast. Political and media commentators referred to him as "a mench [a decent human being] with a kafiya." But, alas, Hussein had been one among few exceptions.

98 Yoel Marcus, "Truth Serum on the Tip of a Missile," *Haaretz*, June 17, 2003.

99 As quoted by Draper 1968, p. 98.

100 Gluska 2004, p. 395.

101 Ibid., p. 14.

102 Ezer Weizman later reminded his fellow officers that, "Because we had all lived in the shadow of the 1956 Campaign, none of us believed that on conquering territories we would be able to retain them." Ibid., p. 262.

103 Oren 2002, p. 176.

104 Ibid., p. 187.

105 Shlaim 2000, p. 244.

106 Oren 2002, p. 229.

107 Teveth 1970, p. 281.

108 Segev 2005, p. 460. Rabin's speech received widespread approba-

tion but in truth it was largely drafted and inspired by Colonel Mordechai Bar-On. On the other hand, it contained nothing that did not conform to Rabin's own notions and way of thinking.

109 Ibid., p. 584.
110 As quoted by Oren 2002, p. 317.

Chapter 1 The Early Aftermath of the Six-Day War

1 As quoted by Dayan 1976 (Hebrew edn), p. 494.
2 Segev 2005, pp. 421–3.
3 Morris 2001, p. 331.
4 Segev 2005, p. 426.
5 Weizman 1975, p. 297.
6 Dayan 1976, p. 398.
7 Ibid.
8 See Oren 2002, pp. 313–14.
9 Shlaim 2000, p. 254.
10 Rabin 1979, p. 265.
11 Segev 1993, p. 468.
12 As quoted by Kurzman 1983, p. 461; emphasis in the original.
13 Shaham 1998, p. 276.
14 Oren 2002, p. 314.
15 Segev 2005, p. 535.
16 Ibid., pp. 536–41.
17 See *Haaretz*, October 15, 2010.
18 Eban 1978, p. 430.
19 Ibid., p. 433.
20 Quandt 2005, p. 46.
21 See, for instance, Shlaim 2000, pp. 258–9.
22 As quoted ibid., p. 259.
23 As reproduced by Laqueur and Rubin 2001, p. 116.
24 Eban 1978, p. 451.
25 As quoted by Korn 1992, p. 33.
26 Eban 1977 p. 453.
27 As quoted by Eban 1978, p. 452.
28 Korn 1992, p. 38.
29 Shaham 1998, p. 301.
30 As quoted by Gilboa 1968, p. 262; emphasis added.

31 Burkett 2008, p. 231.
32 Shaham 1998, p. 304.
33 Shlaim 2000, p. 287.
34 Shaham 1998, p. 305.
35 As quoted ibid., p. 308.
36 Korn 1992, p. 141.
37 Eban 1992, p. 465.
38 Shaham 1998, p. 288.
39 Ibid., p. 313, Quandt 2005, p. 68.
40 Rabin 1979, p. 271.
41 As quoted by Korn 1992, p. 159.
42 Ibid., pp. 163–4.
43 Shaham 1998, p. 313.
44 Ibid., p. 296.
45 Korn 1992, p. 211.
46 Ibid.
47 As quoted by Morris 2001, p. 365.
48 Segev 2005, pp. 522–3.
49 Morris 2001, p. 366.
50 Segev 2005, p. 617.
51 In this context, it is worth mentioning that, while Jordanian border units were generally not involved directly in PLO actions, they did at least extend support to the saboteurs by way of helping them to cross the Jordan River, providing them with covering fire, and on occasion even shelling Israeli settlements. See Dayan 1976, p. 415.
52 Morris 2001, p. 369, suggests that 240 Arabs were killed, 250 were wounded and 141 were captured.
53 Tessler 1994, p. 425. Morris 2001, p. 369, suggests that Israel lost 33 dead and 161 wounded.
54 Dayan 1976, p. 417.
55 See Morris 2001, p. 370.
56 See Kadi 1969, pp. 137–41.
57 http://palwatch.org/main.aspx?fi=506&fld_id=506&doc_id=4037.
58 Morris 2001, p. 307.
59 Shaham 1998, p. 300.
60 Dayan 1976, p. 406.

61 Shaham 1998, p. 310.
62 *Jerusalem Post*, July 20, 2006 (article by Dan Izenberg).
63 Morris 2001, p. 377.
64 Dayan 1976, p. 431.
65 Ibid.
66 http://news.bbc.co.uk/onthisday/hi/dates/stories/june/9/new sid_4461000/4461735.stm.
67 Ibid.
68 Morris 2001, p. 374.
69 Rabin 1979, p. 311.
70 Kissinger 1979, p. 595.
71 Ibid., p. 626.
72 Morris 2001, p. 375.
73 Dayan 1976, p. 433.
74 Ensalaco 2007, p. 28.
75 Morris 2001, p. 370; emphasis added.
76 Ynetnews.com, January 26, 2008.
77 The Red Army Faction epitomizes the fact that, in essence, there is essentially little difference between extreme leftists and extreme rightists. One of its founding members, Horst Mahler, is currently a virulent anti-Semite and Holocaust denier. When asked in an interview about his transition from the extreme left to the extreme right, Mahler replied that his beliefs had not basically changed, since the enemy remained the same. See Stauber 2003.
78 Morris 2001, p. 382.
79 Shaham 1998, p. 330.
80 Kissinger 1982, pp. 626–8.
81 Ibid., p. 628.
82 Shaham 1998, p. 278.
83 Eban 1992, p. 462.
84 Morris 2001, p. 332.
85 As quoted by Mann 1998, p. 46.
86 Segev 2005, p. 610.
87 Ibid., p. 611.
88 Shaham 1988, p. 295.

Chapter 2 The War of Attrition and the Prelude to the Yom Kippur War

1 Shaham 1998, p. 280.
2 As quoted ibid., p. 281.
3 Korn 1992, p. 56.
4 Ibid., p. 63.
5 Shaham 1998, p. 297.
6 Korn 1992, p. 98.
7 Shaham 1998, p. 303.
8 It is not clear how many soldiers were to be posted to each fort. Figures variously suggested range from fifteen to thirty.
9 Dayan 1976, p. 451.
10 Bregman 2010, p. 98.
11 Korn 1992, pp. 101–4.
12 Heikal 1975, p. 45.
13 As quoted by Bregman 2010, p. 96.
14 Bar-Joseph 2001, p. 55.
15 www.yadlashiryon.com/Info/hi_show.aspx?id=51099&t=3.
16 Korn 1992, pp. 169–70.
17 Ibid., pp. 175–6.
18 Morris 2001, p. 353.
19 Korn 1992, p. 174.
20 Heikal 1975, p. 55.
21 Bar-Joseph 2001, p. 56.
22 Shaham 1998, p. 315, Morris 2001, p. 355.
23 Korn 1992, p. 173.
24 Ibid., p. 174
25 Kissinger 1979, p. 569.
26 Korn 1992, p. 191.
27 Ibid., p. 5.
28 Shaham 1998, p. 315.
29 Dayan 1976, p. 435.
30 Korn 1992, p. 194.
31 Ibid., p. 183.
32 Morris 2001, p. 357.
33 Korn 1992, p. 192.
34 See ibid., p. 231.
35 Ibid., p. 232.

36 Schueftan 2004, p. 147.

37 Shaham 1998, p. 311.

38 As quoted by Korn 1992, pp. 215–16.

39 Shaham 1998, p. 307.

40 As quoted by Korn 1992, p. 221.

41 Burkett 2008, p. 280.

42 Korn 1992, p. 241.

43 For details pertaining to the first plan, see chapter 1.

44 Korn 1992, p. 255.

45 Shaham 1998, p. 317.

46 Ibid., p. 317.

47 Bregman 2010, p. 101.

48 Korn 1992, p. 117.

49 Ibid., p. 114.

50 Ibid., p. 116.

51 Ibid., p. 6.

52 As quoted by Yehuda Avner in the *Jerusalem Post*, August 16, 2008.

53 Shaham 1998, p. 318.

54 As quoted by Korn 1992, p. 269.

55 Morris 2001, p. 361.

56 Bar-Joseph 2001, p. 64.

57 Braun 1992, p. 12.

58 Dayan 1976 (Hebrew edn), p. 569.

59 Bregman 2010, pp. 103–4.

60 Rabin 1979, p. 345.

61 Shaham 1998, p. 321.

62 Ibid., p. 322.

63 Ibid.

64 Korn 1992, p. 277.

65 Braun 1992, p. 16.

66 As quoted by Bartov 1981, p. 170.

67 Kissinger 1979, p. 1279.

68 See Bar-Joseph 2001, p. 89.

69 Kissinger 1982, p. 215.

70 Heikal 1975, p. 201.

71 Rabinovich 2004 p. 12.

72 Bar-Joseph 2001, p. 123.

73 Shaham 1998, p. 328.

74 Heikal 1975, p. 175.

75 Kissinger 1982, p. 220.

76 Shaham 1998, p. 329.

77 Bartov 1981, pp. 175–7.

78 Rabinovich 2004, p. 43.

79 As quoted ibid.

80 Shaham 1998, p. 338.

81 Bar-Joseph 2001, p. 155.

82 *Haaretz*, July 17, 2008.

83 Bregman 2010, pp. 108–9.

84 Bar-Joseph 2001, p. 93.

85 As quoted ibid., p. 46.

86 Ibid., p. 117.

87 Ibid., p. 173.

88 Golan 2004, p. 159.

89 Bregman 2010, p. 116.

90 Schiff 1974, p. 7.

91 Bar-Joseph 2001, p. 225.

92 Dayan was prone to make Pollyannaish forecasts that were shortly disproved. For example, in April 1967, while addressing Harvard academics, he predicted that there would not be any outbreak of serious hostilities for at least another ten years. Two months later the Six-Day War arose.

93 Bar-Joseph 2001, p. 229.

94 Rabinovich 2004, p. 28.

95 As quoted by Nakdimon 1982, p. 17.

96 As quoted by Bar-Joseph 2001, p. 230.

97 Golan 2004, p. 160.

98 Dayan 1976 (Hebrew edn), p. 571, and Bartov 1981, p. 229. Note: the number of Syrian planes destroyed was confirmed as twelve and not thirteen, as is commonly cited.

99 Dayan 1976, p. 472.

100 Rabinovich 2004, pp. 33–4.

101 Bar-Joseph 2001, pp. 190–1.

102 See ibid., p. 189.

103 Braun 1992, p. 39.

104 Dayan 1976 (Hebrew edn), p. 571.

105 Bar-Joseph 2001, p. 244.

106 Bregman 2010, p. 119.

107 Rabinovich 2004, pp. 48–53.

108 Bartov 1981, p. 239.

109 *Jerusalem Post*, September 25, 1998.

110 Braun 1992, pp. 44–5.

111 Bar-Joseph 2001, p. 252.

112 Rabinovich 2004, p. 57.

113 Ibid., pp. 69–70.

114 Haber 1987, p. 20.

115 Bar-Joseph 2001, p. 258.

116 Nakdimon 1982, p. 62.

117 Braun 1992, p. 46.

118 Rabinovich 2004, pp. 58–9.

119 As quoted ibid., p. 60.

120 As quoted by Bar-Joseph 2001, p. 155.

121 Amos Gilboa, in *Maariv*, September 29, 1998.

122 Bar-Joseph 2001, p. 267.

123 Ibid., p. 269.

124 Ibid., p. 272.

125 Ibid., p. 205.

126 Ibid., p. 203.

127 Bartov 1981, p. 231.

128 Rabinovich 2004, p. 56.

129 As quoted ibid., p. 65.

130 Dayan 1976, p. 475.

131 Braun 1992, p. 53.

132 Rabinovich 2004, p. 66.

133 Heikal 1975, p. 31.

134 As quoted by Braun 1992, p. 58

135 Bar-Joseph 2001, p. 289.

136 As quoted by Rabinovich 2004, p. 75.

137 According to Nakdimon 1982, p. 54, Sadat fully briefed the Soviets as early as September 22.

138 Bar-Joseph 2001, p. 292. On the other hand, Heikal 1975, p. 24,

holds that the Egyptians provided the Russians only with a general warning that war was imminent.

139 Bar-Joseph 2001, p. 314.
140 Ibid., p. 325.
141 Ibid., p. 333.
142 As quoted by Braun 1992, p. 64.
143 As quoted by Bar-Joseph 2001, p. 334.
144 Bartov 1981, p. 266.
145 Bar-Joseph 2001, p. 363.
146 Rabinovich 2004, p. 5
147 Dayan 1976 (Hebrew edn), p. 583.
148 Article by Motti Ashkenazi in the *Jerusalem Post*, October 3, 2003.
149 As quoted by Nakdimon 1982, p. 81.

Chapter 3 The Yom Kippur War

1 Bar-Joseph 2001, as translated by the author.
2 Haber 1987, p. 13.
3 Nakdimon 1982, p. 107.
4 As quoted by Bar-Joseph 2001, p. 327.
5 As quoted by Rabinovich 2004, p. 87.
6 Dayan 1976 (Hebrew edn), p. 575.
7 As quoted by Braun 1992, p. 71.
8 Ibid., p. 74.
9 Ibid., p. 69.
10 As quoted by Bartov 1981, p. 279.
11 Haber 1987, p. 14.
12 Kissinger 1982, p. 451.
13 Ibid., p. 477.
14 Dayan 1976 p. 464.
15 As quoted by Bar-Joseph 2001, p. 352.
16 As quoted ibid., p. 375.
17 As quoted by Braun 1992, p. 74.
18 Nakdimon 1982, p. 113.
19 Haber 1987, p. 28.
20 As quoted by Slater 1991, p. 348.
21 As quoted ibid., p. 349.
22 See Rabinovich 2004, p. 99.

23 Schiff 1974, p. 46.

24 Ibid., p. 108.

25 Dayan 1976 (Hebrew edn), p. 615.

26 The Egyptians wanted to commence fighting at 6 p.m., whereas the Syrians were keen to strike out at dawn. The actual timing of 2 p.m. turned out to be a compromise solution.

27 Rabinovich 2004, p. 242.

28 Ibid., p. 54.

29 Ibid., p. 55.

30 As quoted by Bar-Joseph 2001, p. 360.

31 As quoted by Braun 1992, p. 87.

32 *Maariv*, September 29, 1998.

33 As quoted by Heikal 1975, p. 29.

34 Ibid., p. 207.

35 Bregman 2010, p. 133.

36 Bar-Joseph 2001, p. 134.

37 Braun 1992, p. 81.

38 Bartov 1981, p. 294.

39 Braun 1992, p. 83.

40 Heikal 1975, p. 15.

41 Bartov 1981, p. 204.

42 As quoted by Morris 2001, p. 419.

43 As quoted by Bar-Joseph 2001, p. 386.

44 Ibid., p. 389.

45 Bregman 2010, p. 134.

46 Dayan 1976 (Hebrew edn), p. 504.

47 Dunstan 2007, p. 33.

48 Dayan 1976, p. 480.

49 According to Heikal 1975, p. 43, there no fewer than 110,000 graduates of universities and institutes of higher learning in the Egyptian armed forces.

50 Bar-Joseph 2001, p. 371.

51 Dayan 1976 (Hebrew edn), p. 618.

52 Dayan 1976 p. 486.

53 Dayan 1976 (Hebrew edn), p. 595.

54 Rabinovich 2004, p. 175.

55 Ibid., p. 177. It was not the first time that Dayan, as minister

of defence, had bypassed the chief of staff to direct orders for a military engagement. During the Six-Day War, he intervened by contacting Elazar, then head of Northern Command, to attack Syria without first consulting with Rabin, then chief of staff.

56 Bar-Joseph 2001, p. 378.
57 Rabinovich 2004, pp. 189–90.
58 Sharon 2006 pp. 4–5.
59 As quoted by Morris 2001, p. 406.
60 Schiff 1974, p. 93.
61 Dunstan 2007, p. 171.
62 Bar-Joseph 2001, p. 390.
63 Dayan 1976 (Hebrew edn), p. 598.
64 Braun 1992, p. 98.
65 In those early days of the war Meir reputedly had contemplated suicide. See Bar-Joseph 2001, p. 394.
66 Nakdimon 1982, p. 143.
67 Rabinovich 2004, pp. 219–20.
68 Bar-Joseph 2001, p. 391.
69 *Time*, April 12, 1976, p. 13.
70 Morris 2001, p. 405.
71 As quoted by Braun 1992, p. 179. The Egyptians had used chemical weapons with impunity in Yemen.
72 Not enough time had transpired to assemble the requisite numbers for a more decisive battle.
73 Rabinovich 2004, p. 240.
74 Ibid., p. 246.
75 As quoted by Braun 1992, p. 122.
76 Morris 2001, p. 418.
77 Braun 1992, p. 109.
78 Dayan 1976, p. 504, and Morris 2001, p. 419.
79 Dayan 1976, p. 505.
80 Schiff 1974, p. 134.
81 Dayan 1976 (Hebrew edn), p. 618.
82 Shaham 1998, p. 347.
83 From the personal memoirs of Chava Keren, one-time communications reservist in the Southern Command headquarters.
84 Dayan 1976, p. 488.

85 Dayan 1976 (Hebrew edn), p. 613.
86 Dunstan 2007, p. 172.
87 Schiff 1974, pp. 194–5.
88 Bartov 1981, p. 473.
89 Shaham 1998, p. 348.
90 Morris 2001, pp. 392 and 410.
91 Braun 1992, p. 161.
92 Morris 2001, p. 392.
93 Heikal 1975, p. 197.
94 From Morris 2001, p. 393, derived in turn from Saad El-Shazly, *The Crossing of the Suez* (San Francisco: American Mideast Research, 1980), pp. 83–4, and from Bar-Joseph 2001, p. 80.
95 Bar-Joseph 2001, p. 138.
96 This was not understood by the Israelis at the time.
97 Dunstan 2007, p. 80.
98 Morris 2001, p. 423.
99 Nakdimon 1982, p. 164.
100 Schiff 1974, p. 205.
101 Rabinovich 2004, p. 323.
102 Nakdimon 1982, p. 165.
103 Ibid., p. 173.
104 Cordova 1977, p. 46.
105 Haber 1987, p. 29.
106 Nakdimon 1982, p. 190.
107 Schiff 1974, p. 198.
108 On this score there is some debate. Some IDF officers believed it to be the case, but others pointed to an absence of tank replacements as well as artillery pieces. As to planes, their amounts fell short of Israeli requests and expectations. See Nakdimon 1982, p. 190.
109 Shaham 1998, p. 351.
110 Braun 1992, p. 190.
111 Ibid., p. 286.
112 Bartov 1981, p. 484.
113 Rabinovich 2004, p. 393.
114 As quoted by Dunstan 2007, p. 98.
115 Morris 2001, p. 425.

116 Schiff 1974, p. 238.

117 Ibid., p. 246.

118 Braun 1992, p. 210.

119 Dayan 1976 (Hebrew edn), p. 654.

120 Ibid., p. 655.

121 Rabinovich 2004, p. 441.

122 Bregman 2010, p. 141.

123 Morris 2001, p. 430.

124 Rabinovich 2004, p. 475.

125 Braun 1992, p. 252.

126 Dayan 1976 (Hebrew edn), p. 662.

127 Braun 1992, p. 242.

128 Kissinger 1982, p. 608.

129 Ibid., p. 610.

130 Dayan 1976 (Hebrew edn), p. 668.

131 Ibid., p. 669.

132 Ibid., pp. 678–9.

133 United Nations, *World Population Prospects: The 2002 Revision Population Database* (New York: United Nations Population Division, 2003).

134 World Health Organization, *World Health Report 2004*.

135 Rabinovich 2004, p. 498.

136 Bregman 2010, p. 142.

137 Bartov 1981, p. 585.

138 Schiff 1974, p. 297.

139 Dorit Gabai, in *Maariv*, September 29, 1998.

140 Mical Amdur, ibid.

141 Sharon 2006, pp. 100–1.

142 As quoted by Braun 1992, p. 341.

143 Rabinovich 2004, p. 271.

144 *Maariv*, September 29, 1998.

145 Ibid.

146 Braun 1992, p. 251.

147 Schiff 1974, p. 89.

148 Sharon 2006, pp. 23, 27, 31.

149 Rabinovich 2004, p. 439.

150 Schiff 1974, p. 174.

151 Yonatan Paz, in *Maariv*, September 29, 1998.
152 See Phillips 2010.
153 Rabinovich 2004, p. 508.
154 Morris 2001, p. 432.
155 Heikal 1975, p. 258.
156 Dayan 1976 (Hebrew edn), p. 692.
157 Bar-Joseph 2001, p. 131.
158 Wistrich 2010, p. 282.

Chapter 4 Major Events over the Years 1974–1979

 1 Nakdimon 1982, p. 262.
 2 Ibid., p. 263.
 3 Shaham 1998, p. 362.
 4 Nakdimon 1982, p. 275.
 5 Ibid., p. 294.
 6 Rabin 1979, p. 411.
 7 Nakdimon 1982, p. 238.
 8 Rabin 1979, pp. 415–16.
 9 As quoted by Bartov 1981, p. 528.
10 Rabin 1979, p. 413.
11 Nakdimon 1982, p. 304.
12 Rabin 1979, p. 416.
13 Nakdimon 1982, p. 323.
14 Shaham 1998, p. 365.
15 Ibid., p. 366.
16 Rabin 1979, p. 417.
17 Ibid., pp. 417–18.
18 As quoted by David Isaac, Arutz Sheva – IsraelNationalNews.com June 28, 2011.
19 Burkett 2008, p. 366.
20 Rabin 1979, p. 433.
21 Ibid., pp. 435–6.
22 www.mideastweb.org/Kahan_report.htm.
23 The term "Palestinian refugee camps" is a deliberate misnomer, since virtually all are built-up areas where people live under bricks and mortar.
24 Rabin 1979, p. 503.

25 Ibid., p. 534.
26 See Peres 1995, pp. 191–9.
27 Rabin 1979, p. 507.
28 Mann 1998, p. 162.
29 Shaham 1998, p. 394.
30 Slater 1991, p. 391.
31 Shaham 1998, p. 357.
32 Ibid., p. 377.
33 Rabin 1979, pp. 486–7.
34 Shaham 1998, p. 378.
35 Slater 1991, p. 397.
36 Ibid., p. 401.
37 See Morris 2001, p. 448.
38 Ibid., p. 451.
39 Shaham 1998, p. 400.
40 As quoted ibid., p. 401.
41 Slater 1991, p. 405.
42 Morris 2001, p. 456.
43 Ibid., p. 457.
44 http://peacenow.org.il/eng/content/officers-letter-march-1978.
45 Morris 2001, p. 463.
46 As quoted ibid., p. 466.
47 Shaham 1998, p. 411.
48 Among those that did not support the resolution were Yitzhak
    Shamir and Moshe Arens. Although the yes vote was carried by 70
    percent of the Knesset members, a survey conducted soon there-
    after indicated that 82 percent of the public supported the Camp
    David Accords. See ibid.
49 Slater 1991, pp. 420–4.
50 Mann 1998, p. 168.
51 Slater 1991, p. 428.
52 Dayan 1976 (Hebrew edn), p. 729.
53 Rabin 1979, p. 549.
54 Ibid.
55 Ibid., p. 551.
56 Peres 1995, p. 198.
57 Shaham 1998, p. 379.

58 Ibid.
59 Rabin 1979, p. 550
60 Slater 1991, p. 399.
61 Shaham 1998, p. 407.
62 Morris 2001, p. 488.
63 Dayan 1976 (Hebrew edn), p. 718.
64 Ibid.
65 Ibid., p. 722.
66 www.jafi.org.il/JewishAgency/English/Israel/Partnerships/Reg ions/Nahariya/News/2007/news-0706-yom-hazikaron.htm.
67 Reprinted speech in Laqueur and Rubin 2001, p. 175.
68 Shaham 1998, p. 370.
70 www.shabak.gov.il/English/History/Affairs/Pages/TheRefriger ator-en.aspx.
71 Ullman 1978.
72 Karmon 2005, p. 94.
73 Rabin 1979, p. 528.
74 Ibid., p. 532.
75 Ibid., p. 533.
76 Shaham 1998, p. 384.
77 "A Sabbath of Terror," *Time*, March 20, 1978.
78 *Al-Hayat Al Jadida*, June 17, 2010.
79 www.ynetnews.com/articles/0,7340,L-3686831,00.html.
80 Shaham 1998, pp. 405–6.
81 Ibid., p. 368.
82 Ibid.
83 Unless otherwise stated, all the data in this paragraph are derived from Karni 1979.
84 See ibid., pp. 68–9.
85 Shaham 1998, p. 419.
86 Elon 1972, p. 310.
87 Werner 1983, p. 629.
88 Ibid., p. 635.
89 Ibid.
90 Rabin 1979, pp. 554–5.
91 Ibid., p. 556.
92 Ibid.

Chapter 5 The Decade of the 1980s

1 Shaham 1998, p. 423.
2 Ibid., p. 425.
3 Ibid., p. 426.
4 Ibid., p. 430.
5 Ibid., p. 439.
6 www.un.org/en/peacekeeping/missions/unifil/.
7 Schiff and Ya'ari 1984, p. 36.
8 Ibid.
9 Shaham 1998, p. 434.
10 As quoted by Morris 2001, p. 498.
11 Schiff and Ya'ari 1984, p. 80.
12 Ibid., p. 82.
13 Ibid., p. 84.
14 Ibid., p. 94.
15 Shiffer 1984, p. 70.
16 Ibid., pp. 70–1.
17 Ibid.
18 Ibid., p. 84.
19 Ibid., p. 87.
20 Shaham 1998, p. 443.
21 Naor 1986, pp. 44–5.
22 As quoted ibid., p. 47.
23 As quoted by Morris 2001, p. 514.
24 As quoted by Naor 1986, p. 49.
25 As quoted by Schiff and Ya'ari 1984, pp. 104–5.
26 As quoted by Naor 1986, p. 50.
27 Ibid., p. 16.
28 Schiff and Ya'ari 1984, p. 109.
29 Naor 1986, p. 51.
30 Gabriel 1984, p. 81.
31 Schiff and Ya'ari 1984, pp. 112–13.
32 Morris 2001, p. 523.
33 Naor 1986, p. 67.
34 Ibid., p. 69.
35 Schiff and Ya'ari 1984, p. 167.
36 As quoted ibid., p. 186.

37 Ibid., p. 193.
38 Naor 1986, p. 88.
39 Schiff and Ya'ari 1984, p. 195.
40 Ibid., p. 209.
41 Ibid., p. 211.
42 As quoted ibid., p. 212.
43 Ibid., p. 213.
44 Ibid., p. 221.
45 Ibid., p. 225.
46 Naor 1986, p. 138.
47 Shiffer 1984, p. 114.
48 Schiff and Ya'ari 1984, p. 228.
49 Shiffer 1984, p. 120.
50 Ibid., p. 122.
51 As quoted ibid., p. 124.
52 As quoted by Schiff and Ya'ari 1984, p. 258.
53 As quoted ibid., p. 252. There is no indication that Schiff actually accepted Sokar's invitation.
54 As quoted ibid., p. 261.
55 Shiffer 1984 p. 125.
56 As quoted ibid., p. 125.
57 As quoted ibid., p. 126.
58 Ibid., p. 448.
59 Ibid.
60 Elliot Jager, "Power and Politics: Breaking Begin," *Jerusalem Post*, July 3, 2007.
61 www.mideastweb.org/Kahan_report.htm.
62 Ibid.
63 Ibid.
64 Schiff and Ya'ari 1984, p. 298.
65 William Smith, "Carnage in Lebanon," *Time*, October 31, 1983.
66 Gabriel 1984, p. 176.
67 Ibid.
68 Shaham 1998, p. 460.
69 Ibid., p. 461.
70 Arens 1995, p. 23.

71 Shaham 1998, p. 466.
72 Ibid., p. 498.
73 Ibid., p. 500.
74 Ibid., p. 503.
75 Ibid., p. 467.
76 Sprinzak 1991, p. 13.
77 Tzomet supported the notion of a separation of state and religion.
78 Sprinzak 1991, p. 86.
79 Ibid., p. 88.
80 Ibid., p. 87.
81 Shaham 1998, p. 423.
82 Sprinzak 1991, p. 98.
83 Karsh 2002, p. 49.
84 Shalom and Hendel 2010, p. 211.
85 "What Happened on Bus 300," *Jerusalem Post*, December 28, 2001.
86 Thomas Friedman, "Syria-Based Group Says it Staged Israeli Raid," *New York Times*, November 27, 1987.
87 Shalev 1991, p. 30.
88 Schiff and Ya'ari 1989, pp. 29-30.
89 Shalev 1991, p. 29.
90 Schiff and Ya'ari 1989, p. 30.
91 Ibid., p. 90.
92 Ibid., p. 97.
93 Ibid., p. 85.
94 Shalev 1991, p. 17.
95 Schiff and Ya'ari 1989, p. 18.
96 Shaham 1998, p. 483.
97 As quoted by Shalom and Hendel 2010, p. 217.
98 Ibid.
99 Amira Hass, "Broken Bones and Broken Hopes," *Haaretz*, November 4, 2005.
100 On February 5, 1988, in the West Bank town of Salim, IDF soldiers forced four suspected riot leaders to lie on the ground and then ordered an army bulldozer driver to push a mound of earth over them. Fortunately, the victims were dug out alive by villagers as soon as the soldiers left. The four IDF soldiers found responsible for that atrocious crime were at first given only suspended

sentences, but after the prosecution appealed they received brief custodial sentences, most of which were fulfilled by time served while awaiting trial.

101 Shalom and Hendel 2010, p. 225.
102 www.news1.co.il/Archive/001-D-206364-00.html?tag=09-17-36 [in Hebrew].
103 Shalev 1991, p. 71.
104 A dunam is a quarter acre.
105 Shalev 1991, p. 79.
106 Shaham 1998, pp. 497–8.
107 Shalev 1991, p. 123.
108 Ibid., p. 7.
109 Ibid., p. 72.
110 Ibid., p. 187.
111 As quoted ibid., p. 132.
112 As quoted by Karsh 2003, p. 51.
113 Efraim Karsh and Asaf Romirowsky, "Land for War," *Wall Street Journal*, August 5, 2011.
114 As quoted by Shalev 1991, p. 140.
115 Ibid.

Chapter 6 The Fateful 1990s

1 Michael Omer-Man, "This Week in History: Deadly Riots on the Temple Mount," *Jerusalem Post*, October, 7 2011.
2 Mark Thomson et al., "Iraq: The Great Scud Hunt," *Time*, December 23, 2002.
3 Shaham 1998, pp. 510–11.
4 Ibid., p. 512.
5 Ibid., p. 514.
6 As quoted by Segev 1998, p. 126.
7 Shaham 1998, p. 516.
8 Israeli 2012, p. 12.
9 Shaham 1998, p. 152.
10 *The Telegraph-Herald*, December 15, 1992.
11 Shaham 1998, p. 524.
12 Ibid., p. 524.
13 Israeli 2012, p. 28.

14 Ibid., pp. 42–3.
15 Carmon 1994, p. 26.
16 Ibid., p. 27.
17 As quoted by Segev 1998, p. 210.
18 Bodansky 2002, p. 96.
19 As quoted by Segev 1998, pp. 213–16.
20 Ibid., p. 216.
21 Israeli 2012, p. 3.
22 Carmon 1994, p. 28.
23 Adopted at the conclusion of the Yom Kippur War and calling for negotiations for the establishment of a just and durable Middle East peace.
24 As quoted by Bodansky 2002, p. 96.
25 Ibid., p. 96.
26 Carmon 1994, p. 29.
27 Karsh 2003, p. 59.
28 As quoted ibid., p. 62.
29 Karsh 2003 (Hebrew edn), p. 17.
30 Ibid.
31 Bruck 1996, p. 72.
32 Levin 2005, p. 322.
33 www.knesset.gov.il/history/eng/eng_hist13.htm.
34 www.mfa.gov.il/mfa/foreignpolicy/peace/mfadocuments/pages/remarks%20by%20pm%20yitzhak%20rabin%20at%20signing%20of%20dop%20-%2013.aspx.
35 See Shalom and Hendel 201, p. 32.
36 Sprinzak 1999, p. 250.
37 Ibid., p. 251.
38 Savir 1998, pp. 139–40.
39 3(3) of article III of annex 1 of the Gaza–Jericho Agreement, reproduced at www.mfa.gov.il/MFA/Peace%20Process/Guide%20to%20the%20Peace%20Process/Gaza-Jericho%20Agremeent%20Annex%20I.
40 Gal Luft, *The Palestinian Security Services: Between Police and Army*, Research Memorandum no. 36, Washington, DC: Washington Institute for Near East Policy, November 1998.
41 Reproduced at www.mfa.gov.il/MFA/Peace+Process/Guide+to+

the+Peace+Process/Agreement+on+Gaza+Strip+and+Jericho+A rea.htm.

42 Michael Parks, "Israel Seeks Arafat Vow to Back Pact," *Los Angeles Times*, May 24, 1994.
43 Ibid.
44 Karsh 2003 (Hebrew edn), p. 8.
45 Harel and Issacharoff 2004, p. 43.
46 www.mfa.gov.il/MFA/Peace+Process/Guide+to+the+Peace+ Process/THE+ISRAELI-PALESTINIAN+INTERIM+ AGREEMENT+-+Annex+I.htm.
47 Associated Press, March 31, 1998.
48 Luft, *The Palestinian Security Services: Between Police and Army*, p. 7.
49 Gal Luft, "The Mirage of a Demilitarized Palestine," *Middle East Quarterly*, Summer 2001.
50 Ibid.
51 Ibid., and Amos Harel, "Revving up for a Confrontation," *Haaretz*, 6 July 2000.
52 Seliktar 2009, p. 57.
53 Leora Frankel-Schlosberg, "The Palestinian New Game," *Columbia Journalism Review*, May–June 1996.
54 Roy 1994, p. 91.
55 Sam Wilson, "The Mystery of Arafat's Money," BBC News, November 11, 2004, http://news.bbc.co.uk/2/hi/middle_east/ 3995769.stm.
56 Ibid.
57 Bergman 2002, p. 125.
58 As quoted ibid., pp. 153–4.
59 Ibid., p. 114.
60 Ibid., p. 115.
61 Ibid.
62 Seliktar 2009, p. 139.
63 Harel and Issacharoff 2004, p. 51.
64 Levin 2005, p. 387.
65 As quoted by Karsh 2003, p. 114.
66 Rabin 1979, p. 583.
67 As quoted by Shaham 1998, p. 546.
68 Sprinzak 1999, p. 276.

69 As quoted by Levin 2005, p. 345.
70 www.iris.org.il/quotes/stockhlm.htm.
71 *Jerusalem Report*, April 4, 1996.
72 Ya'alon 2008, p. 25.
73 Yigal Carmon, "So Now We All Know," *Jerusalem Post*, January 5, 1996.
74 *Jerusalem Post*, March 15, 1996.
75 Seliktar 2009, p. 29.
76 Bergman 2002, p. 88.
77 Karsh 2003, p. 3.
78 As quoted by Schueftan 2011, p. 145.
79 Karsh 2003 (Hebrew edn), p. 42, quoting from Sneh's book *Navigation in a Dangerous Area*, Tel Aviv: Yidiot Ahronoth, 2002, pp. 22–4.
80 As quoted by Karsh 2003 (Hebrew edn), p. 39.
81 Seliktar 2009, p. 43.
82 See for example Levin 2005, p. 523.
83 Ya'alon 2008, p. 75.
84 See Levin 2005, passim.
85 Ibid., p. 283.
86 Ibid.
87 Ibid.
88 Ari Shavit, in *Haaretz*, December 26, 1997.
89 As quoted by Harel and Issacharoff 2004, p. 142.
90 Seliktar 2009, p. 104.
91 As quoted by Segev 1998, p. 16.
92 As quoted ibid., p. 17.
93 As quoted ibid., p. 18.
94 Seliktar 2009, p. 106.
95 See Levin 2005, p. 398.
96 Andrea Levin, "The Media's Tunnel Vision," *Middle East Quarterly*, December 1996.
97 Ibid.
98 Neil MacFarquhar, in *New York Times*, October 4, 1996.
99 Levin, "The Media's Tunnel Vision."
100 Levin 2005, p. 400.
101 Karsh 2003 (Hebrew edn), p. 22.

102 As quoted by Levin, "The Media's Tunnel Vision."

103 Levin 2005, p. 401.

104 Ibid., pp. 403–4.

105 As quoted by Douglas Feith, "Wye and the Road to War," *Commentary*, January 1999.

106 Ibid.

107 As quoted ibid.

108 Levin 2005, p. 410.

109 Indyk 2009, p. 199.

110 "Habash Won't Meet Arafat unless He Remains Committed to Israel's Destruction," *World Tribune*, July 29, 1999.

111 Zeev Begin, "Etched in Their Minds," *Haaretz*, June 4, 2003.

112 As quoted by Khaled Abu Toameh, "Kaddoumi: PLO Charter Was Never Changed," *Jerusalem Post*, April 22, 2004.

113 Levin 2005, p. 411.

114 Harel and Issacharoff 2004, p. 66.

115 Levin 2005, pp. 415–16.

116 Seliktar 2009, p. 138.

117 Yossi Klein Halevi, "An Insane Gamble Turns into a National Disgrace," *Los Angeles Times*, February 3, 2000.

118 Amos Oz, in an interview in *Haaretz*, March 17, 2000, and as quoted by Martin Sherman in Ynetnews.com, October 8, 2006.

119 Levin 2005, pp. 420–1.

120 Bodansky 2002, p. 318.

121 Morris 2009, p. 138.

122 Harel and Issacharoff 2004, p. 68.

123 As quoted by Karsh 2003, p. 162; emphasis added.

124 http://palwatch.org/main.aspx?fi=506&fld_id=506&doc_id=4037.

125 Harel and Issacharoff 2004, p. 69.

126 Bodansky 2002, pp. 320–1.

127 As reported by Schueftan 2011, p. 151.

Chapter 7 *The al-Aqsa Intifada*

1 Harel and Issacharoff 2004, p. 67.

2 Karsh 2003 (Hebrew edn), p. 28.

3 *Al-Hayat* [London and Beirut], November 23–4, 2000, as cited at http://zionism-israel.com/hdoc/Abbas_ROR.htm.

4 Karsh 2003 (Hebrew edn), p. 28.
5 http://cnsnews.com/news/article/israels-sharon-rejects-us-view-his-temple-mount-visit.
6 Shalom and Hendel 2010, p. 239.
7 Harel and Issacharoff 2004, p. 16.
8 Morris 2009, p. 140.
9 Jacob Dallal, "Treasure Lost," *Jerusalem Post*, January 28, 2000.
10 Harel and Issacharoff 2004, p. 19.
11 Bodansky 2002, p. 281.
12 www.mfa.gov.il/MFA/Terrorism-+Obstacle+to+Peace/Palestinian+terror+since+2000/Victims+of+Palestinian+Violence+and+Terrorism+sinc.htm and Harel and Issacharoff 2004, p. 25.
13 MEMRI (Middle East Media Research Insitute), Special Dispatch no. 194, March 21, 2000.
14 Independent Media Review Analysis, at www.imra.org.il/story.php3?id=12196. Al Din can be seen making those remarks on YouTube at www.youtube.com/watch?v=a-WYBPmhm4c.
15 MEMRI TV, December 16, 2012.
16 As quoted by Khaled Abu Toameh, "How the War Began," *Jerusalem Post*, September 19, 2002.
17 Ibid.
18 As quoted by Karsh 2003 (Hebrew edn), p. 23.
19 Ibid. With regard to Barghouti, Amos Oz, Israel's leading novelist and ardent peace advocate, revealed the naivety that typifies Israelis incapable of coming to terms with the reality in which they live. In March 2011 Oz sent Barghouti (currently in an Israeli prison serving a series of life sentences for murder) a copy of one of his books. Included was a personal dedication that ended "Hoping to meet soon in peace and freedom." See www.ynetnews.com/articles/0,7340,L-4043248,00.html.
20 Seliktar 2009, p. 159.
21 Bodansky 2002, p. 317.
22 John Burns, "Palestinian Summer Camp Offers the Games of War," *New York Times*, August 3, 2000.
23 As quoted by Harel and Issacharoff 2008, p. 38.
24 Ibid., p. 64.
25 As quoted by Karsh 2003 (Hebrew edn), p. 36.

26 Ibid.

27 Jeffrey Goldberg, "Letter from Gaza," *New Yorker*, July 9, 2001.

28 Karsh 2003 (Hebrew edn), p. 26.

29 www.mideastweb.org/second_intifada_timeline.htm.

30 Nidra Poller, "Myth, Fact, and the al-Dura Affair," *Commentary*, September 2005.

31 Ibid.

32 Ibid.

33 Ibid.

34 Melanie Phillips, "The Al-Durah Blood Libel," *The Spectator*, November 16, 2007. Melanie Phillips attended the trial.

35 Scholars for Peace in the Middle East, no. 4101, May 29, 2008, http://pjmedia.com/blog/french-court-vindicates-al-dura-hoax-critic/.

36 www.google.com/hostednews/afp/article/ALeqM5jk7Y0jSIRhd UqmhCERYE77n0-xOA?docId=CNG.da5b79e3c3c298d3b7461 781e8a4e77b.7a1.

37 www.ynetnews.com/articles/0,7340,L-4190373,00.html.

38 Harel and Issacharoff 2004, p. 29.

39 Ibid., p. 89.

40 Ibid., p. 97.

41 Ibid., p. 93.

42 Ibid., p. 94.

43 Benny Morris, "Camp David and After," *New York Review of Books*, June 13, 2002.

44 Bergman 2002, p. 66.

45 Bodansky 2002, p. 357.

46 http://news.bbc.co.uk/2/hi/middle_east/956738.stm.

47 Mark Seager, "I'll Have Nightmares the Rest of my Life," *Sunday Telegraph*, October 15, 2000.

48 Lee Hockstader, "Infamous Killer or Mistaken ID?," *Washington Post*, July 7, 2001.

49 MEMRI, Special Dispatch no. 138, October 13, 2000.

50 William Orme, "A Parallel Mideast Battle: Is it News or Incitement?," *New York Times*, October 24, 2000.

51 http://mfa.gov.il/MFA/MFA-Archive/2000/Pages/Coverage%20

of%20Oct%2012%20Lynch%20in%20Ramallah%20by%20 Italian%20TV.aspx.

52 Harel and Issacharoff 2004, p. 99.

53 Ibid., p. 99.

54 Morris 2009, pp. 146–50.

55 Seliktar 2009, p. 170.

56 Harel and Issacharoff 2004, p. 103.

57 Ibid., p. 109.

58 Levin 2005, p. 468.

59 Harel and Issacharoff 2004, p. 127.

60 Ibid., p. 116.

61 Serge Schmemann, in *New York Times*, September 18, 2002.

62 As quoted by Harel and Issacharoff 2004, p. 119.

63 http://mfa.gov.il/MFA/MFA-Archive/2001/Pages/Tel-Aviv%20 suicide%20bombing%20at%20the%20Dolphin%20disco%20 -%201-.aspx.

64 MEMRI, Special Dispatch no. 237, July 9, 2001.

65 As quoted by Podhoretz 2001.

66 Ya'alon 2008, p. 121.

67 Ibid., p. 121.

68 Lawrence Joffe, "Faisal Husseini," *The Guardian*, June 1, 2001.

69 Ibid.

70 Record of Husseini's interview as reproduced by MEMRI, Special Despatch no. 236, July 8, 2001.

71 Suzanne Goldenberg, in *The Guardian*, August 10, 2001.

72 MEMRI Bulletin no. 3157, October 19, 2011.

73 www.mfa.gov.il/mfa/pressroom/2002/pages/prison%20interview %20with%20palestinian%20ship%20captain%20smu.aspx.

74 Harel and Issacharoff 2004, p. 215.

75 http://news.bbc.co.uk/2/hi/middle_east/1904592.stm.

76 Ibid.

77 Harel and Issacharoff 2004, p. 236.

78 As quoted by Bergman 2002, p. 347.

79 As quoted by Shalom and Hendel 2010, p. 15.

80 Bodansky 2002, pp. 531–2.

81 Bergman 2002, p. 17.

82 Ibid., p. 532.

83 Harel and Issacharoff 2004, p. 262.

84 www.israelnationalnews.com/News/News.aspx/140503.

85 www.jewishvirtuallibrary.org/jsource/History/defensiveshield. html.

86 Harel and Issacharoff 2004, p. 249.

87 Ibid., p. 254.

88 Ibid.

89 Matt Rees, Bobby Ghosh, Jamil Hamad and Aharon Klein, "Untangling Jenin's Tale," *Time*, May 13, 2002.

90 Ibid.

91 Jonathan Cook, "The 'Engineer,'" *Al-Ahram Weekly Online*, no. 582, April 18–24, 2002, http://weekly.ahram.org.eg/2002/582/6inv2. htm.

92 See CNN Wolf Blitzer Reports, April 17, 2002 (for Erekat), http:// edition.cnn.com/TRANSCRIPTS/0204/17/wbr.00.html, and Ian Black, "Israel Faces Rage over 'Massacre,'" *The Guardian*, April 17, 2002.

93 BBC News, April 18, 2002, 10.44 GMT.

94 Phil Reeves, "Israelis Try to Pin Blame for Jenin on Suicide Bombers," *The Independent*, April 19, 2002.

95 Phil Reeves, "From the Ruins of Jenin, the Truth about an Atrocity," *The Independent*, April 20, 2002.

96 www.adl.org/israel/jenin/jenin.pdf.

97 Gold 2004, pp. 212–13.

98 Harel and Issacharoff 2004, p. 257.

99 www.Intifada-palestine.com/tag/former-finnish-president-martti- ahtisaari/.

100 Charles Krauthammer, "Red Cross Snub," *Jewish World Review*, March 27, 2000.

101 www.peacewithrealism.org/wmbdfp3.htm.

102 Harel and Issacharoff 2004, p. 260.

103 Ibid., pp. 266–7.

104 http://articles.cnn.com/2002-06-24/politics/bush.mideast. speech_1_palestinian-state-borders-and-certain-aspects-palestin ian-parliament?_s=PM:ALLPOLITICS.

105 As quoted by Seliktar 2009, p. 86.

106 Harel and Issacharoff 2004, p. 276.

107 Ibid.
108 Ibid., p. 278.
109 Jeff Jacoby, "Arafat the Monster," *Boston Globe*, November 11, 2004.
110 Bergman 2002, p. 20.
111 Jacoby, "Arafat the Monster."
112 Harel and Issacharoff 2004, p. 138.
113 Shalom and Hendel 2010, p. 46.
114 Calculated from timeline of events presented at www.mideastweb. org/second_intifada_timeline.htm.
115 ICT Middle Eastern Conflict Study Project, at http://212.150. 54.123/casualties_project/stats_page.cfm.
116 See Shalom and Hendel 2010, p. 13.
117 Karsh 2003 (Hebrew edn), p. 40.

Chapter 8 Beyond the al-Aqsa Intifada

1 Also to be evacuated were four small isolated settlements in the West Bank.
2 Harel and Issacharoff 2004, p. 322.
3 As quoted by Peters 2010, p. 33.
4 www.jewishvirtuallibrary.org/jsource/Peace/sharon_1203.html.
5 Joshua Hammer and Dan Ephron, "Guns over Gaza," *Newsweek*, April 5, 2004.
6 Ari Shavit, in *Haaretz*, October 6, 2004.
7 http://articles.latimes.com/2004/may/03/world/fg-likud3.
8 www.ynetnews.com/articles/0,7340,L-3118275,00.html.
9 www.economist.com/node/4267246.
10 www.foxnews.com/story/0,2933,147749,00.html.
11 www.cija.ca/issues/2005-israeli-withdrawal-from-gaza/.
12 www.msnbc.msn.com/id/9331863/ns/world_news-mideast_n_ africa/t/looters-strip-gaza-greenhouses/.
13 Ibid.
14 Pnina Sharvit-Baruch, in Alan Baker, *Israel's Rights as a Nation-State in International Diplomacy*, Jerusalem: Jerusalem Center for Public Affairs, 2011.
15 Ibid.
16 Peters 2010, p. 38.

17 www.danielpipes.org/blog/2007/01/admitting-israels-unilateral-withdrawals-a

18 Ibid.

19 As quoted by Even 2009, p. 44.

20 www.foxnews.com/story/0,2933,170386,00.html.

21 Harel and Issacharoff 2008, p. 69.

22 www.haaretz.com/print-edition/news/peres-quits-Labour-joins-kadima-1.175611.

23 Harel and Issacharoff 2008, p. 69.

24 Cohen-Almagor and Haleva-Amir 2008, p. 37.

25 www.ynetnews.com/articles/0,7340,L-3359150,00.html.

26 www.jewishvirtuallibrary.org/jsource/biography/mordechai.html.

27 www.globalsecurity.org/military/world/palestine/pa-elections2006.htm.

28 http://conflictsforum.org/articlepdfs/failure-of-the-national-unity-government.pdf.

29 *Haaretz*, quoting from Associated Press, June 10, 2007.

30 www.camera.org/index.asp?x_context=7&x_issue=20&x_article=1618.

31 www.vanityfair.com/politics/features/2008/04/gaza200804.

32 Barsky 2005, p. 3.

33 Reproduced in *Jerusalem Quarterly*, Fall 1988.

34 *New York Sun*, March 11, 2005.

35 http://www.camera.org/index.asp?x_context=7&x_issue=11&x_article=1151.

36 www.youtube.com/watch?v=8-jh2R-_eQY.

37 www.ynetnews.com/articles/0,7340,L-3284744,00.html.

38 Larsen, as mentioned in chapter 6, was instrumental in furthering the Oslo Accords. Peres always insisted that he was a great friend of Israel.

39 Gold 2004, p. 205.

40 Ibid., p. 206.

41 www.jewishvirtuallibrary.org/jsource/UN/UNcoverup.html.

42 http://mfa.gov.il/MFA/MFA-Archive/2001/Pages/Israelis%20Held%20by%20the%20Hizbullah%20-%20Oct%202000-Jan%202004.aspx.

43 Harel and Issacharoff 2008, pp. 1–15.

44 Ibid., p. 10.
45 As quoted by Bregman 2010, p. 274.
46 Harel and Issacharoff 2008, p. 101.
47 Ibid., p. 108.
48 Ibid., p. 98.
49 As quoted ibid., p. 86.
50 As quoted ibid., pp. 121–2.
51 Hanan Greenberg, "Why Did Armoured Corps Fail in Lebanon?,"
    Ynetnews.com, August 30, 2006.
52 Ibid., and Bregman 2010, p. 291.
53 Harel and Issacharoff 2008, p. 44.
54 See ibid., p. 138.
55 www.hrw.org/news/2006/08/01/israellebanon-qana-death-
    toll-28.
56 Bregman 2010, p. 282.
57 As quoted ibid., p. 284.
58 Harel and Issacharoff 2008, p. 188.
59 Bregman 2010, p. 285.
60 Ibid.
61 Harel and Issacharoff 2008, pp. 189–90.
62 Ibid., pp. 193–4.
63 Ibid., p. 196.
64 http://mfa.gov.il/MFA/ForeignPolicy/Issues/Pages/Behind%20
    the%20Headlines-%20UN%20Security%20Council%20
    Resolution%201701%2012-Aug-2006.aspx.
65 See Ya'alon 2008, p. 209.
66 As quoted by Harel and Issacharoff 2008, p. 213.
67 Ibid., p. 227.
68 http://mfa.gov.il/mfa/foreignpolicy/terrorism/hizbullah/pages/
    israel-hizbullah%20conflict-%20victims%20of%20rocket%20
    attacks%20and%20idf%20casualties%20july-aug%202006.aspx.
69 U. Rubin, "Hizballah's Rocket Campaign against Northern Israel:
    A Preliminary Report," *Jerusalem Issue Brief*, 6(10), August 31,
    2006.
70 Bregman 2010, p. 291.
71 www.cfr.org/israel/winograd-commission-final-report/p15385.
72 http://mfa.gov.il/MFA/PressRoom/2007/Pages/Winograd%20

Inquiry%20Commission%20submits%20Interim%20Report%2030-Apr-2007.aspx.

73 Cohen-Almagor and Haleva-Amir 2008, p. 41.
74 Harel and Issacharoff 2008, p. 70.
75 www.cbc.ca/news/world/story/2006/08/27/nasrallah-abduction.html.
76 As quoted by Inbar 2007.
77 www.mythsandfacts.org/article_view.asp?articleID=87&order_id=6.
78 Yaakov Katz, Herb Kleiman and Tovah Lazaroff, "IDF Reservists to be Handed to Israel after 2-Year Captivity," *Jerusalem Post*, July 16, 2008.
79 http://news.sky.com/home/world-news/article/15038494.
80 http://content.time.com/time/world/article/0,8599,1218760,00.html.
81 "A Searing Contrast," *Jerusalem Post*, July 16, 2008.
82 Harel and Issacharoff 2008, p. 75.
83 Human Rights Watch, *Rockets from Gaza*, 2009, www.hrw.org/sites/default/files/reports/ioptqassam0809web.pdf.
84 Ibid.
85 Ibid.
86 Cordesman 2009.
87 www.camera.org/index.asp?x_context=2&x_outlet=35&x_article=1581.
88 *Haaretz*, January 12, 2009, www.haaretz.com/print-edition/news/sources-hamas-leaders-hiding-in-basement-of-israel-built-hospital-in-gaza-1.267940.
89 http://defense-update.com/newscast/1208/analysis/271208_israel_operation_leadcast.html.
90 Tovah Lazaroff and Yaakov Katz, "UN: IDF did not shell UNRWA School," *Jerusalem Post*, February 1, 2009.
91 Yaakov Katz, "World Duped by Hamas Death Count," *Jerusalem Post*, February 15, 2009.
92 Cohen 2009.
93 Y. Lappin, "IDF Releases Cast Lead Casualty Numbers," *Jerusalem Post*, March 26, 2009.
94 www.google.com/hostednews/afp/article/ALeqM5hF7u6SVbHf

ZSeLKnM97LlsaGWg_Q?docId=CNG.af5a1cb25e03ecc70924
e5a7787c7aa3.831.

95 www.btselem.org/gaza_strip/20091227_a_year_to_castlead_oper
ation.

96 www.btselem.org/download/20090909_cast_lead_fatalities_eng.
pdf.

97 R. McCarthy, "UN Presses for Prosecutions in Damning Report
of Hamas and Israel Conduct," *The Guardian*, September 15, 2009.

98 David Makovsky, "Preliminary Assessment of Israel's Operation
Cast Lead," www.washingtoninstitute.org/templateC05.php?CID
=2997.

99 Cohen 2009.

100 Ibid.

101 Martin Sherman, "A Reality Check: Israel Suffered Diplomatic
Defeat in Gaza, while Hamas emerged Victorious," YNetnews.
com, December 12, 2009.

102 Amnesty International, *Israel/Gaza: Operation Cast Lead: 22 Days of
Death and Destruction*, July, 2, 2009, pp. 10–13.

103 As cited at http://blog.unwatch.org/index.php/2009/07/02/
why-mary-robinson-rejected-the-mandate-accepted-by-judge-
goldstone/. See also www.stonegateinstitute.org/803/un-
investigation-of-israel-discredits-itself-and-undercuts-human-
rights.

104 Ibid.

105 www.juancole.com/2009/01/this-letter-of-attorneys-and-academ
ics.html.

106 Christopher Anderson, "UN Official: Israel Depriving Palestinians
of Basic Rights," *Jurist*, October 11, 2005.

107 Alan Dershowitz, "Double Standard Watch: An Anti-Israel
Extremist Seeks Revenge through Goldstone Report," *Jerusalem
Post*, February, 14, 2010.

108 Ibid.

109 As quoted at www.middleeastmonitor.org.uk/articles/62-europe/
625-qgaza-is-the-only-gulag-in-the-western-hemisphere-main
tained-by-democracies-closed-off-from-food-water-airq-says-
colonel-desmond-travers-co-author-of-the-goldstone-report-in-
an-exclusive-memo-interview.

110 http://unispal.un.org/UNISPAL.NSF/0/F4CB07EBCC6183828 525757F004FD965; emphasis added.

111 As quoted by UN News Centre, at www.un.org/apps/news/story. asp?NewsID=32057.

112 Ibid.

113 Berkowitz 2010.

114 "IDF Phones Gaza Residents to Warn Them of Imminent Strikes," *Haaretz*, January 2, 2009; emphasis added.

115 Cordesman 2009, p. 21.

116 As reproduced in the *Jewish Chronicle*, May 23, 2011. See www. thejc.com/blogs/jonathan-hoffman/col-richard-kemps-speech-we-believe-israel-conference-london-15-may.

117 Ibid.

118 www.cbsnews.com/stories/2009/01/19/world/main4734072. shtml?source=related_story.

119 Cordesman 2009, p. 36.

120 Hamas MP Fathi Hammad, MEMRI TV no. 1710, February 29, 2008.

121 Human Rights Watch, *Rockets from Gaza*, pp. 21, 23.

122 Martin Sherman, "Why are Military Ops in Gaza, Kosovo Judged by Wildly Disparate Criteria?" Ynet.com, January 14, 2009.

123 http://online.wsj.com/article/SB10001424052748704025304575 284081264400448.html?mod=WSJ_hpp_MIDDLETopStories; see also http://www.mfa.gov.il/mfa/pressroom/2010/pages/equip ment_aid_gaza_flotilla_7-jun-2010.aspx.

124 According to *Al-Ahram Weekly* [Egypt], June 17–23, 2010, as indicated by MEMRI Special Dispatch no. 3859, May 24, 2010.

125 Al-Manar TV, May 17, 2010, as indicated by MEMRI Special Dispatch no. 3859, May 24, 2010.

126 MEMRI Special Dispatch no. 3007, June 8, 2010.

127 www.youtube.com/watch?v=pxY7Q7CvQPQ.

128 www.terrorism-info.org.il/data/pdf/PDF_19068_2.pdf.

129 United Nations, *Report of the Secretary-General's Panel of Inquiry on the 31 May 2010 Flotilla Incident* [Palmer Report], September 2011, p. 57.

130 Mona Charen, "Flotillas and Falsehoods," June 1, 2010, www.
nationalreview.com/articles/229863/flotillas-and-falsehoods/
mona-charen.

131 The reader can readily view videos of all that and other incidents
at www.camera.org/index.asp?x_context=7&x_issue=52&x_article
=1859.

132 See 3, "Raid," and then 3.1, "Mavi Marmara boarding," at http://
en.academic.ru/dic.nsf/enwiki/11698521.

133 See "Examinations of weapons found on Mavi Marmara," at:
http://www.terrorism-info.org.il/en/article/18042.

134 Ibid.

135 Emphasis added.

136 "UN Members Decry Israeli Raid on Gaza Aid Flotilla," June 1,
2010, www.bbc.co.uk/news/10200351.

137 http://cnsnews.com/news/article/un-human-rights-council-con
demns-israel-then-calls-investigation-flotilla-raid.

138 Ibid.

139 William Shawcross, "An Irrational, Obscene Hatred," *Jerusalem
Post*, June 8, 2010.

140 www.telegraph.co.uk/news/worldnews/middleeast/palestinian
authority/7790151/Israel-attack-on-gaza-aid-ship-US-deeply-
regrets-loss-of-life.html.

141 *Hurriyet* (English edn), June 7, 2010.

142 Ibid.

143 Josh Rogin, in *Foreign Policy*, June 4, 2010.

144 Joshua Teitelbaum, "Turkey is Calling for a Jihad against Israel,"
The Guardian, June 8, 2010.

145 Britain Israel Communications and Research Centre, September
12, 2011.

146 Migdalovitz 2007, p. 1.

147 Greg Sheridan, "Ehud Olmert Still Dreams of Peace," *The
Australian*, November 28, 2009.

148 Aluf Benn, "Olmert's Plan for Peace with the Palestinians,"
Haaretz, December 17, 2009.

149 Ibid.

150 Sheridan, "Ehud Olmert Still Dreams of Peace."

151 Ibid.

152 Ibid.
153 Chief Palestinian negotiator Saeb Erekat: "Abu Mazen Rejected the Israeli Proposal in Annapolis like Arafat Rejected the Camp David 2000 Proposal," MEMRI, March 27, 2009, www.memritv. org/clip_transcript/en/2074.htm.
154 See, for example, Inbar 2010, passim.

Chapter 9 Social and Economic Developments

1 Jones 1996, p. 19.
2 See, for example, Gal Beckerman, "Highjacking Their Way out of Tyranny," *New York Times*, June 17, 2010.
3 Jones 1996, p. 23.
4 See ibid., p. 44.
5 Ibid., p. 49.
6 Ibid., p. 1.
7 Khanin 2010, p. 6.
8 Ibid., p. 7.
9 Galili and Bronfman 2013, p. 28.
10 Ibid., p. 74.
11 Jones 1996, p. 123.
12 Ibid., p. 125.
13 Gitelman 2004, p. 96.
14 Almog 2012c, p. 17.
15 Cohen 1990, p. 12.
16 Almog 2012c, p. 17.
17 Ilana Golem, as quoted by Galili and Bronfman 2013, p. 23.
18 Friedgut 2004, p. 190.
19 Galili and Bronfman 2013, p. 152.
20 Ibid., p. 159.
21 27.9 percent of the Russian Jews had second degrees compared with 7.5 for Israeli-born Jews. See ibid., p. 23.
22 Ibid., p. 12.
23 Gitelman 2004, p. 96.
24 Khanin 2010, p. 27.
25 Galili and Bronfman 2013, p. 22.
26 Friedgut 2004, p. 206.
27 Galili and Bronfman 2013, p. 49.

28 www.cbs.gov.il/reader/newhodaot/hodaa_template.html?hodaa= 201211307.

29 Spector 2005, p. 3.

30 Kaplan and Rosen 1993, p. 38.

31 Spector 2005, p. 5.

32 Almog 2012b, p. 3.

33 As quoted by Spector 2005b, p. 10.

34 Almog 2012b, p. 5.

35 Spector 2005, p. 11.

36 www.moia.gov.il/English/FeelingIsrael/AboutIsrael/Pages/miv tzaMoshe.aspx.

37 William Safire, "Interrupted Exodus," *New York Times*, January 7, 1985.

38 Unless otherwise stated, all the information in this and some of the successive paragraphs is derived from Spector 2005.

39 Ibid., p. 42.

40 Ibid., pp. 100–1.

41 Ibid., p. 175.

42 Louis Rapoport, "Ethiopian Jewry Rescued," *Jerusalem Post*, June 1, 1991.

43 Hila Weisberg, "Ethiopian Immigrants Earning 30%–40% Less than Arabs," *Haaretz*, March 5, 2012.

44 As reported by Puriya Gal, "Bleak Wedding," *Maariv*, April 25, 2003.

45 Abe Selig and Ron Friedman, "Deal Reached on Petah Tikva Ethiopian Olim," *Jerusalem Post*, September 1, 2009.

46 Stein 2009, p. 101.

47 As quoted by Selzer 1965, p. 15.

48 As quoted by Bernstein 1980, p. 32.

49 Ed Rettig, "Ethiopian Jews and the IDF," *Times of Israel*, February 15, 2013.

50 Rosenthal 2008, p. 170.

51 Smooha 2004, p. 41.

52 Ibid., p. 43.

53 Peleg and Waxman 2011, p. 22.

54 Stendel 1996, p. 39.

55 Ibid., p. 41.

56 Halkin 2009, p. 31.
57 Smooha 2004, p. 48.
58 See Peleg and Waxman 2011, p. 9.
59 Smooha 2004, p. 45.
60 Peleg and Waxman 2011, p. 41.
61 "The Official Summation of the Or Commission Report," September 2, 2003, www.jewishvirtuallibrary.org/jsource/Society_%26_Culture/OrCommissionReport.html.
62 Smooha 2004, p. 37.
63 Schueftan 2011, p. 618.
64 Ibid., p. 684.
65 Ibid., p. 634.
66 Ibid., pp. 705–7.
67 Almog 2012a, p. 17.
68 Ibid.
69 Schueftan 2011, pp. 718–30.
70 Stendel 1996, p. 47.
71 Ibid., p. 48.
72 Schueftan 2011, p. 620.
73 Peleg and Waxman 2011, p. 33.
74 Ibid., p. 34.
75 http://data.worldbank.org/indicator/SE.ADT.LITR.ZS.
76 Peleg and Waxman 2011, p. 34.
77 Stendel 1996, p. 76.
78 Schueftan 2011, pp. 620–1.
79 www.mideastyouth.com/2012/06/10/coexistence-envoys-or-occupational-hazard-israel-posts-two-arab-diplomats-to-norway/.
80 www.haaretz.com/print-edition/features/head-to-head-why-are-so-few-arabs-in-higher-education-1.369967.
81 See www.wgh.org.il/_Uploads/dbsAttachedFiles/RH.pdf.
82 www.raymondcook.net/blog/index.php/tag/arab-doctors/.
83 Almog 2012a, p. 3.
84 Schueftan 2011, p. 639.
85 For example, see Peleg and Waxman 2011, p. 7.
86 In this regard, see Schueftan 2011, passim.
87 Moshe Ma'Oz, in Stendel 1996, p. vi.
88 As quoted by Schueftan 2011, p. 45.

89 Halkin 2009, p. 34.
90 Editorial, *Jerusalem Post*, April 1, 2001.
91 Ibid.
92 The Haifa Declaration, http://mada-research.org/en/files/2007/09/haifaenglish.pdf, p. 3.
93 Ibid., pp. 14–15.
94 As cited by Schueftan 2011, pp. 180–1.
95 As quoted ibid., p. 205.
96 Peleg and Waxman 2011, p. 119.
97 As quoted by Schueftan 2003, p. 73; emphasis added.
98 From Peleg and Waxman 2011, p. 7.
99 See Yakobson and Rubinstein 2010, passim.
100 As reported by Halkin 2009.
101 Berman 1998, p. 5.
102 Schueftan 2011, p. 653.
103 Berman 1998, p. 7.
104 Y. Hess, "America's Jews are Worried," Ynet, August 2, 2012.
105 Berman 1998, p. 2.
106 Ibid., p. 9.
107 "Yeshivas to Receive State Funds without Teaching Basic Subjects," Ynet, July 27, 2008.
108 A. Shoan, "The Haredi School Scam," Ynet, July 14, 2010.
109 Aner Shalev, "The Haredi State," *Haaretz*, January 4, 2012.
110 Berman 1998, p. 7.
111 See Schueuftan 2011, pp. 658–9.
112 E. Bystrov and A. Soffer, "Israel: Demography 2012–2030," University of Haifa, June 2012, p. 61, table 6.
113 Schueftan 2011, p. 671.
114 Soffer 2001, p. 13.
115 A. Harel, "Number of Ultra-Orthodox Men Exempted from IDF Service Reaches All-Time High," *Haaretz*, October 31, 2012.
116 www.loc.gov/law/help/haredi-military-draft.php.
117 Ibid.
118 www.haaretz.com/weekend/anglo-file/canadian-woman-beaten-on-egged-bus-joins-high-court-petition-1.211790.
119 M. Wagner, "Declaring Bride's Conversion Treif, Rishon Lezion Rabbi Nixes Marriage," *Jerusalem Post*, August 12, 2009.

120 A. K. Sommer, "Indian Community Furious at Rabbi's Refusal to Okay Marriages," *Jerusalem Post*, November 6, 1997.

121 Sprinzak 1999, p. 94.

122 http://failedmessiah.typepad.com/failed_messiahcom/2012/07/woman-baby-stoned-by-haredim-in-beit-shemesh-123.html.

123 I. Asher, "Compulsion in the Sky: Haredim Covered a Screen Because of a Movie," *Maariv*, August 8, 2002.

124 See Rosenthal 2008, p. 189.

125 www.ynetnews.com/articles/0,7340,L-3865890,00.html.

126 Ben-David 2011, p. 23.

127 www.haaretz.com/business/israel-s-unemployment-rate-drops-to-32-year-low-1.415453.

128 Senor and Singer 2009, p. 11.

129 Ibid., p. 153.

130 Ibid., passim.

131 Asher Zeiger, "2012 Breaks Record for Incoming Tourism," *Times of Israel*, December 23, 2012.

132 Eduard Gismatullin and Calev Ben-David, "Israel Finds $240 Billion Gas Hoard Stranded by Politics: Energy," *Bloomberg Businessweek*, August 10, 2012.

133 Interview with Professor Stanley Fischer, governor of the Bank of Israel, and Mr Richard Quest at the Globes Israel Business Conference, Tel Aviv, December 10, 2012.

134 The coefficient ranges from 0, perfect equality (everyone has the same income), to 1, complete inequality (only one person receives income).

135 Ben-David 2011, p. 116.

136 Ibid., p. 133.

137 Ibid., p. 137.

138 Ibid., p. 38.

139 Kleiman 1996, p. 2.

140 Dan Levin, "Israel Grows Uneasy over Reliance on Migrant Labor," *New York Times*, July 4, 2010.

141 Ibid.

142 www.irinnews.org/Report/86808/ISRAEL-New-report-highlights-exploitation-of-migrant-workers.

143 Ben-David 2011, p. 37.

144 See, for example, Kleiman 1996, pp. 4–5.
145 Talila Nesher, "Israel to Announce Names of Foreign Children Set for Deportation," *Haaretz*, February 15, 2012.
146 Ben Hartman, "Eilat Worries over Rising Tension with Migrants," *Jerusalem Post*, October 6, 2012.
147 Ibid.
148 www.kibbutz.org.il/eng/.
149 Near 1977, p. 345.
150 Ibid., p. 346.
151 Mort and Brenner 2003, p. 27.
152 Ibid.
153 Near 1977, p. 348.
154 Mort and Brenner 2003, p. 176.
155 Near 1977, p. 347.
156 Mort and Brenner 2003, p. 40.
157 Amnon Rubinstein, "The Return of the Kibbutzim," *Jerusalem Post*, July 10, 2007.

Conclusion

1 Nakdimon 1982, p. 11.
2 As quoted by Teveth 1972, p. 357.
3 As quoted ibid., p. 358.
4 www.fmep.org/settlement_info/settlement-info-and-tables/stats-data/comprehensive-settlement-population-1972-2006.
5 Michell G. Bard, "Facts about Jewish Settlements in the West Bank," www.jewishvirtuallibrary.org/jsource/Peace/settlements.html.
6 As quoted by Palestine Media Watch Bulletin, July 25, 2013.
7 As reported by Palestine Media Watch Bulletin, July 6, 2010.
8 PA TV August 10, 2011, and reported in Palestine Media Watch Bulletin, August 17, 2011.
9 As quoted by *Times of Israel*, July 31, 2013.
10 As quoted by the *Huffington Post*, May 22, 2013.
11 Inbar 2013, p. 5.
12 *The Economist*, September 28, 2013.
13 Inbar 2013, p. 10.
14 Ibid.

References and Bibliography

Works in English

Al-Haj, M. (2004) "The Status of the Palestinians in Israel: A Double Periphery in an Ethno-National State," in A. Dowty (ed.), *Critical Issues in Israeli Society*, Westport, CT: Praeger.

Alexander, E., and Bogdanor, P. (2006) *The Jewish Divide Over Israel: Accusers and Defenders*, New Brunswick, NJ: Transaction.

Anderson, C. (2005) "UN Official: Israel Depriving Palestinians of Basic Rights," *Jurist*, October 11.

Appelbaum, D. M. (2013) "Islamic Supremacy Alive and Well in Ankara," *Middle East Quarterly*, 20(1): 3–16.

Arens, M. (1995) *Broken Covenant: American Foreign Policy and the Crisis between the U.S. and Israel*, New York: Simon & Schuster.

Avneri, A. (1972) *The War of Attrition*, Tel Aviv: Olive Books.

Baker, A. (ed.) (2011) *Israel's Rights as a Nation-State in International Diplomacy*, Jerusalem: Jerusalem Center for Public Affairs.

Bar-On, M. (1994) *The Gates of Gaza: Israel's Road to Suez and Back, 1955–1957*, Basingstoke: Macmillan.

Bar-On, M. (ed.) (2004) *A Never-Ending Conflict: A Guide to Israeli Military History*, Westport, CT: Praeger.

Bar-Siman-Tov, Y. (1980) *The Israeli–Egyptian War of Attrition, 1969–1970*, New York: Columbia University Press.

Barsky, Y. (2005) *Hizballah: A Mega-Terrorist Organization*, New York: American Jewish Committee.

Bartov, H. (1981) *Dado: 48 Years and 20 Days*, Tel Aviv: Ma'ariv Book Club.

Becker, J. (1984) *The PLO: The Rise and Fall of the Palestine Liberation Organization*, London: Weidenfeld & Nicolson.

Ben-David, D. (2011) *State of Nation Report: Society, Economy and Policy in Israel 2010*, Jerusalem: Taub Center for Policy Studies in Israel.

Ben-Gurion, D. (1971) *Israel: A Personal History*, New York: Funk & Wagnalls.

Benson, M. T. (1997) *Harry S. Truman and the Founding of Israel*, Westport, CT: Praeger.

Berkowitz, p. (2010) "The Goldstone Report and International Law," *Hoover Institution Policy Review*, no. 162.

Berman, E. (1998) *Sect, Subsidy and Sacrifice: An Economist's View of Ultra-Orthodox Jews*, Working Paper no. 6715, Cambridge, MA: National Bureau of Economic Research.

Black, I., and Morris, B. (1991) *Israel's Secret Wars: The Untold History of Israeli Intelligence*, London: Hamish Hamilton.

Bodansky, Y. (2002) *The High Cost of Peace*, Roseville, CA: Prima.

Bregman, A. (2010) *Israel's Wars: A History Since 1947*, London: Routledge.

Bruck, C. (1996) "The Wounds of Peace," *New Yorker*, October 14.

Burkett, E. (2008) *Golda*, New York: HarperCollins.

Carmon, Y. (1994) "The Story Behind the Handshake," *Commentary*, March: 25–9.

Cohen, E. (1972) "The Black Panthers and Israeli Society," *Jewish Journal of Sociology*, 14: 93–102.

Cohen, R. (1990) *Soviet Jewish Emigration to Israel*, Washington, DC: Refugee Policy Group.

Cohen, S. A. (2009) *The Futility of Operation Cast Lead*, Perspectives Papers no. 68, Tel Aviv: Begin–Sadat Center for Strategic Studies, www.biu.ac.il/SOC/besa/docs/perspectives68.pdf.

Cohen-Almagor, R., and Haleva-Amir, S. (2008) "The Israel–Hezbollah War and the Winograd Committee," *Journal of Parliamentary and Political Law*, 2(1): 27–44.

Cordesman, A. (2009) *The Gaza War: A Strategic Analysis*, Washington, DC: Center for Strategic and International Studies.

Dalin, D. G., and Rothmann, J. F. (2008) *Icon of Evil: Hitler's Mufti and the Rise of Radical Islam*, New York: Random House.

Dayan, M. (1976) *The Story of My Life*, London: Sphere.

Dershowitz, A. (2008) *The Case against Israel's Enemies: Exposing Jimmy Carter and Others who Stand in the Way of Peace*, Hoboken, NJ: John Wiley & Sons.

Dowty, A. (ed.) (2004) *Critical Issues in Israeli Society*, Westport, CT: Praeger.

Draper, T. (1968) *Israel and World Politics: Roots of the Third Arab–Israeli War*, New York: Viking.

Dunstan, S. (2007) *The Yom Kippur War: The Arab–Israeli War of 1973*, Oxford: Osprey.

Eban, A. (1978) *An Autobiography*, London: Weidenfeld & Nicolson.

Eban, A. (1992) *Personal Witness: Israel through My Eyes*, New York: Putnam.

Elon, A. (1972) *The Israelis: Founders and Sons*, London: Sphere.

Ensalaco, M. (2007) *Middle Eastern Terrorism*, Philadelphia: University of Pennsylvania Press.

Even, S. (2009) "Israel's Strategy of Unilateral Withdrawal," *Strategic Assessment*, 12(1): 29–45.

Eytan, W. (1958) *The First Ten Years: A Diplomatic History of Israel*, London: Weidenfeld & Nicolson.

Fallaci, O. (1976) *Interview with History*, New York: Liveright.

Flapan, S. (1987) *The Birth of Israel: Myths and Realities*, New York: Pantheon.

Friedgut, T. (2004) "Immigrants from the Soviet Union: Their Influence and Identity," in A. Shapira (ed.), *Israeli Identity in Transition*, Westport, CT: Praeger.

Gabbay, R. (1959) *A Political Study of the Arab–Jewish Conflict: The Arab Refugee Problem*, Geneva: Droz.

Gabriel, R. A. (1984) *Operation Peace for Galilee: The Israel–PLO War in Lebanon*, New York: Hill & Wang.

Gavron, D. (2000) *The Kibbutz: Awakening from Utopia*, Lanham, MD: Rowman & Littlefield.

Gelber, Y. (2006) *Palestine 1948: War, Escape and the Emergence of the Palestinian Refugee Problem*, 2nd edn, Brighton: Sussex Academic Press.

Gitelman, Z. (2004) "The 'Russian Revolution' in Israel," in A. Dowty (ed.), *Critical Issues in Israeli Society*, Westport, CT: Praeger.

Golan, S. (2004) "The Yom Kippur War," in M. Bar-On (ed.), *A Never-Ending Conflict: A Guide to Israeli Military History*, Westport, CT: Praeger.

Golani, M. (1998) *Israel in Search of a War: The Sinai Campaign, 1955–1956*, Brighton: Sussex Academic Press.

Gold, D. (2004) *Tower of Babble: How the United Nations Has Fueled Global Chaos*, New York: Crown Forum.

Gordis, D. (2009) *Saving Israel: How the Jewish People Can Win a War that May Never End*, Hoboken, NJ: John Wiley & Sons.

Hacohen, D. (2003) *Immigrants in Turmoil: Mass Immigration to Israel in the 1950s and After*, Syracuse, NY: Syracuse University Press.

Halevi, N., and Klinov-Malul, R. (1968) *The Economic Development of Israel*, New York: Praeger.

Halkin, H. (2009) "The Jewish State & its Arabs," *Commentary*, January.

Harel, A., and Issacharoff, A. (2008) *34 Days: Israel, Hezbollah and the War in Lebanon*, New York: Palgrave Macmillan.

Heikal, M. (1975) *The Road to Ramadan*, London: Collins.

Herzog, C. (1975) *The War of Atonement*, London: Weidenfeld & Nicolson.

Horowitz, D. (1967) *The Economics of Israel*, Oxford: Pergamon Press.

Hurewitz, J. C. (1950) *The Struggle for Palestine*, New York: Norton.

Inbar, E. (2007) "How Israel Bungled the Second Lebanon War," *Middle East Quarterly*, 14(3): 57–65.

Inbar, E. (2010) "The Decline of the Labour Party," *Israel Affairs*, 16(1): 69–81.

Inbar, E. (2013) "Time Favors Israel: The Resilient Jewish State," *Middle East Quarterly*, 20(4): 3–13.

Indyk, M. (2009) *Innocent Abroad: An Intimate Account of American Peace Diplomacy in the Middle East*, New York: Simon & Schuster.

Isaac, R. J. (1993) "The Real Lessons of Camp David," *Commentary*, December: 34–8.

Israeli, R. (2002) *Poison: Modern Manifestations of a Blood Libel*, Lanham, MD: Lexington Books.

Israeli, R. (2012) *The Oslo Idea: The Euphoria of Failure*, New Brunswick, NJ: Transaction.

Jones, C. (1996) *Soviet Jewish Aliyah, 1989–1992: Impact and Implications for Israel and the Middle East*, London: Frank Cass.

Joseph, D. (1960) *The Faithful City: The Siege of Jerusalem, 1948*. New York: Simon & Schuster.

Kadi, L. S. (1969) *Basic Political Documents of the Armed Palestinian Resistance Movement*, Beirut: Palestine Research Centre.

Kaplan, S., and Rosen, C. (1993) "Ethiopian Immigrants to Israel: Between Preservation of Culture and Invention of Tradition," *Jewish Journal of Sociology*, 35(1): 35–48.

Karmon, E. (2005) *Coalitions between Terrorist Organizations*, Leiden: Martinus Nijhoff.

Karni, E. (1979) "The Israeli Economy: 1973–1976," *Economic Development and Cultural Change*, 28(1): 63–76.

Karsh, E. (2002) "What Occupation?" *Commentary*, July–August.

Karsh, E. (2003) *Arafat's War: The Man and his Battle for Israeli Conquest*, New York: Grove Press.

Karsh, E. (2008) "1948: Israel and the Palestinians," *Commentary*, May.

Khanin, V. (2010) *Aliyah from the Former Soviet Union: Contribution to the National Security Balance*, Jerusalem: Interdisciplinary Center Herzliya Institute for Policy and Strategy.

Kimche, D., and Bawly, D. (1968) *The Sandstorm: The Arab-Israeli War of June 1967: Prelude and Aftermath*, London: Secker & Warburg.

Kimche, J., and Kimche, D. (1960) *Both Sides of the Hill: Britain and the Palestine War*, London: Secker & Warburg.

Kissinger, H. (1979) *White House Years*, Boston: Little, Brown.

Kissinger, H. (1982) *Years of Upheaval*, Boston: Little, Brown.

Kolakowski, L. (2008) *Main Currents of Marxism*, New York: Norton.

Korn, D. A. (1992) *Stalemate: The War of Attrition and Great Power Diplomacy in the Middle East, 1967–1970*, Boulder, CO: Westview Press.

Krauthammer, C. (2000) "Red Cross Snub," *Jewish World Review*, March 27.

Kurzman, D. (1983) *Ben-Gurion: Prophet of Fire*, New York: Simon & Schuster.

Kyle, K. (1991) *Suez*, London: Weidenfeld & Nicolson.

Laqueur, W., and Rubin, B. (2001) *The Israel–Arab Reader: A Documentary History of the Middle East Conflict*, New York: Penguin.

Levin, K. (2005) *The Oslo Syndrome: Delusions of a People Under Siege*, Hanover: Smith & Kraus.

Lorch, N. (1961) *The Edge of the Sword: Israel's War of Independence, 1947–1949*, New York: Putnam.

Luttwak, E., and Horowitz, D. (1975) *The Israeli Army*, London: Allen Lane.

Meinertzhagen, R. (1959) *Middle East Diary, 1917–1956*, London: Cressett Press.

Migdalovitz, C. (2007) *Israeli–Palestinian Peace Process: The Annapolis Conference*, Washington, DC: Congressional Research Services.

Morris, B. (2001) *Righteous Victims: A History of the Zionist–Arab Conflict, 1881–2001*, New York: Vintage.

Morris, B. (2008) *1948: A History of the First Arab–Israeli War*, New Haven, CT: Yale University Press.

Morris, B. (2009) *One State, Two States: Resolving the Israel/Palestine Conflict*, New Haven, CT: Yale University Press.

Mort, J., and Brenner, G. (2003) *Our Hearts Invented a Place: Can Kibbutzim Survive in Today's Israel?* Ithaca, NY: Cornell University Press.

Near, H. (1997) *The Kibbutz Movement: A History*, Vol. 2, London: Mitchell.

Oren, M. (2002) *Six Days of War: June 1967 and the Making of the Modern Middle East*, New York: Oxford University Press.

Oz, A. (2004) *A Tale of Love and Darkness*, Orlando, FL: Harcourt.

Pappe, I. (2006) *The Ethnic Cleansing of Palestine*, Oxford: Oneworld.

Peleg, I., and Waxman, D. (2011) *Israel's Palestinians: The Conflict Within*, New York: Cambridge University Press.

Peres, S. (1995) *Battling for Peace*, New York: Random House.

Peters, J. (1984) *From Time Immemorial*, New York: Harper & Row.

Peters, J. (2010) "The Gaza Disengagement: Five Years Later," *Israel Journal of Foreign Affairs*, 4(3): 33–44.

Phillips, M. (2010) *The World Turned Upside Down: The Global Battle over God, Truth, and Power*, New York: Encounter.

Podhoretz, N. (2001) "Oslo: The Peacemongers Return," *Commentary*, October.

Poller, N. (2005) "Myth, Fact, and the al-Dura Affair," *Commentary*, September.

Quandt, W. B. (2005) *Peace Process: American Diplomacy and the Arab–Israeli Conflict since 1967*, Washington, DC: Brookings Institution Press.

Rabin, Y. (1979) *The Rabin Memoirs*, Boston: Little, Brown.

Rabinovich, A. (2004) *The Yom Kippur War: The Epic Encounter That Transformed the Middle East*, New York: Schocken Books.

Rosenthal, D. (2008) *The Israelis: Ordinary People in an Extraordinary Land*, New York: Free Press.

Roy, S. (1994) "The Seeds of Chaos, and of Night: The Gaza Strip after the Agreement," *Journal of Palestine Studies*, 23(3): 85–98.

Sadat, A. (1977) *In Search of Identity: An Autobiography*, New York: Harper & Row.

Savir, U. (1998) *The Process: 1,100 Days That Changed the Middle East*, New York: Random House.

Schechtman, J. (1952) *The Arab Refugee Problem*, New York: Philosophical Library.

Schiff, Z. (1974) *October Earthquake: Yom Kippur 1973*, Tel Aviv: University Publishing Projects.

Schiff, Z., and Ya'ari, E. (1984) *Israel's Lebanon War*, New York: Simon & Schuster.

Schiff, Z., and Ya'ari, E. (1989) *Intifada: The Palestinian Uprising – Israel's Third Front*, New York: Simon & Schuster.

Schueftan, D. (2003) "Voice of Palestine: The New Ideology of Israeli Arabs," *Azure*, Winter.

Schueftan, D. (2004) "The Israeli–Egyptian 'War of Attrition,' 1969–1970," in M. Bar-On (ed.), *A Never-Ending Conflict: A Guide to Israeli Military History*, Westport, CT: Praeger.

Segev, S. (1998) *Crossing the Jordan: Israel's Hard Road to Peace*, New York: St Martin's Press.

Segev, T. (1993) *The Seventh Million: The Israelis and the Holocaust*, New York: Hill & Wang.

Seliktar, O. (2009) *Doomed to Failure? The Politics and Intelligence of the Oslo Peace Process*, Santa Barbara, CA: Praeger Security International.

Selzer, M. (1965) *The Outcasts of Israel: Communal Tensions in the Jewish State*, Jerusalem: Council of the Sephardi Community.

Senor, D., and Singer, S. (2009) *Start-Up Nation: The Story of Israel's Economic Miracle*, New York: Twelve.

Shalev, A. (1991) *The Intifada: Causes and Effects*, Tel Aviv: Jaffee Center for Strategic Studies.

Shalom, Z. (1996) "Kennedy, Ben-Gurion and the Dimona Project, 1962–1963," *Israel Studies*, 1(1): 3–33.

Shapira, A. (ed.) (2004) *Israeli Identity in Transition*, Westport, CT: Praeger.

Sharon, A. (2006) *Ariel Sharon: An Intimate Portrait*, New York: Palgrave Macmillan.

Sharon, G. (2011) *Sharon: The Life of a Leader*, New York: Harper.

Sheffer, G. (1996) *Moshe Sharett: Biography of a Political Moderate*, Oxford: Oxford University Press.

Shepherd, R. (2009) *A State beyond the Pale: Europe's Problem with Israel*, London: Weidenfeld & Nicolson.

Shlaim, A. (2000) *The Iron Wall*, New York: Norton.

Slater, R. (1991) *Warrior Statesman: The Life of Moshe Dayan*, London: St Martin's Press.

Smooha, S. "Arab–Jewish Relations in Israel: A Deeply Divided Society," in A. Shapira (ed.), *Israeli Identity in Transition*, Westport, CT: Praeger.

Sobel, L. A., and Kosut, H. (1974) *Israel and the Arabs: The October 1973 War*, New York: Facts on File.

Soffer, A. (2001) *Israel, Demography 2000–2020: Dangers and Opportunities*, Haifa: Center for National Security Studies, University of Haifa.

Spector, S. (2005) *Operation Solomon: The Daring Rescue of the Ethiopian Jews*, Oxford: Oxford University Press.

Sprinzak, E. (1991) *The Ascendance of Israel's Radical Right*, New York: Oxford University Press.

Sprinzak, E. (1999) *Brother against Brother: Violence and Extremism in Israeli Politics from Altalena to the Rabin Assassination*, New York: Free Press.

Stauber, R. (2003) "Continuity and Change: Extreme Right Perceptions of Zionism," in D. Porat and R. Stauber (eds), *Anti-Semitism and Terror*, Tel Aviv: Stephen Roth Institute for the Study of Contemporary Antisemitism and Racism.

Stein, Leonard (1961) *The Balfour Declaration*, London: Valentine-Mitchell.

Stein, Leslie (2009) *The Making of Modern Israel, 1948–1967*, Cambridge: Polity.

Stendel, O. (1996) *The Arabs in Israel*, Brighton: Sussex Academic Press.

Tal, D. (2004) *War in Palestine 1948: Strategy and Diplomacy*, London: Routledge.

Talmon, J. L. (1981) *The Myth of the Nation and the Vision of Revolution*, London: Secker & Warburg.

Taub, G. (2010) *The Settlers and the Struggle over the Meaning of Zionism*, New Haven, CT: Yale University Press.

Tessler, M. (1994) *A History of the Israeli–Palestinian Conflict*, Bloomington: Indiana University Press.

Teveth, S. (1970) *The Tanks of Tammuz*, London: Weidenfeld & Nicolson.

Teveth, S. (1972) *Moshe Dayan*, London: Weidenfeld & Nicolson.

Teveth, S. (1990) "The Palestine Arab Refugee Problem and its Origins," *Middle Eastern Studies*, 26(2): 214–49.

Ullman, R. H. (1978) "Human Rights and Economic Power: The United States versus Idi Amin," *Foreign Affairs*, 56(3): 529–43.

Van Creveld, M. (1998) *The Sword and the Olive: A Critical History of the Israeli Defence Force*, New York: Public Affairs.

Weizman, E. (1981) *The Battle for Peace*, New York: Bantam Books.

Weizmann, C. (1949) *Trial and Error*, London: Hamish Hamilton.

Werner, S. B. (1983) "The Development of Political Corruption: A Case Study of Israel," *Political Studies*, 31(4): 620–39.

Wistrich, R. (2010) *A Lethal Obsession: Anti-Semitism from Antiquity to the Global Jihad*, New York: Random House.

Yakobson, A., and Rubinstein, A. (2010) *Israel and the Family of Nations: The Jewish State and Human Rights*, London and New York: Routledge.

Ye'Or, B. (2005) *Eurabia: The Euro-Arab Axis*, Madison: Farleigh Dickinson University Press.

Zertal, I., and Eldar, A. (2007) *Lords of the Land: The War over Israel's Settlements in the Occupied Territories, 1967–2007*, New York: Nation Books.

Works in Hebrew

Almog, O (2012a) "Arabs in Israel: A Representation of the Situation," March, www.peopleil.org/Details.aspx?ItemID=30275&noCacheDi gest=f222.

Almog, O. (2012b) "Ethiopians in Israel: A Representation of the Situation," April, www.peopleil.Org/Details.aspx?ItemID=30274&nocacheDigest=e270.

Almog, O. (2012c) "The Russian Immigration: Historical and Sociological Landmarks," December, www.peopleil.org/Details.aspx?ItemID=30155&noCachDigest=b186.

Bar-Joseph, U. (2001) *The Watchman Fell Asleep: The Surprise of Yom Kippur and its Sources*, Lod: Zmora-Bitan.

Bar-Zohar, M. (1975) *Ben-Gurion: A Political Biography*, Tel Aviv: Am Oved.

Ben-Gurion, D. (1969) *The Restored State of Israel*, Tel Aviv: Am Oved.

Bergman, R. (2002) *Authority Given: Where Did We Go Wrong? Thus did the Palestinian Authority Turn into a Conveyor Belt of Corruption and Terror*, Tel Aviv: Yedioth Ahronoth.

Bernstein, D. (1980) *The Ma'abarot in the 1950s*, Haifa: University of Haifa.

Braun, A. (1992) *Moshe Dayan in the Yom Kippur War*, Tel Aviv: Edanim.

Cohen, A. (1964) *Israel and the Arab World*, Tel Aviv: Sifriat Hapoalim.

Cordova, Y. (1977) "The Political Background to the American Airlift in the Yom Kippur War," *Maarachot*, 256.

Dayan, M. (1976) *Milestones: An Autobiography*, Jerusalem: Edanim.

Galili, L., and Bronfman, R. (2013) *The Million that Changed the Middle East*, Tel Aviv: Matar.

Gilboa, M. (1968) *Six Years – Six Days: Origins and History of the Six-Day War*, Tel Aviv: Am Oved.

Gluska, A. (2004) *Eshkol, Give the Order! The Israeli Defence Force and Government on the Road to the Six-Day War, 1963–1967*, Tel Aviv: Ma'arahot.

Gross, N. (1997) "Economics of Israel," in Z. Tzameret and H. Yablonka (eds), *The First Decade*, Jerusalem: Yad Yitzah Ben Zvi.

Haber, E. (1987) *Tomorrow War Will Break Out*, Tel Aviv: Edanim.

Harel, A., and Issacharoff, A. (2004) *The Seventh War*, Tel Aviv: Yedoit Ahronot.

Harkabi, Y. (1967) *Israel's Viewpoints in its Conflicts with the Arabs*. Tel Aviv: Dvir.

Karsh, E (2003) *The Oslo War: An Anatomy of Self-Deception*, Tel Aviv: Begin–Sadat Center for Strategic Studies.

Kleiman, E. (1996) *Does Israel Need Foreign Labour?* Jerusalem: Maurice Falk Institute for Economic Research, Hebrew University.

Lissak, M. (1999) *The Great Immigration in the Years of the 1950s: Failure of the Melting Pot*, Jerusalem: Bialik Institute.

Mann, R. (1998) *It's Inconceivable*, Or Yehuda: Hed Artzi.

Milstein, U. (1989) *The War of Independence*, Vols 1–2, Tel Aviv: Zmora Bitan.

Milstein, U. (1991) *The War of Independence*, Vols 3–4, Tel Aviv: Zmora Bitan.

Nakdimon, S. (1982) *Low Probability: The Story of the Dramatic Events Both Preceding and Following the Yom Kippur War*, Tel Aviv: Revivim-Yediot Ahronot.

Naor, A. (1986) *Government at War: The Functioning of the Israeli Government during the Lebanon War (1982)*, Tel Aviv: Lahav.

Schueftan, D. (2011) *Palestinians in Israel: The Arab Minority and the Jewish State*, Or Yehuda: Kinneret, Zmora-Bitan, Dvir.

Segev, T. (2005) *1967 and the Country Had a Change of Face*, Jerusalem: Keter.

Shaham, D. (1998) *Israel – 50 Years*, Tel Aviv: Am Oved.

Shalom, Z. (1995) David Ben-Gurion: The State of Israel and the Arab World 1949–1956, Beersheba: Ben-Gurion University.

Shalom, Z., and Hendel, Y. (2010) *Allow the IDF to Prevail: A Self-Realizing Slogan*, Tel Aviv: Yediot Ahranot.

Shapira, A. (2004) *Yigal Allon: Spring of His Life*, Bnei Barak: Kibbutz Hameuhad.

Shiffer, S. (1984) *Snow Ball: The Story Behind the Lebanon War*, Tel Aviv: Yediot Ahranot.

Tzameret, Z., and Yablonka, H. (eds) (1997) *The First Decade*, Jerusalem: Yad Yitzah Ben Zvi.

Weizman, E. (1975) *Go to the Sky, Go to the Land*, Tel Aviv: Ma'ariv.

Ya'alon, M. (2008) *A Long Short Way*, Tel Aviv: Miskal-Yediot Ahranot.

INDEX